Euripides, Freud, and the Romance of Belonging

Euripides, Freud, and the Romance of Belonging

Victoria Pedrick

The Johns Hopkins University Press
Baltimore

The Johns Hopkins University Press
2715 North Charles Street
Baltimore, Maryland 21218-4363
www.press.jhu.edu

Library of Congress Cataloging-in-Publication Data

Pedrick, Victoria.
   Euripides, Freud, and the romance of belonging / Victoria Pedrick.
      p. cm.
   Includes bibliographical references and index.
   ISBN-13: 978-0-8018-8594-5 (hardcover : alk. paper)
   ISBN-10: 0-8018-8594-9 (hardcover : alk. paper)
      1. Euripides. Ion. 2. Psychoanalysis and literature. 3. Ion (Greek
mythology) in literature. 4. Identity (Psychology) in literature. 5. Self in
literature. 6. Freud, Sigmund, 1856–1939. 7. Pankejeff, Sergius, 1887–
1979. I. Title.
   PA3973.I6P43 2007
   882'.01 — dc22
                                                          2006033571

A catalog record for this book is available from the British Library.

Contents

Acknowledgments

I had just begun work on this book when my son was born; he is now twelve. The book finally appears thanks to the help and encouragement of many colleagues and friends. Three people deserve my special thanks, Molly Myerowitz Levine, Jane Brown Gillette, and John Glavin. Early on, Molly shared with me her own store of evidence and reflections on the ancient practices of abandonment, a gift that helped me advance much more quickly than I might have otherwise. She generously commented on subsequent drafts at crucial stages. At critical moments, Jane's shrewd reading cut to the heart of the book's underlying goals. John also gave me invaluable resources, especially on Freud, and read versions of the manuscript. He also gave me crucial encouragement; to sum up his role, when I told him that the book was appearing, he said simply, "I have always believed in this book."

My thanks go as well to my colleagues in the Classics Department at Georgetown University, Cathy Keesling, Charlie McNelis, Erika Nesholm, Josiah Osgood, and Alex Sens, who were unflagging in their encouragement and advice. Alex, in particular, read individual chapters in draft and caught many an error. Among our excellent students at Georgetown, Ben Jasnow was an extraordinary reader of the final project, and Courtney Evans generously proof-read the ancient Greek. Benjie Barron also helped with proof-reading. All remaining errors are my own. I am especially thankful to Amanda Rawson, whose effortless assistance keeps me on the ball in so many ways.

My university has supported this project over the years with three summer grants. I wish to thank particularly Jane McAuliffe, dean of the College, for special aid in the final stages. The Center for Hellenic Studies made me welcome and gave me a place to work; my thanks go to Gregory Nagy, the Center's director, and Temple Wright, librarian for acquisitions. John Gibert, David Konstan, and Kevin Lee were also kind enough to read chapters at early stages, and Steve Oberhelman gave me much encouragement. The people at the Johns Hopkins University Press have been helpful and gracious throughout the process, especially Michael Lonegro and Kim Johnson, and I thank Peter Dreyer for his careful eye as copy editor.

Perhaps with any study that brings Freud or psychoanalysis to bear there remains the unstated question of exactly whose neurosis is on the couch. My principal aim is to get a better sense of how and why the origin of identity matters to both Euripides and Freud, but readers may also wonder why it matters to me. Just what is there in the representation of children and their parents by Euripides and Freud that moves me? The truth is that there is a personal element. As the mother of an adopted son, I do not think with complete detachment about a hero's lack of natal parents; questions of belonging matter to me in a particularly personal sense. It is just as well to acknowledge this from the outset, but since one of the guiding issues of this book is that none of us is ever completely free of the longing to know our origins, in my first chapter I suggest signs in contemporary culture that this longing is wider than my own.

My son has lived with this book his whole life, and the vagaries of its production have affected our relationship in ways that he cannot have understood or appreciated. I can never give him back the time it took or excuse my moods. I can only thank him for his patience and love, and I dedicate this book to my parents for theirs.

Note on Names, Texts, and Translations

I transliterate most names following the Greek alphabet — thus Kreousa and Xouthos — except where the Latinized form of the name is especially familiar, as with Apollo. Freud is quoted from the *Standard Edition*, cited as *SE*, and from his *Gesammelte Werke*, cited as *GW*. Quotations from Freud by page number only are from the case history of the Wolf Man, "From a History of an Infantile Neurosis," published in volume 17 of *SE*. Euripides' Greek text is the Oxford text of James Diggle (1981), except where noted. All translations from the Greek, unless otherwise noted, are my own.

Euripides, Freud, and the Romance of Belonging

Introduction

Despite their disparity, the two texts I study in this book grapple in similar ways with the question of how and why our origins affect our identities. The first is Euripides' *Ion*, a tragedy about a young boy's reunion with his mother, a princess of Athens, who exposed him as an infant. With disasters thrillingly averted, Ion heads from Delphi, where he was raised, to Athens as its future king. The *Ion* concerns the riddles of origins and destiny, but with a melodramatically happy ending, making it is very unlike its more familiar cousin, Sophocles' *Oedipus Tyrannus*. The second text is Freud's "From the History of an Infantile Neurosis," the case history of the Wolf Man, in which Freud describes his discovery of a fundamental theoretical construction—the primal scene, that moment when a very young child witnesses its parents having intercourse.[1] This case provided the evidence and theory that established Freud's version of psychoanalysis, at least for him. Thus it is also about origins: the trauma that begins a neurosis and the foundation of psychoanalysis itself. Like the *Ion*, this Freudian case history is fundamentally performative. Both texts engage their audience in the drama of incessantly recreating or repeating the origin of suffering. In this repetition, they capture the human longing to grasp identity's origins, and read together, they raise a spectral peril of foreclosing that longing too quickly.

It is fair to ask why, out of all the texts that deal with identity and its origins, I have brought together these two. Obviously, Freud himself inextricably linked one ancient tragedy in particular, Sophocles' *Oedipus Tyrannus*, to psychoanalysis. Studies by Sarah Winter (1999) and Richard Armstrong (2005) clarify how antiquity influenced Freud as he developed his theory and how he in turn exploited it.[2] Winter spells out Freud's own structure of the relationship between ancient tragedy and psychoanalysis:

> Freud's scenario posits the primal parricide as the "original" traumatic "Deed" (*Tat*) of culture ([*Totem und Taboo*], 161), but this "Deed" has been forgotten or repressed until the deferred action of the historical appearance of psychoanalysis itself unleashes its traumatic effect, witnessed to by the resistance of both patients and the scientific experts to the "universal destiny" of Oedipal sexuality. But psychoanalysis

follows its model of tragedy in this, since tragedy also functions to reenact the primal parricide in a disguised form and arouses its own particular "tragic effect," which Freud calls Oedipal. The difference that psychoanalytic theory claims to make to the "history" of culture is that it discloses to historical consciousness this originary traumatic act—it supersedes tragedy, which merely repeats the parricide through dramatic representation.[3]

Tragedy was that pre-psychoanalytic moment when the oedipal heart of the unconscious erupted into public view, rather than making its more usual appearance through the dreams or neurotic affect of the individual.[4] Like tragedy, psychoanalysis gives the unconscious an audience, in the person of the analyst, but its project gives it a special status: it intends to intervene in and explain the trauma it brings to light.[5] Armstrong studies how Freud relied on Greek tragedy, as a key part of the "ancient archive," to buttress and define his own findings. Using the Derridean notion of "archive," which situates texts within an authorizing structure, Armstrong studies the full ramifications of antiquity for Freud's psychoanalytic project. Ancient texts and their purposeful comprehension collude to give psychoanalysis its ability to understand the meanings that emanate from tragedy in terms of that authorizing structure (Derrida's "archontic principle"). That structure in turn institutionalizes psychoanalysis.[6]

A further link for Freud between Greek tragedy and his own work was the degree to which both tragedy and psychoanalysis allowed for suffering to be dramatized publicly. However different from one another fifth-century Athens and late nineteenth-century Vienna were, Freud appreciated both as historical moments that did not hide the reality of psychic pain. Insofar as tragedy dramatizes the primal suffering of the unconscious for an interested audience, it could serve as a model for the work psychoanalysis itself does to make plain that realm and its mysteries.[7] As both Winter and Armstrong show, Freud's nineteenth-century education taught him that Greek tragedy dramatized ancient legend in terms of confrontation and conflict, with the individual standing against the group. He also learned the Aristotelian principle that the spectators' emotional engagement with the drama is key. For Freud, the overt goal of tragedy was to inculcate an individual's proper sense of identity and, as he notes in *The Interpretation of Dreams*, "submission to the divine will and realization of his own impotence."[8] Freud conceptualized the spectator's response to the performance in terms that would both serve as a model for and ultimately be replaced by psychoanalysis, conceived of as the means to liberate the individual from such submission.[9]

Freud performs his role as the founding hero of psychoanalysis nowhere more stirringly or with greater educative intent than in his case histories. Donald Spence, in his 1994 study of psychoanalytic rhetoric, notes that Freud characterized his letdown on finishing his case study of Dora as feeling "short of a drug."[10] Case histories are Freud's special means of recollecting the drama of analysis, which cannot otherwise be experienced by an audience, and if he had not chosen to write them up, a crucial body of evidence for the efficacy of psychoanalysis would be lacking.[11] The individual analyses of patients whose psychic turmoil helped Freud define the fundamental nature of the unconscious were made up of three precious, otherwise irrecoverable things: talk, which could not be recorded; affect, which was perceptible only to the other participant; and the analyst's interpretation, which grew out of the moment. Freud's case histories are designed to capture these things in a way that is educative and persuasive — authoritative. Structurally and by design, the case history replaces tragedy.[12] The intrinsically performative nature of both genres allows us to consider how each engages its audience on the matter of identity, especially how both demand that the audience watch and believe what is seen or told about origins.

Regarding origins, the star figures of Euripides' tragedy and Freud's case history stand in provocative contrast to each other: one is a hero abandoned at birth; the other is a child who witnesses, symbolically at least, his own engendering. Ion suffers as an abandoned child, in direct contrast to the Wolf Man's trauma of seeing his parents in the act that brought him into being. Ion's tale as an abandoned child in effect inverts the primal scene's staging of the oedipal and thus interrogates identity from a perspective that opposes the master narrative of psychoanalysis. Oedipus himself is also a hero abandoned at birth, but he is not easy to use for such a contrast, because as Freud's chosen hero, he is hard to strip of his psychoanalytic baggage. But Ion is Oedipus's shadowy twin, with a remarkable twist: while each is a hero abandoned at birth and must make his way back into his family and kingdom, Ion's career is very different from Oedipus's, such that his tale visualizes the trauma of abandonment and reunion themselves (rather than Oedipus's peculiarly horrible pollution).[13] At the same time, the drama of the Wolf Man sometimes recasts him as an abandoned hero. Subtle threats and occasional mention of paternal preferences unexpectedly parallel Ion's tale in ways that Freud does not imply in psychoanalytic theory.[14]

What finally unites the *Ion* and "From the History of an Infantile Neurosis" as the subject of fruitful study is that both texts take seriously questions about our identity and its roots in the past. When it comes the first half of the problem — what is it about the past that makes us who we are? — both Euripides and Freud have answers. Freud was certain that the primal scene of parental sexual embrace made the neurotic who he was by dramatizing the oedipal heart of his unconscious. Euripides strongly suggests that abandonment forces the creation of contradictory and irreconcilable identities for the foundling. Yet despite the transparency of these findings, both authors obscure what these answers mean by refusing to answer the second question, *why* the past is the key to the present, as dogmatically.[15] Why does it matter whether we know where we came from and who bore us? Or, to frame the question differently, if the past is the key, why do we seek to know the exact moment when our past began? Both texts approach this second question, but their refusal — or failure — to answer it suggests that something profound and elusive lurks in the problem.

For our postmodern culture, the problem of identity has been reframed theoretically in order to answer at least the first question: it is our culture's past, not our own, that matters. We have come to understand that if we wish to investigate who we are, we must look at social and cultural structures outside ourselves as determinative. One theory for considering our constructed identities derives from the anthropology of Pierre Bourdieu and concerns what he calls a person's *habitus*. I review it as a particularly apt example, because it has been fruitfully applied to Freud himself. Richard Armstrong provides a definition of Bourdieu's concept of *habitus:*

> "systems of durable, transposable dispositions," a person's "embodied history" that incorporates sets of expectations, possibilities, and objectives inculcated by particular conditions of familial and social life. Embodied history in *habitus* is an "infinite yet strictly limited generative capacity," that is, a process of formation and productive agency, and a predictable yet flexible repertoire of assumptions and behaviors — *not* a fixed inheritance provoking mere mechanical repetition.

And:

> *Habitus* produces the strategies of everyday life and social interaction that involve, not a "conscious, rational calculation," but rather "a practical sense as a feel for the game, for a particular, historically determined game . . . acquired in childhood by taking part in social activities."[16]

Habitus accounts for and thus precludes our sense of autonomy, because even that sense (as embodied for instance in Freud's notion of the unconscious) is formed by our engagement with our families and culture. The value of such a notion of constructed identity is manifold, particularly given the flexible nature of Bourdieu's *habitus*, which explicitly rejects the mechanistic and embraces the play of choice and the role of "improvisation" in our behavior and experience.[17]

Thus, to understand who Freud is and where he came from, scholars now reexamine him in light of his *habitus* as it developed in nineteenth-century Europe. In the study of this father of psychoanalysis, *habitus* provides an alluring, extra-psychoanalytic purchase from which to assess the man and his work. "From our post-Freudian perspective, it is obviously difficult to examine Freud without using the very tools he gave us," Armstrong notes.[18] Given a need to understand the influences that shaped Freud's thinking, a study of his education at home and in school and his experiences as a young man helps articulate how he learned to think as he did. We identify what was *possible* for him to learn or think (and, by implication, what was impossible).[19]

Sarah Winter also stresses the need for a nonpsychoanalytic point of view when assessing Freud's development: "In order to examine psychoanalysis historically, it is necessary to step outside of its dominant psychological frame of reference, with which every event is interpreted as a psycho-dynamic scenario, however personalized, impelled by desires defined as arising 'from within' the individual and the mind."[20] While she acknowledges that some of Freud's "institutionalizing strategies" (i.e., those forms of argumentation and documentation that enable him to fix psychoanalysis as an institution) were "quite conscious and purposeful," others would have arisen from the whole complex of experiences that made him a creature of late nineteenth-century Vienna, and these, she argues, are precisely those historical and sociological matters that Freud sought to subordinate to the "universal and originary subjective categor[ies]" of psychoanalysis itself, particularly sexuality. Her goal is to break the "theoretical impasse" arising from the assumption that the "psychological constitution of the subject *precedes* social and cultural formation."[21] On that assumption, all the categories are Freudian and the deck seems stacked against us unless we extricate ourselves from privileging the psychological.

Yet does the focus on cultural structures as the source of our self answer the whole problem of identity? In the study of Freud, not everyone is convinced that he is best comprehended by his *habitus* or any similar framework. Louis Breger, a recent biographer, remarks that his earliest efforts to validate his mistrust of Freudian psychoanalysis began with his study of "cultural and historical factors." He initially blamed Freud's failings on "the influence of outmoded nineteenth-century scientific assumptions, Victorian attitudes toward sexuality, social prejudices about masculinity and femininity" rather than on anything in Freud's own "personality."[22] Breger asserts that his own study found, however, how very different Freud was from much of Victorian and Viennese culture. A psychoanalyst by training and practice, Breger applies current theory on childhood development in order to understand the effects of Freud's "very traumatic, impoverished, and difficult childhood" on his later career.[23] Breger also harshly assesses Freud's purposeful deployment of his own history and his formidable intellectual cabinet to shape psychoanalysis in his own image.[24] Breger insists that a site firmly within psychology is the only vantage point from which to perceive both Freud's blindness to his own psychosexual development and his willful (mis)representation of himself. The singular features of the man matter.

Studies of Freud himself thus suggest a choice when it comes to thinking about identity. We can aim to know what made him who he was in terms of cultural forces and experiences. Through as close an inquiry into Freud's *habitus* as the evidence permits, to use Bourdieu's categories for instance, we see a man whose behaviors conform to the world in which he lived.[25] Or we can analyze the man in terms of his own seemingly unique behavior and look at him as an autonomous agent whose past is uniquely traceable in its effects. This approach interprets cultural forces and experiences from a set of psychological priors that, as noted above, shape or slant the analysis—which presents a particularly acute problem in the case of Freud, the founder of psychoanalysis.[26] Yet either strategy seems to rely on an illusion that we have achieved either methodological certainty or individual specificity. Whether we assume that our identity is a social construction or a matter of psychological imperative, our chosen theoretical structure provides a starting point in the past, however vanishingly small in the case of culture or ancestry, that stands in relation to our present such that the need for further inquiry into our origins seems to be forestalled.

This illusion conceals what is finally not answered about Freud's identity (or anyone else's): the sense that something remains hidden. There is a point of origin left unaccounted for.[27] Either choice requires that we also accept that there is something we don't need to know, namely, why we look for an "ultimate cause" that might be the very beginning. Both perspectives conceal the deeper problem of why that very beginning is so crucial to knowing who we are. We have an anxiety about our origins that both psychoanalysis and cultural studies strive to make sense of.

Rather than explore this question further theoretically, I propose to read Euripides' *Ion* and Freud's "From the History of an Infantile Neurosis," for their examination of origins. Each responds to the constraints of its own genre—

tragedy and case history — in its answers, but both suggest how complicated the answers are. Both acknowledge that we are in some sense constructions. Each also posits that we are something else, something intrinsic to our parents — those who brought us into being. These texts also lay bare stratagems of concealment about the whole problem and express an urgency about identity that mirrors our own regarding these questions (an urgency I argue for in greater detail in Chapter 1). Reading closely in some sense replicates the dramatic nature of tragedy or case history as we experience their effects without the distancing shield of theory. Whether we are convinced that our culture plays the determinative role in our sense of self or that our parentage plays that role, an anxiety lingers that something has been missed. Neither Euripides nor Freud is willing to paper over this dichotomy between intellectual certainty and visceral dread, although they expose it and handle it very differently. And in the end, both were keenly aware of the need to shut down the dread at some point, yet the strategies they use to stop the question are patently that — strategies, not final answers. Euripides and Freud, I suggest, deserve to be taken seriously on the problem of why we long to know who we are, because their approaches do not rob us of the sense that the question matters precisely because it cannot be answered.

Another way to articulate the problem of identity's origin is to recognize that there is trauma at the source. Both texts dramatize the trauma while also normalizing it. The Wolf Man's neurosis originates in a spectacle that incorporates all the anxiety and suffering that he experiences and repeats as he grows up, yet the event itself — a young married couple making love — is "banal," to use Freud's own term, and its oedipal core is, according to him, the destiny of us all. Kreousa, who suffers dreadfully at Apollo's hands, passes that suffering on to her son when she abandons him, yet these are the circumstances that allow Ion to be the heroic figure that the foundation of Athens requires. What does it mean that the normal human condition originates in pain? Yet if it is so, the unanswered question of why we need to know exactly where we came from is less surprising. If we can get at the site of pain, we can see who was there and who was perhaps responsible. Both Freud and Euripides *suggest* what this site looks like and what happens there, but when we follow the pain to its origin, we do not necessarily see what we wish to see.

One further link between these texts is that they address the origin of identity in a most concrete form — a child's view of his parents — which, despite its simplicity, becomes a remarkable metaphor. The Wolf Man, Freud tells us, begged him to write his case up as a narrative of his adult suffering, but for Freud it was the infantile neurosis, and its beginnings between baby and parents, that mattered, that was to be determinative, not just of this man's identity, but of psychoanalysis itself. Euripides' interest in the identity of Athens is profound, but he gets at what it means through the person of a boy who begins the play without a mother or father and ends up having to accept that he needs more than the standard issue of two. Both the psychoanalyst and the ancient dramatist knew that asking about our identity in its most specific and ancient form enlarges the question's frame.[28]

The history of classicists' engagement with Freud and psychoanalysis is checkered. Mark Griffith (2005) provides a useful survey of attempts to apply psychoanalysis to tragedy. On the problem of whether and how to address dramatic characters as if they have coherent inner lives — a seeming requirement for psychoanalysis — Griffith argues that the dramatic character has a coherent reality in terms of the audience's apprehension of it.[29] The effort to read ancient culture through psychoanalysis, to understand in a sense the unconscious of the ancients, has been the subject of several larger studies.[30] C. Fred Alford (1992) finds the perspective of psychoanalysis valuable for reading ancient anxieties in Greek tragedy about key human questions, such as how we can live morally; why we can feel "contaminated" by ourselves or others; how we face death, not in the moment, but in our lives.[31] His process is self-avowedly eclectic, and his results are accordingly valuable to the degree that one accepts the psychoanalytic blend he develops. Page duBois (1988) provides a feminist critique of the patriarchal structures that support both psychoanalysis and classical studies.[32] In a sense, her attempt to assess the risks and costs establishes a perimeter to be mindful of when thinking about tragedy through psychoanalysis.

Victoria Wohl (2002) engages in the delicate process of studying the collective unconscious of Athenian male culture through literary texts as artifacts of that culture. The evidence of repression working on desires too unruly to be acknowledged lies in certain disruptive moments. It is here, Wohl suggests, that we can glimpse the Athenian unconscious.[33] Armstrong (2005) has reversed the interpretive perspective, addressing how Freud appropriated the "ancient archive" for his project of shaping psychoanalysis. For Armstrong, the matter concerns "how psychoanalysis still participates in the uncanny after-work generated by the archive of ancient culture."[34] Armstrong raises the prospect that in our increasing inability to comprehend ancient tragedy lies a concomitant deafness to those modern thinkers whose work is informed and invigorated by their appropriation of the genre.

The present book studies a specific example of the uncanny link between tragedy and psychoanalysis. On the matter of identity, as I argue, Euripides and Freud are both caught up in the powerful reverberations of a question that fascinates them—how the origin of a family affects the identities of everyone in it—but one that both perceive cannot finally be answered.

As a classicist, I take it as self-evident that Euripides is still worth reading, but Freud may be teetering on the bring of theoretical oblivion (into which some would say he has already fallen). That makes for a piquant irony in a study of identity that focuses on the choice to embrace or abandon a child, since we, his intellectual descendents, must assess how relevant Freud remains.[35] To ask whether and how we can still "use" Freud—or, for that matter, Euripides—is another way of asking about our own identity. Are these two points in our past that hold a key to who we are? If psychoanalytic theory can free itself from Freud and his categories, is that theory and its wider culture—including those who reject the categories—in danger of dismissing a past that still shapes us? We are caught in acts of choosing whether to affiliate ourselves or not. Has our culture used up these parts of our past? I think not. Freud's case of the Wolf Man and his primal scene should not be forgotten. The trouble with Euripides and his *Ion* is that outside a narrow set of classicists, we have not fully made this tragic vision a part of our past. One goal of this book is to insinuate both texts and the issues they raise more decisively into our thinking about identity.

Chapter 1 surveys the texts and contexts that inform the subsequent studies, in Chapters 2, 3, and 4, on identity in "From the History of an Infantile Neurosis" and the *Ion*. Presumably, readers may be familiar with one of these texts but not the other, so I summarize both in some detail. I also propose a structure for the tale of origin in a choice between abandonment and embrace, which I call a "romance of belonging," as an adaptation of and challenge to Freud's family romance. A romance of belonging recreates the moment when identity is on the line and the participants choose what happens next. As such, it is very different from the family romance, which is a tale of perception, not decision, and the choices that establish belonging have consequences far more traumatic and de-stabilizing than Freud's theories were inclined to allow. This chapter also presents a context I believe to be crucial for the study—the status of infant abandonment as a reality and as a myth in ancient and modern culture—because it suggests that our own need to know points of origin is unceasing.

Chapter 2 explores how the romance of belonging destabilizes identity in both Freud and Euripides and disallows an authoritative account. The full structure that constructs or denies belonging with an embrace or abandonment cannot fully appear as a site of terrifying choice; only one outcome, and the course of action it sets in motion, can ever be seen. We lose sight of the other choice and its possibilities. Traces of the work of the full romance, however, survive to destabilize the structures of identity built upon whichever outcome of the choice seems to be operational. Freud's primal scene, although it is discovered to account for the identity of the Wolf Man and of psychoanalysis itself, cannot be recovered as memory. It is always a fantasy, a construction whose contours are in the control of its inventor. Freud constructs complementary identities for himself and his patient that illustrate the scene's fundamental necessity as the master narrative of psychoanalysis, but he cannot resist the temptation to use further constructions of the primal scene rhetorically to buttress his arguments as a "secret weapon" against his adversaries. Once that rhetorical power is activated, others also use the primal scene as a weapon against Freud regardless of his claims to authority, as an encounter with Carl Jung illustrates. Tragedy can dramatize the romance of belonging, and in a very real sense, this genre has the duty to rehearse the irresolvable clash between embrace and rejection. Yet spectators do not witness the whole scene; instead, one outcome — abandonment — drives the dramatic action — toward the climax of the other — the embrace of mother and son. The *Ion* is constructed out of abandonment, such that it seems to start a process in which no reliable account of identity can be written. Authority figures such as Hermes or the human adult in the event, Kreousa, cannot construct a tale of Ion's exposure without the intrusion of others' concerns, which lead in tangential but compelling directions. I examine in particular the two competing accounts of Ion's abandonment that open the play, Hermes' in the prologue and Kreousa's fictional tale of her "friend" in the first scene. Neither version can withstand the dynamics of construction: exposure, in deliberately severing the natal union (or preventing its construction), prevents attempts to recall itself.

Chapter 3 examines the romance of belonging for the economic transactions that occur in it. Both texts are profoundly interested in the costs of union or abandonment; both also show signs of the psyche's longing to conceal how profits and losses are calculated, so that terms of belonging become theoretically acceptable or inherent. Accounts are hard to keep in this romance when its processes must be effaced. Freud eliminates abandonment as a theoretical possibility from the family romance but finds that he cannot avoid using it to create the primal scene. He is entangled in conflicting structures of possession. I briefly outline these structures to make plain what Freud longs to believe about familial identity, and what terms of possession he cannot avoid. Fundamental tensions in Freud's economic reckonings affect the Wolf Man, who is entangled in the conflicting structures, constantly poised to accept or resist the notion that all his identities are collapsed into one. In the *Ion*, the juxtaposition of treating children as objects either for investment or for veneration is quite startling and needs sorting out to see just what the play thinks the costs are of rearing a child or exposing it. I provide background on two contexts. First, I consider how the ancient Athenian informally accounted for profits and losses. I then consider Herodotus's thematic deployment of the royal child as an incalculably precious object of destiny. Both contexts suggest that Euripides' Athenian audience brought to the *Ion* a complicated understanding of the value of a child in the play. Mortals calculate in a familiar manner about the possibility of profit or loss when it comes to raising a child or getting rid of it before it consumes other resources, but they also refuse to acknowledge that they have made these calculations. The gods treat children as pure objects, things safely stashed in boxes or entrusted to the care of snakes and virgin priestesses: what matters is what comes out as a token of destiny. For both the case history and the tragedy, economics provide another perspective from which to see how the origins of identity are confounded by the longing to repudiate the cost-counting that determined the choice.

My final chapter examines that moment when we wish to cease the seemingly endless speculation about our origins. The focus of Chapter 4 is on recognition and embrace. Both psychoanalysis and tragedy suggest that the way to stop the romance is to apply typology to enable recognition and then foreclose further inquiry with an embrace. The site chosen for the stereotype is the body of the mother, and I provide a brief background on her typologies in psychoanalysis and in ancient mythic thought. One odd congruity in both tragedy and case history is the use of fiery images to mark the cessation of speculation. Fire has a powerful symbolic capacity both to burn on its fuel and to conceal it; it can mark that which must be perceived but cannot be seen. In the case of both the Wolf Man and Ion, fire burns on identities that are inversions of each other and instantiations of both (re)union and abandonment. But there is a significant difference that finally distinguishes tragedy from psychoanalysis. Freud's construction makes sense of fundamental neurotic fragments at the cost of imprecisely marking their origins. Euripides can dramatize the originary moment, but the ephemeral nature of dramatic epiphany means that it cannot last long enough for us to understand the full implications of the construction. Both strategies, of dramatist and psychoanalyst, enjoy a measure of success in comprehending the terrifying nature of the primal suffering, but each strategy leaves something irrecoverable.

CHAPTER ONE

The Romance of Belonging

Texts and Contexts

Κρέουσα· ἔκτεινά σ᾽ ὄντα πολέμιον δόμοις ἐμοῖς.
Ἴων· οὔτοι σὺν ὅπλοις ἦλθον ἐς πὴν σὴν χθόνα.
Κρέουσα· μάλιστα· κἀπίμπρης γ᾽ Ἐρεχθέως δόμους.
Ἴων· ποίοισι πανοῖς ἢ πυρὸς ποίᾳ φλογί;
Κρέουσα· ἔμελλες οἰκεῖν τἄμ᾽, ἐμοῦ βίᾳ λαβών.
Ἴων· πατρός γε γῆν διδόντος ἣν ἐκτήσατο.
Κρέουσα· τοῖς Αἰόλου δὲ πῶς μετῆν τῆς Παλλάδος;
Ἴων· ὅπλοισιν αὐτὴν οὐ λόγοις ἐρρύσατο.
Κρέουσα· ἐπίκουρος οἰκήτωρ γ᾽ ἂν οὐκ εἴη χθονός.

Kreousa: I killed you as an enemy of my house.

Ion: I didn't attack your land under arms.

Kreousa: You certainly did, and you were going to set fire to the house of Erechtheus.

Ion: With what torches or with what flame of fire?

Kreousa: You were intending to inhabit my possessions, taking them from me by force.

Ion: No, but by my father giving the land which he acquired.

Kreousa: How would someone of Aeolus have a share of Pallas's possessions?

Ion: By arms he protected your land, not by words.

Kreousa: Yet an ally wouldn't be an owner of this land.

EURIPIDES, *Ion*

[I]t may be maintained that analysis of children's neuroses can claim to possess a specially high theoretical interest. They afford us, roughly speaking, as much help toward a proper understanding of the neuroses of adults as do children's dreams in respect to the dreams of adults. . . . In the present phase of the battle which is raging around psycho-analysis the resistance to its findings has, as we know, taken on a new form. People were content formerly to dispute the reality of the facts which are asserted by analysis; and for this purpose the best technique seemed to be to avoid examining them. . . . people are now adopting another plan — of recognizing the facts, but of eliminating, by means of twisted interpretations, the consequences that follow from them, . . . The study of children's neuroses exposes the complete inadequacy of these shallow or high-handed attempts at re-interpretation.

FREUD, "From the History of an Infantile Neurosis"

If you look at everything critically, there isn't much in psychoanalysis that will stand up. Yet it helped me. He was a genius. Just imagine the work he did, remembering all those details, forgetting nothing, drawing those inferences. He may have had six, seven patients a day, and all the things he wrote. He was witty, a very intelligent man, there's no disputing that. And that he made mistakes. . . . to err is human. And it's also clear that he overestimated his work. . . . If he hadn't overestimated it, he might not have done it.

THE WOLF MAN (Sergei Pankejeff)

Euripides' *Ion* and Freud's "From the History of an Infantile Neurosis" are both clearly deeply concerned with foundation, of the city of Athens and of psychoanalysis, and each has been studied as a master narrative authenticating that foundation. Both texts also suggest the problematic of constructing an authoritative account. Kreousa's flat claim of murder is eerie, since she plainly has not killed Ion. As they argue about terms of ownership and being truly an Athenian, something in the language troubles their argument beyond the irony of their natal relationship. Pankejeff, the subject of Freud's case, is not willing to accede to the absolute certainty his analyst maintains; he senses that the help he got from psychoanalysis did not come from theoretical correctness but from some sort of overestimation. Both tragedy and case history invite an inquiry into what undermines them. The very structure of the *Ion* puts spectators on their interpretive guard: the play's action notoriously contradicts the prologue's predictions, while its conclusion institutionalizes the deception of the foreigner Xouthos as an essential element of Athens's foundation myth. Although Freud shapes his case history as a masterly statement of psychoanalytic doctrine, later readers have sensed that he missed, or misjudged, something crucial about the Wolf Man's illness. George Dimock puts the defiance in these terms: "The strongly partisan character of my reading verges, perhaps, on the willful. Yet I take my cue from a curious intransigence and resiliency that seem to lie near the core of this patient's history of debility."[1] Intransigence and resiliency are good words for both texts — there is something weird about them, which is both familiar and unfamiliar — uncanny, or *unheimlich*, as Freud would say.

In this chapter, I summarize Freud's case history and Euripides' tragedy and then explore how they have been discussed as master narratives. I outline another tale of origins that lies concealed in the dominant narrative, a romance of belonging in which parent and child look at each other and wonder, is this worth it? In Freudian psychoanalysis, a romance is a tale that the patient creates to make sense of his origins; the romance uses fantasy to challenge reality and protect the patient from its consequences. I examine Freud's own formulation of this sort of tale — the family romance — below. But I also propose that we read Euripides' *Ion* and Freud's case history of the Wolf Man as two sides of another tale of origins, the romance of belonging. In this romance the crucial issue for belonging is choice, a concept these master narratives distort, contradict, or deny because the process of choosing destabilizes their enterprise. I also study the basis for my claim that a dread troubles contemporary reflections on identity, whether these rely on the psychological or the social. Despite our intellectual conviction, a sense that we have missed something leads us to keep asking about the origins of who we are. Thus this chapter delves into texts, contexts, and the drive that informs the rest of this study. The summaries seem necessary because the book presupposes readers from two disparate communities, classicists and students of psychoanalysis, who may not be equally familiar with both the tragedy and the case history. For the benefit of this readership I have also been selective in my examination of other critical studies. While scholarship on the *Ion* is comparatively compact, I draw particular attention to discussions that particularly address the nature of the authority wielded by gods and mortals within the tragedy.[2] As for studies of Freud's aims in constructing psychoanalysis, I discuss those that are particularly suggestive about how and why "From the History of an Infantile Neurosis" involves that uncanny sense of something missed.[3] When it comes to our never-ceasing need to ask about our identity, both sets of readers, classicists and psycho-analysts, are implicated in my claim, and I take care to establish that need and to propose the structure of the romance of belonging that perpetuates it.

Freud's "From the History of an Infantile Neurosis": An Overview

Freud published "From the History of an Infantile Neurosis," the longest and most complicated of his five celebrated case histories, in 1918.[4] He considered it especially important for its description of how he discovered the primal scene and for its incontrovertible evidence, as far as he was concerned, for two cardinal tenets of psychoanalysis: the power of the sex drive as the source and substance of the unconscious; and the infantile origin of the sex drive. The case also gave Freud fresh insight into the mechanism by which both fantasy and reality reside in the unconscious, since it turned on the relationships among the elements of a patient's dream, the events lying behind that dream in his unconscious, and the ability of the analyst to construct those events.[5] These tenets and principles were under assault by Freud's former associates Alfred Adler and Carl Jung, but armed with his new findings, he believed himself able to expose the shortcomings of their arguments.[6]

I should emphasize at the outset that the "primal scene" appears in this case history in Freud's original sense of the term: as a very young child's witnessing of its parents having intercourse. Later psychoanalysts apply the term more broadly, depending on many factors.[7] The notion of a primal scene can be used more broadly still in interpretive vernacular to signify originary or foundational moments of many different sorts. Thus, for instance, Arthur Little applies the term to the coupling of Othello and Desdemona as the origin of miscegenation for Shakespeare's audience.[8] Adding to the possibility of confusion, insofar as "From the History of an Infantile Neurosis" articulates Freud's master status vis-à-vis his patient, subsequent studies of the case history treat it as a "primal scene" of psychoanalysis itself.[9] My summary of the case history, however, uses the term in its original narrow sense.

The patient under analysis was a wealthy Russian nobleman named Sergei Pankejeff, given the moniker "the Wolf Man" because of a key dream he had. Pankejeff lived until 1979 and remained in contact with the psychoanalytic community, so that Freud's declared successes in his treatment could be tested long after the analysis ended. Pankejeff was proud of his place in the foundation of psychoanalysis and even called himself the Wolf Man in his own writings. He wrote an account of his treatment with Freud as well as an autobiography, and, in his final years, he permitted an Austrian journalist to interview him.[10] Thus alongside Freud's magisterial case history, the patient's own voice survives, sometimes awed at his analyst's brilliance or petulant over details, but always both grateful and, on certain points, adamant that Freud missed something. If "From the History of an Infantile Neurosis" silenced Freud's contemporary critics, at least to his own satisfaction, it also initiated a seemingly interminable dialogue between him and his most famous patient.[11]

The case began in 1910 when Pankejeff, aged twenty-five and crippled by mental illness, sought Freud's help. He remained in analysis for four and half years, a very long analysis at that time.[12] Freud briefly treated Pankejeff again in 1919–1920 when his symptoms reappeared. In 1926, when the Russian needed treatment for a psychotic episode, Freud referred him to his protégé Ruth Mack Brunswick.[13]

The case history's introduction explains three peculiarities that Freud believes make the case difficult to describe. First, he wishes to focus on his patient's childhood illness, although he expects readers to be wary of an infantile neurosis only captured through the analysis of an adult. Second, the sheer length of the analysis makes it "impracticable" to give readers a comprehensive summary. The complicated nature of the analysis also prevents him from giving either a chronological account of the neurosis or a thematic discussion, so that his readers must allow him to weave together events and theory.[14] Finally, he predicts that readers will find the primal scene an implausible construction, but he consoles himself with the confidence that psychoanalysis has given him to construct it. And nothing less than psychoanalysis itself is at stake, because his adversaries are twisting the "findings" of psychoanalysis to come up with their own interpretations (*SE* 17: 9; subsequent references to this case history are by page number only to this volume).

Freud first summarizes his patient's general history and characteristics. The Wolf Man, who spent his earliest years largely under the care of servants, was a toddler of model obedience. At three and a half, he became violent, prone to fits of wild anger and terrified not only of large animals but also of insects, which he enjoyed dismembering. Succeeding this "naughty" phase was a period in which the Wolf Man was obsessively pious, with many rituals to perform, although he harbored blasphemous thoughts. The Wolf Man was both afraid of his father and jealous of his sister for his affection. Between the ages of eight and ten, these "phenomena" cleared up, although the patient's adult symptoms stemmed from them.

Freud now outlines the "riddles" posed by his initial summary (17–18). Why did the Wolf Man's behavior suddenly change? What was the significance of the perverse behavior and fears that accompanied his naughtiness? What was the origin and meaning of his obsessive piety, and of the "ceremonials"? These are the questions to which the primal scene is to be the best and only answer.

Freud next discusses the Wolf Man's memory of sexual molestation by his sister when the boy was not yet four, an incident that was a plausible cause of the onset of the child's wild anger. He does not deny the importance of an event that plainly confounded his patient's psychosexual maturation in complicated ways, but he does not consider it sufficient to account for the entire range of infantile symptoms. This sister was two years older than the Wolf Man and, being especially talented, was preferred by their father. The Wolf Man felt "mercilessly oppressed" by his sister and believed that his lifelong attraction to women of servile status was due to his need to humble her.[15] Her suicide appeared to leave the Wolf Man unmoved, except for the thought that he would not have to share his inheritance with her. Freud found this sentiment and the Wolf Man's lack of affect remarkable, but eventually located the displaced emotion. Some trauma must exist deeper than the Wolf Man's conflict with his sister.[16]

Freud then turns to the anxiety dream from which he constructs the primal scene. On Christmas Eve, the night before his fourth birthday, the Wolf Man had a terrifying dream. I quote Freud's summary of the dream:

I dreamt that it was night and that I was lying in my bed. (My bed stood with its foot towards the window; in front of the window there was a row of old walnut trees. I know it was winter when I had the dream, and night-time.) Suddenly the window opened of its own accord, and I was terrified to see that some white wolves were sitting on the big walnut tree in front of the window. There were six or seven of them. The wolves were quite white, and looked more like foxes or sheep-dogs, for they had big tails like foxes and they had their ears pricked like dogs when they pay attention to something. In great terror, evidently of being eaten up by the wolves, I screamed and woke up. My nurse hurried to my bed, to see what had happened to me. It took quite a long while before I was convinced that it had only been a dream; I had had such a clear and life-like picture of the window opening and the wolves sitting on the tree. At last I grew quieter, felt as though I had escaped from some danger, and went to sleep again. (*SE* 17: 29; the dream material is in Freud's own italics, as usual)

Freud recognized that this dream, whose surface material derived from folktales, pointed to a castration fantasy, but a more comprehensive interpretation of the dream took years until he was able to construct the primal scene itself. I quote his construction in full again:

What sprang into activity that night out of the chaos of the dreamer's unconscious memory-traces was the picture of copulation between his parents, copulation in circumstances which were not entirely usual and were especially favourable for observation. . . . He had been sleeping in his cot, then, in his parents' bedroom, and woke up, perhaps because of his rising fever, in the afternoon, possibly at five o'clock, the hour which was later marked out by depression. It harmonizes with our assumption that it was a hot summer's day, if we suppose that his parents had retired, half undressed, for an afternoon *siesta*. When he woke up, he witnessed a coitus *a tergo* [from behind], three times repeated; he was able to see his mother's genitals as well as his father's organ; and he understood the process as well as its significance. Lastly he interrupted his parents' intercourse in a manner which will be discussed later. (*SE* 17: 36–37)

Freud recognizes the enormity of this construction and notes that he does not expect to be believed. Rather, he asks for "a *provisional* belief in the reality of the scene" (39; his italics), so that he can explain how it accounts for all the patient's symptoms.

The vision of the Wolf Man's parents enjoying themselves became a source of his own longing to give and receive such pleasure. The primal scene, activated through the anxiety dream by deferred action, also conveyed conflicting sexual facts that the Wolf Man did not sort out but absorbed and maintained simultaneously through an enormous expense of psychic energy. He showed signs of a "normal" oedipal phase, but the experience of being sexually molested by his sister inculcated in him a preference for the "passive role." Like his mother, he could please his father in this role within the primal scene; but he would have to suffer castration to do so, which his "male ego" repudiated. The desire for such sexual satisfaction was repressed, leaving anxiety in its wake and an opening for the obsessional neurosis.

Freud now breaks off the case itself to engage his adversaries. Specifically, in order to show the fallacies and limitations of Carl Jung's theories, he imagines how his former protégé would interpret the primal scene as constructed from the dream. Freud also anticipates other rationalized interpretations of the primal scene, including the possibility that it is his own fantasy. He establishes an identity between recollection and construction that is crucial to the primal scene, given its deep antiquity in the Wolf Man's life, and he reminds readers that "dreaming is another kind of remembering," so that to interpret a dream has the same truth value as recovering a memory. But Freud has come up against an intractable problem. For him recollection, construction, and dreaming may be "absolute equivalents" (51), but the question is forever open whether the Wolf Man's primal scene actually occurred or not.[17] In a section added in 1918, Freud is still struggling with the question, although he claims it matters little to him, and he offers another rationalized source for the dream that he says may be the most obvious one.[18] Even so, he refuses to yield, although he must pronounce *non liquet* on the matter (60): such "real" bases for the anxiety dream explain the Wolf Man's symptoms less well than the primal scene.

The heart of the Wolf Man's infantile illness, the obsessional neurosis itself, developed when his mother and his beloved Nanya (his *Kinderfrau* or nurse) decided to introduce him to religion as a means of "distracting and elevating him" from his "irritability and apprehensiveness" (61).[19] Freud examines the child's obsessive preoccupation with religion as a map of the Wolf Man's sexual development. In particular, the Wolf Man's systematic introduction to the stories of Christ's passion gave him the opportunity to "become Christ," Freud determines, with the same need to suffer unjustly at his father's hands and thereby please him. When the Wolf Man was ten, the obsessional neurosis resolved itself under the influence of a German tutor, who relieved him of his excessive piety by introducing "an enthusiasm for military affairs" (69).

Having completed an account of the Wolf Man's infantile neurosis, Freud examines the same events from two thematic perspectives. First, he sketches the role of "anal erotism" in the Wolf Man's development and the decisive role played by money and gift-giving for the neurosis. He then introduces "fresh material," the Wolf Man's earliest memories of a long-forgotten nursery-maid, which provides the "solution" to the whole puzzle and confirms the existence of the primal scene.

In his discussion of the Wolf Man's relationship to money and its libidinal equivalents, feces and babies, Freud focuses on the severity of the Wolf Man's "disturbed" relations with money and on their idiosyncratic nuances. Money was a sign of his father's affection, and he was extraordinarily competitive about it with both his sister and, after his father's death, his mother. Freud considers the link between money and feces particularly pronounced in the Wolf Man and he traces it in detail, because "intestinal problems" were the Wolf Man's most enduring psychosomatic problem. Plagued by a lack of bowel control as a toddler, he suffered from persistent constipation as an adult. Because the child knew of his mother's chronic intestinal troubles, he saw in the primal scene her suffering as well as her pleasure in her castrated genitals. The Wolf Man's own disordered bowels as a child expressed his "feminine attitude toward men" (80), which arose from his sister's molestation, and his identification with his mother. Freud reveals a final detail of the constructed primal scene, which he has postponed until now so that its meaning is more apparent. The infant had interrupted his parents' lovemaking by passing a stool and crying out. A sign of sexual arousal, the feces are also a gift, parallel to the baby a woman gives in exchange for sexual satisfaction. Feces and babies are the coin of recompense the Wolf Man offers for the sexual satisfaction he wishes to give to or receive from his father.

The "fresh material" that unravels the final puzzles of the primal scene involve the Wolf Man's earliest memories of a nursery-maid on her knees, with a pail and broom, scolding him. Using material from throughout the analysis, Freud eventually constructs the full encounter with these details: the Wolf Man saw this adored servant on her knees, urinated in his sexual excitement, and was then threatened with castration. This incident replicated the events of the primal scene, with the Wolf Man playing the role of his father, and it determined the Wolf Man's inclination for women of servile status. The Wolf Man also recalled dreaming of a wasp he mutilated. Freud linked this dream to the early scene of enacted sexual desire and retaliatory threat of castration involving the nursery-maid. The incident clearly indicates that the child's earliest sexual proclivities were to imitate his father in the primal scene, not his mother, but that his sister's sexual abuse of him "drove him into passivity" (94). Armed with this early confirmation of the primal scene, Freud can explain the Wolf Man's summary description of his adult malaise, that his view of world was constantly obscured by a veil that was torn only after an enema-induced bowel movement. This symptom encapsulates the Wolf Man's complicated response to the primal scene as an adult. The Wolf Man always made much of the fact that he had been born covered by his amniotic membrane, so to view the world through a veil was a "fulfilled wishful phantasy" of escape back into the womb. Freud reads this wish as more than an obvious desire for rebirth or a "phantasy of incestuous intercourse with the mother" (100); it is also a sign that the Wolf Man wanted to enjoy intercourse with his father from within the womb and to present his father with the compensatory child. The primal scene, activated by the wolf dream, enacts the sexual satisfaction sought by the Wolf Man from both parents.

In his conclusion to the case history Freud again summarizes the Wolf Man's early childhood, now with all incidents appearing in their proper chronological order and assigned their proper psychosexual values. He also elaborates on the Wolf Man's identification with Christ as a religious symbol of the tangle of responses the Wolf Man has toward his father. This tangle seems precisely the point that gripped Freud, not in its content alone, but as a persistent and remarkable feature of the process itself. Emotionally the Wolf Man was prone to extraordinary ambivalence and "tenacity of fixation," but logically "he betrayed . . . a peculiar skill in unearthing contradictions and inconsistencies." The tension between the Wolf Man's emotional and intellectual life reminded Freud of an abiding archaeological problem: how to make sense of a narrative in which artifacts from an earlier stage are found "side by side" with other, more modern ones, such that one perceives as a plane what one knows is a "solid" (119).

Freud is unabashed about the metaphor: the Wolf Man is a difficult but richly rewarding site for excavation.[20] There was the mess and tedium of painstakingly uncovering every nook and cranny, and his patient is patently more interested in his adult symptoms. Yet the yield is the primal scene, which captures within its compass the universe of erotic possibilities in the oedipal crisis. Freud's notion of the cube behind the plane, by which he understands the Wolf Man's entire childhood neurosis, also fits the drama of the primal scene. Written at a time when his version of psychoanalysis is under serious assault by rivals, "From the History of an Infantile Neurosis" is plainly designed to be a master narrative to silence them:

> This case history was written down shortly after the termination of the treatment, in the winter of 1914–15. At that time I was still freshly under the impression of the twisted re-interpretations which C. G. Jung and Alfred Adler were endeavouring to give to the findings of psychoanalysis. This paper is therefore connected with my essay "On the History of the Psycho-Analytic Movement." . . . It supplements the polemic contained in that essay, which is in its essence of a personal character, by an objective estimation of the analytic material. (*SE* 17: 7n1)

The case history is to be the "objective estimation" after passions have died down, yet Freud also acknowledges the revolutionary nature of what he is proposing. The primal scene itself is remarkable but even more so is the boldness with which he constructs it; particularly provocative is the odd relationship of cause and effect in the deferred action, or *Nachträglichkeit*, between the scene and the dream that activates it. Freud more than once cautions readers to be prepared to believe what he says. His project of proving his version of psychoanalysis once and for all requires his readers to submit to his authority, and he supports this demand through his use of provocative construction and seemingly indeterminate signs that only he can interpret.

In the case history, Freud performs the essential characteristics of fantastic construction and indeterminacy of the primal scene. He insists throughout "From the History of an Infantile Neurosis" that his construction of the primal scene, with its fantastical wealth of detail, is the only true account of the Wolf Man's neurotic origins. Nor is he troubled by the patient's own inability to remember the scene. On the contrary, he prefers the construction, which relies on his interpretive powers coupled with the patient's language, fantasies, affect — in short, with all that psychoanalysis brings out — because he is all too aware of the unreliability of neurotic memory. This very need for the analyst's construction seems to Freud a further guarantee of the validity of the primal scene, which represents a partnership in which the patient supplies the raw data, in the form of memories and dreams, but is finally saved from himself by the daring construction — and the judicious timing in bringing it forth — of the analyst. Freud's version of the primal scene springs from his convictions about the significance of the libidinal and, specifically, the child's oedipal conflict.

Later practicing psychoanalysts have recognized the primal scene as a dramatic metaphor for the oedipal. From the motionless tableau of the nightmare, Freud constructs a drama in which the father asserts his right to the mother before the son's eyes. As the psychoanalyst Harold P. Blum puts it: "The primal scene is a crystallization of the oedipal drama, a condensed representation of passionate attachment and conflict in the oedipal triangle between parents and child . . . [which] inevitably elicits reactions of rejection and exclusion, or of intrusion and inclusion."[21] The primal scene instantiates the child's longing for the mother or for the father, as Freud argues is the case with the Wolf Man, and confirms that the child's rivalry with or attraction to the father is firmly libidinal. And this is how the primal scene is often used in modern psychoanalysis; as Johan Norman describes it in another context: "Even if the child has not seen the sexual act, it creates a fantasy that contains the realization that his parents are physically involved with each other. This primal fantasy is built up gradually with various elements that characterize the child's fantasies about his parents and their relationship."[22] Thus while the primal scene dramatizes the official oedipal myth of psychoanalysis, it is also a potent antidote to a concealed anxiety about the identity of one's parents.

Freud identifies deferred action in this case history as the mechanism by which the trauma inherent in a seemingly trivial event occurs only after subsequent events. He is explicit that the primal scene does not cause the later dream (43–44). The scene's capacity to cause harm has to be "activated" by the dream, which itself has complicated origins in the Wolf Man's sexual development, his exposure to cultural artifacts such as folktales and farming, and even his phylogenetic heritage (44): "We shall further bear in mind that the activation of this scene (I purposely avoid the word 'recollection') had the same effect as though it were a recent experience. The effects of the scene were deferred, but meanwhile it had lost none of its freshness in the interval between the ages of one and a half and four years." And throughout his discussion of the primal scene, Freud makes it plain that it is the interpretation of the four-year-old that activates the trauma — or, more precisely, the words of the twenty-five-year-old who, under analysis, can finally articulate the trauma first felt by the child. The infant witness merely "receives an impression to which he is unable to react adequately" (45n1).

The case history of the Wolf Man, with its dramatic constructions and deferred action, has enjoyed a greatly varied career since 1918.[23] Freud's immediate successors take his findings for granted, as can be seen from the fact that Ruth Mack Brunswick, who reanalyzed the Wolf Man in 1926, called her case history "A Supplement to Freud's 'History of an Infantile Neurosis' "[24] In more recent psychoanalytic practice, the primal scene may be acknowledged to be a crucial feature, because it dramatizes the oedipal crisis so vividly, as noted above. But so ubiquitous is its application that psychoanalysts wonder about its real utility; as one critic puts it, "the primal scene explained everything — and therefore nothing."[25] And later psychoanalytic theory has a complicated reaction to the case.[26] Jacques Lacan cites the "exceptional importance" of the case for the identification of the primal scene as a site of where fantasy and memory could be so traumatically blended. He considers deferred action to be one of Freud's most brilliant intuitions about the workings of the unconscious, because of the linked but noncausal relationship between events that thoroughly confounds linear, causative temporality. Lacan further elaborates Freud's notion that only the present act of speaking by the patient preserves the dream wherein the primal scene lies, waiting to be effected, so that analysis becomes the final act in the drama of the neurosis.[27] Other theorists have had greater reservations. Gilles Deleuze and Félix Guattari, for instance, challenge the entire oedipal premise for which the primal scene is a staging.[28]

Not only have detailed challenges of Freud's account have arisen, but inasmuch as the writings of the Wolf Man himself have been published, his independent voice has contributed to a strange afterlife for the case.[29] In some instances, the assumption is that Freud missed a crucial detail or, through his ignorance of Russian language and culture, misinterpreted what he heard. Based on such reasoning, the psychoanalysts Nicolas Abraham and Marie Torok argue that the primal scene witnessed by the Wolf Man was the spectacle of his father having sex, not with his mother, but with his sister, a scene that the patient did remember, because it occurred significantly later in his early childhood.[30] Other analysts see evidence of Freud suppressing or distorting material that did not fit the case; perhaps the most famous of these is Jeffrey Masson, who argues, based on his editing of Freud's letters to Wilhelm Fliess, that Freud suppressed or misrepresented evidence in the Wolf Man's case that would have supported his old, discarded "seduction theory" of neurosis.[31] Finally, critics have detected strong evidence of a sort of reverse transference whereby Freud addressed his own repressed needs in his construction of the primal scene. For instance, Lawrence Johnson develops a fundamental thesis of his book on the case of the Wolf Man: "It will be my contention that this repressed material [Freud's] found its reflection (its mirror image and its exact opposite) in the Wolf Man's crypt, leading Freud to posit the Wolf Man within his own internal drama as a rival for the control of psychoanalysis." Johnson's use of the term "crypt" is borrowed from Nicolas Abraham and Maria Torok; it signifies a sealed-off portion of the unconscious in which repressed material permanently and irrecoverably resides.[32]

Elements from the case of the Wolf Man have also been deployed as tools for literary interpretation, sometimes in a straightforwardly Freudian sense. For example, David Grene reads a famous incident in Herodotus, Gyges' observation of the Lydian king's naked wife (*Histories* 1.8–12), as a primal scene. Grene maps the politics of dynastic succession as an erotic triangle. "There is . . . the fantastic crime-stained rise to supreme power by someone who has no claim to it. There is, as bedrock in Herodotus' version, a murder of the king-father and the incest with the mother in a wholly paternalistic eastern monarchy." The Freudian notion of the primal scene shapes Grene's attempt to articulate a "deep mythical" basis for the psychological significance of the tale for Herodotus and his readers.[33] But the primal scene as an interpretive structure can also take on the theoretical coloring of its new setting. For instance, Ned Lukacher develops a deconstructive notion of the primal scene that highlights its indeterminability. In Henry James's *The Turn of the Screw*, for example, it is not the sight of sex between the master and the former governess — which, if it were narrated, would be a depressingly familiar act of social power — that haunts the tale. Rather, the construction of an inability to see is what horrifies. Lukacher also deploys Freud's notion of deferred action in this reading, again as a deconstructive destabilizer of cause and effect.[34] Writing about Shakespeare's *Othello*, Arthur Little deploys both concepts once again, but in service to understanding how shared cultural experiences as well as customs, beliefs, and attitudes, activate the latent meanings in the script for the audience.[35] Little suggests that deferred action operates between the primal scene on stage and the audience's own "pre-cognition" of miscegenation. The horror in Othello and Desdemona's marital embrace is not there until the audience makes it horrible by its own reaction; spectators are thus implicated in and made responsible for the violence.[36]

Feminists have challenged Freud's case history precisely because it inculcates the primal scene and deferred action into our modern intellectual cabinet as structures of patriarchal hegemony. In *The Spectral Mother*, Madelon Sprengnether discusses the effacement of the Wolf Man's mother by other feminine figures and suggests that deferred action supports "patriarchal culture from which the mother is effectively excluded as an agent," because it strips the mother of her status as subject/agent in the primal scene by placing responsibility for the child's trauma on its later encounter with the father in its oedipal crisis.[37] The primal scene itself enshrines the oedipal triangulation of the family structure in a hierarchy that privileges the father or, as Page duBois has argued, the oedipal narrative is "an instrument of repression" that begins in gender but extends throughout capitalist culture.[38]

This range of criticism may suggest, among other things, the degree to which "From the History of an Infantile Neurosis" denies its readers their own share in its interpretation. Freud deliberately develops an initial lack of clarity or closure regarding certain key theoretical constructions that, in the end, only he can make sense of. The primal scene is not only posited as a reality that could be remembered but also constructed as a fantasy; it thus becomes a site in which the status of both memory and construction are problematic. As noted above, Freud is happy to construct the contours of the scene from many perspectives (a process studied in greater detail in the next chapter). Furthermore, Lawrence Johnson notes that the process of deferred action is built into the structure of the case history, such that the analyst's progress fortifies what was already there.[39] Yet Freud takes for granted that he can—and does—finally make sense of everything, freezing all this instability and slippage between memory and construction, cause and effect, into a case history that does what he set out to do. "From the History of an Infantile Neurosis" remains *his* master narrative of psychoanalysis, one that defies the attempts of others to appropriate it in order to rewrite it.

I approach this case history by reading it as a romance or, at least, half of a romance (see further below). We can likewise analyze the case history as Freud's presentation of origins, with things ordered—included and excluded—both by design and perhaps not by design, but ordered nonetheless. If the Wolf Man's neurosis is due to a primal trauma and there is, as Freud claims, an originary moment for that trauma, then we can certainly detect that something is missing or left out at the heart of the case. Freud posits that the primal scene is about parental embrace and the child's longing to enter that embrace; he omits consideration that such an embrace predicates its opposite, that parents may choose not to embrace their infants but instead abandon them. Leave out abandonment, as the primal scene most determinedly does, and its effect on a family's identities is obscured. The concomitant urgency to secure both parents and child safely within a dramatization of identities within the family is also apparently unfounded or apparently disproportionate. Effacing abandonment does not make the urgency to belong dissipate or vanish; rather, it inheres within the master narrative that seeks to found psychoanalysis within an embrace.[40] Viewing "From the History of an Infantile Neurosis" as both a master narrative, intended to control and direct its story for (Freud's) ideological purposes and goals, and as a romance, with structures of fantasy and memory set alongside each other with an intent not fully expressed, allows me to read its language for evidence about the nature of that concealed urgency and intent.[41]

Euripides' *Ion:* An Overview

The hero Ion was a founder of Athens whose parents were, according to our earliest sources, a Thracian king, Xouthos, and a royal princess, Kreousa. Ion's chief mythic accomplishment prior to the fifth century was to give his name to the Ionians, Greeks who had once lived on the Peloponnesian peninsula but, when forced out by the Dorians, first received refuge in Attica and then migrated to islands in the eastern Aegean. Because of their sojourn in Attica, the Athenians assumed a close affinity to the Ionians and claimed a right of alliance with them. By the middle of the fifth century, there was also a story that Ion was a foreigner who became an early military leader of Athens.[42] Euripides' tragedy presents a different set of origins for this hero.[43]

The god Hermes opens the play with this prologue. Kreousa, daughter of the Athenian king Erechtheus, was once raped by the god Apollo and, fearing to tell her parents of her pregnancy, gave birth secretly in the palace. Placing the child in a basket with tokens of its royal identity, she exposed it in the cave of Pan at the foot of the Acropolis, expecting it to die. But at Apollo's request, Hermes himself took the child in its basket to the sanctuary at Delphi, where it was discovered by the Pythia, an oracular priestess. The child grew up in ignorance of his identity. Kreousa is now married to Xouthos, who became king of Athens by aiding the city in a recent war, and the couple wishes to consult the oracle about their childlessness. Apollo plans to use this opportunity to bestow his child on Xouthos as the mortal's own son, so that the youth can inherit rule in Athens. Only later, once the boy is in Athens, does the god plan to reveal his true natal identity to Kreousa. The events leading to the boy's recognition by Xouthos are what we are about to see, says Hermes, and they will lead to his special name, Ion.[44] This is not, however, what happens.

Ion enters next singing about his contentment and duties as a temple slave. He welcomes the entering Chorus of the queen's serving women and the lady herself.

Ion and Kreousa establish a warm rapport with one another. She indulges his curiosity about Athens's legendary founders, and he is sympathetic to her childless plight. Under her prodding Ion shares what he knows of his own tale, and Kreousa finally confides her reason for preceding her husband to the shrine. She wants to ask about the fate of a baby born to a "friend" who was raped by Apollo and forced to expose it. Ion is both appalled and strangely stirred by the story, but he refuses to let Kreousa ask the oracle about this child. If it is true, to ask the god to incriminate himself by revealing the child's fate would be wrong. Kreousa subsides, Xouthos now enters to consult the oracle, and soon all characters exit.

After a choral song praying for a good prophecy and celebrating the blessings of children, Ion reenters to meet Xouthos, who hurries from the shrine with the thrilling news that the first person he meets — in fact, Ion himself — is his very own son. Ion is skeptical, but as he comes to accept this oracle, he wonders about the identity of his mother, about whom Xouthos was too excited to ask. The two men decide that she was a maiden of Delphi whom Xouthos seduced when drunk at a festival of Dionysus. Ion then turns to the painful new realities awaiting him if he goes to Athens. Citizens there will have various reasons for despising him, and Xouthos's wife, as his childless stepmother, will hate him. Xouthos dismisses these doubts by reminding him that he is now a king's son and wealthy. As for Kreousa, they will use a combination of deceit and time to let her become accustomed to Ion's new status in her husband's life. Xouthos exits to sacrifice in honor of his newfound son, and Ion goes to prepare a feast for his friends. The Chorus sings once more before an empty scene about the fresh grief about to engulf Kreousa and expresses outrage that an alien no-name is about to enter Athens as the heir apparent.

Kreousa enters, accompanied by her ancient tutor, to learn from the Chorus the terrible news that Xouthos has gotten a child from Apollo while she is to remain childless. Kreousa is speechless, but her tutor has a ready interpretation of this turn of events: Xouthos begat Ion as some slave's child and gave him to an ally in Delphi to rear in secret, as part of a plot to take over the royal house of Athens. Finally Kreousa herself bursts out into a song that is a travesty of a hymn. She subverts praise into a condemnation of Apollo for this newest betrayal of her, for his long-ago rape, and for the death of their child. Afterwards, under the tutor's questioning, Kreousa repeats her tale, especially her anguish when forced to expose her baby. She and the tutor then plot revenge, but neither against the god himself nor against her husband, who has been kind up until now. They decide instead to murder Ion, using an ancient poison handed down in her royal family.

After a final prayer to protect the royal house of Athens from pollution, the Chorus learns that the plan failed; Ion is now coming to kill Kreousa. The queen takes refuge on Apollo's altar as Ion and his men enter. The ensuing confrontation is furiously angry, but just as Ion is about to defy Kreousa's suppliant status and have her dragged from the altar, the Pythia who rescued him long ago enters with the box in which she found him. She urges him to use the tokens to look for his mother, now that his father has appeared and he is leaving for Athens. As Ion's attention turns to this new puzzle, Kreousa bursts off the altar in excitement. She recognizes the special container and when she is able to answer Ion's suspicious questions about the tokens inside it, he is thrilled to embrace his long-lost mother. Ion now has new questions, concerning the identity of his father. Once Kreousa swears that she is telling the truth about Apollo, Ion wonders why the oracle said that he was Xouthos's true son. The queen has a ready answer — because Ion needs acceptance by a mortal father to secure his rule in Athens — but such a finesse of the truth is not enough for this longtime temple servant. He cannot believe that the god gave a deceptive oracle, and he needs to ask Apollo directly, is he the god's son or Xouthos's? Did the god lie or not? As he turns to enter the temple, a deus ex machina appears. Athena has come on behalf of Apollo, who chooses not to appear, lest the mortals blame him, and reports that Kreousa's story is correct. The goddess foretells the youth's glorious future as founder of the Ionians. Kreousa and Xouthos are not left out of the blessing; they will have two sons together, who will be founders of the Dorians and Achaeans. Athena closes by proclaiming that Apollo has managed all things well. Kreousa and Ion accept the news and exit in procession to Athens.

No summary does justice to the *Ion*'s elegant and compelling structure, which relies on a double set of recognitions combined with reversals that ironically invert one another.[45] Ion is first "recognized" by his "father" Xouthos in a reversal that seemingly changes his status to one of blessing and power, but this false recognition motivates Kreousa to make her deadly plans. Kreousa's plot, in turn, leads to the true recognition of mother and son and another reversal, this time of affection and loyalty as well as status, as Ion emerges with an even securer royal inheritance in Athens. The *Ion* delights in the irony of spectators constantly knowing more both about the past and about unfolding events than characters themselves. The tone of the play is often frankly comedic, but its substance is subtle and deep.[46] The forced happiness of father and son is encircled and balanced first by the agreeable rapport of Kreousa and Ion as strangers, and then by their deadly anger, which turns into the genuine happiness of mother and child.

Their final joy is only achieved through a tangle of suspicion, rage, and attempted murders that altogether overwhelms in its intensity both Xouthos's superficial delight and Apollo's contorted planning. Spectators may witness slapstick and a "happy" ending, but the tragedy as a whole enacts the tumult of human emotion that does not neatly resolve itself.[47] Because the play engages big questions, about divine outrage and destiny or about the founding of families and cities, it is also intellectually engaging. We are in presence of knotty interpretive problems, especially how to understand the relationships between human and divine action and between the past and present.

Earlier critics sought the play's meaning in issues raised by human suffering and divine planning. Some saw in the *Ion* Euripides' indictment of Apollo and official religion as it was enshrined at Delphi. For these critics, Kreousa's pain predominates, as well as Ion's confusion at the deceit practiced by Apollo to "manage all things very well" (1595). The intervention of Athena papers over a botched divine plan, devised without consideration of Kreousa's suffering, which would have resulted, if left to run its natural course, in familial murder. Other critics have seen the play as a confirmation, if not celebration, of divine benefi-cence, which finally brings good out of human suffering. In such readings, Apol-lo's seeming distance must be balanced by the impetuosity of human characters. Had mortals waited and obeyed the dictates of the oracles, the anger and at-tempted murders need not have occurred. One feature of such a focus is the degree to which it emphasizes Apollo as if he were a character in the play; instead, of course, he is an absence that is present only in the words of others and in Kreousa's memories.[48]

More recently, critics have preferred to situate the tragedy within the context of the larger contemporaneous Athenian intellectual project that attempted to define the city and its destiny by contrast with other cities and peoples.[49] In particular, the play's deeper meaning is found in its depiction of the obscure eponymous figure of Ion as an icon of Athenian autochthony. Autochthony is the birth from the earth itself of a founding hero, and such stories were often told of a city or people's foundation as a means of establishing claim to the land. Athens enjoyed at least two autochthonies: Cecrops, the first king of Athens, who took the form of a snake from the waist down; and Erichthonius, born from the earth after Hephaestus's attempted rape of Athena.[50] Once taken as simply part of the patriotic tone of the play, the intricate and numerous references to Athens's founding myths are now seen as the heart of the matter. Beneath the romantic action of recognition and reunion, the *Ion* is a study of Athens's origins. As such it offers its audience either a cautionary tale about how the violence that attends the founding of a city is concealed in the celebratory myths or a complicated but finally triumphant founding of Athens that validates its present glory.[51]

Yet if the play is principally *about* Athens, it also displays a peculiar propensity for violence, among both mortals and gods, that has recently received greater critical attention.[52] The violence done to Kreousa, and contemplated by her, generates great sympathy and is a serious roadblock to our understanding of the play's triumphal ending. Nancy Rabinowitz, for instance, attempts to uncover the play's continuing interest in Kreousa's violated body as "a strategy of displacement to satisfy the (misogynistic) Greek male desire to reproduce male from male." This ancient need serves the dramatic purpose of cementing the alliances of fathers and son that are necessary for Ion's status as a founder of Athens.[53] Stanley Hoffer examines the play's violence as part of its cultural structure; he assumes a culture's dependence on violence at every level — personal, familial, political, and military — and attempts to read the effects of these on the protagonist, Ion, himself, "the chaste temple servant." He concludes: "Ion's fairy tale reunion with Creusa may serve as an immediate escape from the tragic crescendo of violence, but not even the simple jingoism of Athena's speech can entirely hide the political realities that Ion has already described. Only through strife and suppression will Ion rule Athens and become the eponymous hero of Ionian culture and Athenian imperialism."[54]

My focus upon what I call the romance of belonging is sympathetic to both Rabinowitz's and Hoffer's approaches to the play's violence. The romance, as we shall see, is a site that deploys violence to create or deny family. But both Rabinowitz, whose emphasis upon the woman's body, and Hoffer, who reads larger injustices within Athenian culture, address the suffering in the *Ion* from a perspective that can obscure other sources of pain.[55] My study attempts to bring both sides of the suffering together as complementary parts of the engagement with the audience.

The tragedy's emotional heart of turbulence and pain, beneath the surface brilliance of structure and the symbols of Athenian glory, is to be found in the ancient tale of abandonment, in which all parties suffer.[56] Ion's abandonment is the source both of the natural sympathies human characters feel for one another and of the pain they inflict on each other. His exposure also generates tension in the dramatic action, which is built out of repeated reconstructions of it. In every scene and in nearly every choral passage, at least one character and usually two construct a tale of an abandoned infant, who is sometimes Ion but can also be a shadowy figment. No two of these reconstructions are alike, even when they immediately succeed one another. The differences can lie in small details — for instance, once Kreousa imagines that her child was eaten by birds, then, a scant thirty-five lines later, she says he was lost to wild animals. Such variations suggest a kaleidoscopic spin of emotions as Kreousa first tries to contain her ancient pain and then finally admits it.[57] And as Kreousa and Ion begin to take an active role in uncovering the past and reuniting with a lost child or parent, they participate in a reciprocity of dangerous ignorance about the past that leads them to the verge of disaster. Yet the cumulative effect of the differences throughout the play is to deny fixity to an authoritative vision of the event, a process studied in greater detail in Chapter 2.

The *Ion* is a play whose protagonist is a sign of destiny for Athens but also of choice and loss within a family. Because this family includes the ancient founders of Athens, the trauma experienced by Kreousa and Ion is also a mark of deadly choice at the origin of Athenian culture. A common and cherished foundation myth — the abandonment of the infant hero — becomes a tale of how both affirmation and loss may be situated at the foundation of the kingdom. In miraculously reuniting Kreousa and Ion as mother and son, Euripides' play authorizes Athens's special heritage as a foundation perfected by the gods, but their entire tale entangles spectators in their own kaleidoscope of emotions, as they witness versions of Ion's abandonment that are sometimes mythically distant and at other times disturbingly real and close to home.[58] The audience's own anxiety about origin is engaged by the spectacle of abandonment, and the *Ion* thus forms an eerie pairing with Freud's "From the History of an Infantile Neurosis," which builds its case for foundation on a tale of family union. In both texts we can read a larger romance of belonging, in which the full peril of creating identity is felt however much the drive to establish the foundation, of a city or an intellectual empire, seeks to conceal the suffering. I turn now to defining this romance and suggesting ways in which it still haunts us.

The Romance of Belonging — The Realities of Infant Abandonment

The romance of belonging is a tale of the moment when a choice secures the identity of everyone involved. The reality that obtains (here, either a family is created with parents and baby, or it is not) is dramatized and tested by the fantasy of choice, whether to accept or reject, because inherent in the choice is a peril whose lingering effects can suffuse the results.[59] The fantasy of the moment allows fluidity about who does the choosing and who is the chosen, and the lines of action stemming from choice are also fluid and reversible.[60] The romance of belonging as such can operate in any context in which we might wonder about the origins of an identity, what its constraints were and who made the decisions, but as suggested above in the Introduction, in Euripides and Freud the romance operates within the family, where the choices and their consequences are particularly immediate and traumatic.[61] That is what makes both the tragedy and the case history particularly appealing for investigation. In effect, life-and-death issues lie beneath the social constructions defining the roles of parent and child. Parents either pick up their newborn or throw it out, to death or worse. To state the choice in its starkest terms, for the formation of the family it comes down to an embrace or a murder. As will become clear in my discussion of the historical practice of infant abandonment below, abandonment is by no means the equivalent of murder, since it seeks to avoid the direct violence and pollution of murder. Nevertheless, sometimes the romance constructs abandonment as if it were murder (or the embrace as if it were something equally ghastly). And that is another key element in the romance of belonging: its capacity to construct and reconstruct its terms, to reflect its impact with differing degrees of intensity.

The term "romance of belonging" deliberately recalls a theoretical construction of Freudian psychoanalysis, the family romance, and challenges the premises of that construction. As Freud defined it, the family romance is a tale created by the neurotic child, which it uses in moments of anger to make sense of its origins in such a way that it can discount its parents: "His sense that his own affection is not being fully reciprocated then finds vent in the idea, often consciously recollected later from early childhood, of being a step-child or an adopted child. . . . the child's imagination becomes engaged in the task of getting free from the parents of whom he now has a low opinion and of replacing them by others, who, as a rule, are of higher social standing" (*SE* 9: 238–39).

Overwhelmed by feelings of neglect, the child consoles itself with the belief that its "real" parents are not the harsh, humble folk who foster it, but people who are nobler and its by birthright. This fantasy does not come from nowhere. The child originally thought its parents were omnipotent beings of inestimable value; these abandoning parents of its fantasy are an expression of its regret that it no longer believes in that earlier construction. Through psychoanalysis, the child recognizes that these two contrasting sets of parents are one and the same, and the fantasy is part of the reality, both as its precursor and screen. The family romance is a tale about origins that begins as a fantasy that defies the real and ends in a reality that although once screened by fantasy, overtakes and subsumes it. The fantasy is crucial as a site in which the child's conflicting images of its parents can be managed, but its lack of reality is never in doubt. Also unexamined as such is the child's fantastical longing for parents who did not want it and threw it out, although this longing is at the heart of an anxious wavering between desire and rejection. Freud does not reflect on the paradox of the child wanting parents who did not want it because, after all, there were no such parents — the implied gesture of rejection is merely the fantasy.[62] Freud does not allow abandonment to exist within his theoretical structure, even though that structure is only made possible by abandonment.

I do not construct the romance of belonging simply as a theoretical antithesis to Freud's family romance. In early human history, there seems to have been a moment of genuine peril for a newborn — and for the structure of the family his or her acceptance would create. In *Mother Nature*, a book about mothering among primates, Sarah Hrdy identifies the physical attachment of the human mother and newborn as the critical hurdle for the child's survival under the earliest living conditions for the human species in the Pleistocene period.[63] After any birth, a mother had to make an immediate decision, whether to pick this child up and suckle it, or discard it in favor of producing another child, and since the commitment was arduous both physically and emotionally (and other opportunities for producing children in more favorable circumstances or with better mates had to be foregone), Hrdy argues that a decision in favor of any particular child was neither "instinctive" nor "natural." Concomitantly, the human newborn evolved to be born with an arsenal of tactics for swaying that decision in its favor:

> Over tens of thousands of years, in worlds where infant survival often depends on maternal calculations, tradeoffs, choices, and prioritizing, an infant had to be appealing in order to extract more rather than less care from his mother, or in extreme cases to be cared for at all. . . . If, from a mother's point of view, deciding to suckle any one child means sacrificing some other option (usually the option to conceive again in the near future), . . . then survival from a human infant's point of view means being born sufficiently attractive to its mother to lure her into the first, largest, step toward lifelong commitment: the establishment of lactation.[64]

Here may be a physical basis for the primal trauma at the heart of belonging, an intrinsic link between the choice of abandonment and family that denies the "natural" in nurturing, especially that of the mother. In constructing the romance of this traumatic moment, I take account of both parents and study the relationship between father and son in particular in my second chapter's discussion of "From the History of an Infantile Neurosis." I consider the maternal role in the romance in greater detail in my final chapter.

Freud's elision of abandonment differentiates the family romance from the romance of belonging, in which abandonment is plainly the opposite of acceptance. In the romance of belonging, the outcomes of abandonment can vary from the miraculous (rescue by a god) to the gruesome (being eaten by dogs or birds), but they are all in opposition to the embrace, which is the physical gesture of acceptance. The choice is made from a remarkable perspective in which the parents can visualize both abandonment and embrace, but either outcome then forecloses further speculation. Whether the child is thrown away or embraced, its parents can no longer look at it from that perspective in which the decision is made, since the embrace brings them so very close to the child while the abandonment puts it far beyond view. The choice also eliminates that perspective for the child, who, whether separated or embraced, can no longer see its parents as the people who contemplated it and made their choice with a cold eye. Because the choice inevitably changes the perspective, from one of contemplation to one in which it is difficult or impossible to see the prior view, the full range of movement in the romance of belonging can be overlooked, elided, or written out of reality, so that parents and child (if it survives abandonment) can regard either belonging or abandonment as the natural or inevitable reality.

For instance, Freud's primal scene begins the child's trauma when it sees a moment of parental embrace. Later events in the child's psychosexual development activate this trauma, such that it longs to give up its position as simple witness and actually join in the embrace in complicated and perverse ways, but the process originates in observation. Freud's use of the term "scene" reverberates powerfully, because key here is the multitextured drama witnessed by the child. The primal scene enacts parental pleasure but it also dramatizes the economic transactions that allow the pleasure, through reciprocities of gifts and denial. The primal scene displays paternal power over the mother, the object of the child's own desire, as well as her suffering. It is also a mimicry of the child's greatest fear, castration at the hands of the father. Yet for all its trauma, the primal scene is a strangely comforting construction, because it dramatizes those actions that engendered the child. The primal scene puts to rest the question of a child's identity by allowing it to visualize its natal embrace.

Euripides' *Ion* dramatizes the other outcomes of the romance, those that eventuate from the child's abandonment, and the play's happy outcome projects the best possible fantasy under the circumstances.[65] Abandonment generates a world of dangerous possibilities that do not fade away in the presence of reality, and it even perverts language, to talk about fantastical — even impossible — outcomes. For example, in the first epigraph to this chapter, Kreousa's assertion that she killed Ion is an example of the durability of abandonment's fantasies. The queen twice strangely states, "I killed you" (ἔκτεινά σ'; 1291 and 1500), in a verb tense, the aorist, that is not normally used to talk about attempted or failed actions.[66] Yet in neither instance is Kreousa's claim true, because when she abandoned him, Ion was rescued, and when she tried to poison him, her plot was discovered. Kreousa's talk about the irreal as if it were real may be nothing more than a hyperbole, the starkest fantasy made possible by abandonment, which alienates the unwanted child in ways as good as murder. But the perversion of language made possible by abandonment does more than that. While the form and "happy" ending of *Ion* suggest that attempted murder does not really matter if it fails, the play also insinuates that for some things, intent is accomplishment. I killed you, says a mother to her child: such words have a reverberation between parent and child that is hard to stop.[67]

The romance of belonging also has a strange tendency to obscure responsibility. Although common sense would suggest that only the parents have a choice in the matter and are the agents at fault, while the child is either the victim or the beneficiary, the moment of observation and choice affects everyone traumatically, at least at some level. While the infant, strictly speaking, has no "choice" in the decision whether it is abandoned or raised, it exercises seductive power in the moment and then becomes relentlessly powerful as a result of the choice. For the child either begins a systematic consumption of the family's resources or exacts terrifying psychic costs in its absence, including the mutually antagonistic senses of terror of and longing for return. Although the parents' power seems paramount at the instant of the decision, if they choose abandonment, as we see below, they must live never quite knowing its fate, whether it lives or is dead, whether it can come back, and in what ways.

Such is the nature of a romance in which choice is fully active. Fantasy and reality are not so far apart, parent and child are both agents, and either outcome has chilling effects. This is the structure of what is at the heart of both the tragedy and the case history, and that such is the site of our beginnings is an intolerable notion, because either outcome turns out to be so painful. This last claim needs to be clarified. Are we really to believe that the embrace that seals a parental promise of devotion and care can be characterized as traumatic? And isn't the notion of abandoning a child, stated as such, so self-evidently traumatic that nothing further needs to be said? Matters are not so simple in either case.

Both the parental embrace and abandonment have been co-opted into the larger discourse of child development in perverse ways. On the one hand, the embrace is at the heart of the oedipal and as such, it becomes a peril whose self-evident dangers may blind us to other problems. On the other, in the talk about a child's maturation, those processes that enable the child to stand as an independent and morally autonomous individual, abandonment can be used as an equivalent term for less profound notions such as loss and separation. Such assimilation, however, changes a ghastly act into a necessary and heroic stage and denatures abandonment of its inherent physical violence. We need to destabilize our perception of both outcomes of the romance of belonging if we are to experience the traumatic effects of Euripides and Freud, and this task now takes us down two different paths.[68] First, I review one particularly provocative challenge to the oedipal family structure, with its privileging of the child's traumatic experience, which suggests how we can view the parents' peril in this romance of belonging. Then I turn to the status of abandonment in the affirming rhetoric of the child. Such rhetoric has a long history in our culture, stretching all the way from the mythic type of the hero or god abandoned at birth to modern talk of the necessary losses a child must experience in its growth. However, its status can be challenged by a look at a recent and surprising turn of events in our society, the legalization of newborn abandonment. These disparate paths come together in a twofold purpose: to suggest the fundamentally traumatic nature of the romance of belonging; and to remind us that, whether we are fully aware of it or not, we have inherited the visions of both the ancient tragedy and the Freudian case history. The abandoned child's longing for embrace haunts our psyche as surely as the prurient terror of the primal scene, because each conceals a larger horror in our identity.

I have suggested above that Freud's primal scene is something of a ruse: masquerading as originary trauma, it consoles the child about his identity by dramatizing his engendering. In the next chapter I explore the ways in which Freud needed this focus on the child's trauma, in part to silence Carl Jung as his rival. In her feminist study of Freud's (non)handling of the mother, Madelon Sprengnether has also challenged the oedipal privileging of the child as part of a patriarchal structure:

In "The 'Uncanny'" Freud comes close to acknowledging a condition of estrangement at the heart of being. Had he committed himself to such a vision, instead of vacillating between an image of mother as source of terror and of ultimate gratification, he might have conceived the process of individual development in less phallocentric terms. Had he meditated further on the condition of separation as a given of ego formation, recognizing in the body of the (m)other the indwelling of the uncanny which characterizes both memory and desire, he might have offered a model of preoedipal relations which would include the possibility of maternal discourse. Instead, psychoanalytic theory has remained predominantly a discourse of childhood, fixated on issues of male subjectivity, and the elaboration of patriarchal culture from which the mother is effectively excluded as an agent.[69]

While Freud identifies the mother's body as a site that is familiar and strange, comforting as well as terrifying, Sprengnether rightly perceives that he elides the "inherent double nature" of that site by viewing the neurotic experience as a process of repression:

> It often happens that neurotic men declare that they feel there is something uncanny about the female genital organs. This *unheimlich* place, however, is the entrance to the former *Heim* [home] of all human beings, to the place where each one of us lived once upon a time and in the beginning. . . . whenever a man dreams of a place or a country and says to himself, while he is still dreaming, "this place is familiar to me, I've been here before", we may interpret the place as being his mother's genitals or her body. In this case, too, then, the *unheimlich* is what was once *heimisch*, familiar; the prefix *"un"* is the token of repression. (*SE* 17: 245)

As Sprengnether rightly emphasizes, sequence is important for Freud here: he constructs a stage for the child when there was no separation from its mother's body, making it the primal "familiar," while later engagement with the father's phallus (re)generates her body as different and unfamiliar, a dissonance handled through repression. Sprengnether suggests that this "discourse of childhood" buttresses the patriarchal project because the oedipal language privileges the father's body as the origin of the child's trauma. The mother's body exists only as a passive site onto which the (male) child maps his experiences sequentially.

To clarify the traumatic nature of the parent's embrace, I build further on two insights to be derived from Sprengnether's discussion. First, the uncanny is better understood through simultaneity: both the familiar (of a caring embrace) and the strange (of that embrace now turned erotic) must reside inherently in the same site. The strange does not follow upon the familiar through deferred action. Sprengnether reads the familiar as the mother's nurturing embrace, the strange as that embrace turned erotic; in Chapter 4, I read the notions less erotically and more as a desire for belonging. Nevertheless, Sprengnether's defiance of the principle of deferred action — *Nachträglichkeit* — reinstates the mother as an independent will in the child's development, such that we gain a concomitant sense of multilateral wills, of both parents and child. My second insight depends on Sprengnether's sense that calling the child a victim is a crucial aspect of the patriarchal project. If our sole focus is on the child's suffering and our investigation is only into its sources, we shall naturally regard the adults as traumatic agents.[70] Within a mutuality of will and intent that emerges once the hierarchical structure is deposed, however, all participants can be constructed as suffering the primal trauma.[71] In a very real sense, the structure of the child as victim returns us to the very problem that haunts us, that our past is responsible for who we are; reinserting the adult as sufferer destabilizes that assumption sufficiently to allow us to see the traumatic site more thoroughly.[72]

Focusing primarily on the child's development has long been a dominant way of thinking about the family and has important implications for this study, particularly regarding abandonment. Euripides, for instance, can take for granted that his audience's intellectual and emotional equipment includes stories about gods, heroes, and even historical figures exposed at birth. These tales suggest the inherency of survival, despite natural danger, human cunning, or divine spite, as a sign of coming glory. Exposure, survival, and glory are not sequential but intrinsically linked as an epiphany of divine or heroic identity. In a recent study of the theme in Euripidean tragedy, Marc Huys notes: "Without ἔκθεσις [exposure], without separation and abasement, no glorious return, recognition and rehabilitation would be possible. The extraordinary and superhuman capacities shown by the abandoned infant through his survival in wild nature make his later successful career inevitable."[73] The god's or hero's abandonment at birth is his first test and proof of his divine or heroic status. Survival marks him as a child of destiny while his destiny ensures and necessitates his survival, such that cause and effect are not strictly linear but interconnected within every layer of the mythic narrative. Huys articulates the familial decision within the narrative as an ambiguity: "Exposure, as 'an attempt at infanticide that is not intended to succeed,' is an intrinsically ambiguous act, a threat to the life of the hero child which is always overcome and gives way to a new and more glorious revival."[74] Exposure is inevitably motivated, at least in Greek myth, by familial fear or guilt. A close relative, often a grandfather, *wants* this child dead; or its mother fears that others will torment or kill it if it lives. They choose exposure as the means to effect its removal without personal pollution.[75] The intent that blocks its success, however, is divine, and the heroic or divine child's destiny is further marked by the defiance of its natal kin.[76]

This structure of abandonment is a powerful narrative for child development, one that anchors the very impulse for growth in the child's destiny and identifies its past as that which would stop it. Not surprisingly, this narrative structure is ubiquitous in literature, and abandonment is not an absolute but can be rewritten as an accidental loss, the death of a parent, or other, more (physically) benign forms of separation. However their absence is handled, the parents are the past and only relevant for the movement of present into the future.[77] The loss of the buttresses the family provided stimulates the child's own resources for survival and causes it to construct alternative relationships, prudently or not, as substitutes for the missing parents. These quests inevitably lead the child back to its natal family as the authority of the past, an inevitability that, because of the confrontation with the child's "true" origins, is the final test of its hard-earned sense of self.[78] The past, in the form of the natal family, also provides the template that accounts for the nature of the child's foster mentors, whether positively or negatively.[79] This essentialization of destiny can reflect larger political ideologies, particularly the process by which these succeed one another. Farah Mendelsohn argues that nineteenth-century fiction sentimentalizes the figure of the abandoned prince-to-be, "[a] popularization of absolutist monarchy just as it was about to disappear from the European political stage, overwhelmed by the demands of the new capitalist aristocracy. Ironically, the true message of this romanticism, the assumption that fitness to rule is genetic, was essential to the establishment and co-option of this new order. Capitalism needed romance to establish it as a normative value."[80] The new order feeds on the assumptions of the old, particularly regarding destiny ("genetic" fitness), while it also celebrates the self-invention or creation of the abandoned child as a model of individual enterprise and success.

The structure of abandonment is also a subject for theorists in fields ranging from anthropology to folklore and, of course, to psychology and psychoanalysis.[81] Bruno Bettelheim, for instance, charts the motif of the child separated from its parents as an impulse that may emanate either from the child's wish for independence or the parents' desire to help it develop.[82] Yet parental motivation as a positive force is rarely the issue; helplessness in the presence of dire need or brutality are more likely but often relatively irrelevant.[83] The focus remains on the child's progress toward independent maturity.[84] Abandonment in this context is part of growing up, the most intense expression of anxiety about being left alone, but naturalized as part of the scale of separation experiences. Freud himself illustrates how the hyperbole that appropriates the language of abandonment renders its perilous effects virtually meaningless: "In cases in which the two children are so close in age that lactation is prejudiced by the second pregnancy . . . what the child grudges the unwanted intruder and rival is not only the suckling but all the other signs of maternal care. It feels that it has been *dethroned, despoiled, damaged in its rights*" (my emphasis).[85] This sense of violent displacement has little real meaning within the confines of the family in which the child is not seriously at risk of being put out on the street. The ubiquity of abandonment as a developmental motif situates it within a discourse that conceals the most dangerous aspects of the real-life practice; instead, the motif of the child separated from its natal roots becomes shorthand for how children grow up. It is a useful vehicle for representing the process because it supports the assumption that we do not grow unless and until we have to do so on our own.[86] Parents are meant to be left behind — abandoned — if not outright overcome. Yet often the key to such tales of identity lies in acceptance of those natal origins just as Freud predicts in the family romance. Parents neither help us as much as we'd like nor hinder us as much as we assume and resent — they're just parents; we are the ones who need to grow up. Our thinking about "abandonment" is assimilated to this larger, positive goal and thus robbed of a sense of peril.[87]

The motif of the abandoned child in contemporary fiction is so common as to be stale, but it can still display the flexibility of a living — or at least an undead — metaphor. Fascination with Harry Potter, a recent instantiation of the motif, may be due in part to J. K. Rowling's shrewd reworking of it.[88] Predictably, Harry derives his exceptional power as a wizard from his very lack of parents, but that act also makes him perilous because it establishes his archenemy, the evil wizard Voldemort, as a foster figure. As the case of Oedipus, the most famous foundling of all, reveals, the terrifying thing about the orphaned or abandoned child is that he can end up with too many intimate connections. His parents give him an identity that can never be eradicated; but without their nurture, the hero becomes someone else as well through the choices and design of those who foster him. Rowling insinuates randomness at this point for understanding Harry's identity, through a prophecy that Voldemort himself chooses one of two boys to be his rival. This ambivalent outcome is not one that would have been recognized by the ancient Greeks, for whom the fulfillment of prophecy was overdetermined, with signs in nature and the cosmos replicated in the mortal figure. By tying Harry's connection with evil to the randomness of human choice, Rowling denies the inherent cause and effect of natal blood and foster nurture. Her strategy is refreshing but not a little alarming. If we accept that our identity is a matter of random choice, have we laid to rest concealed anxieties about identity? Is a random choice better after all than a studied one?

If the motif of the abandoned child resonates within our culture as a sense of autonomous destiny, we may believe that the resonance is fading into little more than a ghostly echo, given the current understanding of culture's pervasive structuring of who we are. Yet to judge from a largely unheralded revolution in thinking about what to do with babies found in the trash, abandonment may pack more of a psychic punch than we realize. The language used here tells a complicated tale of a culture recoiling from deeply troubling issues. We recoil at the suffering of innocent newborns when they are exposed, of course, but our newfound solution suggests that our psyches recoil at something else as well. The real and full horror of the abandoned child raises the specter of a lost identity far beyond the comfortable clichés of the development motif.

In the autumn of 1999, after eleven babies were abandoned in ten months in the city of Houston, the state of Texas enacted a "safe haven" law decriminalizing the abandonment of infants at emergency rooms of hospitals or fire stations. Marjory Williams was an early advocate who urged the entire nation to consider this option more seriously: given the much larger problem of neglected and abused children, she writes, "to steer this tiny minority of desperate mothers toward emergency rooms instead of trash cans seems merely common sense." But Williams feared that our society's "most sacred beliefs about motherhood" would hamper efforts to decriminalize abandonment. She reasoned that since mothers are by nature supposed to love and want the children they bear, it seemed doubtful that anyone would want to give them the legal opportunity to demonstrate otherwise.[89] Events have proven Williams wrong, however; with stunning speed all but four states and the District of Columbia had, by June 2006, legalized some version of infant abandonment.[90]

It is not clear how our culture so quickly ironed out its complicated reactions to the problem of unwanted children, reactions ranging from opinions about abortion and adoption to concerns about inadequate foster care, as well as those nostalgic beliefs about motherhood.[91] Texas had its epidemic shock — five newborns were abandoned in one two-week period — but elsewhere, any rise in the number of exposures has been more gradual and largely invisible.[92] Some suggest that the trend toward legalization was fueled by the contradictory handling of two cases of newborn abandonment in Delaware, in which the judge rebuked prosecutors for seeking longer prison terms for a Filipino couple who cooperated with police than for a white couple who did not.[93] The Internet may have accelerated the popularity of the movement, with web sites to guide expecting mothers through the process. For instance, Illinois advertises its "safe haven" law with the promise of blank anonymity: "You're afraid. You don't want to keep this baby. You just want someone to take it, keep it safe, make sure it gets a good home. Don't panic. There are people who will help you with no questions asked. At all. Ever."[94] This Internet advertisement presents leaving an infant anonymously in a safe location as the *alternative* to abandonment, but other sites call these laws "legalized abandonment."[95]

In some states single voices have plainly had a disproportionate influence, and one woman in particular, through reenvisioning dead exposed infants, brought a new and persuasive rhetoric about abandonment into wide prominence throughout the United States.[96] Debi Faris began her mission to give burial to abandoned babies, a mission she calls divinely inspired — "It was as if God tapped me on the shoulder and said, 'Debi, would you stop here for a second?'" — after she heard of a newborn found strangled in a duffel bag and wondered who would bury him. She claimed the child as a member of her own family and arranged for his funeral, only to learn from the coroner's office that two more dead children were about to be buried in a mass grave — would she like to take care of them as well? She has since buried many abandoned children. Faris's mission expanded to get California's "safe arms for newborns" law passed. Faris was motivated by this paradox: "'Right now, it's a felony for a mother who can't care for her baby to leave him in an emergency room. . . . She's prosecuted for doing the right thing." Nationwide attention and accolades have followed for Faris and her mission.[97]

The language in which the issues were discussed by Faris and by the media points to the change in our thinking about newborn abandonment that made legalization possible. We can also discern the strategy by which we made the change. In an extraordinary act of cultural and legislative will, abandonment has been systematically redefined: it is no longer an illegal sign of failed love by "desperate" parents, but rather "the right thing" and the ultimate act of love. The title of the *Parents* magazine column on Faris, "Giving the Love They Lacked," itself condenses the entire act of abandonment into emotions that simplify our response. Love encapsulates Faris's motivation to rescue dead infants from mass graves. And all the feelings and conditions that may account for any parent's choice to abandon a child illegally — shame, fear, helplessness, ignorance, poverty, and substance addiction — are distilled into a lack of love. Making a complex problem into a matter of love allows for the necessary redefinition of abandonment for legalization to take place. Instead of effectively destroying newborns, abandonment becomes the process that saves them, and it thereby no longer defies our convictions about the sanctity of motherhood but confirms them. The language of love allows the abandoning parents to redeem themselves, at the very moment when they are repudiating that title of parent as a sign of failure, because our culture agrees to redefine the abandonment as an act of love.

Of concern has been that this redefinition may exert enormous pressure to "do the right thing" on a new mother hesitating over whether she can care for a newborn. The alternative version of the abandoning mother, however, demands this risk. This is a mother of great moral indifference who, unfettered by the law, would simply throw away a child she might otherwise choose to rear. The specter of such a monster haunted some in the debate over legalization: no law could be changed with *her* in mind.[98] And so an alternative version of the desperate mother had to be constructed: bad, maybe, in contemplating abandonment, but waiting to be good under a law that transforms her anguish into love even as it obliterates her as a mother. For this is the cost of the transformation that legalizes abandonment: it deliberately and irrevocably severs the natal bond in an assurance to the parents that they can act anonymously. Under most of these laws, there is no medical history for the baby, little opportunity for the mother to change her mind, and virtually no chance for the natal father to intervene with his claim.[99]

Redefined, legalized abandonment breaks a link that has always seemed unbreakable and yet is a source of anxiety. How did our modern culture quiet that anxiety? And why would we want to do that? The means of calming ourselves is clear in the rhetoric used to argue the issue. Once the abandoned child loses its natal identity, it can become anything someone wants to make it, simply through redefinition or reconstruction. Faris offered to bury that first dead infant she heard about as "a member of her family," an extraordinary redefinition, but only the first such transformation presented in the coverage of her work. In *Parents*, for instance, that membership in a family allows a murdered child to be redefined as a loved child by virtue of its burial. Throughout the larger discussion, any legally or illegally abandoned child becomes a series of abstractions. The unwanted and abandoned child is first a token of someone's desperation and failure, but it can become a token of having done the right thing, and then, through adoption, it becomes "someone else's blessing," Faris's phrase for the child whose mother has the courage to abandon her child properly.[100]

The expression "blessing" makes abandonment sound nearly like an economic transaction, and if we so hear it, we can suddenly discern not only who really profits but from whose perspective the whole transaction is constructed in the first place. Turning unwanted children into others' blessings is not just a matter of life and death for the children, but a matter of profit for the society as a whole, which is empowered to perform this nearly magical transformation legally. Morally and socially, our culture profits because we have addressed even one aspect of the problem of uncared-for children, but there is an emotional benefit as well. Illegally abandoned children are stark reminders of identity's fragility: because they have lost that which is assumed to give the best or truest sense of self, natal parents, they can all too easily become nothing but garbage. Through the law, the abandoned child's indeterminacy turns out to be a useful tool to prevent this ghastly transformation. With the past deliberately obliterated, the child is ready to bless another family and thereby, the larger society. The ease and swiftness with which abandonment has been legalized, although it has been steeped in sentimental goodwill, suggests the urgency felt about solving the ancient problem.[101]

And yet the taint of the ancient is there, if we judge by the language that transforms abandoned children. Faris performed one last transformation on the strangled child she took into her custody: she buried it in a cemetery plot that she named the Garden of Angels. In defiance of their brief fate as mortals, abandoned children enjoy a final, remarkable conversion into beings of power and beneficence.[102] In death as angels or in a life blessed by legality, abandoned children receive from the state an identity that no longer indicts the community for its indifference and incompetence. It is not simply that we've saved such a child, but that we have done the best possible thing for it — and how often does a society get to believe that about itself? But society has also stepped in and stopped the otherwise ceaseless, random swings of identity that remind us of what happens when we are unstuck from our origins. Legalizing abandonment means that unwanted children trouble us no more, as long as we are willing to obliterate the natal parents who were the evidence of that lack of desire. Yet the whole process of rescuing the infant and effacing the natal parent has to be legalized and made a formal and public part of our culture under the law, thereby suggesting that nothing is simple about obliterating the past. There is always the abyss created by the loss of natal identity.

Freud disavows the abyss altogether. On the one hand, his primal scene requires a natal bond among all participants and thereby essentializes natal identities.[103] On the other, his theoretical consideration of abandonment in the family romance defines it out of existence as nothing more than a neurotic fantasy. Freud was handling within the psyche what had been an overwhelming interest in abandonment (broadly conceived in terms of separation from parents) in the nineteenth-century literature that formed the basis of Freud's education and intellectual formation. But although he was an avid reader of the world's literatures and found them a source of provocative examples, he could not permit the delicate balance by which the past offered both the model for and confrontation with identity. The earliest template for identity — the child's natal origins — is not the model of later constructions of family and authority; it *is* all later constructions. As I discuss further in the next chapter, the psychic task is not to confront parallels and differences in an effort to understand the self, but to evaluate properly in each setting the single, unitary identity that is the constant.

Freud's stake in this theoretical identification of a past reality with later fantasies can be clarified by comparing it with his younger rival Jung's insistence on the reality of the phase of separation for his archetype of the Child. In their fight over the older man's authority, both Freud and Jung theorized about the family romance and its issues in a predictable way: the younger man postulated a real and independent experience of separation from the parent as crucial in the psyche's development. Freud's younger rival and former pupil maintained the reality of the isolation as a crucially fruitful moment in psychic development: " 'Child' means something evolving towards independence. This it cannot do without detaching itself from its origins: abandonment is therefore a necessary condition, not a concomitant symptom."[104] Not for Jung is Freud's explanation that the child's sense that it once had different parents is pure fantasy. Instead, Jung speaks of a longing or "fascination" in consciousness for the solution that Freud so neatly defined out of existence. The "child's" miraculous survival in its abandonment provides a triangulation between differences that are otherwise irreconcilable: "For the conscious mind knows nothing beyond the opposites [that represent an 'agonizing situation of conflict from which there seems to be no way out'] and, as a result, has no knowledge of the thing that unites them. Since, however, the solution of the conflict through the union of opposites is of vital importance, and is moreover the very thing that the conscious mind is longing for, some inkling of the creative act, and the significance of it, nevertheless gets through."[105] While Freud resolves the conflict through his vision of origins, Jung finds resolution in the "redemptive effect" of perceiving the abandoned child as a necessary reality, but one that is finally incomprehensible to consciousness.

In Greek myth, the abyss of lost identity in abandonment is circumscribed by the guaranteed reunion of the hero with his natal family, whether the result is ruin or glory. The vast range of possibilities between the lost past and the present reality is compressed into just two: the hero who knows his roots; or one who is temporarily without parents, but whose eventual reunion with them is taken for granted. Both possibilities bespeak the fact that one is never without natal parents.[106] But what about Euripides' spectators—what did they think about abandoning newborns? A plausible construction of what Athenians did with children they did not want and what they thought about what they did helps frame the context for the anxiety as it appears in the *Ion*.[107]

We can infer from notices of Solon's laws in the early sixth century that it was legal for Athenians to abandon newborns, even legitimate offspring, under certain circumstances, although we have no sense of how many infants were exposed.[108] In fact, we do not have much information at all about the practice from the fifth and early fourth centuries, but social historians recognize that technical questions about the number of exposures and their manner may not be the right ones to ask when trying to assess the effect of the custom on a culture.[109] Even when somewhat reliable statistics about the frequency of abandonment first become available—not until the eighteenth century of this era—they do not give a sense of how the choice affected any individual nor how the society as a whole registered the practice.[110] But the early evidence is particularly suggestive about the questions that most concern us, namely, why the Athenians exposed newborns and how the practice registered with them emotionally.

Ritual evidence suggests that the act of abandonment was not without moral gravity, while other references in literature reveal two crucial moments of evaluation and decision.[111] The first moment seems to have been the midwife's. In a famous metaphor in the *Theaetetus*, Socrates casts himself in the role of an intellectual midwife, whose task is to scrutinize new ideas and discard those not worth rearing:

> Apply, then, to me, remembering that I am the son of a midwife and have myself a
> midwife's gifts, and do your best to answer the questions I ask as I ask them. And if,
> when I have examined any of the things you say, it should prove that I think it is a
> mere image and not real, and therefore quietly take it from you and throw it away,
> do not be angry as women are when they are deprived of their first offspring. For

many, my dear friend, before this have got into such a state of mind towards me that they are actually ready to bite me, if I take some foolish notion away from them. (151b–c)[112]

As Cynthia Patterson argues, the metaphor has point only if such an inspection of a newborn was familiar to Plato's readers.[113] Soranus, a second-century c.e. medical writer, also instructs midwives on how to determine a baby is worth rearing: "Now the midwife, having received the newborn, should first put it upon the earth, having examined beforehand whether the infant is male or female, and should make an announcement by signs as is the custom of women. She should also consider whether it is worth rearing or not."[114] The procedure seems based on what midwives normally do, although the elaborate list of criteria that follows expects too much of any newborn.[115] Soranus does not indicate here whether the midwife herself disposes of a defective child, but he later suggests that she did, perhaps by drowning it.[116]

If in the first instance it is the midwife who decides about the life of the child, perhaps regardless of the "passions" of the parents, we may see a hint of a ritual in her laying the child upon the ground, as a precursor to the cardinal gesture of acceptance, picking it up. This gesture lies at the heart of the next moment of scrutiny and decision, when the parents themselves pass judgment. Again in the *Theaetetus*, Socrates continues with his metaphor of the idea as a newborn, now with an allusion to the ritual that formally introduced it to the household's gods, the *amphidromeia*:

> Well, we have at last managed to bring this forth, whatever it turns out to be; and now that it is born, we must in very truth perform the rite of running around with it in a circle — the circle of our argument — and see whether it may not turn out to be after all not worth rearing, but only a wind-egg, an imposture. But, perhaps, you think that any offspring of yours ought to be cared for and not put away; or will you bear to see it examined and not get angry if it is taken away from you, though it is your first-born? (160e)

Within a week of birth, the newborn's father picked it up and carried it around the family's hearth as a sign of his acceptance.[117] Socrates' reference to the indignation and anger felt at this moment corroborates our intuition that parental anxiety, particularly for a firstborn, could be high at this moment of choice. The decision to dispose of a newborn was not an emotionally neutral one, however legal.

Parents were guided in their decision about a newborn by complicated reasons, such as the infant's sex, the family's economic circumstances, or suspicion about paternity.[118] The role of the first two factors is hard to judge. Whether a disproportionate number of girls were exposed is a notoriously thorny problem for which the evidence is conflicting. Patterson warns against using the pervasive Greek misogyny as an argument, since this was aimed at wives, while a marriageable daughter could be a valuable political commodity in Athenian culture, and her dowry was less likely to be a burden than is normally assumed.[119] The dramatic evidence seems to provide the best picture, but it is a problematic guide in either direction. Tragedy deals with the careers of male heroes exposed at birth, but this evidence may be less relevant because of its mythic content.[120] Comic jokes in the fifth century about the substitution of illegitimate babies assume a ready supply of abandoned male babies, but in later comedy a typical plot device is that of a baby girl being abandoned and rescued. It is difficult to know what to infer about the popularity of this plot device. Scholars argue the diametrically opposing explanations, with some asserting that it was out of the ordinary and therefore spiced up a story, while others arguing that its commonness made it a plausible turn of events.[121]

The role played by financial circumstances in a family's decision to expose a child was not simply a matter of making ends meet. Patterson argues that when economics were a factor in parents' decision about rearing a child, a desire to preserve riches might be as crucial as worry about meager resources.[122] Hesiod articulates both aspects of the paradox in his advice to his brother in *Works and Days* 376–380, when he suggests that rearing one son is a way to foster one's wealth, but numerous children are good for sharing the work. Other factors might still influence the decisions of impoverished families, which are usually out of the reckoning of high status accounts. As Plutarch comments: "When the poor do not rear children it is because they consider poverty the greatest of evils and do not wish to share it with their children; it is as though poverty were a contagious and dangerous disease."[123] In Chapter 3, I explore further how economic reckoning operates in the romance of belonging.

Concern about a newborn child's legitimacy might lie at the heart of a decision whether to rear it.[124] A new father had to bear public testimony to the legitimacy of a son by enrolling him in his phratry or clan, and the rituals surrounding a child's birth were crucial evidence of a father's acceptance of the newborn into his household. Both the *amphidromeia* and the more public *dekatē* are used by orators to indicate that a man was a legitimate citizen.[125] Although we have no evidence that exposure was the automatic consequence of doubt, the father's gesture of lifting his child up and carrying him or her around the hearth suggests, in the words of Mark Golden, "a reversal of the alternative, exposure (ἀπόθεσις or ἔκθεσις)." Both possibilities, acceptance or rejection, are situated in the ritual life of every citizen *oikos* and thus in the state itself.[126] The reality of both possibilities invigorates the Platonic metaphor of a newly born idea suffering the same jeopardy as a newborn child and, as suggested above, may underlie the midwife's first act of laying it on the ground for inspection.

Aristophanes' jokes about infant substitution in the *Thesmophoriazusae* further illuminate the crisis of legitimacy enacted in the rituals that begin (or end) a newborn's sojourn in a family.[127] The Kinsman, a character masquerading as a woman, describes the whole process:

> Then I know of another woman who pretended to be in labour for ten days, until she was able to buy a baby, while her husband was going round buying birth-charms. An old woman brought it in — the baby, I mean — in a pot, with its mouth stopped with a piece of honeycomb so it wouldn't cry. Then, when the old woman nodded, straightway she cries, "Go away, husband, go away, I think it's going to come right now!" (The baby had given the pot a kick in the stomach.) He ran out of the room, delighted; she pulled the thing out of the baby's mouth; it bawled. Then the wicked old woman who'd brought in the baby runs to the husband with a beaming face and says, "You're the father of a lion, a lion! He's the very spitting image of you." (502–516)[128]

Jane Gardiner plausibly argues that such a scenario exploits a ubiquitous fear of the husband that his offspring might not be his own. Instead, his wife introduces an alien child, either to fulfill her "duty" to the *oikos* of producing heirs or to hide her infidelity.[129] The Aristophanic jokes about infant substitution also insinuate an unsavory commercial air into the process. A woman can circumvent her husband's efforts to secure the integrity of his *oikos* by relying on economic transactions rather than sex. By buying a baby a woman can make herself into a mother (and her husband into a father).[130] Abandonment lies at the heart of such a fantasy, with its capacity to turn children into whatever coin is needed. And that transformative power creates a further, profound paradox lurking within the emotional and social tangle of Aristophanes' jokes. A newborn is exposed because its father suspects its legitimacy, but it thereby becomes another woman's final means to fulfill, however spuriously, her wifely function of producing an heir.[131] The exposure saves one household from taint but makes possible, at least potentially, the illegitimate alien that is feared by every other father and that undetectably pollutes the entire polis.[132] In the presence of this anxiety, the real numbers, or the frequency of supposition, are beside the point: the taint to the state is the same even if only one such child is inflicted upon it.[133]

The references to infant substitution in the *Thesmophoriazusae* suggest one further piece of information to be inferred about the ancient practice of abandonment: the availability of newborns on which the jokes depend supports the assumption that abandoned children did survive. Perhaps this seems an obvious point, but given the ease with which modern discussions assimilate exposure to infanticide, it needs to be stressed.[134] Parents might decide not to rear a child, but that decision did not guarantee, or perhaps even intend, its death. Later evidence suggests that natal parents did assume that their abandoned infants survived: Roman law even regulated how such children could later be recovered by their natal families.[135] For fifth-century Athens the evidence that parents could believe, if they chose, that their exposed infant survived has to be drawn from otherwise seemingly extraneous details found in contemporary literature.[136] Despite the tenuousness of the evidence, however, the distinction between abandonment and infanticide should be carefully maintained.[137] If exposure kept alive the possibility, however unlikely or unwelcome, that an abandoned child was not lost forever through death, then the parents faced a complicated set of sensations: their child was both gone and yet remained as something that could potentially be returned or recovered. Mythic and dramatic treatments of heroic and divine exposures certainly play on this reality, but Athenian spectators may also have felt a similar tension in reality.[138]

Ancient spectators would thus have watched the *Ion* with a complicated awareness of infant exposure. As it really happened in their lives, abandonment addressed concern for the preservation and integrity of institutions — the private *oikos* and the polis itself — at the expense of the individual. The exposure of an infant was still emotionally charged for parents and might be accompanied by pain and anger, as well as anxiety about the possibility that an abandoned child might survive, for better or worse. This real-life experience of infant exposure is not synonymous with the mythic images of exposure, where it is the equivalent of attempted infanticide. Ancient parents probably did not consistently assume that they were consigning their children to death, although they could imagine far more dismal outcomes for their abandoned children than myth and tragedy offered.[139] Viewers also expected to see an exposed hero survive and grow to glory — for how else could there be a story? Part of that glory lay in his reunion, fatal or joyous, with his natal family, since this is an invariable feature of Greek myth, at least.[140] But evidence (and common sense) suggests that this mythic imperative was contradicted by a reality in which abandoned babies suffered very different fates, such as being reared to be slaves or prostitutes, if they did not die. Mythic survival in drama conceals a wider truth about the outcome of exposure: that it was not bipolar, with death the only alternative to (re)union.

Methods of Reading

This book juxtaposes two texts, from disparate moments in Western culture, that explore an anxiety about identity's irrevocable link to the past. The past is variously figured: concretely, in parents, who decide whether to accept or expose a newborn; mythically, in a city's founding; or abstractly, in the right theoretical construction of the unconscious. That past, however concrete, mythic, or abstract, proves to be the site of an originary choice that established identity traumatically. The romance of belonging could tell the entire tale of both choices, to abandon or to embrace, as their consequences radiate out from the originary moment, but that moment itself seems to be so terrifying that both texts make it hard for us to grasp. They conceal one or the other outcome, or obfuscate it in repetitions that continually suggest what happened but always deny it. In what follows, I read both the *Ion* and "From the History of an Infantile Neurosis" closely for this repetition. As inheritors of Freudian thought, we parse repetition as an attempt by our unconscious to communicate what it has concealed as too traumatic to lay to rest. Repetition offers an enjoyment that momentarily releases the anxiety, but it is also an attempt at therapy that cannot succeed. Both texts famously rely on repetition to build either dramatic action or case history.[141] Tragedy enacts the trauma for that release in its spectators; psychoanalysis presents itself as the therapeutic solution, the setting that will replicate the trauma not for anxiety's sake but for knowledge and healing. Both texts finally shut down the seemingly incessant repetition of the originary moment through an act of will—the tragedy's deus ex machina or Freud's final pronouncement about what the primal scene means.

Yet it takes this act of will, and the preceding spectacle of repetition lingers after it, surviving the fiat to haunt the audience. This is the dynamic that becomes problematic for the viewer of the drama or reader of the case history. Besides questions about the moment itself and why it is so hard to grasp, the audience has its own preconceptions about and experiences of abandonment and familial embrace entangled in the action of the play or narrative. Their repetitions awaken and interact with the audience, such that the anxiety suggested by recollection and reconstruction is communicated to the audience and further heightened by it. The trauma of origins is not merely to be contemplated by either Euripides' or Freud's contemporaries — nor, I have suggested, by us. Thus I read the repetition both for the trauma it evokes and for the ways in which it eludes the projects of tragedy and psychoanalysis.

My effort to interrogate repetition for the anxiety it preserves parallels the work of Victoria Wohl's *Love Among the Ruins* (2002), which suggests how in reading fifth-century texts as eruptions of the Athenian unconscious, the work of fantasy is crucial. Fantasy represents the individual's engagement with ideology, the effort to bring the ideal or "a contingent and artificial, 'fictional' set of social arrangements," into reality. In this structure, Wohl suggests, with Judith Butler, that we understand the "collective unconscious" of the Athenians as that part of ideology that the individual (or group) cannot consciously accept and has repressed.[142] She seeks signs of what must be repressed by citizens about the erotics of democracy in those moments of slippage in Thucydides, Aristophanes, or Plato where the sequence of logic is defied by something else, a topic out of joint. Wohl reads that something else as evidence of the tension between citizens' fantasy of democracy and their own resistance to that fantasy.

I agree that Athenian drama, history, and philosophy are sites in which a sort of collective unconscious of the Athenians can be read. Instead of interrogating further the construction of desire, however, I seek to understand Euripides' tragedy as the site of an anxiety whose nature is worth inquiry. Repetition seems key for this anxiety, and in a sense, this book's origins lie in a fascination with the rhetoric of certain kinds of repetition that appear in Greek tragedy. Why is it that in some tragedies concern for a family's identity is reconstructed over and over as a single long-past event? Take Agamemnon's murder, for instance. Electra and Orestes, in whatever play one finds them, must constantly rehearse his death and their suffering thereby. Why does such repetition seem to drive their tragedies? The *Ion* is another, more pronounced example of a play whose action is driven by attempts to recollect or reconstruct the moment of the protagonist's abandonment, yet which ends in a constructed (re)uniting of the family torn apart by that ancient trauma. As such, it offers a rich site for studying anxiety about the past of belonging.

Freud's case history of the Wolf Man is equally susceptible to an inquiry into his uses of repetition. His notion of the primal scene, as an originary drama of neurosis that replicates itself relentlessly until it can be calmed by psychoanalysis, seemed initially to be a provocative model for thinking about why a certain kind of drama seems to require the repetition of an originary traumatic act. Yet Freud's notion of the primal scene is no simple analytic tool. Because Freud repeats versions of it so often in his narrative, the scene becomes implicated in its own restless blend of reality and fantasy, memory and construction. The primal scene as a narrative device self-destructs as an entity in its efforts to dramatize the union of family.

The rhetoric of repetition seems then to be an expression of a neurotic anxiety, but in what ways can we measure how the audience becomes implicated in this anxiety? The psychoanalytic critic Peter Brooks proposes a relationship between a text and its readers in which readers collaborate with the "constructions" of the text in a process that is inherently repetitive:

> Through the rethinkings, reorderings, reinterpretation of the reading process, the analyst/reader "intervenes" in the text, and these interventions must also be subject to his suspicious attention. A transferential model thus allows us to take as the object of analysis, not author or reader, but reading, including of course the transferential-interpretive operations that belong to reading. Meaning in this view is not simply "in the text", nor wholly the fabrication of a reader . . . but in the dialogic struggle and collaboration of the two, in the activation of textual possibilities in the process of reading.[143]

The text's voice, like that of the patient, employs language that is articulate to the analyst/reader, not itself, particularly as readers apprehend what is transferred to themselves as symbols. Readers, like the analyst, need to account for these transferred symbols by constructing persuasive scenarios. Thus Brooks recommends a rhetorical study of the text itself as the proper locus for the psychoanalytic interpretation, for it is there that text and reader struggle and collaborate to determine meaning.

Brooks's identification of the analyst and reader is telling, however, as is his intimation that transference is a part of the process that the reader can control to some extent.[144] His process of construction as a means to understanding a text's rhetoric is benevolent — constructive, as it were — and aimed, as Freud says, at "explanation and cure":

> As Freud writes in the last sentence of another important essay, "The dynamics of the transference," "for when all is said and done, it is impossible to destroy anyone in

absentia or *in effigie*" (Freud 1958a, p. 108). The statement appears paradoxical in
that it is precisely "in effigy" — in the symbolic mode — that the past and its ghosts
may be destroyed, or laid to rest in analysis. What Freud means, I think, is that the
transference succeeds in making the past and its scenarios of desire relive through
signs with such vivid reality that the reconstructions it proposes achieve the effect of
the real. They do not change past history — they are powerless to do that — but they
rewrite its present discourse. Disciplined and mastered, the transference ushers us
forth into a changed reality. And such is no doubt the intention of any literary text.[145]

Thus a text may repeat obsessively what it cannot lay to rest. Readers can intervene, however, with scenarios — readings of the text's symbols — made vivid by
their own experience, and their intervention brings forth the reality of text.

Yet to equate the reader with the analyst, as Brooks suggests, produces a
disturbingly tidy semblance of hierarchy and orderliness. Readers bring to the
text their own matters they cannot lay to rest, as Freud surely did, such that the
relationships of mastery, reader over the text, may not operate within the transference that Brooks predicts. As I have suggested in this chapter on the matter of
infant abandonment, both ancient practice and our own newfound taste for laws
that "legalize" it, must make some profound difference in how the repetition of
the act affects an audience.[146] Freud's theoretical insistence on the irreality of
abandonment and the primacy of the oedipal embrace must also be taken into
account as context for a case history whose didactic purpose everywhere assumes
an audience well versed in such matters. Thus in either case, repetition may elicit
anxiety in the audience as well as its interpretative intervention.

This matter of the audience's context is not confined simply to abandonment
or acceptance, and each successive chapter also predicates other matters that
trouble clear lines of reception between text and audience. Chapter 2 thus engages in greater detail the construction of a master narrative or account out of
fantasy: the establishment of authority is at stake, and the audience's assumptions
about that process trouble the matter. Chapter 3 examines the costs and rewards,
in economic terms, of giving birth to identity; again, when fantasy is where these
accounts are kept, they are hard to balance. The audience's sense of commerce
comes into play here. Finally, the need to stop the unstoppable, to put to rest
questions that cannot be answered, the subject Chapter 4, engages the audience's
sense of acceptable final resting places; these turn out to involve motherhood.

The rhetoric of repetition is something else besides neurotic; it is inherent in
the action of both tragedy and case history, action that can be untidy in its

intricate repetitions and at the same time insistent about itself. As Bert O. States remarks, arguing against the notion of subtlety in dramatic signification, "the play does far more than is necessary in order to mean whatever it may mean."[147] Freud also shaped his case history of the Wolf Man so that his readers themselves experience the repetition of the primal scene, although as a tool of analysis. We cannot just submit to the neurosis of the repetition in an effort to master it; we have to engage it as a rhetorical structure as well, as a matter of self-conscious choice by Euripides as tragedian and Freud as educator and agent provocateur of psychoanalysis. The net result, I think, is a discussion that at times reads as if it were psychoanalytic and at others as if it were another, more pragmatic analysis of what the text is up to. The distinctions are based on my intuitions, guided by the findings of other scholars and readers.

One feature of my discussion that will be apparent to those familiar with the literature on the case of the Wolf Man is the degree to which I try to steer clear of reanalyzing it. I am referring in particular to the inclination I alluded to earlier in this chapter, of trying to see in what ways and why Freud missed the correct construction of the primal scene. Was it actually the Wolf Man's molestation by his sister, as he himself came to believe? Or was it the father's incest with Anna, his sister, as is most notably argued by Abraham and Torok? Or was there no scene at all, given what we now know about childhood development and youthful memories, as suggested in the recent biography by Louis Breger? Given how much we know about Freud and his patient and about Freud's habits of argumentation and theorizing, such attempts are tantalizing to make, but I have tried to avoid the temptation. To begin with, the evidence reveals less than is often imagined, as suggested by the contradictory versions that have appeared. We might also recall Freud's own warning about the dangers of analyzing enemies from their writings; it cannot be done, he says, because true psychoanalysis requires the consent of the one being analyzed, as well as submission to the analyst's authority.[148] Attacks on Freud's construction of the primal scene often read (and are meant to be read) as reanalyses of either him or his patient, and as such they have that hegemonic drive for authority. The reality of any such mistake or deliberate deception on Freud's part is less useful than a study of his rhetoric in the case history itself, if we wish to think about what he was trying to achieve. Nevertheless, I am aware that the language of (re)analysis creeps into my discussion, perhaps a testament to the hegemony of the psychoanalytic frame of reference that Freud did so much to establish. When I have detected such lapses, I have done my best to reframe them as rhetorical analysis.

Finally, Brooks's optimistic project of collaboration between text and reader is compromised by a ghostly absence in both texts. Guiding the directions of this study is my sense that the encompassing structure of the romance of belonging is not fully or directly engaged by either text because it cannot be. Full contemplation of the romance is foreclosed by its completion. Nevertheless, both text and audience engage this romance as a matter of longing for identity, and in my interpretation, I bring the romance in as an analytic model, to recover as best as I can the felt consequences of romance as these remain in the text.

CHAPTER TWO

Competing Accounts

All that I mean to say is this: scenes, like this one in my present patient's case, which date from such an early period and exhibit a similar content, and which further lay claim to such an extraordinary significance for the history of the case, are as a rule not reproduced as recollections, but have to be divined — constructed — gradually and laboriously from an aggregate of indications. . . . I am not of the opinion, however, that such scenes must necessarily be phantasies because they do not reappear in the shape of recollections. It seems to me absolutely equivalent to a recollection, if the memories are replaced . . . by dreams the analysis of which invariably leads back to the same scene . . .

FREUD, "From the History of an Infantile Neurosis"

Ἴων· γῆς ἄρ' ἐκπέφυκα μητρός; Ξοῦθος· οὐ πέδον τίκτει τέκνα.
Ἴων· πῶς ἂν οὖν εἴην σός; Ξοῦθος· οὐκ οἶδ', ἀναφέρω δ' ἐς τὸν θεόν.
Ἴων· φέρε λόγων ἁψώμεθ' ἄλλων. Ξοῦθος· τοῦτ' ἄμεινον, ὦ τέκνον.

Ion: Was I born from the earth as my mother? *Xouthos:* The ground does not bear children.

Ion: Then how can I be your son? *Xouthos:* I don't know; I refer it to the god.

Ion: Come, let's get hold of different accounts. *Xouthos:* That's better, my son.

EURIPIDES, Ion

But it is interesting that he should have said, "Don't criticize, don't reflect, don't look for contradictions, but accept what I tell you, and improvement will come by itself." That's how he succeeded in bringing about a total transference to himself. Is that a good thing, do you suppose?

THE WOLF MAN (SERGEI PANKEJEFF)

The romance of belonging destabilizes attempts at an authoritative account of its operation and goals; its outcome immediately obscures the process. Yet the desire to belong needs this obscurity, because it makes the resulting identity seem inherent and tidy. Freud's "From the History of an Infantile Neurosis" and

Euripides' *Ion* both suggest that belonging desires simplicity but the process makes it impossible. In both texts there is a longing for a simple account and an anxiety about it. The turmoil and conflict of the Wolf Man's childhood are to be understood through the single prism of the primal scene, whose very existence is confirmed most of all by the fact that it accounts for everything in ways that other explanations do not. Yet phantom recreations of that scene haunt the case history and confound the image of the single parental embrace that is supposed to explain everything. Meanwhile, such is the nature of abandonment that to wonder about Ion's origins is to find the possibilities endless. The abandoned infant can become anything — a temple slave, food for birds, or a king's son — and these fates conceal his natal origin in such a way that other constructions of his past become plausible. Abandonment is a slippery vehicle on which to build an authoritative account of the founding of Athens.

This chapter studies how constructing a narrative of primal identity troubles lines of authority, whether that narrative explains a patient's childhood trauma or a hero's abandonment. The romance of belonging establishes identities for its figures — father, mother, and child — either within the structure of family or deliberately outside of it. The process is an alchemic blend of reality, in the form of a choice, and fantasy, to manage the consequences of that choice. Can a theoretical framework account for the relationship between memory and construction? Freud provides one in a scene whose oedipal nature insists on natal identities. He begins his understanding of the primal scene by girding it to the familial structure, which serves both his therapeutic goals and his efforts to cement his control over psychoanalysis; he can then work backward to prove that construction confirms memory. In the process Freud sets up a scene that proves inherently unstable. Because the primal scene holds both construction and memory, both fantasy and reality, its contours can be constantly recreated or restated. Freud finds this power valuable rhetorically, but he cannot finally control its drive to repeat or replicate the traumatic drama, either within his case history or within the master narrative of psychoanalysis itself. I look first in the case history at how Freud constructs identities for himself and his patient in the discovery of the primal scene. A site in which the hierarchy of authority should have been clear — even overdetermined — becomes unstable when Freud uses it as a supple rhetorical weapon to buttress his version of the primal scene and psychoanalysis itself. I then use this shifting sense of the primal scene to interpret Carl Jung's staging of his falling-out with Freud: where Freud perceived a theoretical structure of family that confirmed an oedipal hierarchy, Jung saw a myth of the rebellious son.

Ancient tragedy stages what Freud's case history engages theoretically. The

Ion dramatizes the romance of belonging through recreations of abandonment, while driving toward embrace. The play projects the future by reconstructing the past, a dramaturgy that reveals how much kinetic energy there is in the question of Ion's origin. The *Ion* constructs the birth and abandonment of its hero primarily through dialogue: one character's recollection is set beside another's conjecture and interpretation; appeals to reason are juxtaposed with deference to authority. It is striking how many such constructions there are, with no two alike enough to establish a definitive version.[1] It takes nothing less than a deus ex machina to stop inquiry into Ion's identity: Athena imposes a future on the past and assures Ion of his rightful place in Athens's destiny. The construction of a narrative that accounts for Ion is a process that, once set in motion, cannot otherwise be stopped. I examine the beginning of this process in Hermes' opening monologue and then study the use of dialogue to construct versions of Ion's birth, particularly in the first episode. Dialogue unpacks the problematic of such construction into two voices, one of memory and the other of inference, in the form of fantasy or speculation. The voices may collaborate, as Ion and Xouthos do in the second epigraph to this chapter, or they may compete for authority, as Ion and Kreousa subtly do in their first encounter, but with collaboration and competition embedded in the very structure of each scene, no sense of primacy emerges for any single account of Ion's abandonment.

Psychoanalysis predicates a pervasively hierarchic relationship between doctor and patient in which transference recreates the oedipal therapeutically. This analytic moment exploits both construction and memory, but Freud is clear about which is to be provided by whom: the analyst's role is to construct; that is what gives him power. The analyst's repetition (through construction) of the patient's trauma thus acquires an extraordinary ontological status, because although drawn from the patient's account, the repetition has a greater claim to the truth that can break through all other neurotic recreations and thereby heal. Moreover, Freud's case history is a genre developed to extend that power beyond the domain of the couch into the discipline itself. "From the History of an Infantile Neurosis" is a particularly rich site for studying the process in both regards, because the primal scene, the very structure intended to deploy the analyst's power, cannot guarantee his authority; rather, it creates challenges to it.[2] Within Freud's conceptualization of the official roles of patient and analyst, we can see both his self-confidence and the reasons why those roles become so fraught in the context of the primal scene.

In *The Interpretation of Dreams*, Freud explains the need to inculcate good reporting habits in the patient, who must learn, not to apply "criticism" in recounting his memories and dreams, but to produce simple "self-observation." Otherwise, the patient's critical faculties discount and discard details or events as irrelevant, meaningless, or unimportant. Ironically, a discussion that illustrates the problem particularly well is one in which Freud quotes his self-interpretation. He dreams he saw a picture of a friend who, in the dream, was also his uncle (as usual, Freud italicizes dream material): " '*R. was my uncle.*' What could that mean? I never had more than one uncle—Uncle Josef. There was an unhappy story attached to him." And then, in a note: "It is astonishing to observe the way my memory—my waking memory—was narrowed at this point, for the purposes of the analysis. Actually I have known five of my uncles, and loved and honoured one of them. But at the moment at which I overcame my resistance to interpreting the dream I said to myself that I never had more than one uncle—the one that was intended in the dream" (*SE* 4–5: 138).

Freud's nonanalytic interpretation censors details, but since he is both patient and analyst, he can use the experience to remark on the power of the unconscious over memory.[3] The psychoanalytic truth is what matters here, not the reality of five uncles, and this unique patient understands that. In a normal analytic setting, the patient cannot be allowed such liberties, since his neurosis precludes the reliability of his own constructions, which will merely foster and perpetuate the neurosis: "He [the patient] must adopt a completely impartial attitude to what occurs to him, since it is precisely his critical attitude which is responsible for his being unable, in the ordinary course of things, to achieve the desired unraveling of his dream or obsessional idea or whatever it may be" (*SE* 4–5: 101). And in any case, shutting down such critical faculties enables the patient to concentrate better on simple observation and produce many more "ideas."

Freud wants the patient's frame of mind to be a kind of midway state between dreaming and wakefulness. The patient relaxes his critical faculty, as if falling asleep, but also "purposely and deliberately abandons" that tendency in sleep to convert "involuntary thoughts" into "visual and acoustic images" as dreams. Instead, the patient "attentively follow[s] the involuntary thoughts which now emerge, and which—and here the situation differs from that of falling asleep—retain the character of ideas. *In this way the 'involuntary' ideas are transformed into 'voluntary' ones*" (*SE* 4–5: 102; emphasis in the original). Freud encourages his patients to convert memories and details from their unconscious, not into the drama that is dreaming (in "visual and acoustic images"), but into verbalized ideas, which the analyst interprets through constructions that may account for them. Given the patient's illness, the analyst must do what the dreaming state does for all of us and become the dramatist of the unconscious.[4]

Although Freud recognizes that patients may suffer too great a resistance to bringing out "involuntary ideas," he asserts that by and large, a patient's ability to suspend all critical judgment is manageable (in fact, "by no means difficult"; *SE* 4–5: 103). He points out that other moments in our psychic life, such as the process of artistic creation, require a similarly free release of "involuntary thoughts," and appropriates a metaphor for the process from Friedrich Schiller, quoting a letter to a friend of Schiller's in 1788:

> It seems a bad thing and detrimental to the creative work of the mind if Reason makes too close an examination of the ideas as they come pouring in — at the very gateway, as it were. Looked at in isolation, a thought may seem very trivial or very fantastic; but it may be made important by another thought that comes after it, and in conjunction with other thoughts that may seem equally absurd, it may turn out to form a most effective link. Reason cannot form any opinion upon all this unless it retains the thought long enough to look at it in connection with the others. On the other hand, where there is a creative mind, Reason — so it seems to me — relaxes its watch upon the gates, and the ideas rush in pell-mell, and only then does it look them through and examine them in a mass. You critics, or whatever else you call yourselves, are ashamed or frightened of the momentary and transient extravagances which are to be found in all truly creative minds and whose longer or shorter duration distinguishes the thinking artist from the dreamer. You complain of your unfruitfulness because you reject too soon and discriminate too severely. (*SE* 4–5: 103)

Freud claims that Schiller is describing an "exactly similar attitude" at work in the creative process as in psychoanalytic interpretation.[5] Both art and the psychoanalytic setting thrive on the mind's capacity to pour out a profusion of ideas, and both must beware of a censor in the thought processes that stifles creativity, a censor that can either be admired as Reason or understood as shame or fear of the mind's extravagance. Both art and psychoanalysis require an avoidance of premature interpretation of details or ideas in isolation, since both are grounded in the belief that something may become meaningful only in a later context.

Freud finds Schiller's language an attractive distillation for the collaborative work in psychoanalysis, but there is a fundamental difference between the views of the artist and of the psychoanalyst. Schiller asserts that when our censor, whatever we call it, relaxes its guard, the mind itself performs a creative act, fearlessly turning extravagance into art or dream. Freud wants only the extravagance — ideas in profusion but not dramatized or interpreted. The patient must be fearless or trusting enough to relax his own role as censor, so that the psychoanalyst can become Reason at the gate. The patient's illness mitigates any struggle for authority in this division of effort between the two participants in psychoanalysis, and the hierarchy is normalized by the "fundamental law," as Freud terms it, that the patient must say whatever comes to mind; otherwise, there is no psychoanalysis.[6] Yet there remains a tension about what flows forth when Reason stops its watch on the gate: is it art or merely the raw material for constructing art? For Freud, the memories found in the patient's extravagant profusion of talk are not privileged as such but are simply more ideas for him to dramatize.[7]

Officially, Freud's construction of the primal scene follows from these principles. The scene dramatizes and authenticates the unconscious as a place where the distinctions between reality and fantasy are irrelevant because their collaboration, either to traumatize or to heal, is what is key. Thus Lacan can claim that the "exceptional importance" of the Wolf Man's analysis lies in its capacity to illustrate the principle that "the real supports the phantasy, the phantasy protects the real."[8] The patient's memories likewise are interpreted by the analyst's constructions, and elsewhere Freud considers such constructions principally to be goads for further revelations from the unconscious, as he notes in his case history of the Rat Man: "It is never the intention of such discussions to call forth conviction. They are only supposed to introduce the repressed complexes into consciousness, to kindle the conflict about them on the soil of conscious mental activity, and to facilitate the emergence of new material from the unconscious" (*SE* 10: 181n).[9] But in "From the History of an Infantile Neurosis," Freud's "discussions," his constructions of the Wolf Man's infantile experiences, take on an authoritative status beyond this therapeutic strategy. At the heart of the primal scene is a competition of body and will that Freud calls the oedipal, and here there is no ambiguity: the oedipal drama confirms a hierarchy of identities within the natal family. Furthermore, Freud insists on an absolute equivalence among his construction of the primal scene, the dreams that activated it, and the Wolf Man's memory:

> I am not of opinion, however, that such scenes must necessarily be phantasies because they do not reappear in the shape of recollections. It seems to me absolutely equivalent to a recollection, if the memories are replaced (as in the present case) by dreams the analysis of which invariably leads back to the same scene. . . . It is this recurrence in dreams that I regard as the explanation of the fact that the patients

themselves gradually acquire a profound conviction of the reality of these primal scenes, a conviction that is in no respect inferior to one based on recollection. (*SE* 17: 51)

Intellectual conviction can replace memory for Freud, a conviction that he has the authority to inculcate in his patient, however gradual the process.[10]

Collaboration and contest are in tension in the master narrative of psycho-analysis, whose constructions depend upon everyone's choosing to participate in the paradox. As I suggested in the previous chapter, many critics have speculated on the sources of this tension, whether Freud missed something in the Wolf Man's past, deliberately suppressed what did not fit his theory, or was actually working out his own infantile trauma and imposed his anxieties on this case. I argue that it is the presence of a romance of belonging — a longing for a complete tale of origins — that is at work here. The programmatic insistence that the primal scene dramatizes the oedipal embrace requires the elimination of the other possible outcome, the abandonment of the child. What is left behind is an anxiety about belonging that destabilizes the identities set up for both patient and analyst. The presence of this anxiety is revealed in the restless permutation of the primal scene, which is constantly repeated and restated in varying terms that change identities subtly.

To understand why Freud presents the matter as he does in "From the History of an Infantile Neurosis," we need to keep in mind that the political struggles of the early psychoanalytic community, in the throes of its first major crisis of leadership, were a constant pressure on the construction of the primal scene. Freud's adversaries are ghosts of earlier tales of origins that he once entertained, pupils banished from the fold but not gone. While authority is an issue from the outset in "From the History of an Infantile Neurosis," the Wolf Man is not presented as the source of the conflict.[11] Freud characterizes his patient as ideal, "obliging," and intelligent in his own recollections; he could also be persuaded about his doctor's construction of the primal scene.[12] Instead, it is Freud's bitter struggle for authority with two of his inner circle that gives the case history its thrilling tone. Alfred Adler, who had been part of Freud's earliest attempt to promote sustained discussion of psychoanalysis, was one of these opponents. In a formal and irrevocable split in 1911, Adler left the fold to pursue his own version of psychoanalysis, which, to Freud's relief, he finally called "individual psychology."[13] Shortly thereafter, Freud found himself in an even more painful and momentous struggle with Carl Jung, his most brilliant follower and chosen successor. By late 1913 he faced the prospect that Jung, who had become hardly less well known than himself, would end up in control of psychoanalysis. Eventually, Jung was only too happy to distance himself from Freud's version of psychoanalysis, rather than redefine it as his own, but Freud could take no chances. In his first explanatory footnote to it (*SE* 17: 7), he characterizes "From the History of an Infantile Neurosis" as the sober, scientific corollary and frame to his "On the History of the Psycho-Analytic Movement," published in 1914 (*SE* 14: 7–76).

Freud's attacks on Adler and Jung in "On the History of the Psycho-Analytic Movement" are detailed and direct, but he rejects the notion that one can refute one's enemies by analyzing them.[14] Too detailed a dive into the psyches of Adler or Jung would be both dangerous and not genuine psychoanalysis: "Analysis is not suited... for polemical use; it presupposes the consent of the person who is being analysed and a situation in which there is a superior and a subordinate. Anyone, therefore, who undertakes an analysis for polemical purposes must expect the person analysed to use analysis against him in turn" (*SE* 14: 49). Freud does not attack Adler and Jung directly in the case history because lack of hierarchy and of their consent prohibits it from polemicizing against them. Instead, he builds them in as imaginary challengers to the primal scene, as replicas of their real threat to his control of psychoanalysis. Since Freud cannot silence the "twisted re-interpretations" of Adler and Jung, which are not innovations in his view but attempts to alter the truth by skewed blends of reality and fantasy, he constructs voices of dissent to the work he presents.[15] It is a delicious staging, since the men who have been twisting his voice are now incorporated into his argument as parallels he can dismiss.[16]

The case history also carefully frames the issues of consent and hierarchy within the primal scene as a rebuke to those challenging Freud. Proper authority is to be both the solution to the mystery of the Wolf Man's infantile neurosis and the essence of (and antidote for) what is discovered to be the primal scene. The narrative characterizes the Wolf Man and his analyst as endowed with the complementary qualities needed for successful analysis. Freud appears as a healer wielding his authority benevolently, and the Wolf Man becomes the traumatized child. Freud explicitly refuses to write a case history that addresses the Wolf Man's adult symptoms and career, despite the Wolf Man's request that he do so. Instead, the case history focuses on a child whose perceptions and recollections offer no challenge. The primal scene can be recovered, it is implied, because analyst and patient are in a proper therapeutic hierarchy.

To get at the nature of the identities constructed for Freud and the Wolf Man, we can focus first on the recovery of the primal scene itself and then on how

Freud deploys it as a construction to prove its validity. Early in his analysis, the Wolf Man recalled the dream for which Freud gave him his pseudonym: he was sleeping (in the dream) when the window next to his bed suddenly flew open, waking him up and revealing white wolves perched immobile but menacing in a tree just outside. Freud recognized the importance of this early anxiety dream, which he dated to the eve of his patient's fourth birthday, but interpretation of its complete significance eluded him. Freud constructs this problem as the responsibility of the Wolf Man, who, after three years, was too comfortable with the analytic process:

> The first years of the treatment produced scarcely any change.... The patient... remained for a long time unassailably entrenched behind an attitude of obliging apathy. He listened, understood, and remained unapproachable.... It required a long education to induce him to take an independent share in the work; and when as a result of this exertion he began for the first time to feel relief, he immediately gave up working in order to avoid any further change, and in order to remain comfortably in the situation which had been thus established. (*SE* 17: 11)

Freud breaks through this apathy with an ultimatum — an irrevocable date for ending the analysis.

Freud describes this impasse and its resolution as part of his prefatory material in the case history, and it initiates our perception of the Wolf Man in a series of oppositions: obliging but apathetic, intelligent but unwilling to take risks, capable of being taught, but only up to a point. At first glance, this does not sound like the ideal patient who has relaxed his censor at the gates of his mind, but this oppositional structure conceals a congruence that, once rewritten in the primal scene, will reveal the identity of the Wolf Man as a tautology. Apathy becomes longing; an unwillingness to take risks becomes a needy drive; the barrier to further understanding, a leap into the tangle of embraces in the primal scene. The transformation of opposition into congruence is, of course, a figure of the psychoanalytic patient, whose presence in the analyst's office as an adult predicates a neurotic toddler. In the Wolf Man's case, this toddler in turn marks and conceals an infant witness of the primal scene. They are all the same person, such that when Freud refuses the adult symptoms in favor of the infantile, he is not really leaving them out. But the figure of opposition masking identity is, as Freud remarks more than once, what is most extraordinary about the patient:

> I shall now bring together some peculiarities of the patient's mentality which were revealed by the psycho-analytic treatment but were not further elucidated and were

accordingly not susceptible to direct influence. Such were his tenacity of fixation, . . . his extraordinary propensity to ambivalence, and (as a third trait in a constitution which deserves the name archaic) his power of maintaining simultaneously the most various and contradictory libidinal cathexes, all of them capable of functioning side by side. His constant wavering between these (a characteristic which for a long time seemed to block the way to recovery and progress in the treatment) dominated the clinical picture during his adult illness. . . . This was undoubtedly a trait belonging to the general character of the unconscious, which in his case had persisted into processes that had become conscious. (*SE* 17: 118–119)

Under the guise of describing his patient's "peculiarities" Freud insinuates the larger image of the Wolf Man as a figure for the unconscious. In constructing this patient's identity as a child whose "obliging apathy" is really terrified longing and relentless will, Freud gives readers a figure who is essential to the primal scene; it is a crucial part of the oedipal family—the infant who watches his parents' (sexual) interactions and desires to intervene, to replace either his father or his mother.

To break through to the ideal patient, Freud's role as analyst, through transference, is constructed to replicate the ideal father in the primal scene. Freud does not construct himself as the patient's father, who appears in the case history as simultaneously remote and vigorously present. The Wolf Man's father is constructed out of memory and theory to be a figure of arbitrary power and terrifying mystery. He torments his wife with sexual intercourse, which the child does not understand; privileges a sister for reasons that are all too obvious but impossible to assail—her cleverness and beauty; and commands both rebellion and submission in the toddler. Threats of castration, all of which explicitly come from women in the Wolf Man's family, emanate from his father by reason of phylogeny. This father also uses money to reward his favorites. The Wolf Man resents it when he sees his father give such a present to his sister and later fights with his mother over the estate that his father has left in trust to both. Above all, the Wolf Man's father is gone—he dies just before the patient enters analysis.

Freud offers in transference a more reliable father, one who can maintain his distance but also keeps his promises.[17] Such a figure is integral to the primal scene but also key to its recovery. The case history reveals that Freud made two crucial promises to the Wolf Man. First, in order to remove the Wolf Man's doubt about the efficacy of psychoanalysis, "the patient's strongest weapon, the favorite expedient of his resistance," he promises the Wolf Man sure relief from his bowel problems (75). Sure enough, as the Wolf Man's bowels recover their function, his doubts also dwindle away. The sequence — promise, fulfillment, cooperation — gives Freud "satisfaction," and it is one he uses on other patients as well.[18] In this case, although Freud does not comment on the parallel, the sequence also replicates the dynamic assigned to feces in the primal scene by the Wolf Man's libidinal fantasies. They are an offering to his father, a substitute for the child that a woman can offer, in exchange for sexual satisfaction. The Wolf Man can never learn what his father would do if his fantasy came true, because his terror of the required castration paralyzes him, but he does learn from Freud what a fulfilled promise feels like: relief. A promise meant to secure confidence in the psychoanalytic process also secures the operation of the primal scene.

The second promise is actually a threat: to break through the Wolf Man's comfortable stagnation, Freud fixes a deadline for ending the analysis. The results are once again gratifying to the analyst: "Under the inexorable pressure of this fixed limit his resistance and his fixation to the illness gave way, and now in a disproportionately short time the analysis produced all the material which made it possible to clear up his inhibitions and remove his symptoms" (*SE* 17: 11). This gesture remains a most controversial feature of Freud's relationship with this patient, but prudent or not — and Freud defended his gamble to the end — its effect on the construction of the primal scene was evidently crucial.[19] Only then did the Wolf Man produce the material that Freud used to unravel the puzzle of the dream of white wolves and construct the primal scene.[20] Ruth Mack Brunswick, who later treated the Wolf Man for psychosis, acknowledges the utility of a time limit in the case of a patient who is "glad . . . to retain one last bit of material," but she recognizes a peril:

> Perhaps sometimes the pressure actually brings out all that is there; but I can imagine that an inaccessibility which necessitates a time limit will most often use this limit for its own ends. Such seems to be the case with the Wolf-Man. . . . There was no way of meeting [his] resistance other than the removal of the [analytic] situation itself. This resulted in the patient's bringing sufficient material to produce a cure, but it also enabled him to keep just that nucleus which later resulted in his psychosis.[21]

Brunswick perceives a crucial feature of this patient, his resourcefulness in analysis (further examined in Chapter 3).[22] As with the promise regarding his patient's constipation, Freud replicates the dynamics of longing felt by the Wolf Man for his father in his construction of this first primal scene. When Freud exercises his analytic authority by setting a time limit, he produces the circumstance in which his patient is glad to collaborate. (The Wolf Man himself also recalled a third promise, which he said Freud made but did not keep — that he would remember the primal scene; see below.)

Such are the seemingly passive child and reliable father who collaborate to discover the primal scene. While Freud explicitly refuses to give a clear chronology of the analysis and its vagaries, his narrative suggests that prior to his ultimatum, they had gotten this far with the dream: "*A real occurrence — dating from a very early period — looking — immobility — sexual problems — castration — his father — something terrible*" (*SE* 17: 34; Freud's emphasis). The ultimatum produces "spontaneous work" by the Wolf Man that proved key (33).[23] Freud quotes his patient's epiphany: "It must mean: 'My eyes suddenly opened.' I was asleep, therefore, and suddenly woke up, and as I woke I saw something: the tree with the wolves" (34). From the Wolf Man's realization that the window's opening represented his own real awakening, Freud can construct the primal scene: the Wolf Man, at the age of eighteen months, while suffering from malaria, had awakened from an afternoon nap in his parents' bedroom and had seen them, partially dressed in their white undergarments, having intercourse *a tergo*.

In the collaboration to recover the primal scene, the Wolf Man's role is commensurate with his infantile characterization. He cannot remember the scene itself; he can only recall the malaria, a detail that helped Freud date the primal scene and explained the parents' presence during their son's nap.[24] Instead, the crucial thing the Wolf Man recognizes is that the primal scene is exactly that — something that he witnessed.[25] At the originary trauma of his neurosis, he was merely a spectator — what else could make such sense if he was indeed an infant? Only later psychosexual events turn that infant into a participant through fantasy. Yet the implications of his recognition are telling. Here in therapeutic guise is the shock of witnessing the sexuality of the father, but the Wolf Man cannot recover a real spectacle behind the fantasy. As he articulates what the first part of his dream means (that he awoke in real life), he superimposes the symbol of the wolves in the tree onto the vanished memory. He uses fantasy to mark the site of it, even when talking about the real event. The memory that the Wolf Man cannot find must then be supplied by Freud, who infers that there must be an infantile event to account for his patient's neurosis. For one thing, the Wolf Man's memories as a two- and three-year-old were clear enough — full of turbulence both externally and internally — but nothing struck Freud as capable of being the origin of it all.[26] Naturally enough, given his social class and circumstance, the Wolf Man's memories of these years have to do with the female servants rearing him, such as his nanny and the governess, and with his sister. Later analysts would argue that the absence of the Wolf Man's mother is also crucial. Freud considers his patient's interactions with these women as deriving from an earlier trauma that must have involved his father.[27]

Freud is guided here by his psychoanalytic convictions: he is expecting to find a scene that enacts the oedipal drama. These convictions flow from his sense of the healing power of psychoanalysis, or, put differently, they flow from his sense of what must be healed. The dramatization of the oedipal in the primal scene, while it is later activated as a crisis of libidinal identity, is in fact a confirmation of familial identity grounded in the father. Under the turmoil of the primal scene lies a tableau that guarantees the identity of the father, for if the primal scene is to have oedipal force, the man in it must be the father. The oedipal conflict requires and confirms paternal identity; the primal scene allows the child to see its father doing the very thing that engendered it. The father is no longer an abstract or invisible sexual rival. Yet the primal scene shows the child the hierarchy, too, for the child is the infant witness only, while the father is enjoying something *banal* (Freud's word), something as normal as sex with his wife. Deferred action will make this hierarchy traumatic, but analysis restores the healing vision of a father asserting his proper rights (to sexual relations with his wife).

If the primal scene is to dramatize this essence of the oedipal and thus serve as the master narrative of psychoanalysis, it is plain why Freud must construct his patient and himself as he does. The child needs everything the scene promises to reveal about the father. From this perspective it is also no wonder why Freud was so persistent in constructing the scene and using it on the Wolf Man's behalf. His words about the original appearance of the wolf dream during the analysis suggest the influence he seems to have had: "The patient related the dream at a very early stage of the analysis and very soon came to share my conviction that the causes of his infantile neurosis lay concealed behind it" (*SE* 17: 33). Freud has to have confidence in his own power of discernment about what is crucial; otherwise, psychoanalysis offers nothing more than the "free, conversational exchange" that the Wolf Man has already tried and dismissed.[28] As Freud constructs the scene to offer an epiphany of the oedipal, it also becomes a narrative between patient and analyst with authority properly deployed.

Yet this official construction of the primal scene, with its suffering infant witness and purposefully active, reliable father, is not the only construction offered in "From the History of an Infantile Neurosis." Freud explicitly ventures into a region of the unconscious where fantasy and memory are equivalents, and here there are seemingly endless possibilities for constructions of the primal scene. It is a site both of pleasure, reflected in the parents' faces and the infant's feces, and of terror, reflected in genitals. It is a commercial site, where an exchange of gifts reckons the value of sexual favors, but it also involves an exchange of physical abuse and sexual suffering.[29] Freud grasps the protean nature of the primal scene and freely restates it from various perspectives, such that it becomes a tableau of the mother's feelings, a site of future anal-erotic turmoil, and so on. Throughout his case history, Freud remains fully confident that these constructions serve to confirm, either positively or negatively, the veracity of his authoritative account.

Freud understands that all this construction creates a problematic about authority:

> But what is argued now is evidently that they are phantasies not of the patient but of the analyst himself, who forces them upon the person under analysis on account of some complexes of his own. An analyst, indeed, who hears this reproach, will comfort himself by recalling how gradually the construction of this phantasy which he is supposed to have originated came about, and, when all is said and done, how independently of the physician's incentive many points in its development proceeded; how, after a certain phase of the treatment, everything seemed to converge upon it, and how later, in the synthesis, the most various and remarkable results radiated out from it. (*SE* 17: 52)

In this version of the analyst, he is someone who, his enemies claim, is deluded by his own constructions. But Freud presents this version only to assert himself as an analyst who has an altogether different sense of himself and his science, one fully equipped to defend the primal scene. The case history gradually reveals, too, how such a defense is mounted. In a favorite rhetorical strategy, Freud concedes that his own master construction of the primal scene is incredible. "Many details, however, seemed to me myself to be so extraordinary and incredible that I felt some hesitation in asking other people to believe them" (*SE* 17: 12). He even concedes that it is his construction itself that will beggar belief, as he pulls together a scenario from out of "the chaos of the dreamer's unconscious memory-traces": "I have now reached the point at which I must abandon the support I have hitherto had from the course of the analysis. I am afraid it will also be the point at which the reader's belief will abandon me" (36–37). Yet Freud has further strategies for convincing his readers. He says repeatedly that he checked details with the Wolf Man to see whether he, through his affect, accepted them or could simply contradict them, and he claims to have discarded material in this way.[30] He disavows the notion that preconceived ideas colored his constructive attempts, saying, "Readers may at all events rest assured that I myself am only reporting what I came upon as an independent experience, uninfluenced by my expectation." He also asserts his claim to larger understanding by paraphrasing Shakespeare: "So that there was nothing left for me but to remember the wise saying that there are more things in heaven and earth than are dreamed of in our philosophy" (12).[31]

Most of all, Freud argues, the scene as he constructs it must be the right one because it is the only one that both accounts for everything in the Wolf Man's past and also leads to relief of his present symptoms (52). Here he ventures into his most compelling and yet potentially dangerous method of fostering the belief. In addition to recasting the primal scene to represent different aspects of the Wolf Man's precise symptoms and fantasies, as noted above, Freud also relies on phantom alternative versions of events to suggest alternative explanations for these symptoms and fantasies.[32] He then argues for the essential validity of his version, because these more "plausible" scenes of primal trauma, although they are more clearly motivated by events that the Wolf Man remembers, occur later in the patient's childhood or fail to account for all his symptoms.

Freud thereby unleashes precisely that aspect of the scene that undermines any authoritative account: its ability to redefine or reidentify participants according to the tone or perspective. The danger arises because these alternate versions remain in his narrative, constructed there and possibly able to offer readers other realities. This aspect is surely linked to the play of fantasy and memory at work in the scene, but it also reminds us that the guarantee of identity that the primal scene was supposed to provide — to make visible, in fact — is nonexistent. Parental embrace is the beginning for any child, but the embrace within the primal scene turns out not to be the absolute or guaranteed beginning, because there it can turn all the participants into other versions of themselves.

For instance, Freud constructs a primal scene as Jung or his adherents might do:

> [They assume that] the causes of neuroses [reside] almost exclusively in the grave conflicts of later life; [and] . . . that the importance of childhood is only held up before our eyes in analysis on account of the inclination of neurotics for expressing their present interests in reminiscences and symbols from the remote past. [Such assumptions lead then to primal scenes that] . . . are not reproductions of real

occurrences, to which it is possible to ascribe an influence over the course of the patient's later life and over the formation of his symptoms. (*SE* 17: 49)

Freud pursues the nature of the analysis that would follow from such a construction, even writing the analyst's dialogue with the patient (50), all the while minutely dissecting its flaws. Finally, he announces: "I may here venture to point out that the antagonistic views which are to be found in the psycho-analytic literature of today are usually arrived at on the principle of *pars pro toto*. From a highly composite combination one part of the operative factors is singled out and proclaimed as the truth; and in its favour the other part, together with the whole combination, is then contradicted. . . . What is left over, however, and rejected as false, is precisely what is new in psycho-analysis and peculiar to it" (*SE* 17: 53). The Jungian analysts are guilty of the very blunders and theoretical errors that Freud insists he is free of. They lead the patient too aggressively, develop constructions out of their own assumptions, and, in short, are unwilling to let the remarkable play of memory and fantasy have free range. As incredible as his own construction of the Wolf Man's primal scene may sound, it is buttressed by these alternative versions, which Freud deliberately constructs to be as fully elaborate as his own and convincing from a certain faulty perspective. Yet despite Freud's confidence that he has dismantled such sturdy structures, their effects linger, because he leaves their remains as a testament to his superior construction.

Freud's problem seems to arise from his admission (or insistence) that there was a *real* primal scene. In a structure that theoretically endorses construction and interpretation as memory's equal, the possibility that the 18-month-old Wolf Man really did see his parents having sex insinuates reality as a fixed point that troubles the otherwise free flow of construction. Freud has already subsumed such a reality to his theory to his satisfaction (see *SE* 17: 51, quoted above): as we have seen, psychoanalysis requires the superior authority of construction in the hands of the analyst. But as late as 1918, Freud was still adding and dismantling alternate versions "by way of supplement and rectification," especially for those who insisted on a connection to reality: "There remains the possibility of taking yet another view of the primal scene underlying the dream — a view, moreover, which obviates to a large extent the conclusion that has been arrived at above and relieves us of many of our difficulties" (57). This most obvious of possibilities — that the source of the dream of white wolves was the young patient's observation of sheep copulating — Freud expects to be the last he must engage, but his own narrative suggests otherwise. It simply stops growing after 1918, with the reality of the primal scene left unclear — *non liquet* (60).

In his discussion of the primal scene, Ned Lukacher juxtaposes Freud's handling of the memory and construction with that of others, such as Heidegger, Lacan, and Derrida. Freud, he maintains, solves the conundrum because he has the figure of the Wolf Man to play off of. With his longing for the reality of primal scene, the Wolf Man serves as a foil to Freud's superior grasp of the unconscious.[33] The patient represents the insufficiently enlightened intellect who insists on congruence between consciousness and the unconscious. But Lukacher also captures for us the poignant figure of the Wolf Man, who went to his grave troubled by his inability to recall the primal scene. Pankejeff swore that Freud promised him that in time he would remember the scene itself, but the analyst does not include this promise among those he made in his bold handling of this difficult and crucial patient. Nor should we believe that Freud omits any mention of the promise simply because the memory didn't come (although if the Wolf Man had recalled the primal scene, presumably Freud would have used that fact to buttress his case). Instead, we should recognize that such a memory would challenge the very premise of the family structures in the primal scene. The father's word had to be authoritative. The Wolf Man's primal scene needs to be beyond recall theoretically, so that he is obliged to rely on his analyst. Yet, explicitly or not, Freud also holds out the promise of remembering the scene as a kind of testament to his authoritative powers of construction.

The irreconcilable difference here suggests an anxiety of the larger romance. Consider the degree to which Freud conceals the full vision of this romance. The scene that essentializes belonging through family embrace, conceals that other option, repudiation. Freud's psychoanalytic praxis, as it is described in the case history, constructs analyst and patient in a relationship that makes repudiation seem impossible. Furthermore, theoretically, through the family romance, Freud also eliminates the notion of repudiation or abandonment. It never happens; it is just the child's strategy for processing his complex feeling about his real parents. But is that other option really gone? To get at the missing parts of the romantic structure, in whose absence the primal scene is an unruly site of infantile neurosis, we turn to the other side of the project spelled out in "From the History of an Infantile Neurosis" — the fight for control of psychoanalysis.

Freud finds the primal scene a remarkably supple weapon with which to enforce his authority over his younger colleagues, because it illustrates the oedipal essence of psychoanalysis. More crucially for our purposes, the primal scene identifies the patient, in the drama and in analysis, as the infant whose role is merely that of observer. At first it is hard to perceive why such a minimal role is important. After all, what harm could the child intend, that it must be constructed first as a mere witness and then as a victim that suffers the effects of what it sees? In light of Freud's political struggles within the psychoanalytic community, however, we can reread the primal scene as a tale of wider suffering that involves the possibility of blaming a more active (and vindictive) child.

In the psychoanalytic structure, the infantile child replicates the primitive human and hence incorporates an inherent violence, that of the frustrated sons against their sexually dominant father. Freud had but lately articulated the analogy in *Totem and Taboo* (1913), but he maintains the identification as late as *Moses and Monotheism* (1939). The primal scene surprisingly absolves the infant of such inherency, since it cannot hurt its father now — or even later. The potential for transgression devolves into self-inflicted harm, which psychoanalysis can heal, but only if it is allowed to exist as Freud constructs it. This foundational myth — the primal scene's enactment of the *proper* resolution of the oedipal crisis as the essential dogma of psychoanalysis — seems thus not to be aimed at the theoretical structure of primitive man. Instead, it rewrites and repudiates Freud's one-time strategy for founding his psychoanalytic realm. In the first decade of the twentieth century, Freud planned to introduce Carl Jung, an outsider and a member of another "race," whose status as such would legitimize the nascent kingdom. "From the History of an Infantile Neurosis" presents the primal scene as an enactment of why that strategy is impossible: to belong, the child has to be engendered within the family.

We can appreciate this secondary reading of the primal scene beyond the case history if we turn to Jung's account of his split with Freud, particularly his description of one critical moment. Jung frames this moment, it appears, with the symbolism of ancient Greek myth, to produce an extraordinary paradox — and a stroke of malicious humor. In 1957, long after his one-time mentor and rival's death, Jung constructed his falling out with Freud as a primal scene, a tempestuous moment when father and son contemplate the father's sex life as a site either for further alliance or for rebellion. In this account, it took place much earlier in their association than Freud might have imagined, in 1909, on a voyage to America, when Jung claims that the "roots" of his irrevocable breach with Freud lay in his mentor's refusal to be forthcoming about his sexual involvement with his sister-in-law:

> From the very beginning of our trip we started to analyze each other's dreams. Freud had some dreams that bothered him very much. The dreams were about the triangle — Freud, his wife, and his wife's younger sister. Freud had no idea that I

knew about the triangle and his intimate relationship with his sister-in-law. And so, when Freud told me about the dream in which his wife and her sister played important parts, I asked Freud to tell me some of his personal associations with the dream. He looked at me with bitterness and said, "I could tell you more, but I cannot risk my authority."

Jung learned of the attachment, he says, from the sister-in-law herself, Minna Bernays, who drew Jung aside on his first visit with the Freud family in 1907 to confess it:

> When, a few days later, I was visiting Freud's laboratory, Freud's sister-in-law asked if she could talk with me. She was very much bothered by her relationship with Freud and felt guilty about it. From her I learned that Freud was in love with her and that their relationship was indeed very intimate. It was a shocking discovery to me, and even now I can recall the agony I felt at the time.[34]

Jung conjures up a remarkable moment. It is during Freud's only trip to America, to receive his first honorary degree and public lionizing. The elder statesman of psychoanalysis and his star protégé stand with the interior life of the father between them, a window into his unconscious opened through a dream. The son knows that he is looking at his father's sex life, but the father, who does not know this, attempts to maintain his authority by censorship.

Ostensibly, Jung is asking Freud for what sex represents in a professional sense: candor in service of psychoanalysis. In fact, the younger man demands that his elder privilege him over anything else, whether human or principle. Freud's answer suggests that he recognizes in the dynamic the father's great peril when his sons grasp everything, including his sex life. He knew that his younger colleagues, both Adler and Jung, chafed at his supreme command of psychoanalysis. In particular, both men took issue with his insistence about the sexual origin of all neuroses. He acknowledges as much publicly when speaking about their goals in challenging his ideas: "they both court a favourable opinion by putting forward certain lofty ideas, which view things, as it were, *sub specie aeternitatis*. . . . with Jung, the appeal is made to the historic right of youth to throw off the fetters in which tyrannical age with its hidebound views seeks to bind it."[35] Freud intuits the mythic nature of Jung's struggle, its primal structure. Yet had he heard Jung's characterization of their fateful conversation on that ship forty-five years later, he might well have wondered at the surviving intensity of the energy generated by their fission. Freud professed always to be willing to share his dreams with his fellow psychoanalysts and, indeed, with the entire world.[36] In *The Interpretation of Dreams*, he insists that in the interest of his science, he has overcome his reluctance to reveal his dream life: "There is some natural hesitation about revealing so many intimate facts about one's mental life; nor can there be any guarantee against misinterpretation by strangers. But it must be possible to overcome such hesitations. . . . And it is safe to assume that my readers too will very soon find their initial interest in the indiscretions which I am bound to make replaced by an absorbing immersion in the psychological problems upon which they throw light" (*SE* 4–5: 105). There were limits, however, as he says in a note: "I am obliged to add, however, by way of qualification of what I have said above, that in scarcely any instance have I brought forward the complete interpretation of one of my own dreams, as it is known to me. I have probably been wise in not putting too much faith in my readers' discretion." Jung saw the matter of discretion differently. From the moment Freud concealed the scene that Jung knew was there behind the veil of his authority, he lost his claim to it with his younger colleague.[37]

In Jung's account of this outcome to the oedipal crisis of psychoanalysis itself, we can discern the impossible, irreal notion of an alliance between father and son over the matter of the son's growing up and overtaking his father. Perhaps such matters always require, as Freud inferred, a perception of the father as tyrant and violence. Certainly, Jung's representation of that onboard confrontation is a sly parody of the primal scene as master narrative. It also resonates, perhaps by Jung's design, with the ancient Greek mythic struggle for succession, particularly in the alliance Jung constructs between consort and son. The cosmogonic struggle in the Greek universe begins with just such a primal scene, deliberately set up by Gaia, mother Earth, who wished to rid herself of Ouranos — Sky — as a mate.[38] Hesiod's *Theogony* conceptualizes the tale as a struggle between the father's needs and those of mother and child.[39] Ouranos wants sexual gratification without its consequence, the birth of children, and his solution is simple: he prevents the birth of his children by shoving them back into the earth. Gaia plots an end to this violence by asking one of her unborn children to castrate Ouranos. Only the bravest, Kronos, is willing to watch the approach of his sexually aroused father. This earliest of primal scenes in Greek literature allies mother and son against father, and as such it captures a deep anxiety of Greek thought about sexual propagation per se that makes it a site of intense struggle between the generations, as fathers try to prevent being supplanted by their sons.[40]

Jung deploys a version of this primal peril as his mythic weapon to account for his rupture with his mentor. He turns Freud's therapeutic tool on behalf of the child — the primal scene — into the means to see what is forbidden and thereby to strip the father of his authority. Freud frames his refusal to discuss his dreams as an appeal to his absolute authority, a reproof by this father of his intellectual son. Jung eroticizes the encounter into a primal scene, however, and wrests his liberation from his erstwhile father by insinuating himself into Freud's sex life. Forty-five years after the fact, Jung turns Freud's discovery on his mentor. The primal scene is not to serve the child's healing. Instead, it is a moment in which the father is entrapped by the combined cunning of consort and heir. As Gaia set her son beside her to wait for Ouranos's descent, so Jung says that he was given the information by Minna Bernays that allowed him to watch for Freud's slip, a task that plainly put Freud's authority in peril.

Peter Gay, one of Freud's recent biographers, confirms this signification of Jung's primal scene by the very terms in which he describes it: it is a question of witness. Outlining various contradictions in Jung's story that cast doubt upon the veracity of portions of it, Gay articulates one argument in a way that eerily reveals the struggle for succession: "it seems quite improbable that Minna Bernays would have confided such an intimate matter to a total stranger — a man whom she had just met and who was alien to her in religion and culture and professional interests. To be sure, she might conceivably have seen an outsider, especially one who would soon depart again, as precisely the right person to confide in. *But I find it virtually impossible to visualize the scene*" (my emphasis).[41] Gay's argument is reasonable in cultural terms. Jung, the guest from Zurich, was alien to Freud's Viennese household in many profound ways. Within the then current founding myth of psychoanalysis, however, Jung is not an outsider or a stranger; he was Freud's "crown prince" and "son," as he calls himself at the height of their intimacy. In recollecting their rupture, Jung visualizes the moment when Freud's illicit consort chose to entice him into betrayal. Gay, who as a biographer has the right to interrogate his subject's sex life, cannot — or will not — visualize the scene. This latter-day devotee writes himself into the story of the voyage to America as the son willing to abide by Freud's silence, thus making himself into the champion of the psychoanalytic legacy into its second century.[42]

In 1909, the Wolf Man's primal scene has yet to be discovered, so neither Freud nor Jung has the construction that makes sense of the shipboard moment. When they do have it, Freud discusses the primal scene in terms of its traumatic effect on the child as witness, and Jung constructs it as an erotic comedy that liberates the son from the father. In either case, the son receives his identity, as belonging or free, from the shock of the moment, such that we can detect the larger structure of the romance of belonging as it operates in ghostly fashion around the primal scene. Such is the uncanny nature of this choice that Jung cannot repudiate Freud without revealing his longing for him. Jung has constructed a primal scene that does not confirm a family with the identification of father and son but instead tears it apart, as the father's choice goes against the son in favor of the reticence he believes will save his identity as authority. In dramatizing his oedipal victory so long after the fact, Jung also, inescapably, displays the voraciousness of the son's need to belong.

In the aftermath of his failed alliance with Jung, Freud felt a great urgency to regain control of the international psychoanalytic community, but in the first bloom of their friendship, he saw the Swiss doctor as "the man of the future," who would "continue and complete my work." It was not just Jung's brilliance. As Gay puts it, one very real attraction for Freud was that Jung was "not Viennese, not old and, best of all, not Jewish."[43] Freud's heir had to be brought in from outside, to provide a wider legitimacy to the enterprise. Freud's efforts with Jung replicate an ancient and time-honored strategy of bringing in an adoptive child who is picked from elsewhere to become the legitimate heir. Or, if no adoption is possible, the state itself can choose someone from the outside to revitalize or redirect its destiny.[44] But Freud discovers painful truths about insinuating an outsider: that, on the one hand, it is difficult to establish the legitimacy of such a suppositious heir, and, on the other, the child himself may wish, for better or worse, to take the kingdom in wholly new direction. Fosterage does not obliterate natal identities. Although Jung was initially delighted to call himself Freud's son, he came to regard that filial status as too closely allied to that of patient.[45] Freud had to continue the foundation of his kingdom on his own resources.

In light of Freud's own rupture with Jung, we can see that the primal scene addresses the question of whether an alien can be constructed as an insider and heir. Any child who is alien to family — or becomes so through abandonment — has other identities, which may be in dangerous tension with natal ties. Can fosterage or adoption ease this tension? Can either sort of non-natal nurture efface the danger by willingly picking up an outcast? In the family romance, Freud has already theorized abandonment out of the picture, obliterating the predication on which such a question is based. The primal scene dramatizes the answer: the son must be identified by and within the natal embrace.

I have read the competing accounts of the primal scene by Freud and Jung as a parable of their rupture, well aware that serious issues of theoretical dispute divided them, as well as Freud's insistence that his disciples adhere unquestioningly to his version of psychoanalysis.[46] Yet Jung's version of the primal scene incorporates these issues, as the terms of Freud's refusal to speak more frankly about his dream suggest. Letting Jung see his sex life was a matter of lowering his authority, which he could not bear, but which Jung needed. To confront the crisis in his nascent kingdom of psychoanalysis, Freud needs to finesse the identity of his successor. Jung must be both a stranger, who therefore cannot expect to see into Freud's inner life, and the son who is allowed to see the father at its very center. But Freud cannot achieve the necessary blur, at least in practical reality. However much he needs a Jung to avoid psychoanalysis becoming too identified with the Jews of Vienna, he cannot be the father that Jung wishes to see when he contemplates the primal scene of psychoanalysis. Freud cannot allow Jung to see him in the very place that would make them father and son — in the primal scene. The younger man, in turn, refuses to see himself as the son and heir.

Freud also cannot finesse the matter of natal belonging in his theory. In an act of psychoanalytic authority, he shapes the Wolf Man's primal scene to conform to the oedipal, both so that it is at the heart of his patient's neurosis and so that it serves as the basis of understanding and healing. Freud also describes the discovery of the scene as a collaboration between two identities that complement each other in a structure of authority that authenticates the therapeutic claims of psychoanalysis. And, at least as he is constructed in the case history, the Wolf Man submits and becomes the son by transference that this father of analysis needs. In the crucial confrontation of "From the History of an Infantile Neurosis," he opens his eyes on command and sees his father. Yet if the patient is all too eager to participate in the oedipal primal scene, the pupil, as we have seen, wants only to escape it and repudiate his status as "crown prince."

Even here, however, the primal scene is a treacherously protean construction. Jung, in wielding a weapon against his mentor that was once intended to silence him, cannot avoid the dramatization of his own desires. Freud also cannot eliminate the alternative versions of the primal scene, even though he introduced them merely to confirm his own, those that suggest the oedipal in all its dangerous nontherapeutic guises. The internal voices constructed by Freud continue to be heard, and long after the analysis, new constructions challenge what he insisted the Wolf Man saw.

The *Ion* dramatizes Athens's official myth of foundation in terms of the embraces that create the boy Ion. This foundering figure requires a blur of paternity similar to the one Freud was seeking, because Athens needed an insider to authenticate its autochthony, its claim of inherency, as well as an outsider (legend had it that the city's early autochthonous kings were no military leaders).[47] In this play we get to watch the assemblage of parents' bodies that makes Ion. Like Freud, Euripides is interested in the infant at the heart of the process, but the analyst's tautological preoccupation with the trauma of familial embrace is leavened by the work of abandonment. Since abandonment creates multiple identities, its centrifugal effects complement the unifying embrace, such that we seem to get the fuller, more encompassing romance of belonging, one that can give Athens its new leader. Scenes of abandonment show more than seems possible in terms of belonging. Yet just being able to contemplate both abandonment and embrace within the same story turns out not to be the full antidote to the anxiety of belonging. Just as Freud cannot finally control the tension he releases in the primal scene between memory and fantasy, so too the *Ion*'s persistent tendency to reconstruct its hero's abandonment reveals an instability in whatever constructed identities emerge.

No single account or voice of authority is accepted until the appearance of the deus ex machina. The report of a participant like Kreousa is not accepted at face value, but is challenged and shaped by a confidant or interlocutor. In this process other versions of the participants and their actions appear: different Kreousas as abandoning mothers, new Ions as exposed infants, and various sorts of gods and mortals as fathers. And these versions are disturbing, because even though they are only simulacra of the on-stage characters, they demonstrate an immense power to influence and effect the dramatic action, as well as to interpret the past. The action of the *Ion* develops out of an urgency on the part of characters to recapture Ion's abandonment, but that act causes the possibilities of identity to careen almost out of control. The spectators experience this tension between memory and interpretation through a perspective colored by their prior awareness of Ion's heroic myth and their own experience of abandonment (as reviewed in Chapter 1).[48] They may long to observe a single coherent version of the moment when Kreousa bore Ion and then abandoned him, because it would explain their past, but the tragedy's constant recreation of abandonment denies them relief.

Katerina Zacharia also studies this longing and its frustration as a phenomenon of repetition in the play and argues that Euripides means it to be salubrious. To seek a simple account, she argues, is to block the notion that what is "inside" Athens might *need* what is outside for its health and continuance. Dramaturgy drives the therapy: "In the end, the audience too is to learn [like Kreousa] to confront honestly the complexity and ambiguity of reality."[49] I agree that the *Ion* forges a link between spectators and its dramatic attempts to bring memory and interpretation into harmony. The play does create a desire for a construction of the past whose present effects are beneficial (or at least not harmful). Ostensibly, the present positive effects are all around the audience, in the presence of Athens with its democratic vibrancy and imperial triumph: the person of Ion, whose identity is forged in this tragedy, brought all this to pass.[50] But I am less convinced that the concomitant denial of the spectators' longing is therapeutic. A sensation lingers of other identities also forged in this tragedy and possibly still in effect. For all that the *Ion* drives toward a climatic embrace of mother and son, because it proceeds through abandonment, with its unstoppable devolution of identity, the play undermines Zacharia's comfortably "humanist" project of lesson-learning. No authoritative identity, however complex or ambiguous, emerges.[51]

Hermes recounts Kreousa's suffering and Ion's exposure merely as background to a dramatic action that is predicted to climax in a recognition by Xouthos that will rescue the youth from the abyss of lost identity and enable his triumphal entry into his Athenian destiny.[52] The god himself is the patron of those of ambiguous status, such as Ion, and prone to lying, like the lies about Xouthos's paternity that salvage Ion's destiny.[53] This figure of deception and trickery suggests that the sense things may not be as they seem is officially sanctioned — the gods construct and endorse ambiguity. Beyond the conventional nature of his opening speech, Hermes has none of the usual reasons gods give for appearing in divine prologues, in that he neither sets dramatic action in motion nor plans further intervention.[54] He comes onto to stage, he says, to see what happens to Ion, a reason similar to the spectators' for entering the theater (76–77).[55] This disjunction between Hermes' spectator-like curiosity and his authoritative status (as god and as a familiar dramaturgical device) sets the audience up for gamesmanship and puzzles. But abandonment troubles the official playfulness from the outset; in fact, it is already at work without, apparently, the god even knowing.[56]

Hermes presents a fantastical abandonment in which there is a mother without trauma, a generous and caring father, and a miraculous rescue (10–36):

... παῖδ' Ἐρεχθέως Φοῖβος ἔζευξεν γάμοις
βίᾳ Κρέουσαν, ἔνθα προσβόρρους πέτρας
Παλλάδος ὑπ' ὄχθῳ τῆς Ἀθηναίων χθονὸς

Μακρὰς καλοῦσι γῆς ἄνακτες ᾿Ατθίδος.
ἀγνὼς δὲ πατρί (τῷ θεῷ γὰρ ἦν φίλον)
γαστρὸς διήνεγκ᾿ ὄγκον. ὡς δ᾿ ἦλθεν χρόνος,
τεκοῦσ᾿ ἐν οἴκοις παῖδ᾿ ἀπήνεγκεν βρέφος
ἐς ταὐτὸν ἄντρον οὗπερ ηὐνάσθη θεῷ
Κρέουσα, κἀκτίθησιν ὡς θανούμενον
κοίλης ἐν ἀντίπηγος εὐτρόχῳ κύκλῳ,
προγόνων νόμον σῴζουσα τοῦ τε γηγενοῦς
᾿Εριχθονίου. κείνῳ γὰρ ἡ Διὸς κόρη
φρουρὼ παραζεύξασα φύλακε σώματος
δισσὼ δράκοντε, παρθένοις ᾿Αγλαυρίσιν
δίδωσι σῴζειν· ὅθεν ᾿Ερεχθείδαις ἐκεῖ
νόμος τις ἔστιν ὄφεσιν ἐν χρυσηλάτοις
τρέφειν τέκν᾿. ἀλλ᾿ ἣν εἶχε παρθένος χλιδὴν
τέκνῳ προσάψασ᾿ ἔλιπεν ὡς θανουμένῳ.
κἄμ᾿ ὢν ἀδελφὸς Φοῖβος αἰτεῖται τάδε·
῏Ω σύγγον᾿, ἐλθὼν λαὸν εἰς αὐτόχθονα
κλεινῶν ᾿Αθηνῶν (οἶσθα γὰρ θεᾶς πόλιν)
λαβὼν βρέφος νεογνὸν ἐκ κοίλης πέτρας
αὐτῷ σὺν ἄγγει σπαργάνουσί θ᾿ οἷς ἔχει
ἔνεγκε Δελφῶν τἀμὰ πρὸς χρηστήρια
καὶ θὲς πρὸς αὐταῖς εἰσόδοις δόμων ἐμῶν.
τὰ δ᾿ ἄλλ᾿ (ἐμὸς γάρ ἐστιν, ὡς εἰδῇς, ὁ παῖς)
ἡμῖν μελήσει.

Phoibos yoked in marriage the child of Erechtheus,
Kreousa, using force, at the north-facing rocks
beneath Athena's hill in the Athenians' land,
which the lords of Attica call the Long Rocks.
And secretly from her father (for it was the god's desire)
she carried her burden in her belly. But when the time came,
Kreousa gave birth in her home and then carried out her newborn child
to the same cave where she slept with the god.
She exposed it, expecting it to die,
in the well-rounded circle of a hollow *antipex*,
preserving the custom of her ancestors and the earthborn
Erichthonios. For beside him the daughter of Zeus
had set a pair of snakes, watchful guardians of his body,
and then she gave him to the maiden daughters of Aglaurus

to protect. From this there arose a custom of Erechtheus's offspring,
to nurture their children amidst gilded serpents.
But once she had fastened onto her child
the finery a maiden has, she left it, expecting it to die.
Thereupon my brother, Phoibos, asked this of me:
"Brother, go to the earthborn host
of famous Athens (for you know the goddess's city)
and pick up a newborn baby from a hollow in the rock,
together with its cradle and the swaddling it has.
Take it to my sanctuary in Delphi
and place it before the very entrance of my temple.
The rest of the matter will be my concern —
for know that the child is mine."

The god's account mutes the physical suffering of Kreousa's rape and her anguish. She conceals her pregnancy from her father and yet gives birth at home, although in other versions, the caves below the Acropolis were the scene of the birth, as well as of the assault.[57] The exposure itself receives greater detail. Kreousa's ability to prepare for it elaborately with ritual objects furthers the sense that the issue here is not her travail but the abandonment. Hermes constructs a maiden with no very clear designs in exposing her child, although he twice uses the ominous phrase "expecting it to die." Her preparations suggest that this phrase expresses less intent than hopelessness, but if mortal intent is frail in expecting death, divine purpose is strong and proactive. Hermes stresses Apollo's planning throughout. The god, who wished the pregnancy to be concealed, almost seems to work with Kreousa to hide her condition, and he carefully plans the baby's rescue and rearing in Delphi. Now Hermes reveals his brother's latest design for bringing his son into his own.[58] Mortal mother and divine father have secured the infant's best interests as far as they can. Both even mark the child with part of his special identity: Kreousa bestows the tokens of the earthborn royal house; Apollo asserts his semi-divine nature.

As part of the intertwining of human and divine purpose, Hermes' account interprets Kreousa's preparations for the abandonment by superimposing parallels from both the human past and divine myth. When Kreousa places the newborn in a ritual chest with special tokens, she is repeating the ancient custom of her household. Athena, who first used this chest, also fastened two golden snakes on the infant Erichthonios to protect him. But it is not clear what sort of link is established between the goddess and Athens's founding fathers, on the one hand,

and a desperate maiden forced to expose her infant, on the other. Is Kreousa somehow redeemed or condemned through the juxtaposition? It has been argued that this alignment is for the sake of contrast: the earlier gestures of Athena and the city's kings remind us that Kreousa is perverting objects designed to protect a child to bring about his death. The political symbolism, however, may connect the acts of maiden and goddess in a more positive association, since Athens's autochthonous heritage is brought into the tragedy from the outset in order to situate Ion in its context as its final founding father.[59] Whatever meaning we find in the juxtaposition, more significant for our purposes is the fact that such parallels obscure Kreousa's gestures but also interpret them. So much prominence is given to the significance of the *antipex*, a ritual basket, and Athena's ancient rescue of Ion's ancestor that we cannot quite see what Kreousa herself is doing. Has she too put golden snakes into this basket? Or just "a maiden's finery"?[60]

Despite this confusion, the overarching meaning of this abandonment is not obscure: it is full of symbols that compel the audience to understand Kreousa's trauma as the beginning of the renewal that is the promised action of the tragedy. And this renewal will obliterate her suffering as well as Apollo's healing intervention. What matters is Ion's future, his belonging to Athens. This is a version of abandonment, in short, that comes very close to its opposite, the familial embrace. It is little wonder that this fantasy is the version with the gods' approval. Hermes constructs it to announce the play's setting; Apollo builds his plans for the coming action based on it; Athena will close the play by confirming it. Also significantly, this is the only version of Ion's abandonment in the play that is not called "sick" in some or all aspects by the character who constructs it.[61]

The effects of abandonment, however, are already at work, beyond even the god's control. Within Hermes' tale of Kreousa and her newborn, another exposure appears, set in the half-light of imagination. The divinely authorized abandonment cannot manage Ion's rescue, it seems, without imagining another version of itself. The Athenian princess is replaced by an anonymous maiden of Delphi, and new energy and design clash with the god's official account. Hermes' construction sets up links between the real and the fantastic, between memory and interpretation, without any sure signs as to which can be considered authoritative.

The overt necessity of the second construction of Ion's abandonment appears when Hermes reaches his own rescue of Kreousa's exposed infant. Once he places the infant's opened basket on the temple steps at Delphi, someone must intervene further (41–49):

κυρεῖ δ' ἄμ ἱππεύοντος ἡλίου κύκλῳ
προφῆτις ἐσβαίνουσα μαντεῖον θεοῦ·
ὄψιν δὲ προσβαλοῦσα παιδὶ νηπίῳ
ἐθαύμασ' εἴ τις Δελφίδων τλαίη χόρη
λαθραῖον ὠδῖν' ἐς θεοῦ ῥῖψαι δόμον,
ὑπέρ τε θυμέλας διορίσαι πρόθυμος ἦν·
οἴκτῳ δ' ἀφῆκεν ὠμότητα, καὶ θεὸς
συνεργὸς ἦν τῷ παιδὶ μὴ 'κπεσεῖν δόμων·
τρέφει δέ νιν λαβοῦσα. . . .

Exactly as the sun was rising the prophetess
happened to enter the god's oracle.
Casting her sight on the hapless baby,
she was astounded that some Delphic maiden
had dared to throw her secret pain into the sanctuary of the god,
and she was eager to banish it beyond the boundaries.
But she set aside her savagery out of pity, and the god
was also at work on the child's behalf so that it not be cast from the temple.
She took up the child and reared it . . .

As she gazes at the basket, the Pythia comes up with a tale that is brief but rich in emotion. The maiden suffered in secret, and her abandonment of her child is an act of daring. She exposed it at dawn in the open sanctuary, an outrage, but a sure sign of her intent, which is very different from Kreousa's. Although both maidens choose sacred sites, the Athenian princess takes her infant into the dark of Pan's cave expecting it to die, while this illusory mother wants the baby to be found.[62] The Pythia also vividly constructs her own feelings. She is outraged by the girl's daring and the pollution, but throwing the child out of the sanctuary — her own impulse — would be another abandonment, and pity overtakes her. Full of the human emotions needed to save an exposed infant, the Pythia's imaginary tale brings Hermes' intervention to fruition, and she picks up the baby and raises it. Through the labels it freely applies, the Pythia's tale also comments on Hermes' official construction: abandonment is an act of savagery — ὠμότητα — even when protecting the god's sanctuary. This emphasis on emotion disturbs spectators' perception of the figures in Hermes' construction.

The Pythia's tale also confounds the apparently secure significance of the symbolic gestures and tokens that endows Ion's abandonment with such portentous meaning as Hermes tells it. The priestess's construction is very Delphic: the two human figures are from there, and Apollo is the august god of the oracle, able to inspire the rescue of the child, as the imaginary maiden hopes, or to be polluted by it, as the Pythia fears.[63] The ritual basket and birth tokens so carefully bestowed by Kreousa are no longer signs of Athens, either. They are still present —Hermes reports that he opened the basket's lid when he left it at the temple, and the Pythia later gives everything to Ion when she enters—but their special nature is gone. The spectacle in the basket assuages the priestess's disgust, but only through pity, not awe or even curiosity. Symbols so intensely Athenian twenty lines earlier, and the centerpiece of Hermes' own vision of the abandonment, seem to be invisible to the temple's priestess.[64] Apparently, the only thing she sees is the child; the Athenian tokens mean nothing at Delphi.

Here is a version of Ion's abandonment, in short, in which the crucial thing— the only thing that matters—is saving the child. Delphi is not, in the Pythia's imagining of this abandonment, just a convenient place to stash a secret treasure (like an exposed royal prince).[65] In fact, the baby is not seen as a treasure by denizens of Delphi; tokens of his identity and links to the autochthony of Athens are effaced—present but unseen. Instead, human agents inhabit this sacred place, both in reality and in fantasy, who exert merely mortal power to save Ion. Yet these agents are also crucial to Ion's career.

This second version of Ion's abandonment is all the more remarkable because it follows a moment of great energy and purpose, when Apollo plainly constructs a deliberate negation or reversal of his son's exposure. Apollo plans for his son to be moved from Athens to Delphi, from dark cave to dawn-lit temple, from death to life. In case we were in any doubt about his concern for this child, he announces, "I'll take care of the rest; for know that the child is mine" (35–36). These could be the very words of a father at his child's *amphidromeia*, when he picks up the infant and by that gesture makes it a part of his *oikos*.[66] Yet the evocation, perhaps even the enactment, of a paternal ritual that would have been enough in an Athenian court of law to vouch for a man's citizenship vanishes in the next instant, overtaken by a fantasy of Delphic abandonment that appears in the mind of the Pythia. Images of Kreousa's abandonment are immediately succeeded by this version of the deed, with an entirely new identity for the child, including an anonymous father.

The maiden imagined by the Pythia is an unlikely but crucial bridge from the divine prologue's version of Kreousa to the character who appears on stage. In Hermes' account the princess seems relatively unscathed and composed, almost stately in her ritualized exposure of her infant. This princess is replaced by a nameless Delphic maiden who in her suffering prefigures the Kreousa who shortly enters. The language of secrecy and daring that surrounds this maiden also appears in the queen's construction of her pain in the abandonment. The Delphic maiden's gesture of casting her child on the god's mercy prefigures Kreousa's claim, in one version of her tale, that she attempted to compel Apollo to intervene on behalf of their child (965). Secrecy, too, which figures in Hermes' account as a pragmatic matter of concealment, is now associated with the maiden's pain and will shortly become a cardinal feature of the on-stage Kreousa's anguish, whether that which she has to practice in bearing and exposing her child (340), or that practiced on her by Apollo and Xouthos (357). Most of all, daring — an ambiguous combination of outrage and intent that expresses suffering — becomes associated with Kreousa's act of abandoning Ion by the end of the play. The Pythia's complicated reaction to the exposure, captured in the single verb for daring, τλαίη (44), forecasts how characters come to view Kreousa's pain.[67] In short, the Pythia constructs an abandoning figure that marks the presence of another Kreousa, one who suffers and dares, hides things and discovers the treachery of others. This Kreousa is very different from Hermes' princess; she is also not the Delphic maiden. But the Pythia's imagination, which prefigures this Kreousa, seems to be as important to the process of bringing the Athenian queen onto the stage as is Hermes' account of the past.

In light of this alternate construction of abandonment in the midst of Hermes' official account, it becomes difficult to ask which Kreousa is the "real" one — Hermes' or the one about to appear on stage. Nor is the reality of either of greater significance than the fiction of the Delphic maiden, because reality is not the point, but rather life and death. For Hermes' Kreousa, abandonment means death, and only a miracle prevents that. The on-stage Kreousa mostly agrees with that equation in the versions of abandonment that she constructs: her despairing assumption is that no miracle intervened. For the Delphic maiden, however, abandonment means a chance. Ironically, that chance proves to be the Pythia. Normally a figure of the god's prophetic power, here she symbolizes the chance or random encounter that saves a life and begins an identity.[68] The Delphic maiden, although she is nothing more than a construction in someone's imagination, proves more effective in her aim than Kreousa, since she does save Ion precisely where she is needed to do so, in the heart of the Pythia.

The Pythia envisions abandonment in conventional terms: a desperate maiden, a kind-hearted stranger, and a remote but beneficent divinity. Restated in familiar generics, the tale comes closer to the Athenian audience's experience of infant abandonment. Spectators may be startled to see that such a familiar act is powerful enough to save a prince, as opposed to the god's official version, which is heavy with symbolism and intent but also curiously ambivalent and ineffective. Similar conflicts between authorization and sheer effectiveness appear elsewhere. Abandonment repeatedly generates new versions of both the abandoning parents and the infant, and the audience must interact with these invented characters, because they have a dynamic power to further the play's action. However insubstantial or fantastical our reason tell us they are, these constructed versions of the individuals involved in abandonment gain a separate significance through their effect, which may be more powerful than of their official or on-stage versions. (I examine this phenomenon further below and in Chapter 4.)

As abandonment strips away natal origins, it defies any authoritative version of the identities it creates once the moment of choice is past. Hermes' monologue means to impose a structure on the relationship that conceals the past as extraneous. The god provides a proleptic explanation for whatever pain the character Kreousa happens to display on stage: it is a mark of older suffering that Apollo has already healed by providing for his son. The suffering is of no further concern, because the drama's action forestalls Kreousa's recognition of Ion until the future has already obliterated her past trauma and its healing at Apollo's hands. For the gods, the past is a platform on which the present can be transformed into a glorious future. This tidy solution is undermined from the outset, however, by many signs that the past is crucial for Ion's identity — the ancient royal tokens of autochthony are merely the first. But of particular interest for us is how the prologue suggests that the construction of Ion's tale must be dialogic, with the give-and-take of memory and inference. The process suggests the highly tensile relationship between the real and the fantastic: they require each other but they do not rest easily side by side, and when the fictional, interpretive element is imposed on the real, it does not completely conceal or obliterate its complement's contours. The reverse is also true: the real, interpreted even by divinely established sanctions, cannot put a stop to or contain the effects of the fantastic. In the next scene, this dynamic is made explicit, as two mortal characters construct new versions of abandonment through a line-by-line repartee that blurs origin.

Ion and Kreousa each have a temporal relationship with their past selves that challenges Hermes' tidy logic. Kreousa's first appearance altogether subverts the god's plan: he predicts a dramatic action centered on male characters, and here instead is a queen.[69] The eyewitness to the ancient events he treated as background insists they are not irrelevant — she sees them still (249–254):

ἐγὼ δ᾽ ἰδοῦσα τούσδ᾽ Ἀπόλλωνος δόμους
μνήμην παλαιὰν ἀνεμετρησάμην τινά·
ἐκεῖσε τὸν νοῦν ἔσχον ἐνθάδ᾽ οὖσά περ.
ὦ τλήμονες γυναῖκες· ὦ τολμήματα
θεῶν. τί δῆτα; ποῖ δίκην ἀνοίσομεν,
εἰ τῶν κρατούντων ἀδικίαις ὀλούμεθα;

But, upon seeing this sanctuary of Apollo,
I retraced some ancient memory,
and though here, I had my thoughts there.
O sufferings of women! O outrages
of gods! What then? To where can we refer our suit,
if we are destroyed by the injustices of those in power?

Kreousa's tears and enigmatic talk of ancient memories confirm that Hermes' official construction of a remote and stately princess has vanished or existed only as a fantasy. The new and visible Kreousa handles her suffering by clinging to past images; she cannot even look at the present with her closed eyes, which Ion notices immediately (241).[70] This eyewitness plainly troubles the predication that the past need be healed only in service of the future.

Kreousa's strategy of refusing to look at the present is also challenged by the presence of physical evidence — nominally, Apollo's temple, but ironically, her son himself. Ion is the crucial figure in the dialogic constructions of the first scene, because he has no relationship to his origins in the past. Ion's monody introduces him as an odd creature, just an artifact of abandonment, a child who explicitly bases his affection on gratitude to those who troubled themselves to raise him (109–111, 136–140):

ὡς γὰρ ἀμήτωρ ἀπάτωρ τε γεγὼς
τοὺς θρέψαντας
Φοίβου ναοὺς θεραπεύω.

For as one born motherless and fatherless,
I serve the halls of Phoibos
that raised me.

Φοῖβός μοι γενέτωρ πατήρ·
τὸν βόσκοντα γὰρ εὐλογῶ,
τὸν δ᾽ ὠφέλιμον ἐμοὶ πατέρος ὄνομα λέγω
Φοῖβον τὸν κατὰ ναόν.

Phoibos is my true father,

for I praise him who feeds me
and I call by the name of father my benefactor,
Phoibos the god within this shrine.[71]

The term "true father" captures the depth of Ion's seeming indifference to the identities of his natal parents, because the adjective more appropriately refers to a child's begetter than to a foster father.[72] The phrase "born motherless and father-less" in 109 is equally strange. How could such a child exist? Because of abandonment, Ion enters this play as an embodiment of a particular kind of constructed self, one utterly of the present, whose natal identity is not simply concealed or amplified by socially and politically constructed identities, but nonexistent.[73]

Despite Ion's seeming indifference, it does not take much to set this youth off on a quest for his "true" identity. He is eager to find his own tale in the grief of the first stranger he meets (just as he later proves willing to find it in the joy of the second stranger he meets). As a foundling without tokens of his past, Ion needs the constructions of others, but their versions do not completely work for him. He continually tinkers with them, as we shall shortly see, with unexpected results. While the drama positions Kreousa, by her first entrance, to challenge the gods' authoritative account, her own eyewitness authority is tripped up by the presence of the very person who needs her tale and whose longing is at its very heart. Because Ion is a foundling and hence a stranger to her, Kreousa employs fiction to obfuscate her "true" tale. More profoundly, because of Ion's questions and promptings, she loses control over this fiction of her ancient suffering, such that its Athenian character vanishes. Abandonment produces a child who needs his story, but, by his very nature as a foundling, he cannot be told it. Ion's concerns and curiosity confound the authority of Kreousa's construction of abandonment, as his interpolations in her account suggest that her strategy for controlling her suffering — by holding it in the past — runs counter to the manner in which abandonment frees the real and the fantastic from fixity.

The first full scene of the play enacts a subtle dialogic struggle between two mortal witnesses of Ion's abandonment: the adult with her painful memories, and the infant who can only construct the scene through inference.[74] Kreousa and Ion construct two versions of his abandonment in rapid succession, the first principally his tale (308–329), the second hers (330–368). Because they speak in *stichomythia* (line-by-line response), each version is directed by the interlocutor's questions and reactions. Although each character's story is also the other's in a very real sense, the resulting constructions do not coalesce into one story. Instead, they diverge to reveal the ever-widening possibilities for identity inherent in abandonment. The struggle for control over the authoritative account does not occur between the characters themselves, who establish a delicate, natural sympathy for one another.[75] Rather, the scenarios of abandonments that each constructs struggle for ascendancy. Ion's is a blueprint of sorts for hunting out the mother he did not realize he needed until now, while Kreousa's is a strategy for blocking just such a hunt, or any attempt to make sense of abandonment, by seeing what its results are in the present.

Ion's construction of abandonment is the first conducted as a partnership: he provides the details; Kreousa's concerns provide the peculiar spin.[76] Under Kreousa's questioning about his identity, Ion is initially as indifferent about his natal parents as he sounded in his monody. He counters her remark about how lucky his mother was to bear him by noting that he is a slave (308–309).[77] Her next attempts to learn more about him are equally unfruitful. Ion sticks to his line of belonging to Apollo and not knowing who his parents are (311). Gradually, the abandoned child's life emerges (318–331):

Κρέουσα·	καὶ τίς γάλακτί σ᾿ ἐξέθρεψε Δελφίδων;	
Ἴων·	οὐπώποτ᾿ ἔγνων μαστόν· ἡ δ᾿ ἔθρεψέ με	
Κρέουσα·	τίς, ὦ ταλαίπωρ᾿; ὡς νοσοῦσ᾿ ηὗρον νόσους.	320
Ἴων·	Φοίβου προφῆτιν μητέρ᾿ ὡς νομίζομεν.	
Κρέουσα·	ἐς δ᾿ ἄνδρ᾿ ἀφίκου τίνα τροφὴν κεκτημένος;	
Ἴων·	βωμοί μ᾿ ἔφερβον οὑπιών τ᾿ ἀεὶ ξένος.	323
Κρέουσα·	ἔχεις δὲ βίοτον· εὖ γὰρ ἤσκησαι πέπλοις.	326
Ἴων·	τοῖς τοῦ θεοῦ κοσμούμεθ᾿ ᾧ δουλεύομεν.	
Κρέουσα·	οὐδ᾿ ᾖξας εἰς ἔρευναν ἐξευρεῖν γονάς;	
Ἴων·	ἔχω γὰρ οὐδέν, ὦ γύναι, τεκμήριον.	329
Κρέουσα·	τάλαινά σ᾿ ἡ τεκοῦσ᾿ ἄρ᾿, ἥτις ἦν ποτε.	324
Ἴων·	ἀδίκημά του γυναικὸς ἐγενόμην ἴσως	325
Κρέουσα·	φεῦ·	
	πέπονθέ τις σῇ μητρὶ ταῦτ᾿ ἄλλη γυνή.	330
Ἴων·	τίς; εἰ πόνου μοι ξυλλάβοι, χαίροιμεν ἄν.	

Kreousa:	And which of the Delphic women nurtured you with milk?
Ion:	I never knew a breast, but she who nurtured me …
Kreousa:	Who, O sufferer? Being sick myself, I have found sickness!
Ion:	Phoibos's prophetess I consider my mother.
Kreousa:	Relying on what sort of living did you reach manhood?

Ion:	The altars feed me, and the guests from day to day.
Kreousa:	But you have a living. For you are well dressed in garments.
Ion:	I am equipped in the garments of the god whom I serve.
Kreousa:	And you weren't eager to search for your parents?
Ion:	No, for I have no evidence, lady.
Kreousa:	Wretched, surely, was she who bore you, whoever she was.
Ion:	I was probably an outrage of some woman.
Kreousa:	Ah! Some other woman suffered as yours did.
Ion:	Who is she? If she could take part in the toil with me, I would rejoice.

At first these details sound like the predictable continuation of the Pythia's construction: such is the life of the child abandoned by that Delphic maiden. But significant differences emerge, introduced largely by Kreousa's interventions, between the life Ion reports and that fleeting fantasy.

The intrepid Delphic maiden constructed in the prologue is now replaced by one who is more melodramatic, under the pressure of Kreousa's concerns, and slightly more sordid, seen through the foundling's eyes. Kreousa's curiosity about the boy's daily life places emphasis on the economics of a foundling's rearing — a calculation utterly missing from the Pythia's story of revulsion and pity. Kreousa's sympathy for Ion and his unknown mother also generates new melodrama and poignancy in abandonment.[78] Kreousa finds Ion's lack of nursing a great sorrow, and the servant's life that Ion celebrates in his entrance song she pronounces "hard."[79] The queen now recognizes that the woman she just blessed, Ion's natal mother, was wretched. Kreousa's concerns do not seem to resonate with Ion, who repudiates the insinuation of a suffering mother into his tale. He simply pronounces himself to be "probably the wrong of some woman."[80] This maiden is quite different from either Hermes' princess or the Pythia's phantom. She prepares her infant in no way for death or for survival, takes no chances, and has no civic identity. She is merely a cipher for the boy, who remembers nothing and can only imagine the worst. And she is the woman Kreousa so wishes herself not to be that the latter's every aside about this wretched maiden insinuates her own story into Ion's. In particular, she infuses Ion's tale with the reality of (her) suffering. Subtly, the audience recognizes, this imagined maiden becomes a version of Kreousa.[81]

At first glance, Kreousa's efforts to distance herself, through pity and regret, from the maiden of this abandonment narrative seem the main source of its dramatic energy and tension. The queen's hint about another such maiden, however, provokes unexpected eagerness in Ion to know her.[82] When, having exposed Ion's need to look for his mother, Kreousa offers to fill that need with the tale of a woman whose sufferings parallel his mother's, Ion's response is electric. In an extraordinary leap of intuition, he seizes on the figure as the very model he needs to find his own lost mother.[83] This young man affects indifference and coolly assigns both gratitude and blame, but the fact is, he has never had the means to do otherwise. Kreousa's eagerness to know about her lost child's life invests Ion's tale of his abandonment with urgency; now his own need to know his mother is activated.[84] And from now on in this tragedy, any construction of abandonment will be heard, by Ion at least, as a treasure map for the hunt.

Kreousa swears that her construction of abandonment is about what happened to "her friend." The ruse is an effective symbol of her prevailing unwillingness to see abandonment's effects in the present, as well as a psychologically realistic impulse.[85] Spectators naturally hear her patent fiction as a version of the "truth": this is what happened to, and was done by, Kreousa herself. This friend was also raped by Apollo, bore a child in secret from her father, and then exposed it; this friend also has never had any other children. As usual, the transparency of the fiction urges the identification, such that this maiden's subsequent actions can be heard as a poignant hint of what Kreousa herself did.[86] She also worried about what happened to the child, returned to the site to hunt for signs, and finally resolved to question the god himself. This, the very first version of her tale that spectators hear from Kreousa, is an unexpectedly sad one, given Hermes' predictions. The queen constructs an authoritative challenge to Hermes with the reactions of the flesh-and-blood mortal who knows for herself what she felt.

Much later in the play, Kreousa will claim that she is revealing her true suffering for the very first time (850). After the queen learns of the perfidy of both Xouthos and Apollo, she bursts into a song that offers another version of her suffering full of bitterness and pain. After it, the Chorus speaks in awe of her "great treasure chest of evils" (923). In the presence of this wave of emotion — another metaphor for what she has just revealed (927–928) — we may wonder about the relationship between her revelations and the fiction she offers Ion at their first meeting. Perhaps Kreousa really is dissembling her own suffering in her fictional account of her friend?[87] The issue of which is more valid, however, is wrongly put: each construction responds to the moment of its creation. Kreousa's tale of her friend appears for this boy; his suffering and her sympathy provoke it. Plus, dramaturgically, Kreousa seems to enter into the lingering aura of those two maidens constructed by Hermes and the Pythia in the prologue, such that her first construction shares details with them. It could hardly be otherwise: Kreousa is still frozen in time and memory, and her first version of abandonment cannot burst forth with the vehemence she later shows.[88]

However fictional, Kreousa's first instantiation of abandonment creates an identity for her friend that suggests the emotional turbulence she is holding in check (340–359):

Κρέουσα·	καὶ παῖδά γ᾽ ἔτεκε τῷ θεῷ λάθρα πατρός.
Ἴων·	οὐκ ἔστιν· ἀνδρὸς ἀδικίαν αἰσχύνεται.
Κρέουσα·	οὔ φησιν αὐτή· καὶ πέπονθεν ἄθλια.
Ἴων·	τί χρῆμα δράσασ᾽, εἰ θεῷ συνεζύγη;
Κρέουσα·	τὸν παῖδ᾽ ὃν ἔτεκεν ἐξέθηκε δωμάτων.
Ἴων·	ὁ δ᾽ ἐκτεθεὶς παῖς ποῦ ᾽στιν; εἰσορᾷ φάος; 345
Κρέουσα·	οὐκ οἶδεν οὐδείς· ταῦτα καὶ μαντεύομαι.
Ἴων·	εἰ δ᾽ οὐκέτ᾽ ἔστι, τίνι τρόπῳ διεφθάρη;
Κρέουσα·	θῆράς σφε τὸν δύστηνον ἐλπίζει κτανεῖν.
Ἴων·	ποίῳ τόδ᾽ ἔγνω χρωμένη τεκμηρίῳ;
Κρέουσα·	ἐλθοῦσ᾽ ἵν᾽ αὐτὸν ἐξέθηκ᾽ οὐχ ηὗρ᾽ ἔτι. 350
Ἴων·	ἦν δὲ σταλαγμὸς ἐν στίβῳ τις αἵματος;
Κρέουσα·	οὔ φησι. καίτοι πόλλ᾽ ἐπεστράφη πέδον.
Ἴων·	χρόνος δὲ τίς τῷ παιδὶ διαπεπραγμένῳ;
Κρέουσα·	σοὶ ταὐτὸν ἥβης, εἴπερ ἦν, εἶχ᾽ ἂν μέτρον. 354
Ἴων·	τί δ᾽ εἰ λάθρα νιν Φοῖβος ἐκτρέφει λαβών; 357
Κρέουσα·	τὰ κοινὰ χαίρων οὐ δίκαια δρᾷ μόνος. 358
Ἴων·	ἀδικεῖ νυν ὁ θεός, ἡ τεκοῦσα δ᾽ ἀθλία. 355
Κρέουσα·	οὔκουν ἔτ᾽ ἄλλον ⟨γ᾽⟩ ὕστερον τίκτει γόνον; 356
Ἴων·	οἴμοι· προσῳδὸς ἡ τύχη τώμῷ πάθει. 359[89]

Kreousa:	And she bore a child to the god, in secret from her father.
Ion:	Impossible! She's ashamed of a misdeed with a man.
Kreousa:	She denies it, and she has suffered miserably.
Ion:	How so? Doing what, seeing that she was yoked with a god?
Kreousa:	The child she bore she abandoned from her home.
Ion:	This abandoned child — where is it? Does it live?
Kreousa:	No one knows. And concerning this I am consulting the oracle.
Ion:	But if it is dead, in what way was it destroyed?
Kreousa:	She supposes that wild beasts killed the unlucky child.
Ion:	Using what sort of evidence does she know this?

Kreousa:	When she went to where she had exposed him, she found him no longer.
Ion:	But wasn't there some drop of blood in the tracks?
Kreousa:	She says not, although she covered the ground repeatedly.
Ion:	How much time is it since this child was done in?
Kreousa:	He would have the same measure of youth as you, if indeed he lived.
Ion:	What if Phoibos took the child and is raising it secretly?
Kreousa:	He commits an injustice, enjoying by himself something shared.
Ion:	The god is now acting unjustly, and the woman who bore him is wretched.
Kreousa:	Indeed, she never bore another child afterwards.
Ion:	Alas! This misfortune is in complete harmony with my own suffering!

This fictional maiden is not as blank a cipher as Ion's creation. Her friendship with Kreousa and the details of her history prevent that kind of anonymity. She is no Kreousa either, although she is also assaulted by a god and acts in secret from her father. She abandons her infant very differently, without a basket or tokens and in no particularly significant site. Finally, she lacks any affiliation with Athenian symbolism or royal destiny. Her physical and emotional energy is concentrated on the aftermath of the rape and abandonment — she is the embodiment of a mother's emotions once she has nothing.

Just as Kreousa's concerns influenced Ion's version of abandonment, so now his new longing skews and shapes her account. Ion's questions about illogicalities in Kreousa's account draw attention to this maiden's confusion and anxiety after the act. Or, perhaps more correctly, his interjections actually *create* them. Her repeated search of the site, while emotionally comprehensible, is an oddly irrational gesture, since once the child vanished it would not reappear. Her imagination assumes the worst: although she found no traces of blood, she concluded that wild animals were the killers.[90] The restless uncertainty of this maiden is very different from the decisive actions of the Pythia's Delphic maiden, who, in risking pollution by exposing her child within the sanctuary, took a deliberate chance that would almost certainly result in a human finding the baby. But her behavior is also very different from that of the figure created by Hermes, who lavishes ritual care on the abandonment itself and then vanishes. Ion's questions insinuate a mortal reality into Kreousa's fiction. He can't believe her tale and tries to challenge it precisely where the divine and miraculous threaten to dominate.[91] Kreousa's friend must be concealing a mortal liaison. Had her child been killed by wild beasts, she would have seen blood. Ion's preoccupation with detail may contrast remarkably to the patent fiction of Kreousa's story, but his questions play a large role in giving her construction its particular sense of helpless suffering and anxiety. Ion's curiosity creates precisely the emotional fragility of the friend that gives this version its poignant air. This aftermath of abandonment is laden with lingering anguish that *feels* very real — like Kreousa's own — but the emotion is there because Ion insists on knowing specific, down-to-earth things about what happened.

The final exchange about the abandoned child's age and the speculation that perhaps Apollo secretly rescued his son are a thrilling piece of theatricality (353–359). As often noted, so obvious are these signals, so close the language to reality, that they suggest spectators are about to witness a recognition that may preempt the gods' design for this play, but Kreousa's emotions block her from seeing the very thing she seeks.[92] Part of the thrill of the moment lies in the remarkable way in which Ion's questions write him into this abandonment, at least as the audience hears it. The strange act of putting himself into Kreousa's construction of abandonment represents a psychic reality: as a foundling, Ion must belong in some construction of abandonment and he immediately molds each new version to include himself, however improbably. "Alas! This misfortune is in complete harmony with my own suffering!" (359).[93] It is an oddly false conclusion to draw — the story of Kreousa's friend could never lead to a temple slave — but abandonment generates neediness. Ion's need erupts as a complement to Kreousa's painful childlessness, even as it forecloses further revelation about this friend who is the embodiment of her need to know what happened in the past.

Given who these two are, of course, Ion's need to hunt for his mother mirrors Kreousa's ancient longing to search for her child. His foreclosing gesture does not simply mark the site of her pain. The audience comprehends that when his need is satisfied, Kreousa's will be as well, and this knowledge may account for our sense of the "natural" sympathy between these two. Yet if Ion is ready for any account of abandonment, since he can fit himself into any, Kreousa is not. She suffers from a sense of childlessness whose source she appears not to apprehend. She abandoned her infant to make herself childless, at least publicly and socially, and thus protect her honor.[94] That act alone did not make her childless; she and Xouthos have had years of fruitless marriage. In fact, abandonment spared her childlessness, because her child lives, but this outcome of her act is still beyond her grasp. The truth of Kreousa's childlessness is not literally so, but it has a present-time verity because of how she articulates it.

Though Kreousa is, at least potentially, the authoritative witness whose constructions could challenge the divine structures of her past, she enters as a woman uninterested in making that challenge. Weeping and with her eyes closed, she is more concerned with preserving herself against pain. Her initial construction of her trauma as a friend's tale accords with that strategy. Yet, as we have seen, abandonment subverts the coherency or cogency of any single account. Even this authority on what happened ends up collaborating with this stranger, yielding to his demands and needs. Their collaboration solves nothing for either, although its irony charms spectators. Ion's eager assertion that this friend's tale sounds like his own does not make it his. Nor does the collaborative construction of an account ease Kreousa's trauma of childlessness, despite the underlying reality of any such that these two should be able to construct. This first on-stage attempt by humans illustrates the poignant fruitlessness of attempting to control a narrative of abandonment.

The encounter between Ion and Kreousa suggests why abandonment and reunion lie very close to one another in the romance of belonging. They are complementary outcomes, and the drive to construct an abandonment that accounts for Ion is another way — in fact, the other way — to write a drama about his reunion with his natal family. The stories of mother and son begin and end with each other and incorporate the suffering and triumph inherent in each. But at this early stage in the action, abandonment scrambles the categories by which these two ought to be able to collaborate and establish the definitive account of what happened to them both. Hermes' monologue is subverted by this first interaction between mortals, suggesting that the gods cannot contrive such an account without the imagination of humans; but mortals cannot come up with the tale either.

Kreousa's experience is nowhere simply her own, in whatever manifestation her memories surface. Her story is overtaken by divine plan, skewed by human curiosity, replaced by stereotype, and concealed within deliberate fiction, such that her gestures are transformed from mildly heroic daring to blank predictability based on human emotions. But both the fictional tale and the stereotypes depend on spectators' own recognition at some level of a story very close to their own experience. The abandonment of infants was a real event for ancient spectators; otherwise it could not work as a site of terror. At the same time, these constructions activate the terror for the audience.[95] The kaleidoscopic representation of Kreousa makes her the locus of this terror, a physical emblem of the ability of abandonment to destabilize identity. We may expect the abandoned child to have no clear sense of self, and the preceding discussion has suggested vagaries in Ion's identity from one construction of abandonment to another. But Kreousa is also denied any inherent fixity of self as a result of the romance of belonging.[96] Representations of Ion's father are considered in greater detail in the next chapter, where the child as an object of investment is studied, but there is more to say about Kreousa's devolution of identity to close this portion of the study.

When Ion and Xouthos construct an abandonment to account for Ion's existence, there is a lot riding on it. This must be the public story by which these two men present themselves as father and son to a city where that relationship is all-important for a man's free status, as Ion worries about in detail (585–647).[97] For this official purpose, the narrative of Ion's origins requires a redefinition, not just of two strangers into father and son, but of other figures as well. When a drunken liaison in Delphi supposedly gives Ion a natal mother, she moves into a relationship with Xouthos that requires Kreousa, as his official wife, also to take on a new identity, that of stepmother, an identity that isolates her from the family (re)created after abandonment.[98] This figure of the stepmother is nothing like the princess Hermes describes, or like the sad and sympathetic on-stage character who forges a genuine bond with Ion himself. But the stepmother type shortly superimposes herself upon both of these earlier images in dangerous ways and nearly commits murder.

Xouthos tries to reconstruct his wife into a figure whom he can both pity, for her childlessness, and deceive, on behalf of his son, until she is somehow finally reconciled to the new reality (654–660). Ion recognizes, however, that any scenario that suits them requires an identity for Xouthos's wife that is not so simple-minded (607–617):

ἐλθὼν δ' ἐς οἶκον ἀλλότριον ἔπηλυς ὢν
γυναῖκά θ' ὡς ἄτεκνον, ἢ κοινουμένη
τῆς συμφορᾶς σοι πρόσθεν ἀπολαχοῦσα νῦν
αὐτὴ καθ' αὑτὴν τὴν τύχην οἴσει πικρῶς,
πῶς οὐχ ὑπ' αὐτῆς εἰκότως μισήσομαι,
ὅταν παραστῶ σοὶ μὲν ἐγγύθεν ποδός,
ἡ δ' οὖσ' ἄτεκνος τὰ σὰ φίλ' εἰσορᾷ πικρῶς,
κᾆτ' ἢ προδοὺς σύ μ' ἐς δάμαρτα σὴν βλέπῃς
ἢ τἀμὰ τιμῶν δῶμα συγχέας ἔχῃς;
ὅσας σφαγὰς δὴ φαρμάκων ⟨τε⟩ θανασίμων
γυναῖκες ηὗρον ἀνδράσιν διαφθοράς.

and to a woman who is childless — one who shared this misfortune
with you heretofore but now has been cut out of the lucky draw
and will bear bitterly this fate all by herself —
how shall I not be reasonably hated by her
whenever I stand near you?
Especially when she looks with bitterness at your blessings,
being herself childless? Therefore either you must betray me as you look to your
    wife,
or you must honor my place while confounding your household.
How many are the slayings and murders from deadly drugs
that women have found for their husbands!

Ion imagines a Kreousa who will be embittered by her change in status. Formerly, she and her husband were partners in their desperation for children, but this miraculous reunion casts different lots for them. Xouthos cannot enjoy common cause with both his new son and his wife, and Ion, while he may pity Kreousa, must also fear her. Xouthos's pallid attempt to construct a largely passive Kreousa cannot stand up to Ion's powerful image, which culminates in a woman ready to murder.

In her next entrance (725), Kreousa begins to embody the typology of the stepmother who plots murder, confirming just how effective the constructed figures within any tale of abandonment can be. The first image of this queen, sadly preoccupied with the past, vanishes in presence of Kreousa as a stepmother ready to kill an opponent. Another set of stereotypes contributes to this new Kreousa. When her loyal retainer, the Old Man, explains the news of Xouthos's new son, he constructs an abandonment characterized by great cunning and calculation (813–824):

ὅστις σε γήμας ξένος ἐπεισελθὼν πόλιν
καὶ δῶμα καὶ σὴν παραλαβὼν παγκληρίαν
ἄλλης γυναικὸς παῖδας ἐκκαρπούμενος
λάθρᾳ πέφηνεν· ὡς λάθρᾳ δ᾽, ἐγὼ φράσω.
ἐπεί σ᾽ ἄτεκνον ᾔσθετ᾽, οὐκ ἔστεργέ σοι
ὅμοιος εἶναι τῆς τύχης τ᾽ ἴσον φέρειν,
λαβὼν δὲ δοῦλα λέκτρα νυμφεύσας λάθρᾳ
τὸν παῖδ᾽ ἔφυσεν, ἐξενωμένον δέ τῳ
Δελφῶν δίδωσιν ἐκτρέφειν. ὁ δ᾽ ἐν θεοῦ
δόμοισιν ἄφετος, ὡς λάθοι, παιδεύεται.

νεανίαν δ᾽ ὡς ἤσθετ᾽ ἐκτεθραμμένον,

ἐλθεῖν σ᾽ ἔπεισε δεῦρ᾽ ἀπαιδίας χάριν.

This man, having married you and entered your city

and home, though a stranger, and seized your entire legacy,

has now been revealed to have gotten secretly the fruit of children

from another woman. I shall explain the manner of his secrecy.

When he perceived you to be barren, he wasn't content

to be equal with you and to bear equally this fate,

but bedded a slave in secret concubinage

and begot this child, which he bestowed as a guest-token on someone of Delphi

to raise. The child, in the halls of the god

ranging freely, grew up thus to be unnoticed.

When he perceived that the child had grown up,

he persuaded you to come here for the sake of your childlessness.

Xouthos is here a treacherous schemer whose partner was some shadowy slave. Ion's "abandonment" was not that at all, but rather a calculated fosterage in Delphi. A new Ion appears, primed to accept tyranny from his father, as well as a pathetic Kreousa, duped and bereft of support in the sorrow of her childlessness (836–838):

καὶ τῶνδ᾽ ἀπάντων ἔσχατον πείσῃ κακόν·

ἀμήτορ᾽, ἀναρίθμητον, ἐκ δούλης τινὸς

γυναικὸς ἐς σὸν δῶμα δεσπότην ἄγει.

And you will suffer the worst evil of all these —

he's bringing into your house as master a motherless,

no-account from some slave woman.

Ion's construction as an ambitious proto-tyrant complements Kreousa's as stepmother and brings them into conflict over Athens.

Is the Old Man merely speculating maliciously or guilty of downright deceit in suggesting such a scenario?[99] It hardly matters, since, as we saw with shadowy alternative mother-figures, this construction of a usurper, however unsavory, is powerful enough to provoke Kreousa's attempt at murder. Ion himself shortly storms onto the stage to kill her. The generic types that establish an official account of Ion's identity take on a strength — a virulence and an onstage reality — that defies attempts to categorize them definitively as fantasy, and in a very real way, they are not fantasies. The identities they develop are not mistaken, since the abandonment that Xouthos and Ion use to make sense of Apollo's oracle ends up with an enduring reality in the settlement that Athena imposes at the end of the play. As far as the Thracian interloper knows, Ion is of any account at all in Athens only insofar as he is his son, and Kreousa is nothing more than his son's stepmother.

The process by which a multiplicity of Kreousas and Ions is set loose in the play begins within Hermes' prologue. To construct an abandonment to account for this child requires a disorientation of identity, and Athena's intervention as deus ex machina does not fully foreclose the reverberations caused by the profusion of versions of both queen and youth. Nor are the goddess's words framed in a manner that suggests they are meant to undo the disorientation. She does not answer Ion's first troubling formulation about Apollo's role: ὁ θεὸς ἀληθὴς ἢ μάτην μαντεύεται; (Does the god prophesy truthfully or falsely? 1537). Instead, she answers his second about whether he is from a mortal father or Apollo (1548). Her pragmatism suggests the naïveté of Ion's questions—yes, Apollo is his real father, but yes, he also needs a mortal father to survive politically, and so he is a "gift" to Xouthos. The goddess's elision of Ion's question about the truth leaves something disturbing in the mix, as a necessary ingredient to the construction of an identity for the abandoned child. Earlier Ion asks about another tale of children and parents with the same turn of phrase: "What then to make of this? Is the tale true or false?" (τί δαὶ τόδ'; ἆρ' ἀληθὲς ἢ μάτην λόγος; 275).[100] At this point he wants to know whether Erechtheus really sacrificed his daughters to secure victory in war and if so, how Kreousa survived. The queen can give straight answers: yes, her sisters died, but she lived, embraced in her mother's arms. The truth is grim but real for the child chosen for survival: if parents plan to kill their children, only their very own embrace can save the infant—such is the murderous closeness of the family. Abandonment is the mechanism that puts the child and its death beyond the reach of the parent, forestalling murder or embrace. As we have seen, such circumstances permit no authoritative account, so Athena must avoid the question of truth.

Case history and tragedy grapple with what is posited to be *the* originary trauma: the parents' sexual embrace or abandonment. These are each an outcome of a moment of larger trauma that is both more deliberate, because it involves evaluation and choice, and more elusive in its effect, because it is immediately effaced. In Freud's theoretical universe, there is no such thing as real abandonment; it is only a phantom representing the reality of parents who can never be what their children first felt them to be — perfect, magnificent beings.[101] The spectacle of sex is the trauma lying at the origin of the child's identity; yet it is also a comfort, because sex itself secures that identity. The primal scene reenacts and thereby essentializes what the child can otherwise never experience, its own conception. The *Ion* does not conceal either outcome of the romance but paradoxically uses abandonment to establish (re)union through parental embrace. But how can one choice lead to its opposite when their results preclude each other? Dramaturgically, the play insists that the boy's abandonment must be continually reconstructed. Every scene requires one new tale about it and sometimes more. The gods in the play assert that the only thing the audience need see is his reunion with his family — or his father (but not his natal father). Hermes tells us this is what we are to see and also tells us what we are *not* to see: the reunion of mother and child. But even if such a phony and incomplete reunion could cement Ion's identity (and, in the end, this reunion does secure Ion's status in Athens, at least publicly), its antithesis and predication, abandonment, makes possible so many other identities for him (and Kreousa) that no single authoritative identity emerges.

The romance of belonging obscures matters of authority, and I have posited that the destabilizing source is the elision or concealment of one outcome from serious consideration. Freud's "From the History of an Infantile Neurosis" illustrates the protean quality of those engaging in the primal scene of embrace, particularly father and son, analyst and patient, in the absence of a larger context of peril to the family or structures of psychoanalysis. Euripides' *Ion* reveals that constructing Ion's originary tale through abandonment constantly changes the identities of the mother and son, whose official embrace is made that much murkier. Each outcome thus appears inherently unstable.[102] I have also suggested that the phantom of the omitted possibility also plays a significant role. For Freud, its absence marks the lost site of choice and leaves behind an anxiety that undermines any sense of authority. Jung's deployment of Freud's primal scene as a site for abandonment reveals the uncanny about Freud's project: through its very insistence on the primal oedipal structures, we can still see the possibility of rejection and a longing to prevent it. In Euripides' *Ion*, the illogical drive of abandonment to its opposite, reunion, leaves in its trail too many identities. The two outcomes have an eerie relationship to each other; they require each other yet do not cancel each other out. Narratives that are intended to settle the issue of origin too easily turn into terrifying sites of lost identity.

On this point, it is worth noting just what sorts of identities are missing: other agents have been effaced or simply constructed to type by the master narrative.

Jung's deployment of the primal scene reinserts the consort as an agent, as one who offers knowledge and gives him a weapon against his intellectual father. In Freud's analysis of the Wolf Man, such a figure is missing. His mother suffers in the primal scene and becomes someone he wishes to replace, but other notices of her elide her agency or deform it. Freud notes she helped the Wolf Man's nanny introduce him to religion (SE 17: 61–62), but that nanny is given a larger role in guiding his toddler affection (cf., e.g., 14–15, 24, 27). The mother is also said to have fought with the Wolf Man over money (72–73). She is a rival, and in that respect, she fades behind the Wolf Man's sister, his more serious challenger for his father's affection and money.[103] Neither mother nor sister offers an alliance to the child, a means for overthrowing the father. This dynamic is no more than we would expect, given Freud's program for the primal scene, but Jung's shrewd parody reminds us of what is missing: the possibility of those other identities based on repudiation, based on choices effaced in the oedipal narrative. Ion's longing for his missing mother eventually, startlingly leads to his willingness to murder her, based on his image of a shadowy Delphic maiden. Her insinuation between Kreousa and her husband creates a new identity for the Athenian queen, also murderous, that provokes violence in Ion on behalf of his new family. The child turns out also to be an agent in the romance of belonging, although the sources of his energy and aggression are only hinted at by the construction of his abandonment tale as we have studied it thus far.

I return to the slippage from embrace to abandonment, or the reverse, in Chapter 4, which looks in greater detail at strategies for stopping the search and accepting an answer as the answer. There we shall discover the Wolf Man's missing mother and the source of Ion's murderous intent. For now, I wish to study the matter of agency from another perspective, one that focuses the finances of the romance. It costs something to belong to somebody — looking at who pays those costs reveals more about the structure of the romance.

CHAPTER THREE

Profit and Loss in Belonging

Ξοῦθος· ἅψομαι· κοὐ ῥυσιάζω, τἀμὰ δ᾽ εὑρίσκω φίλα
Xouthos: I will embrace you — I'm not seizing goods in reparation! I'm finding my own dear possession.

EURIPIDES, *Ion*

Freud was of the opinion that at the end of treatment a gift from the patient
could contribute, as a symbolic act, to lessening his feeling of gratitude and
his consequent dependence on the physician. So we agreed that I would give
Freud something as a remembrance.

THE WOLF MAN (Sergei Pankejeff)

He was in fact unable to pay Freud for his last analysis; on the other hand,
he had formerly as a rich patient paid enough to feel somewhat justified in
accepting gratis treatment now.

RUTH MACK BRUNSWICK

The calculations that determine who belongs in a family can be a matter of life
and death, and afterwards, humans conceal the cost-benefit analysis, if possible.
When Xouthos tries to embrace Ion as his own dear possession (τἀμὰ . . . φίλα),
he contradicts the more legalistic act of seizing goods in reparation (ῥυσιάζω).
Despite his refusal to characterize his new acquisition as such, his denial that he is
"seizing goods in reparation" expresses a reality that cannot be completely re-
futed. Both perspectives are necessary in the final dispositions for Ion; both the
technical and the personal belong in the Athenian royal accounts. Freud and the
Wolf Man are also caught up in a complicated dance of recompense and gratitude. Pankejeff has been paying bills for his analysis for years, but in Freud's
opinion, the flow of indebtedness still runs from him to his doctor. A gift is
proposed to end the calculation of cost and benefit by changing the terms to the
symbolic, but the patient, as we shall see, calculates anyway and chooses an
expensive artifact.

When we study the romance of belonging as a site of transaction, we learn a great deal more about the psychic costs of its choices. Although ancient Athens and early twentieth-century Vienna understood commercial transactions in different terms, Euripides' *Ion* and Freud's "From the History of an Infantile Neurosis" are in agreement that the foundation of a family can be read as a commercial act. For Freud, sex is the ground in which parents give and receive payment, and the infant wants to participate by offering its feces as a gift in order to enter the drama. In the *Ion*, a child is a commodity and parenting is a kind of investment with expectations of future yield. Abandonment is the alienation that stops further resources from being expended on something not worth raising. When parents accept ownership of a child, they are deciding that it will produce sufficient profits or yield (*tokos*, a Greek word that also means offspring). But the romance of belonging is not just about possession of the child, because that child also engages in transactions of desire, with the possession or rejection of its parents at stake. Freud's discussion of the primal scene makes this claim explicitly, and Ion's acquisition of parents is shot through with the calculation of costs against the promises of return. His parents become objects that he needs to possess, both conceptually and in reality. The romance of belonging objectifies those in a family by its reckoning of their worth as possessions, but there is also the self-deceptive longing to conceal the transaction. The slippage between real and psychic cost accounting is another sign of the trauma of belonging—we cannot find the figures that balance costs against gains.

This chapter studies the representation of the romance of belonging in economic terms, as a site in which a decision to own or dispossess is made based on profit or loss; it looks at how cultural differences regarding the alienability of a child once chosen for rearing affect the basis for the calculations. For Freud, while in theory no child can be abandoned, no child is ever fully inalienable. The possession and nurture of a child is always tinged with possibility of cutting losses, and the parent, whether natal or psychoanalytic, can use abandonment as a useful threat to get what is wanted from the child. For the ancients, abandonment was possible, but, once chosen, the child was inalienable, as suggested by the structure of evaluation and choice detectable in birth rituals. Parents have just one moment to decide whether to abandon or rear a newborn. I also study what sorts of self-deception appear with the economic calculations. Both texts count the worth of a valuable object as inestimable and consider its use a matter of destiny. With this scheme, children can be understood in terms seemingly less troubling. I suggest how this perspective manifests itself in both cultures. For Freud's era, I briefly consider how the ownership of a precious artifact shaped the terms of the narrative it inspires. For Euripides, I study parallels in the first book of Herodotus's *Histories* for the deployment of royal children as precious tokens for destiny.

From these two perspectives, a complicated picture of the finances of belonging emerges in both the *Ion* and "From the History of an Infantile Neurosis." In both texts the cost of identity, whether established through an embrace or by abandonment, is endless. Freud discounts abandonment in theory but applies its threat in practice, and what he gets in exchange is nothing less than psychoanalysis itself. This result has costs for both him and his patient that far outlast the case itself. So, too, although the *Ion* is predicated on a natal connection between parent and child that is irrevocable, once abandonment occurs, no account of Ion's origins is ever complete and in balance. The view of the child as a precious object helps counter the troubling costs of belonging, but this strategy works better for the parents than for the child, who can never settle his lack of balance in terms of parents and identity.

In both texts economics are a part of the audience's culture that is unexpectedly activated as it watches the drama or reads the case history. Euripides' spectators were unlikely to associate the heroic myth of infant abandonment with cost accounting; the dramatization of abandonment in intimate but banal economic terms disrupts the surface of their engagement with the tragedy. Nor do Freud's readers expect economics to burst out from the anal-erotic frame with which they are familiar, so that the intricacy of the Wolf Man's neurotic engagement with the financing of belonging is startling.[1] Even as this disruption quickens the audience's prior conceptions about the economics of ownership, the other model of the object bestows a symbolic value of destiny on the child, a value that, since it cannot be bought or alienated, is absolute and incalculable. The collision between versions of abandonment and union as economic transactions or as narratives of destiny exposes the intimate relationship between calculation and self-deception at the heart of the entire romance.

Throughout this chapter, I deliberately speak of abandonment and nurture (the outgrowth of the natal embrace) in economic terms. This may sound like a metaphoric deployment of language that is excessive for the topic under discussion—the rearing of a child. Yet both the *Ion* and "From the History of an Infantile Neurosis" are preoccupied with the child as a possession and with its equivalents in money and other forms of wealth, such that the metaphor is not out of place. Or, more correctly, the language of neither text is metaphoric. In both ancient and modern psyches, the child is a possession that must be managed like any other. Either the child has to be invested, in the hope of further yield, or discarded, to avoid the loss of other resources.

The clutter in familiar photographs of Freud's study reflects his private passion for collecting artifacts from ancient cultures. As is well known, these objects on display for his patients were a critical part of his "intellectual alchemy." "*Saxa loquuntur* — the rocks speak," Freud proclaimed as an early and abiding metaphor for his psychoanalytic work: to find fragments at the deepest layers in the archaeology of the mind was to begin to (re)construct the unconscious.[2] "Intellectual alchemy" is Joseph MacGillivray's phrase for the interaction of artifact and theory in the work of the British archaeologist Sir Arthur Evans (1851–1941), who styled himself a scientist in his reconstruction of ancient Cretan culture and whose work Freud followed avidly. Ownership of the object was key, MacGillivray argues, for Evans's archaeological narrative: "[O]nce the ancient artifact was acquired personally, it assumed a far greater significance than it could ever have had in a museum case or someone else's collection. It gave the collector-scholar the cherished nucleus around which to build a theory, which would both explain the artifact in an ancient context and add to its importance in the modern context, thereby enhancing its value in every way."[3] Freud's obsession with collecting ancient objects suggests that he also found ownership more satisfying than observation of someone else's possessions. Richard Armstrong quotes the American poet H.D. on Freud's sense of the object: "The Professor said that we two met in our love of antiquity. He said his little statues and images help stabilize the evanescent idea, or kept it from escaping altogether."[4] The purpose of these objects was not merely to inspire but to provide the framework for theoretical narrative.

In Freud's time, a scientist provided a convincing narrative of origins to work against the prevailing one — the biblical account — whose persuasive powers might be waning but whose place of privilege was still powerful and buttressed by legal institutions. Those who headed scientific quests of all sorts expected to construct a scientific narrative to account for what was found. Freud too believed that his constructions were essential to the science of psychoanalysis.[5] If the explanatory narrative is based on ownership, however, the scientist had to take care, since the narrative could be skewed if it relied too heavily only on objects that could be acquired. The energy and budgetary discipline Freud exerted (as did Evans) in his acquisitions suggests that he understood the peril of working with too small a sample.[6] In the previous chapter, we saw how Freud shaped the psychoanalytic method so that the analyst would acquire as much raw material as possible from the patient's talk. Freud also took meticulous care to provoke more material by offering up his "constructions." The case histories themselves as a genre were offered as objective corollaries to the theoretical. Freud, like Evans and other scientists of their era, believed in the dispository power of the object to ground the foundational narrative.

This was not the only scientific perspective in Freud's age on the value of the found or acquired object; other ways of thinking about evidence and proof deliberately diminished or effaced the object's value. In her *History of the Modern Fact* (1998), Mary Poovey situates the object within the relationship between the numerical account and theory. In particular, the early modern invention of double-entry bookkeeping had a profound and lasting effect on individuated particles of evidence. According to Poovey, this method of keeping accounts, which requires all transactions to be listed twice, as both loss and gain, generated the problem of "how to conceptualize the relation between the particular (quantifiable) details one could observe in the world and the general theories one could advance to explain them."[7] The status of the object as evidence is significantly affected by the interpolation of the "quantifiable," because the new emphasis on the numerical comes to signify accuracy. Once early developers of double-entry bookkeeping had succeeded in "align[ing] precision with accuracy," the precision of their books itself was the thing that effected accuracy. Fact became what had been precisely recorded, even if its accuracy was not verifiable. Poovey argues that for a business to thrive, its daily practices, or its narrative based on artifacts, had to be deliberately beyond verification. In accounting specifically, numbers and their transparency substitute for and create the verity of the recorded transactions. Details from the narrative of individual transactions that could not and *should* not be verified had to be effaced as "superfluous."[8]

We have, then, two forms of alchemy at work, one that relies on the valuable object, whose details provide the exemplum of theory, and another that deliberately effaces narrative detail based on artifacts in order to create the appearance of or affect accuracy through precision. Contradiction here may be illusory, because by either reckoning, artifacts are marked as valuable (either to help or harm) by whether they are visible or invisible. For the archaeologist, whether of ancient culture or the unconscious, the recovered object suggests the presence of other, lost or still buried objects and inspires narrative. The accountant privileges countable details to produce precision, thus hiding other details that may say a great deal about a business's practices but must be concealed for it to thrive.

Accounting is a self-confirming abstract narrative that replaces the individuated tale. Whether the drive is to imagine what is concealed or to substitute abstraction for what must be concealed, both means of handling objects or details require the narrative as an essential part of their science. It is not enough to amass evidence and let it speak for itself.[9] Possession of the object is a provocative first step to suggesting hidden depths, and the case of the Wolf Man reveals how Freud and his patient acquire things and use them in shaping the narrative that defined their identities.

Freud was theoretically conversant with the economics of human interaction, and within "From the History of an Infantile Neurosis," the primal scene dramatizes the anal-erotic phase of infantile development, as a precursor to the oedipal crisis, in terms of money and gift-giving. It is a vivid if disturbing picture of parents and child buying and selling each other. In this respect, Freud's theory reflects the fact that in late nineteenth-century Europe, the notion of a child inherently belonging to its parents, with a concomitant entitlement to inheritance, had been abrogated. The removal of this traditional tie changed the terms of belonging. Fathers could now choose how they would distribute their wealth.[10] Children earned their inheritance in their fathers' eyes, and more critically, the period of evaluation by the father was for all intents and purposes interminable. No ceremony or moment of final (or initial) risk, like that faced by an ancient newborn, marked the end of judgment. Thus, in theory, the child was no more an inherent possession than any other object: when Freud bought the objects that were metaphors for his intellectual kingdom, he exercised a choice paralleling the evaluation that governed belonging in the lives of the family.

The family romance, however, suggests that in framing his theory of identity, Freud relies on another ideology that is in fundamental conflict with the view of property, whether inanimate or animate, as alienable.[11] From one perspective, the text reveals an economy that always yields the same bottom line — fixity within a family whose values are identical — but the fantasy used by neurotic children to express conflict with their parents relies on structures of evaluation and redress that presuppose modern economic calculus. In their fantasy that they were abandoned by a noble family and are being reared by a humble one, neurotics assigned economic values to affection and rank. Freud supposes that children so afflicted calculate the rate of return on their affection and, when it is not "fully reciprocated," explain the discrepancy in terms of abandonment (*SE* 9: 239). The neurotic constructs abandonment within the structure of wealth, just as fosterage lies within the structure of poverty: throwing away resources is something noble (that is, rich) people do; conversely, the humble and poor pick up the refuse of others.[12] As a therapeutic structure, the family romance suggests that the fantasy resides in the neurotic child's faulty economic reckoning. Psychoanalysis heals this situation by redirecting the neurotic's calculus of identity, such that he sees no return on abandonment, no increase in parents, status, or identities. The union of a family is a steady state, whose wealth and poverty are equal, or so the equation is supposed to run that finally determines identity. And, as a corollary, abandonment has no point, since it yields none of the increase the neurotic child expects. Freud's theoretical economics in the family romance are a stern corrective to the fantastical exuberance that can emerge when the child can expect a big return from his abandonment by trading up from his current misery to rich, socially valuable parents.

But this new calculus begins in an oldest layer of neurotic evaluation that participates in a very different sense of the object. The family romance is really an expression of "regret" for the child's lost original sense of his parents, when they were "incomparable" and unique in their value.[13] Here is the notion of family as destiny: the child finds that his parents are tokens of his own immeasurable value. The parents' uniqueness holds the promise of something extraordinary in terms of destiny, and the child's disdain for its humble family is grounded in this mythic sense. Psychoanalysis exploits this view of the parents as objects in order to shut down the modern reevaluations that the child neurotically repeats. True, the final calculation eliminates this magic of destiny, since the child must discard his earliest evaluation of his parents and learn to be satisfied with parents who are not less hoped for but all that can be hoped for. Nevertheless, psychoanalysis cannot overcome neurotic assessment without it.

Here Freud struggles with a conflict in his theory of identity that he cannot resolve. He is attempting to articulate a fantasy of identity using an economic discourse that is modern insofar as it acknowledges the capacity of a child to be incessantly evaluated.[14] Thus rich parents are imagined to discard a child in these terms (an unstated given) and the child resents his mean parents in similar terms. The value of this discourse is its ability to reward reevaluation and new reckoning: the real is imagined to supersede fantasy by asserting that the transactions of the fantasy that might have enhanced the value of fantastic parents and identities never took place. Yet this propensity to (re)assess is in conflict with those older categories of identity that buttress the ancient inherency between parent and child. If the child's belonging is never a matter of calculating costs versus yield, then its identity is never a matter of choice but is always determined through the certainty of parental identity. Freud's family romance, while it attempts to sub-stitute a new construction of identity, one based on wealth and the commerce that produces it, cannot finally dispel the older, still powerful narrative that based class distinctions on intangible, unobservable factors such as religion and lineage. Furthermore, the romance finally shows that any sort of economic reckoning is wrong-headed and neurotic.

Part of Freud's failure to liberate his theory from the ancient inherency of identity may lie in the fact that such inherency buttresses the premier role he gives to dreams, fantasy, and construction in psychoanalytic theory. They must be the equivalent of recollection. He stakes his theory against those of his rivals on the value of the fantastic for replacing a patient's recollections with therapeu-tic meaning. As he says regarding the Wolf Man, "It seems to me absolutely equivalent to a recollection, if the memories are replaced . . . by dreams the analysis of which invariably leads back to the same scene" (*SE* 17: 51). Freud may have been particularly emphatic about the equivalency of the constructed scene and recollection in the case of the Wolf Man, given the extremely early time of the primal scene in the patient's life (at eighteen months).[15] Nevertheless, his preoccupation with essentialized identity was abiding; it can also be seen in the equation that prohibits abandonment in the presence of identity. The psychic task is not to confront parallels and differences among the child's imagined sets of parents, which might lead to an understanding of the self.[16] Instead, Freud wants the patient to learn to evaluate properly the single, unitary identity that is the constant in each setting. All that changes, because it is all that *can* change, is the sense of worth that the child (mis)assigns to its origins in any setting. Self-realization, then, lies not in a self-directed construction of identity but in the excavation of a buried treasure whose worth is fixed and realizable. The finances of the family romance confirm the structure of authority in Freud's theory: sepa-ration is a sign of neurotic misevaluation by an unruly child; acceptance of the past (and submission to its proper evaluation that lies in psychoanalysis) marks the healthy psyche.

In "From the History of an Infantile Neurosis," Freud's preoccupation with the equivalence of the reality and the fantasy of origins appears in his deployment of money, gifts, babies, and feces as substitutions for one another within the primal scene. This oedipal drama also serves as a site for purchase and exchange, cost accounting and profit-taking. Freud even structures his case history to reveal the deepest levels of meaning in the primal scene only after he has assessed its significance in these anal and economic terms. Money, as payments and gifts, is unusually prominent from a wide array of perspectives in the case of the Wolf Man. The patient's presenting symptom of extreme constipation provides the context in which to articulate the role of money in the anal-erotic phase. Such constipation both expresses the feminine desire for copulation with his father and signals the Wolf Man's repression of that urge. The withheld feces become both the Wolf Man himself, returned to the "womb" in order to enjoy the intercourse, and the child he would bear his father in recompense (*SE* 17: 100–101). In Freud's understanding, feces give the baby its first conscious awareness of loss from its body, and bowel movements are precious to the child, a present worth giving to those it wishes to please, especially the mother. And since sexual intercourse is a commercial matter, with women producing children in recompense for their pleasure, the child needs a gift or payment if it is to participate in the primal scene as more than a witness. Freud determines that the Wolf Man interrupted his parents' lovemaking in the primal scene by a bowel movement that awoke him, which Freud calls the child's "present" (80).[17] But for the Wolf Man, money can also substitute for a feminine gift—whether feces or baby, which are equivalents—by which he can replace his mother in intercourse with his father.[18]

Freud's equation of feces, babies, and money is confined by his prejudices and misapprehension of infantile development, but it also offers a perspective from which to think about the case history's emphasis on wealth, gifts, and recompense.[19] To begin with, this is an equation that Freud believes lies within his control: it is well known to his readers, so that his description of the Wolf Man's complicated adult neurosis surrounding his constipation is meant simply to confirm the role of the anal zone in this case. And since Freud has deliberately chosen to focus on the infantile neurosis, he does not comment on all of its manifestations. For instance, in his opening encounter with the Wolf Man, he reports in a private letter, the patient "confessed the following transferences: Jewish swindler, he would like to use me from behind and shit on my head."[20] On the surface, this coarse assertion of superior social and religious standing is an act of aggression and defiance. Within the context of the Wolf Man's full array of ambivalences, the gesture is an early sign that the wealthy Russian aristocrat recognizes in Freud a new father, with whom he will have a complicated libidinal relationship (even, as usual for him, confounding the male and female roles). Given that Freud and the Wolf Man become entangled in a web of finance and obligation that extends beyond the analysis, as explored below, the offer is also the earliest known gesture by which the Wolf Man tries to become a highly valued object for the father of psychoanalysis. Freud leaves such considerations out of the case history, with its paradigm of infantile neurosis.

At the level of the infant, Freud's case history repeatedly suggests the importance that gift-giving and ownership had within the narrative of the Wolf Man's original analysis.[21] The Wolf Man was born on Christmas, a day to expect gifts, and he recalled a "rage" when he was disappointed with them. But such a birth date meant that he was also a present, just like Jesus, with whom the Wolf Man intensely identified (*SE* 17: 61–69). Meanwhile, his dream of the white wolves occurred on the eve of his fourth birthday, when he saw Christmas presents in a tree and was looking forward to his own. Freud concludes that the wolves of his dream replaced those presents (35–36).[22] The Wolf Man was once enraged when he saw his father give his sister money, and he demanded a share of it. Freud interprets this sibling economic quarrelling as libidinal jealousy: "What had excited him was not merely the actual money, but rather the 'baby' — anal sexual satisfaction from his father" (83). Freud comments more than once on the Wolf Man's lack of apparent grief when his sister commits suicide, as well as his relief that he would now not have to share his inheritance or his father's love.[23] Since Pankejeff desired his father himself, the economic rivalry mimics and masks the sexual. The father's gift was actually money, and this confusion between gift and payment assimilates the Wolf Man's sister to his preferred erotic object of women of low status.[24] The case history relies on the anal-erotic in money and gift-giving to organize its interpretation of the crucial oedipal drama.

Even the Wolf Man's real-life financial situation, so far as it appears in the case history, is subsumed into a symptom: "In our patient, at the time of his later illness these relations [to money] were disturbed to a particularly severe degree. . . . But he had no idea how much he possessed, what his expenditure was, or what balance was left over. It was hard to say whether he ought to be called a miser or a spendthrift" (*SE* 17: 72–73). Freud understands his patient's inability to keep good accounts as an external insouciance that parallels a profound inability to relinquish any libidinal attitude arising from his unconscious, or to resolve his ambivalence. This same inability to separate finances and erotics subsequently becomes a source of abiding collaboration and tension between Freud and his patient, beyond the controlled frame of the text. The first evident marker of the tension is the closing gesture of a present. Freud considers a gift normal at the end of an analysis, but in this case it took an unusual turn, as the Wolf Man reports in his autobiography:

> In the weeks before the end of my analysis, we often spoke of the danger of the patient's feeling too close a tie to the therapist. . . . In this connection, Freud was of the opinion that at the end of treatment a gift from the patient could contribute, as a symbolic act, to lessening his feeling of gratitude and his consequent dependence on the physician. So we agreed that I would give Freud something as a remembrance. As I knew of his love for archeology, the gift I chose for him was a female Egyptian figure, with a miter-shaped head-dress. Freud placed it on his desk. Twenty years later, looking through a magazine, I saw a picture of Freud at his desk. "My" Egyptian immediately struck my eye, the figure which for me symbolized my analysis with Freud, who himself called me "a piece of psychoanalysis."[25]

For Freud, the gift is symbolic recompense for the "feeling of gratitude" and is meant to weaken ties between patient and analyst. When the Wolf Man executes the proposed final transaction of the analysis, however, he appears to wish to strengthen rather than lessen the attachment. By choosing an expensive artifact that he guesses will be particularly attractive to Freud, he plainly means to insinuate himself permanently into Freud's psychoanalytic life.

By itself Freud's proposal of a symbolic closing gift is a strange gesture from an economic standpoint and reminds us that the psychoanalytic partnership is ripe for murkiness in terms of the power established by money.[26] Sarah Winter has studied the way in which Freud presented fees as part of "the moral and professional superiority of psychoanalysis over doctors." Candor about fees and directness in expecting their payment was to be in contrast to the doctor who might "act the part of the disinterested philanthropist."[27] Avoiding the appearance of noblesse oblige was a strategy to inspire confidence. Yet Freud seems to have seen this professional affect about money in hermeneutic terms only. In a psychoanalysis the patient may pay fees for years, but Freud seems to discount the possibility that the transaction imparts any power or authority to the patient, since at the therapeutic level, the doctor asserts control and invites the transferences that create dependence and trust. In the Wolf Man's account of his gift we can read the success with which Freud assumes he has handled everyday economics with this wealthy Russian. He believes he has created a great enough symbolic debt that, far from fearing the patient's sense of entitlement, he assumes gratitude as the potentially overwhelming emotional response. The gift, as a "symbolic" gesture, can ignore the reality of money and payment and redress a presumed imbalance, because it operates purely at the symbolic level and in one direction only.

The Wolf Man subverts this economic calculus when he enhances the symbolism with an expensive gift aimed at a private luxury of his analyst's.[28] He later congratulates himself on his choice: when he sees the statuette on Freud's desk some twenty years later in a photograph, he knows he is still at the heart of psychoanalysis. The object parallels the case history in instantiating his identity as the child in the primal scene. Far from relaxing any ties or feelings of obligation, the Egyptian goddess furthers a sense of entitlement. As Richard Armstrong remarks, "The Wolf Man's parting gift of an Egyptian figurine could therefore bear the sinister allegorical reading of an analysand 'producing' the required artifact for his analyst in order to play the game."[29] Theoretical work on gift-giving has taught us to expect just these consequences; what is remarkable is Freud's assumption that a gift could do otherwise — such is the confidence he has in the therapeutic power of transference.[30]

Ruth Mack Brunswick, who analyzed the Wolf Man in 1926–27, reports that he did feel a sense of entitlement based on his payment for analysis (see this chapter's third epigraph). A few years after the original analysis ended, the Wolf Man's financial circumstances were ruined by the revolution in Russia, and he came to blame Freud for the loss. When he needed further analysis in 1919, Freud provided it without charge and also took up a collection among the psychoanalytic community for the Wolf Man out of a sense of indebtedness to his patient, "who had served the theoretical ends of analysis so well." Freud made this gift for some years in row, and the Wolf Man came to expect it so keenly that he concealed the recovery of some family jewels so that Freud would not withhold one donation. The Wolf Man also conceived the notion that Freud, who was suffering his first bout with cancer, would leave him something in his will.[31] Having been supported by one father and enriched by his death, he expected the other to do the same. But dependence and restitution were not all that were at stake. When Brunswick analyzes the Wolf Man, she interprets the theme of gifts and payments in the context of the patient's illness: "it became clear that the gifts of money from Freud were accepted as the patient's due, and as the token of a father's love for his son. In this manner the patient recompensed himself for the old humiliation of his father's preference for his sister."[32] Love and money are inextricably linked for the Wolf Man, and if he is to replace his sister in his father's affection, he expects to be paid for it, just as she was. Brunswick concludes, "The libidinal significance of gifts runs like a red thread through the entire history of the patient."[33]

Brunswick apparently does not take into account the hidden issue of evaluation and choice that also runs through the Wolf Man's neurosis, which Freud deliberately provoked in his bold gamble over ending the analysis. The irrevocable time limit to the analysis becomes a threat of abandonment. Freud speaks of the gesture in therapeutic terms, as a means to break through what he sees as a profound psychoanalytic lethargy.[34] But from the Wolf Man's point of view, he is pretty well off. He has improved enough to acquiesce in a process that he finds intellectually stimulating: "I can only say that in my analysis with Freud I felt myself less as a patient than as a co-worker, the younger comrade of an experienced explorer setting out to study a new, recently discovered land."[35] Furthermore, the current state of affairs is sexually rewarding, since Freud allows him to renew his relationship with the woman whom he eventually marries, again, with his analyst's permission.[36] Especially in the context of the Wolf Man's powerful transference of his father to Freud, the irrevocable time limit for analysis is analogous to abandonment, in that it threatens permanent severance. Equally seriously, the Wolf Man stands to lose the identities of "co-worker," "younger comrade," sexually active husband, and son properly filial in erotic terms. Freud, however, sees an endangered analysis that he needs to succeed for reasons having to do with his political struggle of control of psychoanalysis, as we saw in the previous chapter.[37] The time limit works, because the Wolf Man produces key details in the wolf dream that Freud needed to construct the primal scene.[38]

This threat of abandonment proves as traumatic as abandonment itself, however, as is clear from the aftermath of the analysis.[39] The most obvious sign of the trauma is an abiding resentment in the Wolf Man, as Brunswick later learns, that is fed by Freud's gifts of free analysis and money. Brunswick concludes that the gifts were inadequate because the transference of the patient's feelings for his father to Freud are stronger than had been recognized by anyone.[40] Careful attention to Brunswick's case history further clarifies the impact of the threatened abandonment on attempts by Freud and the Wolf Man to settle their sense of indebtedness to each other both in financial and emotional terms. Brunswick's record of the entanglement of economics, erotics, and authority beneath her patient's acute psychotic behavior testifies to the residual power of the Wolf Man's neurosis. Even after years of psychoanalysis, these issues restage all too easily the acts of gift-giving that mark and conceal a traffic in sexuality that the Wolf Man cannot make sense of as a child and is forced to replicate wherever he could as an adult.[41]

Brunswick's apparent goal is to relax the Wolf Man's sense of entitlement and attachment—not an easy task, because he for his part makes the analysis itself into a competition with her that restages these issues. From her vantage point as analyst, Brunswick sees the competition as an opportunity to break through the patient's psychotic resistance, which manifests itself as a mixture of condescension and contempt.[42] Behind this affect lies the Wolf Man's real conflict over his relationship with the only "analyst" he would ever acknowledge as such — Freud himself. To penetrate the resistance, Brunswick makes a concerted effort to "attack" the assumptions on which it is based. She emphasizes an alliance between Freud and herself, not just of superior medical and therapeutic understanding, but also of closer friendship and trust; her aim is not humiliation but recognition:

> Again, he stressed the non-professional quality of their relation. I now asked why, if such were the case, he was never seen socially at the Freuds'. He was obliged to admit that he had never met Freud's family, thereby badly damaging his entire case. . . .
>
> So long as he combined his two techniques of satisfaction, on the one hand blaming Freud for the loss of his fortune and therefore accepting all possible financial aid from him, and, on the other hand, maintaining, on this basis, his position as the favorite son, it was impossible to make progress in treatment. . . . My technique therefore consisted in a concentrated attempt to undermine the patient's idea of himself as the favorite son.[43]

Brunswick suggests the degree to which the Wolf Man assumes that a favored status requires gifts as marks or tokens of that favor. Eventually, her attacks work, although with his "megalomania" undermined, the Wolf Man exhibits such fearsome symptoms of psychotic violence that Brunswick is "relieved" when the dreams appear that signify his reevaluation of his troubled economic relationship to Freud. She reports a dream of particular importance:

> The patient is in the office of a doctor with a full, round face (like Professor X.). He is afraid that he has not enough money in his purse to pay the doctor. However, the latter says that his bill is very small, that he will be satisfied with 100,000 Kronen. As the patient leaves, the doctor tries to persuade him to take some old music, which, however, the patient refuses, saying he has no use for it. But at the door the doctor presses on him some coloured postcards, which he has not the courage to refuse.
>
> . . . the patient refuses [the music], only to be presented with the coloured (i. e. cheap) postcards. Certainly these are symbols of the gifts of Freud, now grown valueless to the patient. The meaning is clear: no gift is now sufficient to compensate the patient for the passivity involved in acceptance. Thus at last gifts, which at

the time of the patient's fourth birthday on Christmas Day, had precipitated the wolf-dream and, indeed, the entire infantile neurosis, and had played a leading role in all his later life and analytic treatment, were now robbed of their libidinal value.[44]

Brunswick interprets the dream as an economic staging of the Wolf Man's liberation from Freud. He could no longer accept his subordinate role to Freud as the Father, a relationship that had been buttressed by payments and gifts on both sides. Brunswick does not comment, however, on the fact that the Wolf Man lacks the courage, in his dream, to refuse the postcards, valueless though they have become (see further below).

The Wolf Man's competitive attitude toward Brunswick suggests to later psychoanalysts that he is constructing a triangulation among himself, Freud, and Brunswick as a replica of his ancient rivalry with his sister. Brunswick herself is better situated than the patient to claim the title of favored child, and, as we saw above, she exploits her close professional relationship with Freud as a therapeutic tool during her analysis of the Wolf Man.[45] This triangular tension can be sensed in her sometimes harsh representation of the Wolf Man over the matter of money: "Most striking of all was his total unawareness of his own dishonesty. It seemed to him a matter of no moment that he was actually accepting money under false pretences."[46] The triangular structure is attractive if we assume that the primal scene was actually one of incest between the Wolf Man's father and sister. Lack of comprehension combines with guilt and the need for secrecy in a particularly toxic brew, which might well poison the Wolf Man's unconscious irreparably, as indeed seems to have been the case.[47] Certainly, the urgency of the competition with Brunswick is commensurate with this theoretical reframing of the primal scene. But do we miss something if we assume that the triangulation restages only the Wolf Man's rivalry with his sister?

Brunswick herself presents the triangulation in significantly different terms, with her as a mother-figure, not a sister. While she sees that the Wolf Man's dreams about her suggest his rivalry with his sister, she interprets that evidence in terms of the ancient causes of his passivity. To understand her patient's transference, however, Brunswick imagines herself as the mother in a primal scene:

> In this connection, the patient's idea that he occupied a kind of mid-position between Professor Freud and me is interesting; it will be recalled ... that he had many fantasies about the discussions which Freud and I were supposed to have had about him. He himself remarked that he was our "child"; and one of his dreams revealed him lying next to me, with Freud sitting at his back. (The importance of *coitus a tergo*

is again shown here.) In the language of the womb-fantasy, he is indeed partaking of the parental intercourse.[48]

In Brunswick's construction, the Wolf Man sees himself in a primal scene of the intellect, lying in the middle of private discussions between his psychoanalytic parents. And she interprets another vignette from the dream quoted above, in which the Wolf Man embraced her as a woman (despite her "boyish dress") and placed her on his knees, as signs of the positive, heterosexual transference of recovery from the "remnant of the transference to Freud." Both privileged positions spell out the infant's erotic desires, as far as Brunswick is concerned, and are commensurate with her characterization of her work with the Wolf Man as a continuation of Freud's.[49]

Brunswick's narrative of the Wolf Man's longing to remain important to Freud is structured to display the therapeutic power of the family romance. When she triangulates herself in this second analysis as the mother of the natal family, she forces the Wolf Man to admit her own superior connection to Freud. Brunswick insists that this child of psychoanalysis recognize his "true," unprivileged status. Nevertheless, from the perspective of the family romance we can discern more clearly the effect of the hidden, disallowed abandonment. The dimensions of what Brunswick is forcing the Wolf Man to admit are far greater than she seems to imagine. As we have seen, the Wolf Man seeks identities from Freud and psychoanalysis that he can count on as a reliable yield from his suffering: intellectually equal if junior partner, husband to a wife whom Freud himself bestows, favorite son. He buys these identities from Freud with his payments for analysis, which, Brunswick reports, create a sense of entitlement in him to remain in analysis. Freud's threat to abandon the analysis requires more payment, but in new coin and with a new knowledge about the nature of payments in a romance of belonging: they are necessary but never sufficient in a setting in which abandonment turns out to be a real option. The Wolf Man has to pay by giving up that detail so crucial to the primal scene's discovery, so that he can remain in analysis, but it is heading now to its inexorable end. Such is the initial yield that he comes away with a great sense of debt, as well as anxiety at the failure of payment to secure his identities.

When the Wolf Man falls seriously ill again in the mid 1920s, his sense of indebtedness seems to interact poisonously with his sense that he has paid for identities within psychoanalysis, to which he is entitled. Abraham and Torok blame this relapse at least partially on a letter that Freud wrote to his former patient in June 1926, which asked for confirmation about certain details of the wolf dream. They dramatize the moment vividly. "What an incredible surprise," they write. "A letter in Freud's own handwriting and quite a letter at that. He asks nothing less than a truthful testimony. Freud's illustrious life, salvation, and honor depend on the poor words of a modest Wolf Man."[50] Abraham and Torok are playing here upon the irony of the truth and lies that they believe pervade the Wolf Man's analyses, given their conviction that the true primal scene was the father's incest with the sister. The lure of further inference here is hard to resist: Freud's demands seem to exceed what the Wolf Man can give, particularly at a time when he is receiving annual gifts of money from Freud (one of which was due shortly after this letter).[51] According to Abraham and Torok's chronology, the psychotic episode begins precisely when the coincidence of the demand for knowledge and payment becomes intolerable. The Wolf Man's response suggests the neurotic anxiety of someone fearful that his identity may be taken away unless he pays for it again. The circularity restages the threat of abandonment.

Theoretically, Freud's psychoanalysis cannot acknowledge the force of the threatened abandonment. Instead, Brunswick's reading of the triangulation, with herself as the mother, allows her to restage the family romance and, just as the theory predicts, to exploit the drama to assert that the abandonment never took place. The Wolf Man's distrust of Freud as well as his longing for him are discounted as signs of delusion. His condescension toward Brunswick, in turn, becomes a disdain for foster parents that signifies delusions of grandeur about one's real parents. In speaking about her patient's deceit regarding the concealed jewels, Brunswick remarks: "In his fear of losing Freud's help, it evidently did not occur to him that Freud would never have considered permitting the patient to use up his little capital."[52] Her characterization of the Wolf Man's deceit as an inability to recognize Freud's true identity is part of the discourse of a unified self-identification. Brunswick knows how to exploit the theory by which maturity and reality lie in denying the multiplicity of identities that abandonment creates; she interprets her patient's desire for continued beneficence from his former "father" as a misapprehension of the man.[53]

Brunswick is right to see a "red thread" of economics running through the Wolf Man's history, and we can add an emphasis on cost accounting. These were two men, patient and analyst, who both knew the cost of sex and what it bought. They could articulate these transactions in terms of identities. Freud bought the foundation of psychoanalysis, and with the right gifts, the Wolf Man could be his father's chosen one and the special object of psychoanalysis.

What both men also seem to sense, but cannot acknowledge, is the effect of abandonment on all these calculations. It throws everything out of balance, because nothing is ever settled for good. Freud cannot strictly apply his theory to his practice of analysis and, at the same time, be a parent who does not practice abandonment. Once he threatens to cut off the analysis on a certain date, the Wolf Man always fears abandonment, and so Freud finds that he cannot stop the payments that are temporary antidotes to this ceaseless anxiety. Freud might have been surprised at this characterization of his donations to his former patient, because he thought of the threat as a spectacular therapeutic tool with only a momentary effect. He was certain that he would never repeat this tactic with the same patient. The threat had to hold good unless one wanted to lose all authority. Freud's tag for the tactic says it all: "A miscalculation cannot be rectified. The saying that a lion springs once must apply here."[54] The Wolf Man does not ever grasp this assurance, however, and seems never to relax his anxiety that his belonging to psychoanalysis might be taken away.

Understood in economic terms, Freud's threat reverberates ominously: you *could* be mine, if you give me what I need.[55] What he needs is material for theoretical abstraction, not an individuated memory. Freud had spent too many of his early years, and wasted too much ink on theories about "seduction scenes," to permit the Wolf Man's recollections, whether of his sister's molestation or of some other encounter, to stand as the primal source for infantile neurosis.[56] And in his struggles against his rivals, Freud is looking for "comprehensive solution to all the conundrums" (*SE* 17: 7), a solution that is not the memory of trauma itself and yet is "absolutely the equivalent of memory."[57] Freud wants an account that makes abstraction the exact equivalent of recollected detail. From the Wolf Man's realization that he *saw* something, Freud can develop the primal scene, a construction capacious enough to account for every recollected detail and also able to frame them therapeutically.[58] This was yield enough to warrant the donations to his patient. But the threat of abandonment also has to be paid for, and in this matter, Freud's debt is not merely for having threatened abandonment, but also for having even admitted it as a reality. In theory, abandonment is the neurotic's screen over the larger reality of a single, irrevocable identity, which is safe in its self-enclosing nature. When Freud actually uses abandonment as a psychoanalytic weapon, he teaches the Wolf Man something else: the identity he longs for is subject to withdrawal if he cannot earn it. Brunswick's application of the family romance perversely reinforces this lesson as part of the therapeutic accommodation.

To judge from his writings about his later career, the Wolf Man never stops wondering what he meant to psychoanalysis. His preoccupation with the real contents of the primal scene and with his inability to recall Freud's construction of it are evidence of a restless anxiety that he might not be what Freud told him he was, the special object of psychoanalysis.[59] Even though his neurosis can never lay to rest the sense of impending abandonment, the Wolf Man is as resourceful as any child confronting a father with a choice. With his analysis with Freud ending, he recognizes an opportunity to gain an even greater and permanent yield by creating another identity for himself. The Wolf Man chooses a gift that is not symbolic recompense but a seduction, which works because it is a physical analogue of what psychoanalytic theory suggests. Freud is so taken with the Egyptian statuette that he displays it prominently in his office. The Wolf Man's identity is objectified as a precious artifact. No matter the vicissitudes that wrack the Wolf Man for the rest of his life, he needed only look at pictures from Freud's life to see himself always in the very shrine of psychoanalysis, with an identity no one can take from him.[60]

This account changes our perception of the child's seemingly passive role as witness in the primal scene. To prevent his abandonment, the Wolf Man gives the elusive detail that seduces his analyst into a solution. This presentation is replicated in the gift of the Egyptian statuette; the Wolf Man once again seduces his analyst into keeping him as an artifact of psychoanalysis. Once we look at the entire structure of belonging, we see that the primal scene, with its gifts and recompense, is something like the seduction scene that Freud refused to ground his theory in, but with the child as agent. Inherent in the romance of belonging is the peril of abandonment, with its ability to make of the child anything at all. But the child, given the chance, exploits the instant of peril to become exactly what the parent needs or wants. Freud can construct his primal scene to conceal this seductive power in part because the Wolf Man made it into a site in which natal identity is not a problem but a given: I saw my parents in the very act that engendered me. This was the gift that put Freud so much into the Wolf Man's debt, but the statuette reminds us that the child cannot give up the sense of peril that made him.[61]

Ancient spectators of the *Ion* might have been baffled by the endless need to reassess a child's worth as a possession that drives Freud and the Wolf Man, because they viewed children rather differently. To begin with, once parents decided to raise a child, the link between them was inevitable enough to symbolize immortality. Moreover, abandonment was not a construct to be eliminated theoretically but a real option that at least some in the audience had contemplated or exercised. Furthermore, drama affords the luxury of being able to capture the paradoxical tension between abandonment and embrace by bringing them both into the action, and Euripides' tragedy can thus use both to construct Ion's Athenian identity. That, in a very real sense, is what tragedy does best. Freud, for one, understood the relationship between it and psychoanalysis in these terms: tragedy rehearses the unconscious anxiety that psychoanalysis recreates in order to heal.[62] But for Freud this relationship pertains to the natal triangle of Laius, Jocasta, and Oedipus, not antecedent structures such as abandonment, and as we have just seen, he has a hard time making his accounts of primal trauma balance when he eliminates that antecedent. What happens when tragedy engages abandonment and embrace in economic terms? Does it fare better in reconciling the paradox and the tension, not dramatically (which it can plainly do by the simple expedient of a deus ex machina) but in its engagement with its spectators' unconscious?

Let us consider what spectators brought to the *Ion* in terms of their understanding of the object and the child as an object. Spectators certainly participated in a culture that understood children as valuable objects whose worth could be measured against other forms of wealth. At the same time, children, particularly in myth, could be perilous tokens of destiny and ruin. And sure enough, recreations of Ion's abandonment sometimes sound like crisp accounting narratives and sometimes like narratives laden with symbols of destiny. From either perspective, the child in the romance of belonging acquires an identity that someone has paid for or must bestow as a gift. But if we assume that these competing visions interact with the audience's experience of everyday political commerce, as well as its awareness of the symbolic power of mythic kingship, we still have to wonder what these differing perspectives mean. I approach the nature of this juxtaposition first by examining what we know about what the Athenians thought about objects, and how and why they kept accounts of their wealth. Then I study how children can serve as symbolic markers of kingship and royal power in a text well known to Athenians, the first book of Herodotus's *Histories*.

Possession of the object was a more fluid notion for the ancient spectator than for Freud and his audience. The fifth-century Athenian economy was not liquid enough for us to imagine men purchasing valuable objects simply to fill a collection.[63] A fine object was a form of tangible wealth that could be useful in commercial transactions, but it also had value when conspicuously displayed or consumed on behalf of one's friends or polis, both gestures of high status.[64] An inability to apprehend such gestures, or a too-ready willingness to forgo them, could mark a character in drama or literature as someone of low or alien status. The Athenian was also steeped in literary, artistic, and mythic traditions that might treat the fine object as something more — as a token of greatness and destiny. All of these connotations of the object were related. A gift to a guest was largesse, but it also became the treasure that marked a relationship between two households and might even one day become a token of destiny.[65]

The ancient notion of acquisition could also be rather haphazard — a matter of windfall. Herodotus reports the good fortune of a certain Ameinokles, a landowner of Sepias, who garnered "untold wealth" in gold and silver cups that washed ashore after a Persian fleet ran into a storm off the Chersonese in 480 (7.190). Ameinokles became "exceedingly rich" — presumably far beyond what his land represented — as a result.[66] Men gave each other objects to create obligations or as a form of informal credit, and objects were one aspect of wealth that could be seized.[67] In the first epigraph of this chapter, the technical verb used by Xouthos to describe how he's *not* taking possession of Ion — ῥυσιάζω — signifies the process of taking something in reparation, through violence if necessary, from someone who has harmed a man or owes him.[68]

The notion of "yield," or "return on investment," follows from this complicated sense of the object, and seems crucial in turn for understanding the nature of ancient bookkeeping. Our most detailed information about business and accounting in Athens comes from the fourth century, from which we have parts of court cases that concern financial matters or mention business dealings that affect the case.[69] Although these cases occur after significant changes in Athens's political, social, and economic landscape at the end of the fifth century, they can help us understand the sort of financial accounts that Athenians in Euripides' audiences might have kept.[70] In particular, the sense of formal accounting that we can garner from the fourth century suggests what sort of informal reckonings men made.[71] They kept track of yield (or loss) as moments in narrative time, one in a sequence of transactional moments when something comes into (or passes out of) one's possession.

In a recent study of lending and credit in classical Athens, a specific arena of economic activity in which bookkeeping of some sort would seem to be required, Paul Millett suggests how economic concerns there were intertwined with familial, social, and political matters far more inextricably than we can grasp if we judge ancient financial transactions from our perspective.[72] For instance, the circulation of valuable objects mentioned above, as a means of creating obligations or fulfilling informal loans, might not strike us as a real part of Athenian commerce, but it certainly was. Very ordinary objects could circulate as part of a mosaic of opportunities for borrowing and lending, most of which were highly informal.[73] Relatives, neighbors, or members of the same phratry or clan might help each other out, and the formalities and the expectation of specified return were in inverse relationship to the propinquity of the relationship. Interest was not paid, except under limited and impersonal circumstances. Millett claims, in fact, that borrowing from a banker was the "last resort" for a man in need of money, but even between banker and client, cash or property literally exchanged hands and loans were made without witnesses.[74]

Within this informal system of lending and borrowing, written accounts were not normally kept; instead, participants relied on their memories of obligations incurred and discharged. Athenian bankers did keep written records, however, and the nature of these records suggests the kind of reckoning about investment, loss, and gain that went on informally and formed part of the tragic audience's experience. Let us consider one particularly intricate fourth-century court case that illustrates both what sorts of accounts or financial records men might have kept and why they kept track of what they did.

When suing Timotheus for nonrepayment of a debt, the banker Apollodorus reminded the court about the kinds of records bankers kept, a speech attributed to Demosthenes tells us: "And let none of you wonder if we know these things precisely. For bankers are accustomed to write records for themselves of what money they give, and for what purpose, and of whatever someone might repay, in order that both things loaned out and things repaid might be known to them for their accounts."[75] The apparent simplicity of such records suggests to some historians that Athenian businessmen lacked the means of keeping a true account of a business's overall profitability, because these accounts do not allow one to calculate net versus gross profit. "Even at their most sophisticated, ancient Greek accounts were intended as checks on embezzlement, not as guides to profit and loss," Paul Millett asserts. "It would be foolish to argue that the Greeks had no concept of, or desire for, increased profitability. . . . But the rudimentary nature of [their] accounting techniques reflects the Athenians' inability to balance overall profitability against a rate of interest."[76]

Richard Macve, a student of the history of accounting and bookkeeping, suggests, however, that what appears to be a lack of knowledge about such matters as formal credit or net profit may instead represent a preoccupation with other issues. People keep accounts of what they want to know, he argues, and that is the interesting question to ask—what did the ancient accounts tell businessmen?[77] When Apollodorus says that his accounts tell him what he has given out and for what purpose, and who has paid him back, what is he really interested in learning or remembering?

Current accounting practices derive, as noted above, from the early modern invention of double-entry bookkeeping, which was intended to provide a schematic overview of a business's well-being. Any entry in one column must be accompanied by a corresponding and opposite entry in the other, even when that entry is an arbitrary figure created simply to achieve balance. Double-entry bookkeeping is an early testament to the rising power of numbers, treated as the sole relevant evidence, as opposed to everything else that a business does.[78] Such accounts affect a reliable overview of a business' entire operation precisely because material has been excluded. Looking at neat, even arbitrary balances, both owners and investors sense that they can grasp the larger picture of what is really going on in a business, and can thus predict the likelihood of profit or loss, either overall or in any individual act.[79] As an invention of early-modern Italian city-states in which businesses facilitated complicated overseas trade enterprises, double-entry bookkeeping was a sign of honesty to customers, because it was (apparently) a transparent tool for preventing internal fraud.[80]

In contrast, what the banker Apollodorus says he knows from his records suggests that ancient Athenians were interested in what Macve calls a "chronological narrative" of their commercial transactions in the form of payments and receipts.[81] Given the role of informal lending in cementing social and political relations, the interest is less in an overview of an individual's business than in a sense of where one stood relative to another at any given moment. Such a narrative form of recording-keeping makes particular sense in light of how Athenians understood property or wealth, which they divided into two opposing categories: "visible" (φανερὰ οὐσία), that is, property, such as land, its produce, valuable objects, or coins, that could be seen and counted; and "invisible" (ἀφανής), that is, cash or objects stashed away for safekeeping or invested in loans or ventures that might yield profit.[82] The distinction between visible and invisible wealth was not synonymous with tangible and intangible. Rather, it applied to what could and could not be observed publicly, and objects could move in and out of view. The fluidity with which objects became visible or invisible is crucial for comprehending why the ancients kept accounts in the form of chronological narratives of loans, payments, and motives, so that an Athenian could know where he stood relative to his associates. Bankers' written records, which could be used in court in certain cases, evidently formalized what men already kept track of in their informal dealings with one another. Such narratives allowed it to be known who had acquired things from someone and whether anything had been repaid.[83]

Apollodorus's suit against Timotheus illustrates the value of keeping a chronology of the transactions that move wealth in and out of visibility. In one complication, a merchant Timosthenes deposited two vases at the bank of Pasion (Apollodorus's father) for safekeeping while he was abroad. Here is an attempt to use a bank to render possessions invisible for safekeeping in Timosthenes' absence.[84] What happened next complicated matters. A servant of Pasion's loaned the vases to Timotheus, who had to apply to Pasion for equipment and cash to entertain important guests ([Dem.] 49.22). Timotheus eventually returned some of the goods, but not the vases or the cash, so when Timosthenes returned and demanded the return of his property, Pasion had to make good the loss, since the vases were a formal deposit in the bank. Apollodorus puts the best face on these events. He alleges that his father's reasons for making the loan to Timotheus, while businesslike, were also straightforward and friendly: he appreciated the goodwill he thought existed between himself and Timotheus (27).[85] These same transactions can be read differently, for it is also possible that someone, either the slave or Pasion himself, took advantage of Timosthenes' absence to make an investment on the side whose yield would be the good favor of Timotheus, a prestigious general. If we imagine the ancient account sheet of Timosthenes' interactions with Pasion's bank over the vases, we see the ebb and flow of transactions in which each man expected a return (in monetary profit or good favor) from his manipulation of the visible wealth of the vases (see chart below).

The intermediate transaction of the loan to Timotheus should have profited the banker, at least in goodwill, without loss to Timosthenes, who was only entitled to the full return of his property.[86] Pasion, however, lost money when he could not recover the vases when he needed to, and he was forced to settle up with Timosthenes. In the end, Timotheus presumably had the vases, but whether to display as visible wealth or hide as ill-gotten gains remains unclear. Meanwhile, Timosthenes received restitution, also visible as cash, because the banker's accounts provided the narrative frame that allowed for the value of the vases to be restored. But those same records, if Apollodorus's suit is successful, will secure restitution for the cost of the vases, because everyone can read the incomplete transaction (stage 4 in the chart).

This fourth-century set of transactions, which was formally presented in court, squares well with the picture of informal credit and lending that comprised

Visible and Invisible Goods as Illustrated by [Demosthenes] 49, "Against Timotheus"

Transaction	Status of Goods
1. Timosthenes deposits cash, vases, and bedding in Pasion's bank	invisible for safekeeping
2. Pasion stores cash and goods	visible among the bank's assets
3. Pasion lends cash and goods to Timotheus	invisible as an investment for goodwill (cf. [Dem.] 49.3)
4. Timotheus returns bedding but not the cash and vases	bedding is visible, but the status of the vases and cash is ambiguous; because he does not demand restitution in full, Pasion earns Timotheus's partial goodwill (cf. [Dem.] 49.23–24, 27)
5. Timosthenes demands restitution	Pasion pays Timosthenes the cash value of the vases, reducing his own visible wealth; Timosthenes recovers the cash as visible wealth; Timotheus retains the vases and cash, which he may or may not use as visible wealth

the bulk of transactions among Athenians in the fifth century, as long as we understand that most men kept their records informally and as a matter of memory. Such accounts yielded tales of contracting or expanding wealth, especially visible wealth, which one decides either to expend publicly or hide as an investment, hoping to recover both it and its yield later. Timing can be crucial—a missing link when someone else wants to settle up yields a loss then and there. My schematization of the transactions in the table above, however, illustrates the absolute necessity of a narrative tracking investments and debts, without which Apollodorus's bookkeeping is incomprehensible to us as a picture of his business's success or failure.[87]

As the preceding discussion suggests, Athenian attitudes to objects of wealth turn out to depend on how they are used, as investments or expenditures. Their methods of keeping an account of objects they invested or spent tell the story of where and when they were ahead or behind. But what if the precious object is a child? The child enjoys a similarly complex status as an object of either visible or invisible wealth, but with more troubling consequences. For parents, a child is a form of wealth to be saved or expended as needed. It can become that kind of treasure that represents a personal relationship between two families (through marriage), or a family and its polis (through service in war). The child is also a form of yield; as noted earlier, the chief word in ancient Greek for "yield" or "return on investment" — *tokos* — is in the first instance a word for offspring or child.[88] When the child is a *tokos*, it is the yield of the womb and thus a return on the parents' expenditure or investment (with their bodies). But the child is also that investment itself; once taken into a father's *oikos*, the child cannot be disinherited or otherwise eliminated statutorily from the family.[89]

Abandonment acquires a peculiar power within this structure of ownership, as the single instant when a child can be evaluated and disallowed a place in the family before it takes on this awesome worth. Yet so powerful is the inherency of natal belonging that even a child so abandoned is not a detail that can simply be effaced or utterly eliminated from reckoning. If present circumstances are unfavorable, the child is written off as a loss. If it survives and is recovered, abandonment can then serve as an explanation for unexpected gain. As objects, children turn out to be accountable like any other possession, in a manner of reckoning that is already familiar to audience. And the *Ion* is full of accounts — narratives of transactions — that echo those that ancient spectators could have told about their own circumstances.

Ancient spectators had another view of children arising from the myth of cultural foundation, a view that relies on the inevitability of identity from parent to child and the inalienability of that child, even if it may suffer abandonment. This view of the child is instantiated in the myths in which the child is a token of a household or kingdom's strength, and to gauge the nature and power of this tale within the audience's consciousness, we can turn to the first book of Herodotus's *Histories*.[90] One organizing structure in Herodotus's opening book involves tales concerning children whose fates prove ruinous for themselves or those who engender them, or about whom there are grim omens and warnings.[91] These tales reveal a great deal about parents' motivations.

The two most famous of these tales are familiar examples of Herodotus's vision of how destiny and recompense work in history. First, Croesus's vain attempt to save his one healthy son from a fated early death is a tragic part of the story of this Lydian king, whose imperial ambition results in what Herodotus calls the first acts of aggression that eventually led to the Persian invasion of Greece. Croesus's overthrow is Herodotus's earliest historical example of how a more ancient crime must be expiated.[92] The second tale, the exposure as a baby of Persia's great king Cyrus, opens the centerpiece of the book — the rise of the Persian kingdom. Omens surrounding Cyrus's birth cause his grandfather, the Median king Astyages, to fear his own downfall, and he orders the infant killed, but Cyrus is exposed instead. He is reared by a shepherd and his wife and grows up to overthrow his grandfather's kingdom. The mythic structure of a hero's abandonment at birth provides a Greek frame of meaning to the story of the transfer of power from the Medes to the Persians: Cyrus's glorious career as king is prefigured and guaranteed by his survival as an exposed infant.[93] Yet these are not the only two instances of children used as fatal markers of royal destiny in Herodotus's opening book.[94] The fate of the child becomes a tale of the parents' or grandparents' gain or ruin, as they choose either to preserve their children or put them at risk on behalf of the state, all the while failing to recognize that their children mark their own demise. The spectacle of wasted children warns of the peril of kings and queens trying to calculate how best to use their offspring, for their children are the sign of their own power, over which they ultimately have less control than destiny itself.

The tale of Cyrus's ruin in the book's final episode illustrates the issue (1.205–216). The Persian king's campaign against the Massagetae and their queen Tomyris is marked for disaster by riddles and troubling omens.[95] As the Persian forces approach the Araxes River, which separates their kingdoms, Tomyris issues a challenge that sounds straightforward but is actually a riddle that the Persians do not get: "O king of the Medes, stop this zeal of yours, for you cannot know whether it will be accomplished opportunely for you. But cease and be king over what is your own — and endure seeing us rule over what we rule" (1.206).[96] If Cyrus insists on fighting, though, Tomyris continues, she invites him to choose the location of their battle. Either he should cross the river and march into her country a journey of three days, or she will cross and march three days into Persia. Tomyris is warning Cyrus against acting on partial knowledge — he cannot know how this will come out — but she also threatens him with her own self-confidence.[97] Cyrus and his advisors do not hear this warning; instead, they debate which part of her offer to accept, with all the advisors recommending that Tomyris be allowed to cross into Persia except Croesus, who thinks this dangerous foe should not be let into their territory.[98] Croesus also suggests a trick whereby the Massagetae's vanguard are introduced to the Persian luxury of wine and then destroyed when their guard is down. The trick works, and Tomyris's son Spargapises, commander of the vanguard, is captured as a result.

Upon her son's capture, the queen translates her first, riddling communication into clearer terms. She denounces Cyrus's aggression as an insatiability for blood (212).[99] Tomyris's own restraint becomes a naked taunt: whereas formerly she wished to be left to rule her own, she boasts now that, if Cyrus does not return her son and retreat, even with a third of her forces lost, she will beat the Persians.[100] But it is too late for Cyrus to take her advice — her son has already committed suicide. The queen's battle fury is unleashed, Cyrus's army is utterly defeated, and the king himself killed. The full meaning of Tomyris's first words is now plain: her offer was neither cautionary nor tactical; it was a prediction. It did not matter to Tomyris where they fought, because she knew she would beat the Persians regardless. And she translates her opening riddle one last time, through a horrible vengeance on Cyrus's body. To sate his bloodlust, she stuffs her vanquished enemy's head into a sack of blood.

Tomyris's revenge on Cyrus has been characterized as the excessive recompense of a clever but savage queen — a type that occurs with some frequency in Herodotus. Such a figure uses great cunning and "self-control" to overcome her enemy but then exacts a revenge that, in the words of Stewart Flory, "outstrips in ferocity the degree of insult that provoked it."[101] Cyrus's use of wine to seduce and overcome his enemy is also a provocative symbol of the clash of cultures.[102] As François Hartog notes, "In Tomyris's eyes, Cyrus the drinker of wine is in truth a drinker of blood, so he will be served blood just as if it were undiluted wine."[103] But we should not allow Tomyris's status as a primitive or the Persians' luxury of wine to obscure the significance of her son in calibrating the queen's behavior. When Tomyris commits the outrage against Cyrus's severed head, her taunt is tempered by a sense of her own ruin: "Though I am alive and victorious over you in battle, you ruined me when you took my child through trickery. But I will sate you, just I promised, with blood" (214). The trick of the wine may sting and thus determine the symbolism of her retributive gesture, but the queen's sense of defeat reveals that the gesture against a dead man is worse than simply futile. The brutality supplements her words without satisfying her, because, figuratively speaking, it is her own son's blood that is the intoxicant that has drowned Cyrus. Tomyris's most precious resource — her son — stands symbolically in the place of Persian wine. When cultures fight, they use their entire arsenal, and

Croesus insists that wine is potent part of the Persian weaponry, because it leaves the enemy confused and vulnerable. Tomyris's restaging of the trick makes the blood of children the equivalent weapon.

The matter here seems more than a clash of the cultured with the primitive, although it is certainly that.[104] Herodotus insinuates into this tale another, briefer notice of a son in peril that brings the theme wholly into the realm of the cultured. While organizing his assault on the Massagetae, Cyrus is troubled by another omen of doom, a dream that a courtier's son has wings overshadowing all Europe and Asia. Cyrus interprets this dream as a plot against himself and demands that Hystaspes, the courtier in question, arrange for his son's surrender. Hystapes appears to assent but his retreat to guard his son Darius in fact saves him from the Persian debacle. (Darius does indeed become the Great King, but not until he seizes power many years later from Cyrus's crazy son Cambyses). Even as Cyrus stands on the brink of losing his life in battle, he stirs up the passions that will later end his dynasty through a faulty understanding of another aspect of Persian culture, dream-interpretation and omen-reading.

Tomyris's ignorance of wine causes her to read blood as its equivalent, but the story of Hystaspes and his son suggests that for Cyrus, all signs, whether primitive or cultured, stand in equivalence and point to the same thing — the Persian king has reached his limit. Darius, like Tomyris's son, is a thing of great value to his parent and is put at sudden risk by Cyrus's insatiability: his paranoid desire to protect his rule requires others' children, just as it does unceasing conquest. But this demand, like his campaign against the Massagetae , brings him to the limits of his dynasty. Neither Hystaspes or Tomyris is willing to allow Cyrus to consume his or her child. Hystapes takes advantage of the king's delusion about Darius to flee (and thus survive); the savage queen's true power and intent are revealed when hers dies through the trick.[105] Wine, blood, and dream all mark a peril for children — even grown children — that is really the ruin of Cyrus.

From the perspective of Cyrus's nasty death, the stories about children earlier in book 1, particularly those in which royal parents struggle to preserve or to destroy children marked as fatal by the gods, take on greater meaning. Croesus tries to protect a son whose consumption is predicted, to the point that he prohibits even normal activities for the youth. When the son protests his enforced inactivity, the king insists on preventing his death at least for his own lifetime (34–35); the time frame is an ominous indication that he is badly misjudging the proper use of a prince. Croesus wishes simply to preserve his son as an object of personal value rather than royal worth. He thereby ensures his own termination by forfeiting any benefit from his son's work for Lydia and any heirs his son might have produced.[106] The reverse impulse is no more sensible. Astyages' attempt to destroy his grandson and preserve his own rule is self-destructively futile. Killing his heir to prevent his rise to power both signifies the end of the Median line and brings it about. Astyages' failure to perceive the meaning of the omen confirms its point. His line is at an end, but it will be his own efforts to prevent the seemingly natural succession of a child from his daughter's womb that make Cyrus a Persian, not a Mede.[107]

The royal child, properly understood, is a nonnegotiable and inalienable possession that is a symbolic protection of a king's future because it is the future of the kingdom. The reign of any king is doomed when he receives the omen of a fatal child, since the child that should promise perpetuation of his line suddenly signifies its ruin. Astyages' reaction is illustrative: why should he fear that a grandson will supplant him, since such a succession is normal? His fear is a sign of his doomed state, and his decision to marry his daughter to a Persian, from the perspective of the Medes, is a reprehensible denigration of her. The marriage brings about the transfer of power from the Medes to the Persians precisely because it is such a transfer. At the same time, the royal child's mortal fragility symbolizes the gift and burden of destiny, because no child can be treasured up (or thrown away) forever. Like Tomyris, who makes her own son commander of the Massagetae vanguard, Croesus and Astyages should be prepared to embrace the risk that their children represent: to put them to use on behalf of their kingdom; to hope that they produce heirs for the continuance of royal lines; and to accept that they cannot be redefined as too precious for use or expendable. Instead, each king tries to hedge his bets by manipulating the child's status, and their inability to think beyond a calculation of profit and loss signifies that each is already too blind to see the vicissitudes of fate.

Men who are not royal pursue different strategies regarding the use of children, as an example of a different kind of response to divine destiny illustrates. Herodotus reports that the Athenian Hippocrates, while preparing a sacrifice at the Olympic Games, is startled by the spontaneous bubbling up of the water and meat in the cauldrons before the fire is lit (1.59), an omen that the Spartan Chilon interprets to mean that the Athenian should avoid having a son. Hippocrates should not marry any woman who would bear him one; and if he has a son, he should send him away. Hippocrates ignores Chilon and his son Pisistratus, the future tyrant of Athens, is eventually born. Hippocrates is simply a citizen of Athens, aristocratic, but not royal, and what he hears in Chilon's advice is a kind of social suicide. The willful failure to breed heirs would mean the destruction of his name and household.[108] Unlike the kings who try to circumvent the danger when faced with the prediction of a fatal child, Hippocrates embraces his future, which depends upon children.[109] Similarly, the noble but nonroyal Hystaspes feels no obligation to put his son's life on the line. On the contrary, Cyrus's threat against his son gives him a chance to escape destruction when he goes to guard his son.

In the story of Cyrus's abandonment, the nonroyal couples into whose hands the infant comes plainly calculate what to do with the baby solely on the basis of what is best for their own safety and standing. Harpages, Astyages' lieutenant, and his wife decide to avoid any taint or recrimination by finding a shepherd to kill the child (1.109). Mithradates and Cyno, the poor shepherd and his wife, substitute their own dead child for the body they were supposed to produce to prove that they had killed the prince, so that they can have a living child (1.112). Even more remarkable is how Harpages gets the better of his king when Astyages tricks him into eating his own child as punishment for disobeying orders. Such cannibalism is a gesture fraught with taboo and symbolic of wanton greed, but Harpages denies the outrage by the simple expedient of ignoring it when Astyages taunts him.[110] He waits instead for recompense until he can make common cause with Cyrus. The reactions of nonroyals are pragmatically self-interested. These men can actively protect themselves and their children with an eye to their own prosperity. Herodotus's deployment of royal and nonroyal children suggests that there is a symbolic quality about some possessions — or the possessions of some.

I have surveyed this theme in Herodotus's first book at some length to suggest that children of fatal destiny have a complex symbolic valence in myth and legend. From the perspective of the nascent hero, abandonment signifies coming greatness, but Greek myth also reverberates with parents' choices and their ruin. The audience encounters abandonment in the *Ion* with this complex frame of reference. Ion, as an abandoned child, is destined for greatness and his survival serves as an originary symbol for Athens itself. He is also a royal child, however, and might be one of those incalculably valuable tokens of dynastic destiny and ruin. These two possibilities must quicken the tension of the play: Oedipus's tragic doom suggests that the outcome for Ion is no sure thing. This tension about the nature of the abandoned child is meanwhile troubled by persistent commercial evaluation that thrusts Ion's worth into the sphere of financial reckoning. As we have seen, Athenians kept track of payouts and earnings in a narrative that allowed them to know their debts and credits in both social and financial terms. In the *Ion*, characters display signs of tracking their gains and losses in a process similar to these accounts. From this perspective abandonment becomes a transaction that both discards the child as worthless and renders it, as a possession, an invisible investment, whose yield depends on chance. Spectators are forced to come to terms with characters calculating profit and loss as shrewdly as they themselves might. But these characters also conceal or rewrite their calculations with appeals to other standards that derive from a more mythic or legendary understanding of the child. The familiar accounting narrative is suddenly also a romance of belonging.

From the outset, the gods' version of the romance is plain: Ion is a treasured object that is going to secure Athens's greatness, not ruin. And this is a familiar image throughout the *Ion*, of treasure hidden away, locked up, opened, and rediscovered. Ion's abandonment in an *antipex* with token gold snakes replicates his ancestor's fate, since Erichthonius, one of Athens's autochthonous kings, was also hidden in such a box with snakes. But the image is not simply a symbol of the gods' design. Kreousa's grief and guilt over her lost child finally pour out of her like treasure from an opened safe. For his farewell party in Delphi, Ion builds a fabulous tent that encloses his guests and himself amidst decorations of destiny, from which he will explode when the attempt on his life fails. The Pythia even carries the *antipex* onto the stage at the play's climax, so that the audience can see Ion open it up and Kreousa rediscover her past.[111] Ion's abandonment constructs him as both treasured child and a treasure-store of evil.

Balancing this imagery that associates the child with treasure is the language that calculates the value of children as possessions: cost accounting, return on investment, and the discovery that invisible property has become profit or loss. The language of happiness and pain, good fortune and loss that permeates the play reverberates with financial overtones. One word for the child prominent in the play is *tokos*, which also means "yield on investment," so that, as Mark Golden remarks with regard to children, the "relation of interest and affection" is inextricable.[112] Compounds of the verb "to encounter" (τυχεῖν), "to prosper" (εὐτυχεῖν) and "to fare badly" (δυστυχεῖν), suggest that abandonment is a risky investment that might or might not pay off, as characters speak of their lucky or unlucky chance in the experience. The audience seems primed to feel its own experience in all these financial reckonings, alerted to the concern by the first choral song, which occurs at the juncture between Kreousa's fantasy about her "friend" who abandoned her newborn and Xouthos's equally fantastic and unexpected recovery of an abandoned child. Between these two instantiations of the romance of belonging, the Chorus celebrates the blessing of children as an immense wealth, and we see straightway the competing desire to calculate and to mystify those calculations.

This choral ode has a simple prayer at its heart — for the Athenian royal family, "to get possession of its long-awaited bounty of children" (εὐτεκνίας χρονίου ... κῦρσαι; 470–471). The song's antistrophe, however, elaborates on what this wish means through a sharp calculus of children's value. According to the Chorus, children are a commodity that can be invested with the possibility of an extraordinary and continuing yield, but they also have a worth as a conspicuous symbol of a man's generosity to his *oikos* and polis. It depends on how the investor puts them at risk (472–491):

ὑπερβαλλούσας γὰρ ἔχει
θνατοῖς εὐδαιμονίας
ἀκίνητον ἀφορμάν,
τέκνων οἷς ἂν καρποφόροι
    λάμπωσιν ἐν θαλάμοις
πατρίοισι νεάνιδες ἧβαι,
διαδέκτορα πλοῦτον
ὡς ἕξοντες ἐκ πατέρων
ἑτέροις ἐπὶ τέκνοις.
ἄλκαρ τε γὰρ ἐν κακοῖς
σύν τ᾽ εὐτυχίαις φίλον
δορί τε γᾷ πατρίᾳ φέρει
σωτήριον ἀλκάν.
ἐμοὶ μὲν πλούτου τε πάρος
βασιλικῶν τ᾽ εἶεν θαλάμων
†τροφαὶ κήδειοι κεδνῶν γε τέκνων†.
τὸν ἄπαιδα δ᾽ ἀποστυγῶ
βίον, ᾧ τε δοκεῖ ψέγω·
μετὰ δὲ κτεάνων μετρίων βιοτᾶς
εὔπαιδος ἐχοίμαν.[113]
For he has blessings exceeding
in return for mortals,
a risk-free venture,
for whomever youth in their prime,
fruit-bearing in children,

shine in their father's halls,
because they will receive
a wealth that continues its payoff from fathers
in successive generations of children.
For children are a defense in hard times,
a pleasure amidst prosperity,
and in war they bring a saving defense
to the land of their fathers.
May I find the careful raising of legitimate children
worth more than the wealth of kings' halls.
I loathe the life without children
and I fault the man who prefers it.
May I always, amidst modest possessions,
cling to a life rich in children!

The Chorus moves between talking about children as a form of wealth that is invisible, an investment that pays out a yield in successive generations, and a possession that is visible, wealth spent lavishly on behalf of one's household and state.

The specifically commercial language suggests that children, as property to be invested, have excellent prospects for yield but require the long view.[114] Phrases such as a "risk-free venture" (ἀκίνητον ἀφορμάν), "exceeding in returns" (ὑπερ-βαλλούσας), and "fruit-bearing" (καρποφόροι), suggest an investment, to judge from the fourth-century evidence, analogous to what were called maritime loans (*nautika*). The (usually) overseas nature of these loans made them risky, and their yield could neither be spelled out in advance nor be expected to pay out at a specific time. These loans differed from so-called landed loans or investments (*eggeia*), whose terms of repayment, including yield for the lender and length of term, were a part of the original deal.[115] In overseas operations, as with children, one had to await events, and therefore the investment was uncertain in terms of time but potentially very profitable. The phrase *diadektora plouton* — wealth that continues its own payoff — captures the long view: children are a form of wealth that increases through inheritance and through their heirs.[116] Amidst the enthusiasm for the great wealth that children represent, the Chorus's characterization of them as a "risk-free venture" (ἀκίνητον ἀφορμάν) is an ominous oxymoron.[117] Can a venture be risk-free? This sounds like "a safe bet," which can be safe only when it is no bet at all. So, too, here: one hopes the venture is virtually without risk. But children, like any form of wealth, are plainly not risk-free, since death can carry them off before any yield is gotten.[118]

The Chorus also characterizes children as visible, conspicuous wealth, and now a familiar ideology for the proper use of wealth appears, When children are called a "boon" in poverty or in war, it is a reminder that the good citizen does not stash his children away as investments that pay out in offspring for his own perpetuity. Instead, he spends them upon the immediate needs of his household and state.[119] Within the metaphor of financial language, children are suddenly rehumanized in their value to the *oikos* and the polis. No longer counted in coin, they are seen for what they can contribute as workers, heirs, and soldiers, and this is a value that also increases the parents' wealth. Children can be put on display for neighbors to admire; and in war, they are a parent's sacrifice. In both instances, they accrue good fortune for the parent, provided he is willing to put them at immediate risk. In one of his Nemean odes, Pindar makes the larger point about a man's wealth: if he merely stores it up he gains nothing (*N.* 1.31–32):

οὐκ ἔραμαι πολὺν ἐν μεγάρῳ πλοῦτον κατακρύψαις ἔχειν,

ἀλλ' ἐόντων εὖ τε παθεῖν καὶ ἀκοῦσαι φίλοις ἐξαρκέων.

I do not want to hide great wealth in my home and keep it there,

but to enjoy it as available to me and be said to help my friends.

To spend property on behalf of himself and others earns the citizen a payoff in immediate pleasure and good reputation — which itself is a return with long-term value — and children are no exception.[120] Nor is their complete consumption in this way certain; the parents may still get descendants in their long-term investment. But the risk is higher, when children are available for the household and state to use, that parents get none of the yield in heirs that is the other *tokos* accruing over time.

The curious feature about children is that they have value at one and the same time as conspicuous and as concealed possessions. They are worth a great deal in the present of their lives and they can bring unending *tokos* for the future as well. The expenditure of children in the short term gives parents a return of good repute because it benefits both *oikos* and polis, but the long-term investment has its benefits, too — generations of heirs — and is not to be scorned in the manner in which Pindar dismisses the saving up of other forms of wealth. Truly children are an amazingly versatile form of wealth whose bounty (εὐτεκνία) can become prosperity or good fortune (εὐτυχία) in several ways, depending on how they are put at risk.

Despite the versatility, the Chorus must pray to prefer children to other kinds of wealth. Such a prayer is conventional in tragedy, but the dilemma is real in this instance.[121] After all, children consume resources. To have a life rich in them means settling for fewer possessions of other kinds, and there are always those who prefer a wealthy life without children (488–491).[122] The problem is rehearsed in literature since Homer: one's investment in children can come to nothing if they die young. Dead children are a loss of the resources they consumed without any payoff: no help in poverty or old age; no ornament in prosperity; no heirs. Glory does accrue if a child is killed in war, but again, as early as the *Iliad*, parents are imagined to find this a poor return on their investment.[123] The Chorus creates a momentary vision of investors who compare one commodity with another, and the Chorus's own preference does not quite conceal the attractiveness of the alternative.

In the closing epode of its song, the Chorus sings about children in very different terms, which are lush in legendary and symbolic detail. The song specifically recalls the fictional abandonment that Kreousa created in the previous scene, but its sights and sounds also evoke Athens's royal children long dead and gone. The Aglaurids—later punished for viewing an abandoned baby—are dancing to Pan's syrinx, and a newborn, the outrage of a bitter mating by Apollo, is left to become a meal for wild animals.[124] The swirl of movement and music evokes vestiges of abandonment seen through a mythic lens. That other value of lost children, as symbols of royal destiny and ruin, is glimpsed. These are children who were cherished or sacrificed as flesh-and-blood tokens of something inhuman, remnants of choices made by Athens's royal house. Before we can parse their symbolic power, the Chorus once again abruptly repudiates this momentous, incalculable value (507–508):

οὔτ' ἐπὶ κερκίσιν οὔτε λόγων φάτιν
ἄιον εὐτυχίας μετέχειν θεόθεν τέκνα θνατοῖς.
Nor have I ever heard report, in weaving or in story,
that children born to mortals from a god have a share in good fortune.

The Chorus's assessment of good fortune (*eutuchia*) reinserts the impulse to calculate costs, to compare gains and losses, and gives the myth a price tag. That momentary image of lost royal children signifying Athens's complicated origins is effaced. The Chorus concludes that children born of mortal and immortal are not a valuable form of wealth. In becoming nonnegotiables either as visible wealth or invisible investments, they cannot bring a yield in either status or offspring. Instead, they are an outrage and end up as food for animals.

The peculiar blend of the commercial and the mythic with which the Chorus prays for "the bounty of children" captures the need both to calculate the costs of belonging and to deny those costs. At one level, the prayer is no more than a string of commonplaces about the value of children, but these conventional claims may implicate spectators in their own notions of possessions. To enjoy a bounty of children requires an investment strategy for this form of wealth like any other, but the specificity is disturbing when dramatized. The intrusion of alternate ideologies that make the choices sound less commercial is a relief. At this instant of implication and entanglement, the spectators hear their city's founding myth from a painfully close perspective. In particular, the prayer's pledge to hallow children over other forms of wealth is a commentary on the choices of Athens's royal house. Kreousa's family repeatedly trades or discards children for other valuables. The child of Apollo's rape was not legitimate, and so Kreousa chose the honor of her royal *oikos* over its rearing. Her father, however, did get rid of legitimate offspring (his daughters) in favor of victory in war. Neither of these is an unparalleled or even unreasonable choice, but this particular hard fact about Athens's royal family complicates the emotional entanglement and intellectual dissonance of the first choral ode.[125]

At this somber moment, abandonment is suddenly deployed as a comic accounting maneuver, as Xouthos enters to claim his son. This foreign-born king manipulates his sense of what happens to children carelessly sown: they become another form of investment with windfall yield if they are somehow recovered.[126] Here again is that uncanny nature of an abandoned child as something irrevocably gone but possibly returning, but the play now dramatizes it as slapstick. Abandonment is rewritten as a shrewd investment strategy for a parent who got rid of a child because the costs were too high. But such a child is not utterly gone, since the same act of abandonment possibly converts it into invisible, invested property. Xouthos's ridiculous joy at "recovering" a discarded son illustrates how this investment can pay off. Representation of such a possibility need not be comic, however. The young Kreousa also attempted to hedge her bet by transforming abandonment into a ritualized presentation that challenged Apollo for a reciprocal gesture. When no such reciprocity was forthcoming, she had to write off the child as lost property, a failed investment. As a strategy for managing children, abandonment can range from a largely impersonal transaction involving an anonymous piece of wealth to an intensely intimate exchange between would-be *philoi* (friends and allies), but always with an eye to rendering greater yield in the end.

Despite the differences between Xouthos and Ion in background, experience, and style, neither has much use for the fanciful when it comes to explaining how babies are born. Xouthos dismisses the explanation that Ion might have been born from the earth (542), and Ion does not let Xouthos get away with a vague fling back home. How could such an infant get from Thrace to Delphi, Ion wants to know (548). These are the two practical minds that come up with an abandonment to account for Ion's presence in Delphi as Xouthos's son.[127] In the process it emerges that they want or need very different accounting narratives. Xouthos is so excited by the news that he cannot explain the windfall initially, but at Ion's prodding he simply employs the transaction of abandonment. Since the king's focus is entirely upon this new gain, as he sees it, he isn't worried about the identity of the mother who had to abandon Ion.[128] Ion, however, wants the account to include the gain or yield of his mother. The word he first uses to ask about his birth, *tuchē* (τύχη), literally means "chance," but it soon represents her identity (539, 668). In this play, the word must also interact with its compounds *eutuchein* (εὐτυχεῖν) and *dystuchein* (δυστυχεῖν), which can signify encountering good or bad fortune in a financial sense.[129] Finding his mother would complete Ion's own new bounty, and without that knowledge, he says, he lacks the resources to live (ἀβίωτον; 670). Can a single accounting narrative yield both outcomes? The new father and son construct in rapid succession three scenarios of Ion's abandonment. The first two seem mere false starts; the third is fully fleshed out and becomes as convincing a narrative as Ion can get from an interloper.

Ion's first proposal, that he was born from the earth, goes nowhere because Xouthos, with his lack of imagination for Athenian myth, instantly denies its premise.[130] Xouthos's reckoning is based on an economic truth, however, at least for those outside Athens and its ancient legends. As the earth cannot yield sentient beings like children, so nothing comes from nothing. Instead, a child comes, as the next two scenarios make explicit, from the very human transaction of sex. The second vignette of Ion's engendering is equally brief, at least here: perhaps there was a clandestine liaison in Thrace, which Xouthos freely admits to, "in the folly of my youth" (545).[131] Ion dismisses this scenario as logistically impossible, but both men see it as plausible: young men have sex, and then there may be babies to expose. Only the problem of getting an infant from Thrace to Delphi saves Ion from having to believe that he is the son of a slave. Finally, the two men come up with a version of Ion's abandonment that is both feasible and satisfying: during a festival of Dionysus, Xouthos seduced a Delphic maiden. This tale, involving a freeborn woman, allows Ion to consider himself freeborn as well, much to his relief: "I have escaped slavery!" (556).[132]

Ion's last two constructions encapsulate a significant part of the sexual experiences of males in Euripides' audience, who might have sex with slaves and courtesans, freeborn noncitizen or citizen concubines, and a citizen wife.[133] Xouthos exempts himself from marital infidelity (546); otherwise his sex life sounds normal. Sexual intercourse can produce a child, necessary in marriage for a legitimate heir.[134] But an illicit liaison produces a child that cannot be acknowledged within the *oikos*—a possession that cannot be entered into any account. Abandonment is then the appropriate transaction because it has two effects: it effaces the imprudent expenditure of sex that produced the child; and it renders the unwanted child invisible.[135] As a bonus, abandonment can also account for that child if chance allows for its recovery in circumstances in which, as here, what was once a necessary loss is needed as property. Throughout the construction of a plausible account Xouthos plainly takes for granted this convenience of abandonment. And since it is this anonymous maiden of Delphi who suffered the entire trauma, Ion is as much as a windfall as if Xouthos had had no role in his birth. When Ion wants to know whether he was "engendered as yours or merely as a gift," Xouthos's insistence that both are true—"a gift, but born of me"—makes sense (537). An accounting narrative built around abandonment allows the king to encapsulate both the tricky divine revelation and the (barely) imagined suffering of the Delphic maiden (after his brief drunken encounter with her) in a single short phrase: "a gift from Apollo."[136]

Kreousa also understands the power of abandonment to settle or unsettle accounts regarding children. When Ion poses another set of antithetical equations concerning children, the queen's response reveals his failure to factor in the effect of abandonment (303–307):

Ἴων·   καρποῦ δ᾽ ὕπερ γῆς ἥκετ᾽ ἢ παίδων πέρι;

Κρέουσα·   ἄπαιδές ἐσμεν, χρόνι᾽ ἔχοντ᾽ εὐνήματα.

Ἴων·   οὐδ᾽ ἔτεκες οὐδὲν πώποτ᾽ ἀλλ᾽ ἄτεκνος εἶ;

Κρέουσα·   ὁ Φοῖβος οἶδε τὴν ἐμὴν ἀπαιδίαν.

Ἴων·   ὦ τλῆμον, ὡς τἄλλ᾽ εὐτυχοῦσ᾽ οὐκ εὐτυχεῖς.

Ion: Have you come on account of the land's fruits, or concerning children?

Kreousa: We are childless, though we've had a long-standing marriage.

Ion: And did you never give birth, but are you childless?

Kreousa: Phoibos knows my childlessness.

Ion: You poor thing! How you are not prospering though in other respects you are prosperous!

Kreousa comments bitterly on how males account for a sexual encounter and its yield. Apollo knows the reason for her childlessness perfectly well, namely, that she had to use abandonment to make herself childless. The god's apparent insouciance, which sounds very much like Xouthos, reflects the reality that young men, whether gods or mortals, need worry little about the aftermath of sex.[137] The seduced maiden, however, cannot view abandonment with the same lack of concern as men, since she must write off her body's *tokos* for the gain of reclaimed honor or at least the invisibility of shame. Moreover, the act may make her childless forever, as Kreousa has discovered.[138] Ion has no means to unravel her riddle about Apollo, but his answer at 307 captures exactly how her childlessness registers as a great lack in the midst of prosperity.

The maiden can try to convert her discarded infant into an investment if, instead of a completely anonymous act, she engages in a more personalized form of abandonment by turning the infant into an offering to someone.[139] Then she can hope for reciprocity by defying the inherent drive of abandonment in the other direction, towards severance and anonymity. The maiden in the Pythia's version of Ion's abandonment performs this manipulation by putting her infant near Apollo's temple (45). Her gesture tries to get the god to establish a relationship where none existed before, if not with herself, then at least with her child. This strategy works through a surrogate in the Pythia's change of heart. And, as noted above, Kreousa also frames her child's abandonment as a gesture that was intended to compel Apollo to reciprocate (964–965).

Πρεσβύτης·   σοὶ δ' ἐς τί δόξ' ἐσῆλθεν ἐκβαλεῖν τέκνον;
Κρέουσα·   ὡς τὸν θεὸν σώσοντα τόν γ' αὐτοῦ γόνον.

Old Man: What was your plan in casting out the child?
Kreousa.   I hoped that the god would at least save his own child.

Kreousa does not rely on chance. She takes careful steps to ensure that only her divine seducer can save her baby, since hiding it in a box within a sacred cave leaves little room for a kindly passer-by.[140] Kreousa's abandonment requires the miracle of reciprocity unmediated by human agency.

Like the anonymous Delphic maiden, Kreousa did not expect to profit personally from her illegitimate infant, but she did hope that this secret investment would bring some yield. She wants news that her child survived and is a credit at least to his father, Apollo, and the seeming frustration of her wish is made bitterer by the fact that Ion is to be exactly such a credit to Xouthos. She rages at Apollo (913–918):

Ἰὼ ⟨ἰὼ⟩ κακὸς εὐνάτωρ,

ὃς τῷ μὲν ἐμῷ νυμφεύτᾳ

χάριν οὐ προλαβὼν

παῖδ᾽ εἰς οἴκους οἰκίζεις·

ὁ δ᾽ ἐμὸς γενέτας καὶ σὸς, †ἀμαθὴς†

οἰωνοῖς ἔρρει συλαθείς,

σπάργανα ματέρος ἐξαλλάξας.[141]

O wicked bedfellow,

who did not omit a grace to my husband,

but settled a child in his house;

while my offspring — and yours —

has vanished, ignorant,

ravaged by birds

and stripped of his mother's swaddling.

The Chorus comment on how risky such an abandonment can be when, at the end of the queen's monody, they gasp, "Oh, how great a treasure chest of evils is opening!" (923–924). The metaphor for Kreousa's revelations reverses her abandoning gesture of locking her infant and its tokens away in an *antipex* (19), and the results of her investment are plain: only evils remain in the strong box as *tokos*.[142] The antipex did not save the infant, as it once did Erichthonios, and Apollo did not pick the child up either. Hades got possession of it as a windfall, to be raised in the house of the dead — a ghastly expression of the collapse of Kreousa's investment. When the Old Man reacts to the account, his language sums up the awful yield of this investment, "What accusation are you making against Loxias [i.e., Apollo]?" (τίνα λόγον Λοξίου κατηγορεῖς; 931). Kreousa's attempt to engage the god in reciprocal obligation has ended up in an account (*logos*) that is a denunciation.[143]

The failure of Kreousa's attempt to personalize abandonment means economic ruin for her and her royal house. And a more ancient trouble now surfaces (966–971):[144]

Πρεσβύτης· οἴμοι, δόμων σῶν ὄλβος ὡς χειμάζεται.

Κρέουσα· τί κρᾶτα κρύψας, ὦ γέρον, δακρυρροεῖς;

Πρεσβύτης· σὲ καὶ πατέρα σὸν δυστυχοῦντας εἰσορῶν.

Κρέουσα· τὰ θνητὰ τοιαῦτ᾽· οὐδὲν ἐν ταὐτῷ μένει.

Πρεσβύτης· μή νυν ἔτ᾽ οἴκτων, θύγατερ, ἀντεχώμεθα.

Κρέουσα· τί γάρ με χρὴ δρᾶν; ἀπορία τὸ δυστυχεῖν.

Old Man: Alas, how the prosperity of your household is overwhelmed!

Kreousa:	What are you hiding in your heart as you weep, old man?
Old Man:	I am envisioning you and your father lacking in fortune.
Kreousa:	Such are human affairs; nothing remains as it was.
Old Man:	Let us then no longer cling to this weeping!
Kreousa:	What ought I to do? To lack fortune is to be without resources.

Kreousa's ill fortune (*dustuchein*) and lack of resources are part of the heritage of her house, whose prosperity has suffered because it throws away or sacrifices children.[145] Out of this economic extremity emerges the plot to rob Xouthos of his windfall and prevent the usurper from gaining the royal household of Athens (1036). The Old Man shrugs off moral scruple with an economic assessment (1045–1047):

τὴν δ᾿ εὐσέβειαν εὐτυχοῦσι μὲν καλὸν
τιμᾶν· ὅταν δὲ πολεμίους δρᾶσαι κακῶς
θέλῃ τις, οὐδεὶς ἐμποδὼν κεῖται νόμος.
It's well enough for those who are prosperous
to honor holiness; but whenever one wants to harm enemies,
no rule stands in the way.

Kreousa's failed investment leaves her bound by no rules as she sets about ruining her husband's good fortune.

Once each parent recognizes Ion, they employ a measure of self-deception or fiction to conceal earlier calculations, claiming to have found something dear or precious. But, as noted at the beginning of this chapter, the technical word used in each context — ῥυσιάζειν, "to seize by law property claimed as one's own" — betrays an underlying reality.[146] Both Xouthos and Kreousa *are* claiming property that is the payoff of an ancient investment.[147] Abandonment ostensibly eliminated unneeded or unwanted property; now the natal parents are cashing in on someone else's time and trouble.[148] In reunion, it is natural for Xouthos and Kreousa to wish to define their recovery of Ion in a way that screens what happened to him long ago. After all, abandonment aims to deny the natal identity they are now happy to give him. But the particular joy of each parent's self-deception is peculiar to their circumstances. The drive to conceal that which is inherent in abandonment can generate darker constructions of economic intent and motive. Such is the Old Man's tale of a nefarious plot whereby Xouthos was to acquire all Kreousa's assets and "reap the benefit of children in stealth" (παῖδας ἐκκαρπούμενος / λάθρα πέφηνεν; 815).[149]

Apollo, Ion's natal father, does not rewrite Ion's abandonment after the fact, because he apparently sees matters very differently. The divine perspective in the *Ion* everywhere contradicts the mortal accounting that feels so strongly both the profit and the loss. When the gods contemplate Ion's abandonment, they do not see a child discarded as valueless or invested for windfall yield. For the immortals, Ion signifies destiny. He is a token of coming heroic greatness and Athens's glorious destiny. The gods' actions insist that an illicit, abandoned child is the best kind of possession. Apollo does not (visibly) reciprocate Kreousa's gestures when she abandons her child, because he plans to stash his son away to protect him as a token of royal destiny, just like the golden jewelry Kreousa put in the *antipex*. Apollo appears to believe that an abandoned infant, rendered invisible in this way, grows and produces its yield in destiny as planned, and any human suffering, by mother or child, is irrelevant.

Hermes and Athena, agents of Apollo, create or endorse versions of the child as this sort of token. Such a child is something that can be hidden in a box, literal or figurative. Athena did this with Erichthonios literally, giving no thought for the autochthon's care and feeding. Apollo has done it symbolically, by concealing Ion in the enclosure of his shrine at Delphi until he can be revealed. Of equal unconcern are the details of Ion's revelation, at least from the gods' point of view. Hermes' account mutes Kreousa's suffering, as we have seen, and the final account revealed by Athena freely endorses Xouthos's permanent delusion.[150] Furthermore, Athena's finesse about the false oracle is a sign of its irrelevance. It is not that the gods cannot explain these machinations. Athena does so when human travail makes it necessary, and her terms are very like those used by Kreousa to pacify her newfound son.[151] Instead, the startling symmetry between the divine accounts that frame the action, despite the intervening mortal turmoil, underscores how unconcerned Apollo and his agents are about the messy economic reckoning.[152] The miracle of Ion's survival is all that is important; he exists in his exposure as pure revelation, an object whose value is inherent as a sign of destiny and cannot be altered or alienated, even by events that nearly kill him or make him a matricide.

Despite the dissonance between Apollo's vision of Ion's abandonment and that of Kreousa and Xouthos, no harm accrues to the mortals, such as we might have expected from Herodotus: no punishment for ignorance or arrogance; no end of dynasty. On the contrary, Ion's abandonment and recovery are the start of great things for everyone. Ion ends up wealthier in human possessions than he could have imagined, with a superabundance of parents and a prediction of many offspring. Kreousa and Xouthos are also to have more children, to supplement the one that each believes the other has no share in, and many descendents. Everyone ends up enriched in the coin of children as a result of this abandonment—a transaction turned miracle.[153] Yet in its final tableau, this happy ending itself, with its cheerful indifference to everyone's multiplied, conflicting, and deceitful identities, restages this reality: that with an abandoned child, no account can produce a complete and whole identity. Once a child is cast away it never comes back in the same form. Something is lost or increased; either way, the numbers don't add up. Ion's struggle to establish a complete account of his family illustrates this problem. Throughout the play Ion wants better or different parents who can make him more prosperous, just as they once discarded him in hopes of a better yield in offspring, but he learns that the account of his identity makes more sense or is safer when one or the other parent is eliminated.[154]

In the absence of natal parents, Ion has already calculated his own economic value rather precisely; he reckons familial identity and loyalty in terms of who pays the bills. He gives affection and devotion to Apollo, the Pythia, and even the sanctuary at Delphi, because they took the trouble to provide for him, either financially or physically: "I shall not stop serving those who nurture me" (182–183). Because the foundling cannot give his foster parents either legitimate heirs or honor and status by service to their *oikos* or polis, his sense of relationship is built on immediate and reciprocating return.[155] Lacking these options, Ion is a peculiarly blank slate of a child, "Born motherless and fatherless" (109).[156] Although he sounds joyously content with his life as a temple slave in his opening monody, Ion is ready for the immersion in an accounting narrative that will construct parents of great value.[157] He wants a mother to determine his future and a father to define his past, but what he discovers is that he cannot construct either of them in the presence of the other.[158]

The mother is a figure of that chance (*tuchē*) that brings prosperity or impoverishment through the outcome of any investment. Ion explicitly counts his unknown mother as such (668–670):

στείχοιμ' ἄν. ἓν δὲ τῆς τύχης ἄπεστί μοι·
εἰ μὴ γὰρ ἥτις μ' ἔτεκεν εὑρήσω, πάτερ,
ἀβίωτον ἡμῖν.

I'll go, but there's one piece of fortune I lack:
if I don't find the woman who bore me, father,
my life's not worth living.

The absence of the mother is devastating for the child, who is more than impoverished by the lack. He becomes of no account: he does not accrue as anyone's wealth and can easily slip into unendurable identities.[159] Ion later marvels at the power of *tuchē* to determine one's identity (1512–1515):

ὦ μεταβαλοῦσα μυρίους ἤδη βροτῶν
καὶ δυστυχῆσαι καὖθις αὖ πρᾶξαι καλῶς
τύχη, παρ' οἵαν ἤλθομεν στάθμην βίου
μητέρα φονεῦσαι καὶ παθεῖν ἀνάξια.

O changing fortune, which has before now
made countless mortals both fare ill and then again prosper,
by such a narrow margin of life did I come
to murdering my mother and suffering unworthily!

The slimmest of chances enable him to recognize Kreousa in time and avoid a new identity that would have been intolerable — that of a matricide. The mother's identity determines both yields, either of great misfortune (δυστυχῆσαι) or of prosperity (πρᾶξαι καλῶς).

Thus Ion is not satisfied with the anonymous maiden of Delphi first suggested by Xouthos, because such a mother is insufficient for his future career. Given the dangers and inconveniences awaiting him in Athens, he wants a freeborn Athenian parent who will give him license to move and speak freely as a citizen (623–628):

... τίς γὰρ μακάριος, τίς εὐτυχής,
ὅστις δεδοικὼς καὶ περιβλέπων βίαν
αἰῶνα τείνει; δημότης ἂν εὐτυχὴς
ζῆν ἂν θέλοιμι μᾶλλον ἢ τύραννος ὤν,
ᾧ τοὺς πονηροὺς ἡδονὴ φίλους ἔχειν,
ἐσθλοὺς δὲ μισεῖ κατθανεῖν φοβούμενος.

... For who can be blessed, who can be prosperous,
who stretches out a life in fear
and suspicion against violence? I'd rather live
as a prosperous common citizen than be a tyrant,
who takes pleasure in friends who are wretches
and despises good men in fear of his life.

For the interloper or the tyrant an economic paradox accrues: he cannot truly be prosperous when he fears for his life and misvalues good and bad men. Without a mother to secure an Athenian identity, Ion reassesses his current life more favorably: Delphi, with its foster mother and temple, gives him status, purpose, and privileges (634–639). He is better off here (645–648):

ταῦτα συννοούμενος
κρείσσω νομίζω τἀνθάδ᾽ ἢ τἀκεῖ, πάτερ.
ἔα δέ μ᾽ αὐτοῦ ζῆν· ἴση γὰρ ἡ χάρις
μεγάλοισι χαίρειν σμικρά θ᾽ ἡδέως ἔχειν.[160]
Reflecting on these things all together,
father, I reckon they are better here than there.
Let me live here; the blessing is the same,
whether one welcomes greatness or takes pleasure in modest circumstances.

This strange equation reveals the importance of his mother's identity for his future.[161] If he can't have exactly the one he wants, potential greatness is no greater blessing than present poverty. But as long as Xouthos is his father, such a mother is out of the question. His natal mother must remain shadowy and ill defined for that paternity to work, so a more secure future in terms of Athens is out of the question.

Once Ion has recovered Kreousa as his mother and the situation is reversed, he now longs for the knowledge of the past in terms of his father, but he fares little better with Kreousa than he did with Xouthos. In her first delight, Kreousa is silent about Ion's father, and the boy assumes it is Xouthos. Kreousa must eventually confess to another version of the tale that, because of the false oracle, gives Ion too many fathers. She is as little troubled about this superfluity as Xouthos was about the gap, but Ion states the only account he is willing to accept in another of his flat antitheses.[162] "Either I am a mortal's or I am Loxias's. The god either prophesied truthfully or falsely" (1548–1549). Ion is not seeking a strict equivalency between truth and biology—he admits shortly that Apollo's role was believable enough before Athena confirmed it. He needs an accounting narrative that can make sense of the past: in light of the false oracle, can all the transactions in his identity's origins be squared?

Ion's literal-mindedness at this dramatic moment is at odds with the drive of the drama, which has played cleverly throughout with paternal identity: fosterage, adoption, the symbolism and reenactment of autochthony, all can create fathers beyond biology.[163] And the boy's resistance to the gaming with identity cannot survive. He may compel Apollo, through Athena as deus ex machina, to own up to a Byzantine set of accounts that involve the permanent deception of Athens's king, but eventually Ion himself has to learn a lesson about choice that scrambles any attempt to reconcile accounts.[164] The identity of the father is less about biology than it is about a man choosing his son. This is a strange paradox, given how obsessed ancient Athenians were with the legitimacy of babies born to them, but Ion must face the fact that two fathers claim him, and it is not an either/or situation. Both Xouthos and Apollo have a right to be his father and he needs both of them to take his rightful place in Athens. Xouthos's version of Ion's begetting, with his foundling son legitimated through himself alone, must endure permanently for Athens to survive and triumph, even though Ion is a scion of the city's precious autochthony through his mother and the son of a god. Xouthos got the right to claim Ion as a gift from Apollo, however, and that befuddles the youth until Athena simply insists that all is well, even the false oracle.

When we finally hear from Athena how Apollo solves the equation about Ion's identity, abandonment plays a different role from the one Xouthos gave it earlier (1560–1562; and see 536–537):

ὡς ἥδε τίκτει σ᾽ ἐξ Ἀπόλλωνος πατρός,

δίδωσι δ᾽ οἷς ἔδωκεν, οὐ φύσασί σε,

ἀλλ᾽ ὡς κομίζῃ ᾽ς οἶκον εὐγενέστατον.

This woman bore you with Apollo as your father;

and he gives you to whom he had given you, though that man did not beget you,

so that you might be settled in the house of the noblest lineage.

According to Apollo's construction, neither Xouthos nor Ion had it quite right. Abandonment did not make Xouthos the natal father and Apollo just the revealer; nor was Ion a random lie. Instead, the god bestowed him as a favor that Xouthos did nothing to earn, so that a special relationship could be established as a blessing for Ion himself.[165] Apollo's account reinforces the significance of the father's identity as a benefit the foundling craves, but it makes it a matter of choice and planning. The father's choice is early and determinative of a status for the child, whether it becomes a valueless castoff or an object of wealth for the household, but Apollo asserts once again that there is a third possibility for that special child who is royal and can signify destiny: such a child can be a priceless object beyond any human reckoning.[166] The god can balance the competing claims among the fathers who are to be Ion's by going outside the mortal economies and valuing his son on a completely different scale.

Abandonment never permits a yield that is in balance with the family. Someone is always either missing or redundant. Mythically, abandonment is supposed to signify utter ruin for the natal family, not the beginning of their dynastic and civic glory. The *Ion* turns this stereotype on its head. Yet the tragedy also suggests the cost of making sense of abandonment in defiance of human economies, as the gods do when they treat Ion as a token of destiny. They prefer not to bother with the human details, but if compelled, they can give an account that mortals must accept. The rest of the play suggests why the gods otherwise choose to ignore human needs. Once participants start to reckon returns on abandonment, the fragility of the relationship between calculation and self-deception is revealed. To think about one's costs and gains with regard to a newborn is to end up with too little or too much in the way of yield. The divine view on the matter is more comfortable, and mortal fathers and mothers use self-deception to participate in that view.

Abandonment in the *Ion* implicates ancient spectators in notions of economic calculation and risk because it — nearly — makes explicit the links between the judgments spectators themselves made both about children and about loans and gifts of more impersonal, inanimate objects. There is also a subtle tension between the risk-assessment and self-deception involved in disposing of a child that must also resonate with spectators. Socrates' metaphor of himself as a midwife in the *Theaetetus* suggests both these sensibilities. He insists that parents actually want to cherish "false bags of wind" and need the services of a midwife like himself to evaluate the newborn and make the right decision, the economically prudent choice.[167] Given these sensibilities, when a child is unexpectedly recovered, the parents engage in a kind of revision that may personalize abandonment and screen its essentially obliterating action, or at least screen the calculation. The *Ion*, as often noted, also finesses the details to achieve the founding narrative of Athens: the blessings that are so unexpected for the characters are no surprise for the audience, whose past this is. This is Athens, after all; Ion is the foundation of the spectators' glorious past, which brought about their very presence in this theater. Beneath the triumphant, however, is a residual sense of unease about accounting practices in the tragedy. The reckoning by which these blessings are achieved may work well enough to protect spectators against someone else's fraudulent claims in their ordinary business, but it does not work so well with children.

As we began, the costs of building a family are high, and they are not exacted only from the infant (although its costs are particularly high if it is not chosen to belong). Part of the psychic cost is having even to admit that a choice is being made, and we have seen that Freud and Euripides explore this conundrum with differing focuses and thus different outcomes. But both are aware that to construct an identity, the messy business of analyzing profit and loss has to be concealed, denied, or otherwise eliminated. The problem is, it can't be — residues of the process and the outcome remain in the unconscious permanently to trouble the sense of identity.

The *Ion* has no need to conceal abandonment itself; in fact, it requires the darker choice in the romance of belonging to build its drama. The ancient tragedy can dramatize the cost accounting that plays itself out between abandonment and reunion as a spectacle that horrifies and engrosses the audience, quickens our sense of dread, and then relieves us with melodrama and hegemonic solutions that are not meant to balance accounts. The full symbolic play of the child is at the disposal of the *Ion*, which dramatizes its protagonist's identity as a shrewd investment, a windfall profit, a pathetic plea for reciprocity, and an unchanging, imperishable token of destiny. That there is a flesh-and-blood child in all this is hard to see, except that the very kaleidoscope feels right: this is what a child is, whether we choose to keep this one or try for another. But the *Ion* also dramatizes the need to conceal the choice itself, and so we see the desire of parents to deny the choice at the heart of their child's belonging and therefore identity. Whatever else the tragedy is about, it opens up the poignancy of belonging from the parents' perspective in a way that makes it plain that this adult trauma has no origin in childhood.[168] Kreousa's ancient pain is as real as any that Ion discovers hidden in himself, because both have to live through a romance of belonging in order for this to become Athens's founding tale. The *Ion* insists that we see the cost.

Is Euripides thereby requiring that we also see the high costs of founding and maintaining Athens's identity as an imperial polis? It may be, but it has not been my aim to establish this.[169] To dramatize the psychic cost of belonging, the playwright quickens his spectators' dread and anxiety, that residue left behind within everyone who made it into the family and now makes his own choices about his family. Whether this sensation leads to thoughts, for good or ill, of larger structures lies beyond the scope of this study.

As Sarah Winter has argued so well, Freud understood that tragedy's capacity to restage the trauma of the unconscious was both its triumph and its inherent inferiority to psychoanalysis, which can repeat trauma in terms that finally release it. Such a hegemonic structure of filiation and supplanting, of course, is articulated with regard to the oedipal (and as an oedipal structure itself). We are dealing here with abandonment, but even so, we can discern that tragedy's insistence that spectators must watch and feel its traumatic effects on identity is at odds with Freud's compassion for the theoretical neurotic. In his family romance the child expends great energy trying to maintain both the fiction of a grand past and a present construction of despised parents in mean circumstances. Better, Freud concludes, to have both constructions give way to the reality of one's parents without any gain or diminution of value. Eliminating abandonment as a possibility achieves that identity as a complete unity. But Freud discovered in practice that abandonment is a valuable weapon in the arsenal of the parent and hence in that of the psychoanalyst, even if it is one that he can use only once. Since he and his immediate successors — in the person of Ruth Mack Brunswick — cannot admit the theoretical reality of abandonment in the family, they have to disavow its disorienting effects by eliminating themselves as the source of the cost.

What psychoanalysis makes comprehensible, perversely, are Apollo's actions and identities for his son. The child as a royal, precious object of destiny is necessary. "To lessen feelings of gratitude" and "subsequent dependence on his physician," was how the Wolf Man said Freud put it, a gift is appropriate. The anxious residue of the outcomes of the romance never goes away. It can't, because it seems to be that part of our identity that our unconscious cannot process. But to see the statuette of the Egyptian goddess on Freud's desk is an abiding comfort for both analyst and patient because it embodies the long view of identity, abstracted from the moment of suffering. The analyst sees an artifact that confirms this theory and provokes further ideas. The Wolf Man sees himself fixed in an identity no one can take away.[170]

CHAPTER FOUR

Recognition

Embracing a Deadly Flame

"Father, can't you see I'm burning?" *This sentence is itself a firebrand — of itself it brings fire where it falls — and one cannot see what is burning, for the flames blind us to the fact that the fire bears on the* Unterlegt, *on the* Untertragen, *on the real.*

JACQUES LACAN

Ἴων·   οὗτοι σὺν ὅπλοις ἦλθον ἐς τὴν σὴν χθόνα.
Κρέουσα·   μάλιστα· κἀπίμπρης γ᾽ Ἐρεχθέως δόμους.
Ion: I didn't attack your land under arms!
Kreousa: You certainly did; and you were going to set the house of
           Erechtheus on fire!

EURIPIDES, *Ion*

Fiery images are unexpectedly important for understanding the romance of belonging in both Euripides and Freud, because an odd association of figures comes together in their recognition scenes: stereotype, embrace, and fire. The stereotype substitutes for identity, while the embrace forecloses further inquiry into its nature by changing perspective so that the trauma cannot be seen. Such seems to be the strategy for dealing with the trauma of belonging, which otherwise exhausts the unconscious in attempts to repeat scenes in which it is created. Fire burns at the site of this strategy: what burns is obscured but its presence is made visible by the fire itself. This chapter attempts to make sense of what this collocation means.

In the preceding chapter, my focus was on the more obviously dangerous outcome of the romance of belonging: abandonment. It is the grim choice lurking within calculations of loss, even if people talk out loud in terms of yield. But the outcome of embrace is also traumatic, even the embrace of a mother, and it is time to examine moments in each text when recognitions between parent and child are staged as an embrace. In "From the History of an Infantile Neurosis," a scene plays out between a mother-figure and child that might be seduction or rejection, but Freud does not parse it in either set of terms. Instead, he recognizes a restaging of the primal scene. In the *Ion*, two recognition scenes are the anchors of the play's action, which flows from their pointed antitheses: parody leads to near-disaster; murderous anger leads to the embrace that settles the future of Athens. For both texts, the recognition about mother and child, whether Freud's inspired interpretation of a cryptic early memory or the thrilling embrace of mother and son, is meant to bring to a close the search for the child's identity (although, as we saw in the previous chapter, Ion's literal-mindedness about his father's identity requires a further deus ex machina). The closure is cast as a relief to the repetition that has driven each text thus far, suggesting that when we wish to stop our search for identity, we can turn to a platitude based on stereotype.

Yet it remains unclear why the platitude is deployed just at this point and not somewhere else. Nor can we get behind the stereotype for further analysis, even if we recognize that it marks an earlier, more fundamental layer of identity. When we long to stop asking about our identity, do we sense that we finally know who we are? Or have we simply found the cliché that substitutes for that knowledge and stops our search for something more?

Fire is the strange clue that guides our answers to these puzzles. Freud finally made sense of everything having to do with the Wolf Man's infantile neurosis, he tells us, when his patient's preoccupation with the fiery martyrdom of Jan Hus, who was burned at the stake for heresy in 1415, allowed him to interpret memories of a terrifying butterfly and a beloved nursery-maid kneeling with a bucket and broom.[1] These recollections arose from the earliest recoverable replication of the primal scene: the maid was kneeling before the toddler, who urinated on the floor in his excitement, and she threatened in jest to castrate him for the mess. Here Freud found, to his immense satisfaction, unmistakable evidence of a "normal" oedipal complex, about to be perverted into the Wolf Man's peculiar neurosis as defined by later events but connected with and activating the primal scene. The martyr's fire was the key that pointed to the typology of what the Wolf Man could have been and hence, how he had been so traumatized. Fire also marks recognition in the *Ion*. Minutes before Kreousa and Ion embrace each other, their angry confrontation is awash with flaming imagery. For Ion, Kreousa is a serpent with eyes of murderous flame, while she calls him an invader who attacks with fire. The outlawed queen and the youth see in each other the very types of a murderous enemy—a bitter stepmother or an alien interloper, identities that were created by abandonment but are about to be concealed by an embrace that makes these two into mother and son.[2] Fire has ignited in this alarming image of mortal enemies who are also mother and son. The close of the play celebrates their union as the happy secret of Athens's coming glory, but in this recognition fire incorporates murderous anger into their identities.

As part of this chapter's investigation of the mother's embrace, the stereotype of identity, and the symbolism of fire, I contextualize the stereotype of motherhood and the imagery of fire for each text. I can be brief, since others have discussed both topics well, but I need to set up the means by which we can destabilize the seemingly transparent fictions about nurturing and motherhood in which the longing for a final answer about our identities seems to inhere. The figures of beneficent motherhood are many and pervasive, leading to assumptions about the mother's inborn nurturing of and love for her child. The physical and emotional links between a mother and child are constructed as natural, as opposed to the authoritative and determinative will of the father. But these fictions are exactly what the fire burns on in the case of the Wolf Man and the *Ion*, suggesting that the mother's identity is not a comforting fixed point. In the case of Freud, I consider the images of the mother—both his own and those of subsequent psychoanalytic theorists—that deprive her of agency and will and, paradoxically, strip away the very typology on which those images rest. In the case of Euripides' *Ion*, in order to suggest the tension between life and death as they are instantiated in the hero's mother, I explore the myths of nurturers who control the lives of their fosterlings through fire. The contradictory status of mothers as noncitizens in the Athenian state, although they are nonetheless crucial to their sons' identities, complicates Kreousa's role as founding mother.

To investigate the symbolic status of fire in both texts, I first review the prosaic meaning that Freud attaches to it. In "Civilization and Its Discontents," he links it with urination, and in neurotics, fire marks (infantile) enuresis, which in turn signifies the masculine or active sexual impulse.[3] But there is another, more terrifying image of fire that troubles Freud's foundational discussion of dreams: a burning child who touches his father with a reproach. This image allows us to speculate on how fire marks trauma within the unconscious of psychoanalysis itself, as post-Freudian theorists have argued.[4]

Freud and Euripides employ different strategies for contemplating what part of identity is fueling the flames. Freud very deliberately stops short of seeing what the flame has ignited. He marks the presence of a reality at a site that is plainly off-kilter, near but not right, because he cannot come closer and retain psychoanalysis as he has constructed it, through the body and authority of the father. The Wolf Man's attempted seduction of his nursery-maid follows his primal scene and seems to repeat it in comforting stereotypes, but the flames alert us to the possibility of a ruse. Through the language and the action of embrace, Euripides can dramatize the murderous beginning of mother and child, but only as an ephemeral moment. In the next instant, the glimpse within the fire is gone, and the *Ion* puts aside the longing to replicate and hence sustain the trauma. Characters and audience are finally placed in the reality of their future and Athens's past through the deus ex machina. Both strategies, of psychoanalyst and dramatist, enjoy a measure of success in comprehending the terrifying nature of the primal suffering, but each leaves something irrecoverable. Freud's constructions make sense of fundamental neurotic fragments at the cost of imprecisely marking their origins. Euripides can dramatize the originary moment, but its ephemeral nature means that we cannot understand the full implications of the construction. Hence the power of the stereotype, as a shorthand for the strategic decisions necessary in the presence of the traumatic.

That the moment of choice in the romance of belonging can inhere in the figure of the mother is not unexpected, but this is a hard moment to study in Freud, whose handling of the mother is notoriously shot through with a flawed blend of sentimentalities and structures that requires the passivity of the oedipal mother and the absence of the pre-oedipal.[5] Caroline Dever, for instance, concludes that the Freudian figure of the mother is a "figure at the center of every form of desire" and yet also a passive figure whose absence serves more than her presence.[6] Madelon Sprengnether has studied Freud's case histories for evidence of "displacements and denials" of the mother's influence.[7] In the primal scene itself, the mother is victim and rival, a structure for explaining the effects of the scene through the conventions of a "normal" oedipal relationship. The Wolf Man's real mother is virtually absent from the case history except as victim or rival; signs of her agency or aggression are effaced or translated into other figures. Sprengnether also assesses Freud's drive to assimilate the mother to his patriarchal structures with regard to the originary site of the "uncanny" (Freud's *Unheimlichkeit*). Although he suggests that that eerie sense of both belonging and alienation arises from a tension between the familiar and the alien resident in the single figure of the mother, he makes the alien a supplement to the familiar and identifies its source in the fear of castration, thus ultimately deriving from the father, as that fear always does.[8]

Although we now read Freud through a lens that sharply criticizes his handling of the mother-figure in childhood development, Sprengnether demonstrates how later psychoanalytic theorists participate in Freudian structures despite challenging his emphasis on the oedipal.[9] For example, the theory of object-relations posits a pre-oedipal crisis for the infant, in which the importance of the mother as a figure cannot be overstated. It is against and through her that the infant is forced to learn about and acknowledge boundaries and distinctions, while before this trauma the infant enjoys a physical and emotional attachment to its mother (the primary caregiver who feeds the child) so complete that it has neither a sense of itself as subject nor of the other as object. As Caroline Dever puts it: "the loss of the mother is at once inevitable, catastrophic, desirable, and traumatic. Subjectivity, as well as etiology, springs full-blown from the child's ability to reconcile the polarity of desire and catastrophe."[10] This crisis is driven by the child's needs and perceptions, however, not the agency and will of the mother as an aggressor. And it is worth noting here that although the child's trauma in separating from the mother-figure is felt as loss or even abandonment, object-relations theorists remain convinced of the developmental and therapeutic value of the separation itself.[11] Despite its replacement of the father by the mother as the cardinal figure, object-relations, as Dever points out, requires a lost or absent mother as its theoretical goal. Freud's invisibly passive mother is replaced by an attractive enigma that is still a largely passive figure. Certainly abandonment as the mother's active strategy of family planning is not part of the picture, since the predication is that the child *needs* separation, however traumatic its effect.[12] To counter the structures of the passive mother, Sprengnether argues that, from the mother's point of view, the "symbiosis" conceptualized by psychoanalysis is illusory. Her solution points to the cycle of pregnancy and birth as the site of maternal agency. To the child in her womb, the mother's body is always both home and not-home — in a word, uncanny, which is to say both inherently familiar and also, as Sprengnether says, "alienating."[13]

The romance of belonging predicates a subsequent moment to the uncanny simultaneity of the familiar and the alien of birth, another instant of separate agency. As noted in Chapter 1, Sarah Hrdy has studied that moment after birth in primates and early humans when abandonment is one of two options for the new parent, such that attachment and union are anything but natural. For protection and nurture, the newborn requires physical attachment, whether to its natal mother or to an "allomother," as Hrdy terms other lactating females who might be counted on to help with an infant. But a new mother still faces an arduous commitment, both physically and emotionally, and her decision is no given.[14]

Hence the human newborn is born with many attributes that seem designed to sway her decision. For instance, in the last few weeks of gestation, a fetus bulks up on body fat, so that it is born more pleasing and cuddly to the eye, even though certain key neurological functions only develop once the baby is born. It also has the rather dangerous capacity (in a predatory environment) to make a lot of distressed noise to plead for nurture.[15] Thus, since the origin of the species, human mothers and their newborns have been creatures whose earliest goals were quite distinct and might be in potential conflict. An imperious set of needs comes up against pragmatic choice in a perilous moment of physical and teleological distinction, which began with the bodily separation of birth and involves both conscious choice by the mother and built-in charm designed for survival in the infant.[16]

Hrdy thus posits a human newborn who knows at some level that there is another being that it needs and desires. She further suggests that the embrace of that other being fulfils those feelings as surely as suckling does. Feelings as a token of the newborn's autonomy are also proposed by the psychoanalyst Daniel Stern:

> For [the six-week-old infant], most encounters with the world are dramatic and emotional — a drama that is not obvious to us as adults. . . . he has been born with strong preferences about what he wants to look at, about what pleases him. Among these preferences, intensity and contrast top the list. . . . A baby's nervous system is prepared to evaluate immediately the intensity of a light, a sound, a touch. . . . How intensely he feels about something is probably the first clue he has available to tell him whether to approach it or to stay away.[17]

Both Hrdy and Sterns infer that the physical and emotional needs of the newborn operate irrespective of the mother's feelings (especially if we assume these maternal feelings to be sentimental notions of affection). The embrace is a crucial gesture that gives the child the connection it yearns for and establishes identities within the reciprocal relationship of mother and child. If the mother chooses abandonment, she denies the embrace and the nurture that create the relationship.

This image of mother and child as separate agents challenges stereotypes about what is "natural." The very real possibility of abandonment suggests the source of violence in the romance of belonging, at least on the part of the mother. But we can sense that the child can also be construed as an agent of violence, because if it succeeds, it draws from the mother's body relentlessly. The child satisfies its needs irrespective of hers: her body is taken for granted, subsumed into the newborn's universe of self as a physical resource to be drained for its survival. Embrace and abandonment are an inversion of each other, with the former signifying life for child and diminution for the mother and the latter the reverse.

Such a moment between mother and child of reciprocal will and choice is gone from the case history of the Wolf Man, unless it is that moment marked by fire — his nursery-maid's encounter with him on the nursery floor. Let us turn to that scene in which Freud refigures this woman into the form of the passive mother, despite her active engagement with the toddler, and thereby restages the scene to be a repetition of the primal scene. Freud is perfectly willing to imagine violence at the origin of identity, but only if that violence is oedipal: he insists that the figures in the nursery scene serve as types for understanding the master oedipal narrative.

Very late in his analysis, the Wolf Man suddenly recalled his earliest caregiver in the nursery. The memory "emerged, timidly and indistinctly," and initially the patient confused this maid with his mother: "he must have had a nursery-maid who was very fond of him. Her name had been the same as his mother's. He had no doubt returned her affection" (*SE* 17: 90). Freud and his patient agree that more was going on, and soon the Wolf Man realizes that the maid and his mother do not have the same name. Grusha shares her name with a pear that is striped in a way similar to the wasps that terrify the boy and that he enjoys mutilating (which Freud interprets as part of the Wolf Man's castration anxiety). Finally, this memory emerges: "Very soon after this there came the recollection of a scene, incomplete, but, so far as it was preserved, definite. Grusha was kneeling on the floor, and beside her a pail and a short broom made of a bundle of twigs; he was also there, and she was teasing or scolding him" (91–92). Freud constructs an erotic event in which the toddler recreates the primal scene:

> When he saw the girl on the floor engaged in scrubbing it, and kneeling down, with her buttocks projecting and her back horizontal, he was faced once again with the posture which his mother had assumed in the copulation scene. She became his mother to him; he was seized with sexual excitement owing to the activation of this picture; and, like his father (whose action he can only have regarded at the time as micturation), he behaved in the masculine way towards her. (*SE* 17: 92)

Freud constructs the detail of urination through the Wolf Man's preoccupation with the martyrdom of Jan Hus. Through a dream of a butterfly, the maid's "teasing or scolding" becomes a threat of castration that, although voiced by a woman, registers with the toddler as his father's threat.[18]

Another analyst might have seen in this memory, which could account for much of the Wolf Man's neurotic material, a challenge to the construction of the primal scene. Freud sees the opportunity to illustrate the shrewd application of psychoanalytic fundamentals. For instance, to understand correctly the presence of castration in these earliest memories, Freud divines the symbolism of wasps in relation to Grusha. He exploits a confusion that he and the Wolf Man suffer over the word for wasp. The Wolf Man kept mispronouncing the German *Wespe* by dropping the initial consonant, and Freud could make no sense of the story. Finally, the patient described the insect: "I could now put him right: 'So what you mean is a *Wespe*.' 'Is it called a *Wespe*? I really thought it was called an *Espe*.' . . . 'But *Espe*, why, that's myself: S. P.' (which were his initials). The *Espe* was of course a mutilated *Wespe*. The dream said clearly that he was avenging himself on Grusha for her threat of castration" (94). While the Wolf Man hears himself as the mutilated victim, Freud hears the Wolf Man's mistaken pronunciation as a reenactment of the toddler's retaliatory desire to mutilate his nurse, and stresses again the impact of the Wolf Man's molestation by his sister. The entertaining dialogue illustrates Freud's self-confidence and imagination in dealing with his patient's neurotic talk.

Freud uses this earliest memory to make sense of what had previously been random fragments, those details that can signify the "weightiest secrets that the patient's neurosis has veiled" (89). The infantile arousal at the sight of Grusha on her knees, the effort at seduction, and the threatened castration formed the "solution" to that neurosis and — plainly as important for Freud — confirmation of the scene he had constructed but his patient could not recollect. In addition to a very early instance of a normal oedipal complex, here was the first evidence of how the primal scene worked retroactively through that deferred action that was to wreak havoc on the Wolf Man's psyche at age four when he dreamed of the white wolves. Freud implies that the "weightiest secrets" of the Wolf Man's neurosis lie precisely in the relationship between the primal scene and the Grusha scene (94): "The action of the two-and-a-half-year-old boy in the scene with Grusha is the earliest effect of the primal scene which has come to our knowledge. It represents him as copying his father, and shows us a tendency towards development in a direction which would later deserve the name of masculine. His seduction [by his sister] drove him into passivity — for which, in any case, the way was prepared by his behaviour when he was a witness of his parents' intercourse." The toddler's attempt to seduce Grusha reveals how the primal scene could have formed the basis of his development toward the masculine, but since the primal scene concluded with an interruption that was inherently passive or female — the infant's bowel movement — the trauma of being driven "into passivity" was cemented through the second, and greater, deferred action of the white wolves dream. For Freud, the unremembered, constructed scene of parental copulation must be primal in part precisely because it already incorporates this trauma.

Yet the Grusha incident instantiates much of the neurotic material that haunts the Wolf Man, and Freud is at pains to point out how fundamentally crucial it is. He elaborates the parallels between the barely remembered encounter in the nursery and the entirely constructed primal scene. The existence of both is marked by an episode of anxiety about an animal: the harmless butterfly that turns frightful is a screen memory for Grusha's threat; the dream of motionless wolves in a tree replicates through inversion the father's threatening sexual actions in the primal scene. The transference of the castration complex from the mother-figure to the father is inherent in both, since it is the Wolf Man who dismembered butterflies: "It then appeared that his fear of the butterfly was in every respect analogous to his fear of the wolf; in both cases it was a fear of castration, which was, to begin with, referred to the person who had first uttered the threat of castration, but was then transposed on to another person to whom it was bound to become attached in accordance with phylogenetic precedent" (96).

The phylogenetic as an origin for unconscious anxieties, in which the father's power is supreme, thus carries more force than the ontogenetic mother figure. The two primal events are similar in other ways, which Freud does not spell out, but that the structure of the case history suggests. Both scenes are essentially "commonplace" in themselves, for instance, and only traumatic through deferred action once more information is available to the child (38, 96). And both scenes reverberate in the Wolf Man's language and screen memories throughout the psychoanalysis.[19] The great difference is that Freud shapes his entire narrative to stress the significance of his discovery of the primal scene but condenses the discovery of the Grusha incident into a few pages near the end of his text. His sequence for its recovery and reconstruction is remarkably clear and direct, in contrast to the challenges represented by the primal scene.

Freud gives the scene in the nursery the same rhetorical status that he accords it theoretically: it is a supplement and a decisive confirmation of the real primal scene, not in any way a challenge to it. The scene that "emerged in the patient's memory spontaneously and through no effort of mine" cannot bear the responsibility for the trauma that generates the neurosis. Nor can the Grusha scene preempt the analyst's construction of the primal scene. Instead, it becomes crucial testimony of the child's masculine drive, which itself had to exist to contest and confound the patient's inclination to passivity. His suffering lies in the conflict and ambivalence between these inclinations. The Grusha scene is framed as the missing link between the later evidence of neurotic turmoil and the primal scene: "When once the Grusha scene had been assimilated—the first experience that he could really remember, and one which he had remembered without any conjectures or intervention on my part—the problem of the treatment had every appearance of having been solved. From that time forward there were no more resistances; all that remained to be done was to collect and to co-ordinate" (94–95). Its very appearance is taken as a spontaneous gesture of approval and acquiescence by his patient's unconscious.[20]

Yet the Wolf Man's ability to remember such an early event again raises the question of whether the primal scene itself actually occurred. In light of the contest between memory and construction, Freud once again reminds his readers that:

> I should myself be glad to know whether the primal scene in my present patient's case was a phantasy or a real experience; but, taking other similar cases into account, *I must admit that the answer to this question is not in fact a matter of very great importance.* These scenes of observing parental intercourse, of being seduced in childhood, and of being threatened with castration are unquestionably an inherited endowment, a phylogenetic heritage, but they may just as easily be acquired by personal experience. . . . All that we find in the prehistory of neuroses is that a child catches hold of this phylogenetic experience where his own experience fails him. (*SE* 17: 97; emphasis added)

Thus Freud issues his familiar disclaimer about the status of memory. Not only are fact and fantasy equivalents—a familiar claim—but the ontological and phylogenetic sources are interchangeable. The ontological in fact needs the phylogenetic to make it comprehensible.[21] As usual, theory is better than unreconstructed memory. Yet this fragment of genuine memory troubles the structure, because it is so early and not discernibly part of the suite of troubled, neurotic behaviors that beset the Wolf Man as a toddler. Freud holds the individual memory to confirm the stereotype of oedipal drama, both within the Grusha scene and within the primal scene itself, but he acknowledges that it could be the reverse. Freud attempts to establish an equivalence between individual and type, such that either one may alert us to the presence of the other.[22] The close proximity of individual experience and stereotype becomes a strategic solution to the problem of which really matters more, the construction or the reality.

In effect, the Grusha scene is the first restaging of the primal scene in psycho-analysis, which subsequently learns to see ever-subtler versions of it in the talk of patients. As the patient rehearses the desires of the unconscious in his recollec-tions, Freud learns how to use this nursery drama as what we might call a re-corporation of what cannot be remembered. I use this term "re-corporation" to suggest the ways in which Freud assigns new meaning to the individual corporal details of the Grusha scene, such that they signify the body and will of the father while ignoring the body and purpose of the mother. The Wolf Man's actions as toddler with both Grusha and the butterfly are written to imitate the father in an oedipal enactment. Grusha enacts only the stereotype of the mother as the pas-sive but receptive partner. Even her threat of castration is transferred "by phy-logeny" to the father.[23] The scene still reverberates with suffering that is palpable in the screen memories of the martyr's flames and a terrifying butterfly, but Freud re-corporates the suffering as evidence of a drive to the masculine. This manip-ulation of the Grusha scene captures the essence of psychoanalytic interpreta-tion, which offers therapy by repeating the neurotic in terms that can release the unconscious from its drive to restage.

A sense of suffering or longing lingers in the Grusha scene, but it defies interpretation beyond Freud's. Whatever is happening there might have nothing to do with the father, but the non-oedipal bodies and will of both maid and child are gone.[24] If we set aside Freud's oedipal re-corporation of their postures — both the infantile phallic gesture and the threatened castration — we can but wonder just what has happened or is about to happen on the floor between this mother-figure and child. The intensity of their interaction is suggestive. Their close but oppositional postures recall the moment of decision for the early human mother and newborn, and in this regard the maid's voice, either teasing or scolding, is tempting. Are the two on the verge of embrace or angry withdrawal?[25] An ancient engagement between these two, whether in longing or suffering, lies concealed within the oedipal restaging designed to make sense of it in the newly discovered primal scene. Freud's handling of the Grusha incident denies analysis to what can longer be analyzed, because it can no longer be seen. He makes this denial theoretically acceptable and necessary by marking the boundaries of the psycho-analytic moment with its oedipal stereotypes that explain everything.

The degree to which Freud's psychoanalytic interpretation exerts control on unruly details in the Grusha scene is suggested by how he interprets the presence of fire. The martyr's fiery death is a detail that Freud added to the "spontaneous" memory to bring the libidinal into the nursery incident. The flames transferred from Jan Hus's martyrdom seem to be caught on something more than an accidental puddle on the nursery floor, but Freud's interpretation is theoretically concise and controlled, eschewing the more lurid details of the flames' source. The martyr's torturous death has its own elusive links to the Wolf Man's identity. The Wolf Man had a predilection for identifying himself with suffering martyrs and mutilated beings, from Christ to wasps, a predilection that Freud handles sometimes straightforwardly and sometimes by inversion.[26] In his deployment of the flames in the Grusha scene, he considers them to be "key" to everything, because of fire's equivalence to urination in the neurotic's unconscious. But he does not allow that key to suggest much beyond the enuresis that marks the infant's role in the oedipal encounter. The flames may suggest a reality of suffering that is fuel for the fire, but Freud's re-corporation of the Grusha scene does not permit us to see that suffering. Instead, he insists that we do not need to see beyond or into the flames. We need only sense that something is burning; he can then provide the theoretical construction or interpretation. Even if we suspect that the exact nature of the concealed trauma is other than what Freud discovers in the primal scene, a detailed hunt for what it might be is precluded by the way in which Freud structures his case history. It leads all too well to the primal scene.[27]

In choosing to analyze the relationship of mother and son only in the context of the oedipal, Freud consigns their bodies to embraces that are overseen by the father and do not rival his superior claims. Freud does not contemplate those interactions of their bodies that precede the intervention of the father. The Grusha scene may suggest that mother and child can contemplate one another as allies or antagonists without reference to the father: their gestures of embrace or its denial might enjoy a reciprocity that excludes the father's claims over either body. This exclusion of the father is theoretically impossible for Freud, however, because it destabilizes the basis on which the oedipal drama of identity can play out. The primal scene dramatizes violence and even deadly conflict, but only as they emanate from the father, because for Freud, the male contest is the cardinal struggle in the formation of the unconscious and identity. He does not contemplate the possibility that another site of murderous tension might precede the oedipal.[28]

Freud maintains the oedipal by refusing to look at what the Wolf Man's language insists must be seen (as Hus's martyrdom — a death that bears witness to the truth — implies). He thereby puts psychoanalysis at odds with itself, because psychoanalysis claims a special relationship with the capacity of the unconscious to visualize suffering or anxiety. As Freud observes in "The Interpretation of Dreams," a "dream-thought" is a perception of either physical or psychic experiences while sleeping: "The dream repeated these reflections unaltered, but it represented them in a situation which was actually present and which could be perceived through the senses like a waking experience. Here we have the most general and the most striking psychological characteristic of the process of dreaming: a thought, as a rule a thought of something that is wished, is objectified in the dream, is represented as a scene, or, as it seems to us, is experienced" (*SE* 4–5: 534). What to the consciousness may be an expectation or supposition becomes in dreams a reality fleshed-out with "sensory images." The analytic project allows the doctor to construct scenes out of the random detail and image in the patient's talk, but the doctor must watch the patient's affect, since it is a guide as to whether the construction can be usefully retained.[29]

Lacan also argues that psychoanalysis depends on the recognition that the patient's talk is a demand that the analyst *see* what really happened, and he finds a link between that demand and fire that is most provocative here.[30] Freud claims that his patient's recovery came through his being persuaded to see the entangled bodies of father, mother, and child, but the Wolf Man saw something different — an instant of longing and terror with Grusha. His talk used fire to mark the traumatic nature of this event, and not just any fire, but a fiery martyrdom, as a kind of double appeal that this event be seen. We need to look now more closely at what fire has to do with the problematic of seeing or witnessing in psychoanalysis.

As noted above, Freud fits talk of fire into an erotic structure: flames indicate (infantile) enuresis, which in turn signifies the masculine sexual impulse. As usual, the neurotic restages a primitive moment in human civilization, when the first (male) human refrained from urinating on the communal campfire to extinguish it. That early man thereby gained control over the fire, Freud contended, and also gained mastery over others who lacked his self-control.[31] Fire is an erotic site of self-testing and authority, and that the Wolf Man implicates it in his first restaging of the primal scene is an important sign of his "normal" predisposition. In the judgment of post-Freudian psychoanalysis, fire has a different signification, which draws on its blinding effect, as a terrifying marker for an originary trauma.[32] We can see the flames and *know* that something is burning, but the flames obscure that substance. There seems to be little to link Freud's erotic codes, which focus on male control, with the more intuitive focus on what the sight of fire provokes in us. Lacan, however, in his remarks on the inherent demand for a witness in psychoanalysis, alludes to a provocative dream found in "The Interpretation of Dreams" in which the enticement of watching fire entangles even Freudian psychoanalysis.

Freud offers this dream as a "model" of the fathomless nature of the "psychology of dreams." The dream is part of a sad and disturbing tale:

> A father had been watching beside his child's sick-bed for days and nights on end. After the child had died, he went into the next room to lie down, but left the door open so that he could see from his bedroom into the room in which his child's body was laid out, with tall candles standing round it. An old man had been engaged to keep watch over it, and sat beside the body murmuring prayers. After a few hours' sleep, the father had a dream that *his child was standing beside his bed, caught him by the arm and whispered to him reproachfully: "Father don't you see I'm burning?"* He woke up, noticed a bright glare of light from the next room, hurried into it and found that the old watchman had dropped off to sleep and that the wrappings and one of the arms of his beloved child's dead body had been burned by a lighted candle that had fallen on them. (*SE* 4–5: 509)[33]

Freud considers the everyday sources and meaning of the dream to be transparent: the real event of a glaring candle, the child's final fever, the father's grief and weariness, and anxiety over the possible carelessness of an elderly watchman all are the day's residue for the dream. The nature of the wish fulfilled by the dream, why it occurred at all, "when the most rapid possible awakening was called for" (*SE* 4–5: 510), is also easy for Freud to describe. The father wished his child alive again, and "[if] the father had woken up first and then made the inference that led him to go into the next room, he would, as it were, have shortened his child's life by that moment of time."

Still, Freud takes the dream as a paradigm of how different the dream world is from "waking life." Wishes and suppositions become fact (*SE* 4–5: 534); the father's sheer physical need for sleep generates a "further motive force" for the dream to continue despite its terrifying contents (571). Freud considered this dream a striking example of that force; "*throughout our whole sleeping state we know just as certainly that we are dreaming as we know that we are sleeping,*" he asserts (571; his emphasis). If the state of dreaming is the stage of the unconscious where it gives flesh to the fulfillment of its desires, our physical self is the stage manager, able somehow to exert the force necessary to keep the curtain up or lower it peremptorily. Freud senses that he is on the brink of contradicting himself with this assertion; he insists that an earlier assumption to the contrary, that "our consciousness is never brought to bear on the latter piece of knowledge [that we are dreaming]," is not to be heeded "too much" in this regard (571). This concession must seemingly change our perception of the laws of dreaming, and the very empire of the unconscious itself. Was it wrung from the power of the dream itself over Freud's imagination, such that he is willing to entertain the possibility of deliberately embracing a dream such as this? But why embrace the dream of the burning child at all?

Psychoanalysis — both Freud's and that of later theorists — seems to need this dream.[34] In Freud's case, the source for it is suggestive. A female patient brought him the dream, having heard it in a lecture; it was not hers originally, but she had made it hers by "re-dreaming" it (SE 4–5: 509). Freud makes it his own as well; he reports that the lecturer had correctly interpreted it, but he has more to say about it. And yet he does not say much more about what it might mean, because he recognizes that "other wishes, originating from the repressed, probably escape us, since we are unable to analyse the dream" (571). Instead, he uses the dream to discuss the implications of three key points in the psychology of dreaming: that dreams are wish-fulfillments; that they enact thoughts and suppositions; and that our physical state can dictate how long we dream. Freud has to admit, however, that the father's dream does not actually illustrate the first two points very clearly: "In this particular dream the change made in the thoughts by the conversion of the expectation expressed by them into the present tense may not seem particularly striking. This is because of what can only be described as the unusually subordinate part played in this dream by wish-fulfilment" (534).

As for the third point, concerning the influence of our bodies over our dreams, Freud applies the father's dream as a disturbing, unlikely example of the process. Just as his patient "re-dreamed" this uncanny dream to make it hers, Freud reframes it to serve his discussion. The dream of the burning child marks the beginning of his "endeavour to penetrate more deeply into the mental process involved in dreaming," a moment when "the easy and agreeable portion of our journey lies behind us" (SE 4–5: 511). Despite the momentousness of this pronouncement, Freud turns out only to want an abstracted notion of the dream for his discussion of the general principles of dreaming. He dismisses the dream's meaning as obvious and determines that its individual details cannot yield any psychoanalytic understanding of the father.[35] But his handling of the dream itself suggests that there is something else in it that he wishes to control, and Lacan ([1978] 57, 60) recognizes that the dream of the burning child means something to Freud that remains unexpressed.

Lacan's own discussion suggests that he also feels the uncanny allure of the dream. He notes ([1978] 57–59) that it does not illustrate Freud's notion of the dream as wish-fulfillment well and calls it instead a fantasy of fulfillment only regarding the father's need to encounter what he cannot—his child beyond the flames.[36] As such, the dream is a paradigm for Lacan's notion of *dustuchia*, a missed encounter with the real:

> Between what occurs as if by chance, when everybody is asleep—the candle that overturns and the sheets that catch fire, the meaningless event, the accident, the piece of bad luck—and the element of poignancy, however veiled, in the words *Father, can't you see I'm burning*—there is the same relation to what we were dealing with in repetition. It is what, for us, is represented in the term neurosis of destiny or neurosis of failure. What is missed is not adaptation, but *tuché*, the encounter. [1978] (69)

Lacan surmises that the "missed reality" is that which "caused the death of the child." While this "element of poignancy" perhaps begins with the fever that Freud prosaically posits as the residual source for the dream's fire, it is also something else which causes the father "remorse" (Lacan [1978] 58; cf. 68). Lacan is mapping the terrain in which may be hidden what Freud calls the wish lost through repression, such that he cannot analyze the dream (58). If so, *dustuchia* as a "missed encounter" is a striking expression for that repressed wish.[37]

More crucially, Lacan links this dream with Freud's urgency to recover the "real," and he uses the Wolf Man as his example:

> We have translated [*tuché*] as *the encounter with the real*. The real is beyond . . . the return, the coming-back, the insistence of the signs, by which we see ourselves governed by the pleasure principle. . . . and it is quite obvious, throughout Freud's research, that it is this that is the object of his concern.
>
> If you wish to understand what is Freud's true preoccupation as the function of phantasy is revealed to him, remember the development, which is so central for us, of the *Wolf Man*. He applies himself, in a way that can almost be described as anguish, to the question—what is the first encounter, the real, that lies behind the phantasy? (Lacan [1978] 53–54)

Lacan is preoccupied by two features of the father's dream that Freud leaves unexplored: the flame and the child's complaint that his father doesn't see him. Lacan infers that Freud's oversight is not inadvertent; he knows the originary moment is there—hence the anguish—but cannot see it through the flames. His anguish in the case of the Wolf Man is that he senses he is not seeing the origin.[38]

As the first epigraph to this chapter indicates, Lacan believes that the flames always obscure the real, however surely they mark it. This inevitable inability to see provides a comforting explanatory fiction for the primal trauma of psychoanalysis, its need to label what it cannot see. Flames have a double potency: they signal primal suffering but also unburden the analyst — at least, for Lacan — from the anguish of identifying it. But Lacan also infers that Freud cannot simply embrace the paradox.

The father's dream of his burning child is a terrifying metaphor for the peril of psychoanalysis itself, in that it signifies a failure or inability to see something fundamental. It is easy to see why Freud insists on making such a symbol his own. The dream only fulfils his wish when it has been restaged to fit as well as possible within psychoanalysis, becoming type and model even when it scarcely fits his project. The father's failure to see his burning child, which cannot be analyzed, need not be analyzed; it can serve better as an example. Freud has restaged the dream to make it fit theory.

There are clear parallels here with how he handles the Grusha scene relative to the primal scene. Something about that scene also cannot be brought into the structures of authority, both within the oedipal inherent in the scene and within the psychoanalytic community, so Freud brings Grusha and the toddler as close to the family created in the primal scene as possible. He cannot, or will not, entertain the vision of trauma inhering in the bodies of mother and child, absent the father's will and body. Instead, he restages the individual people and elements of the scene such that everything in the encounter with Grusha becomes type and model. The martyr's death marks a phylogenetic link between urination and fire. Grusha becomes a mother-figure and the Wolf Man his father. Finally, these two together model his parents in the primal scene. As important a discovery as this recollection is, it cannot illuminate with its own light but can only refract the true light of the primal scene.

Freud finesses certainty about the actual instantiation of the primordial trauma in order to speak decisively on theoretical structure, and he brings the Wolf Man to the end of his analysis with as much of his suffering relieved as seems possible.[39] He also cements the destiny of psychoanalysis as an oedipal structure. Such a conclusion conforms to other studies of Freud's habits of mind, but we should recognize that his choice also reflects his clinical experience.[40] Under the constraints of a desperately sick but increasingly complacent patient, and under external pressure from rivals for control of psychoanalysis, Freud found a pattern that approximated the true trauma near enough to serve his purposes.[41] Circumstance compels Freud to stop his search for *the* primal site, although the accretion of explanatory footnotes and remarks throughout the case history suggests the urgency with which he considered alternatives, right up to its publication. Yet, finally, as we have noted before, he ends with a *non liquet* — it is not clear (60). For patient and doctor the romance is over.

When it comes to halting the search for origin in "From the History of an Infantile Neurosis," the entire process seems directed both by Freud's relentless drive to make all evidence conform to theory and by the impingement of external contingency.[42] So, too, the *Ion* is emphatically constructed out of a clash between the contingent and the destined from the very beginning. Of all the odd dramaturgical features of the *Ion*, this may be the strangest: that its divine prologue incorrectly predicts the coming drama.[43] Apollo's plan is to unite Ion with his supposed natal father and to postpone Kreousa's recognition until Ion is safely back in Athens, but the human contingencies of grief, anger, suspicion, and joy disrupt the plan. Once again, tragedy is the complement to Freudian theory. Practical necessity may drive the psychoanalyst to stage the shutting down of inquiry into origins, but the dramatist plots the structure of his play to capture the process by which we finally turn away from the romance of belonging.

The *Ion* is structured around two recognition scenes, both of which turn on an embrace (523; 1404, 1440), so we are once again in the presence of that primal moment of peril. Will each of these parents accept Ion as their son? And, as it turns out more crucially, will he allow himself to be embraced in this new identity? Yet a genuine sense of peril is hardly felt because the outcome is never seriously in doubt in either case. This tragedy is staged largely as melodrama with strong comic elements, so the recognitions can be enjoyed as antithetical turning points in an intriguing set of intellectually engaging paradoxes and puzzles that center on Ion's identity. While we can set out to study how the embrace unsettles the entertainment of watching the pieces all fall together, we must not deny that the *Ion* invests much dramatic energy in piquing our sense of humor and curiosity. Nevertheless, the mind games are setting the spectators up to find out that they are themselves entangled in a fiery embrace.

The constructed nature of Ion's civic identities has been studied thoroughly, with the implications of each turn of events articulated through varying structures. Froma Zeitlin examines the mythic paradigms that inform the multiple fathers Ion needs to establish himself in Athens, with Apollo contributing his heroic status and Xouthos providing the human father a citizen requires. There is, of course, a huge difference between what Xouthos offers — acknowledgment but illegitimacy — and the marriage that any Athenian citizen would have had backing his own legitimate status, but that gap is filled, symbolically and literally, by Kreousa, who contributes a crucial thematic link to Athens's mythical autochthony.[44] From a different perspective, Charles Segal comments on the tensions of Ion's nurture and his natal origin in the context of the boy's maturation. In Segal's view, these tensions stand as a metaphor for the constructed identity of Athens itself. He especially highlights the anomalous role of Kreousa in this construction, which displaces what should be the essential contributions of Xouthos and Apollo as fathers: "Through his contact with Creusa, then, Ion encounters both the primary feelings between mother and child and the possible complexities attendant on heterosexual pro-creation. This powerful role of the mother in the boy's passage from one stage of life to another threatens the legitimization of the son by his father and the civic ideology that insists on the male parent as the source of the son's manhood and his capacities as a future citizen-warrior."[45]

Athenians had strict standards as regards the parentage and virginity at marriage of the mother of any citizen, but what Segal is stressing here is another remarkable aspect of Kreousa' role, namely, how late she has an effect on the development of an Athenian youth. No one in the audience could have imagined that so late in the life of a youth, a mother's identity could play a role in determining his own, which was settled by the rituals after his birth.[46] Modern studies of identity in the *Ion* have established how crucial Kreousa is thematically and symbolically, and how anomalous the solution based on her is in real terms. In her, spectators see something they may recognize from myth but find unimaginable in practical terms. She is, to use Freud's word, an "uncanny" (*Unheimlich*) site for watching the construction of a founding father.

If we turn to the mythic representation of the mother, we find other kinds of uncanniness. The mother occupies the boundary of life and death for the hero. Sheila Murnaghan has studied the ancient Greek association of birth and a mother's care, particularly her nursing, with the hero's death. A mother's life-giving role incorporates death as life's inversion, and a hero's refusal to acknowledge the fragility of his life may take the form of repudiating her care, as Hector does by ignoring his mother Hecuba's bared breast when she begs him to retreat before Achilles' onslaught (*Iliad* 22.249–50). Murnaghan remarks:

> Hecuba's gesture is a claim to authority, a reminder of what Hector owes to her that she hopes will make him willing to listen. It is also the most graphic possible assertion of what both she and Priam want Hector to take into account: his mortal

vulnerability, which makes his encounter with the semidivine Achilles certain to be fatal and thus certain to leave his parents helpless and bereft. But the heroic code to which Hector is bound requires him to ignore even this most persuasive reminder of his mortality.[47]

Others have studied how the mother's prominence at birth situates her symbolically at death as an explanation for the cardinal role of women in ancient funeral lamentation.[48] Significantly for this discussion, mothers are also seen to exercise power over a hero's life. The link may be found in a mother's thoughtlessness: Niobe causes the death of her children by bragging about her superior fertility over Leto's, and in the "Homeric Hymn to Demeter," Metaneira accidentally ends Demeter's attempt to make her son Demophoön immortal when she catches the goddess immersing him in fire. A mother's intervention may be more purposeful. Meleager's mother, Althea saves his life at birth when she rescues a magical log from a fire, but she finally burns it and kills her son in anger at his murder of her brothers.[49]

These last two examples deploy fire at the site where children hover between death and immortality. Because Metaneira cannot bear the sight of her son in flames, she cannot see what the flames are doing to him. Her fear constructs her son as a mortal hero. For Althea, the flames would have hidden the equivalency between the log and her son if passers-by (actually, the Fates themselves) had not dropped the vital hint. Once she knows what is burning, she can intervene and take power over Meleager's life. In both tales, fire hides what is happening to the hero's identity, but it also creates that identity. Althea is the exception that proves the point that mothers make choices about their sons without seeing what the fire is doing. Both her choices — dragging a son from the fire or casting him into it — are deadly in the long run: fire burns on the fact that mothers are as deadly as they are nurturing.

The *Ion* uses flames in each of its two recognition scenes in order to mark changes in identity. Ion must see and embrace what the fire conceals if he is to forestall murder, yet murder itself turns out to have the power to create the same identities. This paradox captures the trauma in the embrace of the romance of belonging. Recognition is something the tragedy insists that we must see for our own eyes; it is not something that can be constructed as a recollection or prophecy. We have to see each mortal parent embrace Ion. Hermes' prologue tries to privilege the paternal embrace, which turns into parody. The recollections of abandonment, however, generate our longing for the maternal embrace, which is paramount in the close of the play.

Ion's abandonment is an event that cannot be left out of his identity, but it defies being seen. Kreousa's grief alerts us to the problem. Although she went to great lengths to conceal her child's abandonment, sealing him in a box in the privacy of night and leaving him in a cave, when she finally speaks directly about her ancient travail, she wishes someone had seen the pathetic moment (954–962):

Πρεσβύτης· τίς γάρ νιν ἐξέθηκεν; οὐ γὰρ δὴ σύ γε;

Κρέουσα· ἡμεῖς, ἐν ὄρφνῃ σπαργανώσαντες πέπλοις.

Πρεσβύτης· οὐδὲ ξυνῄδει σοί τις ἔκθεσιν τέκνου;

Κρέουσα· αἱ ξυμφοραί γε καὶ τὸ λανθάνειν μόνον.

Πρεσβύτης· καὶ πῶς ἐν ἄντρῳ παῖδα σὸν λιπεῖν ἔτλης;

Κρέουσα· πῶς; οἰκτρὰ πολλὰ στόματος ἐκβαλοῦσ᾽ ἔπη.

Πρεσβύτης· φεῦ·

τλήμων σὺ τόλμης, ὁ δὲ θεὸς μᾶλλον σέθεν.

Κρέουσα· εἰ παῖδά γ᾽ εἶδες χεῖρας ἐκτείνοντά μοι.

Πρεσβύτης· μαστὸν διώκοντ᾽ ἢ πρὸς ἀγκάλαις πεσεῖν;

Κρέουσα· ἐνταῦθ᾽ ἵν᾽ οὐκ ὢν ἄδικ᾽ ἔπασχεν ἐξ ἐμοῦ.

Old Man: Who exposed him? For of course it was not you yourself.

Kreousa: No, I did it — by night, after swaddling him in garments.

Old Man: Then was no one your accomplice in the exposure of your child?

Kreousa: Only my misfortunes, and solitary stealth.

Old Man: And how did you dare to leave your very own child in a cave?

Kreousa: How? — by casting many a piteous word from my lips . . .

Old Man: Ah . . .

Bold you were in your daring, but the god more so than you.

Kreousa: If only you could have seen the child stretching out his hands to me!

Old Man: Seeking your breast or trying to reach your arms?

Kreousa: Yes, that very place where, since he was not, he suffered unjustly from me.

In her wish, abandonment is distilled into a tiny space bounded by her newborn's extended hands on the one side and her breast and arms on the other. Her refusal to pick up her child reverses a cliché often found in tragedy, of a child resting safely in its mother's arms. Kreousa herself escaped the fate of her sisters by being held, so it is no wonder that she calls her action unjust. But how does the audience visualize a nonevent that is so private, and meaningful only to the two participants?[50] When Kreousa recreates Ion's abandonment as a moment of opposing gestures, she also creates the specter of the gesture that would have saved him:

her embrace, which becomes the dramatic and teleological goal of the play, replacing the nongesture of abandonment, which cannot be seen.[51]

The play between acceptance and rejection begins with the denial of the mother's breast, and one weird detail in Ion's history, as it appears in this tragedy, is that he was not nursed by anyone.[52] Kreousa does not have the chance, and his foster mother, the Pythia, is too old. Ion's way of putting it stresses the oddity: "I never at all knew a breast; but she who nurtured me . . . " (οὐπώποτ' ἔγνων μαστόν· ἣ δ' ἔθρεψέ με . . . ; 319; cf. 1324). These words are oxymoronic: no one *can* nurture a newborn without nursing it, something the ancient Athenian audience would have understood better than we may be able to, with our modern technologies.[53] Kreousa and Ion later consider what each became when she failed to nurse him (1491–1496):

> Κρέουσα· γάλακτι δ' οὐκ ἐπέσχον οὐδὲ μαστῷ
> τροφεῖα ματρὸς οὐδὲ λουτρὰ χειροῖν,
> ἀνὰ δ' ἄντρον ἔρημον οἰωνῶν
> γαμφηλαῖς φόνευμα θοίναμά τ' εἰς
> Ἅιδαν ἐκβάλλῃ.
> Ἴων· ὦ δεινὰ τλᾶσα, μῆτερ.
> *Kreousa:* Nor did I furnish you with milk, or with my breast
> a mother's nurture, or a bath with my two hands,
> but within a deserted cave as a victim
> and a feast for the jaws of birds
> you were cast — and into Hades.
> *Ion:* O mother who dared terrible things!

Kreousa's choice did more than deny them both their proper natal roles; it transformed them into monstrous perversions of themselves. By refusing to nurse her baby, she transformed it, she fears, into a meal for birds, while Ion equates her motherhood with terrible daring.[54]

Without its natal mother's body to protect and nurture it, the child can become almost anything, depending on who or what picks it up and embraces it. Other versions of the gesture that Kreousa denies represent an identity beyond the natal bond.[55] The gods can transform such an infant into a symbol of power or protection, but when wild beasts or birds get the infant, the transformations are grisly.[56] Athena's treatment of Erichthonios, the second royal autochthon, illustrates how the divine "embrace" transforms a child into a token. She puts him into the ritual *antipex* and provides for his "care" with poisonous snakes inside and ominous warnings for his human foster-nurses, the Aglaurids. The result is hardly a child, and the maidens are thereby placed in an impossible situation: they cannot see or touch what they are supposed to keep safe—a mystery that would be fine for an object but not a newborn. The Aglaurids' failure at fosterage may signify the miraculous nature of Athena the Fosterer (*kourotrophos*), but it also suggests the uneasy fit between Athena's labels and the human reality.[57] The nonmaternal human embrace creates equally profound transformations, even though these are social constructions. For instance, the Pythia's rescue of Ion made him into her foster son in what is plainly a construction—as Ion says, he *deems* her his mother (μητέρ᾽ ὡς νομίζομεν; 321).[58]

All of these embraces, or travesties of embraces, are recollected from the past. Their effects are still felt, but, like Ion's abandonment, they have to be constructed. Yet the embrace can be staged; the first is the broad comic business between Xouthos and Ion in their recognition that reidentifies strangers as father and son. The action between them represents recognition as burlesque: the tender embrace of the child that forms the natal link is parodied in Xouthos's efforts to grab the incredulous Ion. Nevertheless, this parody reverberates with the effects that the embrace or its denial has on the participants' identities.[59] Xouthos is so frantic to claim Ion as his child that he violates Ion's person, tearing at his sacred ribbons and forcing him to jerk back and threaten the king with his bow (519–527).[60] Where the king sees a new family member, Ion sees only a crazy stranger, and his momentary refusal to suffer the embrace signals what he thinks of this one. Embrace momentarily incorporates its opposite—rejection— and also shuts down further serious inquiry into what is going on by directing the actions in one inevitable direction.

Xouthos's happiness is funny, of course, because we know it is a delusion, but the energy behind his drive to embrace Ion is still remarkable. Of course, the king is after a new title, that of father, and so he presses to embrace Ion. But the boy must also accept the reciprocal identity of son, and his initial resistance makes the king's actions into a nearly erotic physical molestation.[61] Xouthos's effort is delusional because it is unanswered by any corresponding expectation, and that delusion is comic because—we know—he has assumed a literal truth where only a manufactured one is planned.[62] His enthusiasm also suggests that one needs to feel passionate about choosing a child. The father's embrace may be the ritualized symbol of new familial and social status, but here it is staged as an act whose enthusiasm compels bodies together even over deep resistance. Once again, Socrates' concern as the metaphoric midwife of new ideas in the *Theaetetus* is worth recalling, that new parents are likely to be irrationally convinced that any child of their must be worth rearing and to become angry at suggestions to the contrary (160e).[63] And once Ion chooses to participate in the delusion, the signification of Xouthos's gestures changes, and they instantly change Ion's identity — from an indignant stranger being treated almost like a beloved (an *eromenos*) into a son and heir.

Ion's initial threat to shoot him with his bow and arrows (524) doesn't dampen Xouthos's enthusiasm for an embrace. On the contrary, the king welcomes the gesture in a hyperbole that finally gets the boy's attention (527–530):[64]

Ξοῦθος· κτεῖνε καὶ πίμπρη· πατρὸς γάρ, ἢν κτάνῃς, ἔσῃ φονεύς.

Ἴων· ποῦ δέ μοι πατὴρ σύ; ταῦτ' οὖν οὐ γέλως κλύειν ἐμοί;

Ξοῦθος· οὔ· τρέχων ὁ μῦθος ἄν σοι τὰμὰ σημήνειεν ἄν.

Ἴων· καὶ τί μοι λέξεις; Ξοῦθος· πατὴρ σός εἰμι καὶ σὺ παῖς ἐμός.

Xouthos: Kill me! Set me on fire! You'll be the murderer of your father if you do.

Ion: What's this about your being my father? Isn't this a joke I'm hearing?

Xouthos: No, but the tale, if it could be run out, would signal to you what I mean.

Ion: And what will you tell me? *Xouthos:* I am your father and you are my son.

Xouthos's tale (*muthos*) is unexpectedly succinct because of his belief in the god's word, but it can also be brief because he hears equivalence in every expression exchanged between him and this youth. Ion's threat, the suspected mockery, and the king's tale all have the same meaning: these two are father and son. Every action or explanation signifies the newly revealed identities (σημήνειεν; 529), and even Ion's threatened violence has the opposite effect from what the youth intends, as Xouthos sees the matter. Potential murder cannot ward off the embrace or forestall new identities for these two, it can only confirm them. If Xouthos's rhetoric says, "Nothing you can do changes who we are to each other," his passion adds, "everything we do now is a sign of our affiliation." This is the happy universe of delusion for those who newly belong to each other.

Xouthos's playful claim that he welcomes Ion's violence also suggests that the embrace can be very close to violence in creating familial identities. If Ion kills Xouthos and sets him on fire, those acts would, like the embrace, make Ion his son, but the results would be more horrific, since they would create that son as a murderer. Ion could only discover both identities after the fact. Such a danger recalls the fate of Oedipus, who was the son of the man he killed in a meaningful way only because he was his murderer — and vice versa. Here, too, the flames, if set upon the "graceless and crazy stranger" — Ion's label for Xouthos (526) —

would mark the king as the site of both identities for Ion, murderer and son, but Ion's assumption would conceal them until too late. Hence the uncanny in Xouthos's ability to call a *mythos* what Ion suspects is a joke by another name. He is, in effect, describing the romance of belonging, in that the embrace, with its suggestion of violence, turns strangers into both father and son, and victim and murderer. It is a terrifying tale.

This comic scene parodies the construction of familial identity, reminding us through burlesque that the possibilities of both abandonment and acceptance reside within the romance. Violence and nurture turn out not to be all that distant from each other. Xouthos's frantic gestures are a travesty of what Kreousa could not do in the moment of her abandonment, and thus they recollect that ancient sorrow by inversion. They are also a hilarious and tantalizing preview of the tender embrace of mother and son we hope finally to see (although that gesture also turns out differently from our imagining). But even in comedy, embrace incorporates or suggests violence, however joking. Xouthos doesn't mean it, of course; he doesn't want Ion to kill him. But Ion did mean it, at least for an instant, and Xouthos marks his meaning with the hyperbole of fire.

The play's first recognition scene provokes attempted murder, a tableau of anger, and finally, another recognition — the one we've been led to long for. Images of fire track the progression. Once Kreousa decides to seek revenge for her husband's betrayal, her accomplice's first suggestion is to set fire to the god's sanctuary (974). It is an extravagant gesture, soon dropped out of fear, but the suggestion insinuates fire into the plotters' sphere of imagery, where it reappears more provocatively. Xouthos departs to sacrifice to Dionysus in honor of his son's many missed birthdays; we learn from the messenger who later describes the murder attempt, that Xouthos went to "where the god's bacchic flames leap" (1125–26). His mission is sacred, but the Chorus has already used just such flames to curse his new son (714ff). Divine fire is a screen of ambiguity behind which Ion's mortal father permanently vanishes. Xouthos's retreat is not only a geographical withdrawal. He vanishes into a dramatic moment in which primal trauma is about to be restaged, and his relationship to Ion remains permanently crucial but never further parsed.[65] Fire next attaches itself to Ion, who is reported to be in a tent that he himself built and decorated. His enemies convert this tent into a recreation of the *antipex*, the first vessel in which Ion's death was intended. As many recent studies point out, the messenger's tale links the tent and the *antipex* in numerous ways, as tokens of destiny once bestowed on a helpless baby are now appropriated by the youth who constructs this space for his coming-of-age party. The symbolic system of the tent represents Ion's construction of himself in his new identity, and its decorations recapitulate and clarify the Athenian autochthony that Ion can now claim.[66]

My interest lies with the complementary images of fire and golden snakes. Ion designs his tent to block the sun's rays, to be shady even against the slanting rays of sundown, but he then lines it with images of fire from the sun and in starry constellations. The concealing purpose of the *antipex* is recapitulated, as are its ritual contents, in the gold of the snake ornaments. The vessel in which Erichthonios was hidden contained live snakes as potent guardians, because they could bite him but did not. Instead, when the disobedient Aglaurids opened the *antipex*, they were terrified at the spectacle and leapt to their deaths. The golden snakes in Ion's infant casket symbolize both that ancient guardianship and that potential for terror and violence. As decorations on Ion's tent, the symbolic system of guardianship comes to fruition as the stars and constellations watch over Ion's miraculous rescue from Kreousa's deadly poison. Yet the messenger's report also replicates the danger inherent in the symbolism of the guardian snakes. A deadly poison from a snake also comes into Ion's tent, venom that Kreousa has had dangling from her wrist all the while.[67] The living snakes, the golden ornaments, and the poisonous venom together instantiate a deadly intent in Athens's foundation, which Kreousa's murder plot attempts to actualize. Because the plot fails, the ancient, divinely established symbolic system remains in the ambiguity of potentiality. If we could see murder effected, perhaps we would understand what the deadly intent means.

Fire marks and obscures events in all three of these appearances. Kreousa's fear will not let her contemplate an attack on her most direct enemy, the god who assaulted her, so she cannot burn down his shrine. Xouthos vanishes into the doom of the eternally deceived. And Ion's murder is now twice attempted — first through the ancient abandonment and then through poison — and its intent seems clear enough, to preserve the purity of Athens's royal household. In both cases, the role of fire obscures something. Is fire protecting him or does it take part in the attempt on his life? Euripides seems particularly to exploit the tragic convention that prevents violence from appearing onstage, so that Ion's murder is not enacted for spectators but only reported in language whose fiery images are hard to fathom.

The longed-for recognition scene begins unexpectedly in a tableau of perfectly balanced anger. Both Kreousa and Ion occupy a position of some moral strength: she is on Apollo's altar; Ion is supported by Delphic allies.[68] The plans of each are equally balanced: Ion wishes to avenge himself on the stepmother who attempted to murder him; Kreousa wanted to prevent an illegitimate foreigner from taking over her household. Each visualizes the other with fiery imagery (looked at more closely below). This entire sense of balance, however, rests on stereotypes the audience knows to be false: Kreousa isn't Ion's stepmother, and he isn't an alien interloper. The scene must titillate spectators with a sense of horror that the fiction might win out and ruin everything, and the tragedy relishes its complete impasse before the Pythia appears as a human agent of divine will, a kind of deus ex machina before the fact. She even has the ancient *antipex* safely in her embrace. An object that once concealed Ion will now serve to reveal him to his mother, as Kreousa's recognition literally springs from this vessel.[69] She willingly leaps from her place of safety to identify the objects inside and thus transforms Ion and herself from mortal enemies to mother and son. Her kinetic energy reverses the momentum short-circuited in the ancient abandonment, in which it was the baby longing to touch its mother. The theatrical energy from a motionless balance of anger to the queen's joyous and one-sided leap must make this recognition scene a thrilling one to witness and worth the wait.

The climactic thrill traps spectators in a disturbing conundrum, however, because the misapprehensions and stereotypes that generate near-murder are shortly revealed to be crucial parts of the permanent settlement. Given that Ion must inherit rule at Athens through Xouthos, mother and son also have to remain mortal enemies, at least publicly. In their anger, Ion and Kreousa see each other as witnesses will see them from now on. Of course, we might comfort ourselves that the underlying identities of mother and son will hold in check the violence inherent in the stereotypes, but that relationship, too, was one born of violence. The mother concealed behind the stepmother did mean the death of her infant, and for the same reasons: an illegitimate child of a father who could not be named was a threat to her household. The distance between the Kreousa of each identity is not great, because the stereotype of stepmother, rather than being an inherent inversion of the mother, dramatizes her motives in large, unmistakable form.

Flames burn on exactly this collapse of distinction between natal roles and social status. Ion's opening words are a vision of Kreousa with fiery eyes, even as she approaches or sits upon an altar surrounded by torches (1261–1265):[70]

ὦ ταυρόμορφον ὄμμα Κηφισοῦ πατρός,
οἵαν ἔχιδναν τήνδ᾽ ἔφυσας ἢ πυρὸς
δράκοντ᾽ ἀναβλέποντα φοινίαν φλόγα,

ᾗ τόλμα πᾶσ᾽ ἔνεστιν οὐδ᾽ ἥσσων ἔφυ
Γοργοῦς σταλαγμῶν, οἷς ἔμελλέ με κτανεῖν.
O bull-formed visage of father Kephisos,
what a serpent is this you have produced, or a
snake, which casts its murderous glance in fire,
such is the utter daring in her, not less than
the ooze from the Gorgon by which she intended to kill me.

Ion's image of his enemy is based on the poison's source, a story that Euripides seems to have invented.[71] During the Gigantomachy, the Earth produced the Gorgon as an ally for the Giants against the Olympians; when Athena killed her, she harvested her blood. Ion's fiery vision of Kreousa decodes the layering of her identities and confirms their equivalence. Heiress to Athens's autochthony, Kreousa also possesses the ambivalent power of that other earthborn, the Gorgon, who was created to fight against the Olympian effort to impose order on the cosmos. Kreousa's implication in Athens's founding heritage of autochthony is affiliated with both blessing and violence.[72]

There is both comfort and danger in this foundation narrative. It affiliates Athens with the earth's ancient maternal power to preserve and protect those children who guarantee her perpetuation. But if threatened, earth can produce a venomous response that does not regard the sanctity of any particular offspring as such. Instead, she fosters one set of children against another according to a seemingly unfathomable choice—why the Giants and not the Olympians? The choice only aims always at her own continuance. In victory, the Olympians appropriate this maternal power.

So, too, does the child who wins its mother's embrace. Ion had to survive two onslaughts by Kreousa against his rule in her city, but once she has chosen him as her son—which the drama stages as a recognition and an embrace—she makes plain that she will do anything to keep him in this role. She accepts her public role as his stepmother; she foists a deceit upon her beloved husband; she willingly calls the god who raped her beneficent. Motherhood as a savage and arbitrary power is captured in Ion's vision of Kreousa as surely as it is in the figure of Althea, guarding the firebrand that is Meleager's life. The difference is that Althea finally abandoned her choice and her motherhood. Here, Kreousa's choices are the permanent solution on which Athens's greatness is founded.

In this recognition fire also marks Ion, who is seen by Kreousa in the typology of foreign invader (1291–1294):

Κρέουσα·   ἔκτεινά σ᾽ ὄντα πολέμιον δόμοις ἐμοῖς.

Ἴων·   οὔτοι σὺν ὅπλοις ἦλθον ἐς τὴν σὴν χθόνα.

Κρέουσα·   μάλιστα· κἀπίμπρης γ᾽ Ἐρεχθέως δόμους.

Ἴων·   ποίοισι πανοῖς ἢ πυρὸς ποίᾳ φλογί;

Kreousa: I killed you as an enemy of my house.

Ion: I didn't attack your land under arms!

Kreousa: You certainly did; and you were going to set the house of Erechtheus on fire!

Ion: With what sort of torches and flame of fire?

When Kreousa envisions an enemy bent on setting her house ablaze, Ion himself supplies the torches in a sarcastic retort that enters into the fantasy.[73] In this dramatic moment, we see Ion as the murderer. He certainly enters intending to kill Kreousa and when invited by her fiery vision, he brandishes torches against Athens itself. This same vision of him as a killer is what summons the Pythia onto the stage and begins the reversal of all ancient suffering, a reversal that concludes with Kreousa's new identity of founding mother. Beyond the ironic thrill, what does this vision of a fire-brandishing murderer mean? How does the helpless, hapless infant get to be a killer, and why does the drama insist on staging him as such, even if the vision immediately yields to its reversal when the Pythia enters? Ion's identity as foreign invader restages the role of the natal child, just as Kreousa's two roles as mother and stepmother replicate each other. The child embraced by the parents as their own becomes the person who overthrows them in the end by consuming precious resources and displacing them from power and authority.

As elsewhere in the tragedy, Euripides uses the ancient tale of abandonment to explore how the child becomes the relentless consumer of his parents' resources. Kreousa's refusal to embrace her infant initially spares her this consumption and passes it on to others. But the Greek mythic imagination understands that even cut loose from his natal identity, the abandoned child still, eventually, consumes it. The hero abandoned at birth always returns to his natal family with fatal consequences, and this outcome is nearly enacted in this play until the Pythia is sent in to prevent it. The near-fatal consequences of abandonment are even spoofed in the play's most comic scene, when Ion threatens to kill a man to avoid his embrace, only to turn around and become his son. But when we finally see the embrace that stories of Ion's abandonment make us long to see, the gesture reveals that Ion and Kreousa are more to each other than we expect. They are mother and son, but they are also deadly enemies, whose toxic relationship is part of the final, public story. The deceit might not be so bad, however, except that the final recognition also suggests that the enmity resides in the natal link as well, because one of them, mother or son, disposes of other as a matter of course.

Now we may begin to understand why, according to Hermes, Kreousa was never meant to embrace her child onstage and in front of the audience. The gods intended instead to dramatize the political and social constructions of Ion, not the gesture that recreates his natal identity. If Hermes' prediction were correct, the tragedy would climax in the travesty of a recognition between Xouthos and Ion. Instead, the reunion of mother and son is lavishly staged, with the proto–deus ex machina entrance of the Pythia and the spectacular image of Kreousa leaping from the altar to embrace the young man who intends to kill her. And somehow the play has taught us that this is exactly what spectators must see. It works at the symbolic level, so rich in irony. Ion cannot go to his rewards in Athens without his mother's saving, redeeming, and identifying embrace — such is the essence of the play's happy message. But what else was there that made it necessary for us to see the leap? Froma Zeitlin articulates the dramaturgical power of the shock by focusing on Hermes' faulty prediction: "Thus when Apollo hands on a son from one father to another and defers the anagnorisis of mother and son to a date beyond the frame of the play, the god would do more than bypass the essential role of the mother in biological, social and emotional terms. He also bypasses the rules of dramatic enactment on which Dionysiac tragedy thrives." The results, she argues, are improvisations on every level: a false oracle is given; the chorus reneges on a promise; a boy undertakes his own initiation rites. Everywhere we see "the freedom to play." And it is in reveling in this freedom that the spectators solve the intellectual puzzles of the drama and find the satisfaction they need to participate properly in the happy ending.[74]

But there may another layer of significance to Apollo's plan. Kreousa's embrace is part of a symbolic system of suffering inherent in identity, such that the creation of the relationship of parent and child creates a creature who relentlessly consumes resources and eventually inevitably displaces. Abandonment is the parent's apprehension of this reality writ large, an effort to do away with his or her doom beforehand. But when fire marks something terrifying by burning on it in the *Ion*, we seem to see that this natal doom is irreversible. Somehow, abandonment does not prevent the parents' fate at their child's hand. Kreousa's embrace stages the heart of belonging (1401–1405):

Κρέουσα· λείψω δὲ βωμὸν τόνδε, κεἰ θανεῖν με χρή.

Ἴων· λάζυσθε τήνδε· θεομανὴς γὰρ ἥλατο
βωμοῦ λιποῦσα ξόανα· δεῖτε δ᾽ ὠλένας.

Κρέουσα· σφάζοντες οὐ λήγοιτ᾽ ἄν· ὡς ἀνθέξομαι
καὶ τῆσδε καὶ σοῦ τῶν τ᾽ ἔσω κεκρυμμένων.

Kreousa: I shall leave this altar even if I must die.

Ion: Grab her! Maddened by the god she has leapt away
and left the images of the altar! Bind her arms!

Kreousa: Go ahead and slaughter me! Even so I shall lay hold of
this vessel and you and the things hidden within!

She welcomes a violent death as an act of extravagant confidence and joy — just as Xouthos did when he realized that he had found a child.[75]

The gods would have concealed this moment by substituting the recognition that creates Ion's political and social identities. These structures, the *Ion* suggests, are those that society arranges in order to conceal the embrace that means death. It seems that Kreousa's human and emotional needs were not beneath Apollo's concern — far from it. Those needs encapsulate or stand for all that the god wants to conceal in order to secure Athens's future. As noted at the end of the previous chapter, the question remains whether Euripides constructs the twisted structures of familial identity to symbolize and thus criticize larger structures in Athens's political culture. Apollo's design of hiding Kreousa's embrace from plain sight might then be seen as an apparatus of Athens's *nomoi*, another of culture's ways of containing the unruly in the family. Again, it has not been my aim to explore this possibility in greater detail, but it may be so. In the Conclusion, I turn to another of Euripides' tragedies, the *Bacchae*, in which the degree to which the familial maps the political is much more transparent.

The *Ion* brings abandonment and embrace very close to each other in terms of natal identity, as close as they can come and still allow for Ion to go on to his destiny in Athens. Kreousa's embrace shuts off the epiphany in which the violent stereotype of stepmother and the natal reality in terms of identity seemed perfectly poised and synonymous. After she is allowed to embrace Ion, she cannot or will not see the problem any longer, and at Athena's direct behest, Ion also shortly gives up his objections. The embrace forecloses further inquiry. Freud constructs this finesse for his case history and tips the balance in favor of theory rather than perfectly poised, irresolvable revelation. Grusha and the Wolf Man cannot be doing anything together, unless it is an equivalent of the primal scene that supplements rather than challenges. In the tragedy, the gods seem to represent the social force that requires trauma to end in favor of identities that serve the larger causes of the state. Plainly, Freud needs a similar outcome, in service to psychoanalysis, and he is the deus ex machina in "From the History of an Infantile Neurosis."

It is remarkable that the mother's embrace is a convenient fiction, not an inherent end point, in the quest for identity. Freud's theory, of course, notoriously elided it from serious consideration, but even the *Ion* makes clear enough the contingent nature of the maternal embrace in the gods' plan to bypass it. Apollo's plan, which is the one that everyone who matters leaves for Athens endorsing, does not need Kreousa's embrace at all. We get it almost as a sop to our sentimentality. Recreations of Kreousa's suffering and Ion's longing to know who he is teach us to crave their reunion as a dramatic climax, but we also have to learn that their embrace is a more torturous and ambiguous moment than we might have imagined it would be at the outset.

Conclusion

"But your parents lived through the Depression — they don't let go of things."

Even if you didn't live through the Depression, it's hard to let go of things. . . .

I realize now that I don't need any of my parents' stuff to hold on to their memory, because the best part of who they are is already inside me and very much alive.

KEVA ROSENFELD

This book has looked at the choices that bind a family together and form a romance of belonging — a tale of the past with present reality. Since that past looked into the future as it made its choices, the present stands in an uneasy relationship to the past. In our consciousness, the present has hegemony over its past, but an unconscious anxiety remains whether this present is the future that the past made its choices by. At the outset, I set Euripides' tragedy beside Freud's case history because, among other reasons, each frames and studies this paradox in the most concrete of ways, as an encounter between parent and child. For the audience of either text, its thrill and anxiety resonate with intimate experience, since we have all been chosen to belong or not.[1] But Keva Rosenfeld's reflections about disposing of his parents' household goods capture the reciprocity of choice that I have tried to illustrate throughout this study: the trauma of the romance of belonging registers for all whose identities are determined in it. The child's trauma is perilous and abiding, but psychoanalysis and tragedy also turn out to agree about this — we can be terrified by our children and what they represent.[2]

Rosenfeld's sentiment can be heard as a kind of Rorschach test. His words can thrill us by making us realize that our child feels he is the best part of ourselves —

what better measure of success could any parent wish for? This seems the happiest outcome of the romance of belonging, with a present that keeps the past alive within itself. Or we can be appalled at a self-centeredness that concludes that once that which is in the child is summed up, nothing else from his parents' lives need be saved. From the children's point of view, it seems, their present is the only prism through which the past is refracted. When we contemplate the spectacle of choice that children make — *this* I will take from my parents, but *that* can go to the yard sale — do we console ourselves with the comfort that it has always been so? This study did not set out to suggest which reaction, which way of hearing the present's triumph, is privileged by Euripides or Freud. Instead, it has examined how both tragedy and case history are romances of origin that arouse unconscious remnants of ancient emotion regarding the whole process of becoming part of a family — or not.

The romance of belonging need not concern an entity as concrete (and intimate) as a family, however. It can also be the tale cultures use to define themselves, or even a history of the ideas that a people embraces as part of its intellectual or spiritual identity. Wherever an anxiety about identity resides within a person or culture — a sense that something crucial lies unmarked and irrecoverable in the past — we can sense the remnants of this romance. We may also perceive the strategies used to quiet the anxiety and thereby learn something further about the neurosis, whether it be in an individual or some larger entity.

To suggest briefly the form these more abstract versions of the romance of belonging can take, let us consider another provocative coincidence between Euripides and Freud. Both turned once again, late in their lives, to a final meditation on a child's origins, and each was thinking in much different terms about the matter. Before they died, Euripides and Freud left their homes for new lands. Like so many other Jews in Austria, Freud could not bring himself to admit his personal peril from the Nazis until it was nearly too late. Even his worst enemies tried to help — Carl Jung offered money for his evacuation — but Freud found his life in Vienna too difficult to leave behind until two of his children were briefly held by the Gestapo.[3] He finally fled to London in 1938, where, dying of cancer, he finished "Moses and Monotheism" in the few months before his physician helped him commit suicide, as agreed.[4] Euripides left Athens after 408 for the royal court of Macedon, where he wrote his masterpiece the *Bacchae*. We don't know why he left. It was said that he got disgusted at losing so often to inferior poets in the annual tragic competition; the year his son produced the *Bacchae*, in 405/404, he won the competition posthumously.[5] This is the sort of precious irony ancient biographers love, however, and other, seemingly more popular dramatic poets were also lured away from Athens. Aeschylus died in Sicily, and Agathon, the tragic poet in whose house Plato's *Symposium* is set, also retired to Macedon.

When Euripides turns to a final traumatic tale of origins with an abandoned child at its heart, it is a return to the mythic typology whereby the child's survival is a sign of his (divine) greatness, and his inevitable return stages his (mortal) family's ruin. As predicted by the mythic typology, the *Bacchae* stages regime change at Thebes in the person of an abandoned child, but that child is Dionysus, and when the child is a god, the nature of change is disturbingly different. The divine signification of human ruin does not stand outside the debacle but is implicated in it.[6] Even Dionysus's separation from his natal family is complicated by his divine nature. His mother, the Theban princess Semele, dies when she demands that her lover Zeus appear to her as he does to Hera. His flaming epiphany burns her up, and Zeus is just able to rescue the child from her womb and stitch it into his own thigh. Upon his "second" birth, Dionysus has to be hidden from Hera's wrath in the far east, and the tales of his inexorable return to Thebes chart his encounters with unbelievers and scoffers, all of whom are made to acknowledge the god's power. Euripides' *Bacchae* dramatizes Dionysus's ultimate encounter with his natal kin in Thebes itself, and it ends very badly for his family. Pentheus's refusal to recognize his cousin as a god entangles him in the worst sort of embrace imaginable, that of a mother who cannot recognize him for who he is. Agave sees only an intruder in the god's mysteries and rips him to shreds. In a disturbing master narrative of a god's dominion, the *Bacchae* deconstructs the very city Dionysus claims by dismembering its king.

Readers of this tragedy have long understood that it concerns the destruction of more than Thebes and is no mere cautionary tale about faithlessness.[7] Dionysus's reunion with his faithless natal city, in the person of Pentheus, exposes the frailty of human resources against such a godhead. This young king, whose mother and aunts are compelled by the god to lead maddened Theban women in Bacchic rites on the mountain in retribution for their unbelief, cannot resist divine challenge to the political structures that define him. He plainly does not have the physical power, and his lack of faith deafens him to the miraculous in Dionysiac worship. Most crucially, he cannot resist his own unruly Bacchic nature. Despite his apparently firmly constructed identity as male authority, Pentheus finds this god irresistibly attractive — disguised in the person of a mysterious stranger with bedroom eyes and long, silky hair — and admits he wants to act the voyeur on his mother's sexual abandon. Theban civic culture cannot contain or account for Pentheus, and neither his sense of authority as the city's king nor the sophistries of his elderly grandfather, Cadmus, and the prophet Tiresias provide him with the means to silence the god's allure. The disproportionality of Dionysiac frenzy defies human acquiescence as well as resistance.

Within the tale of Pentheus's destruction, the *Bacchae* offers an ever-receding horizon of interrogation when it comes to the structures of human culture meant to define (and thereby restrain) individuals. Charles Segal (1997), whose study of the play addresses these structures from several key perspectives, including ritual and gender, finally addresses the very fundamentals of Athenian intellectuality. Dionysus's violent return to his natal origin stages the death of poetic tradition itself as a vehicle for handling, in Segal's words, "the individual citizen's experience and understanding of life."[8] As such the play participates in a wider clash of genres and habits of thought in the late fifth century, as poetry yields to prose and myth to "philosophy and conceptual thought." Segal identifies verse with tradition and prose with the future: "As the function of literary expression changes from transmitting traditional norms to exploring new ideas and opening new intellectual territories, there is an inevitable shift from verse, with its convenient mnemonic devices . . . to prose, which, as the ancient stylists called it, is "loosed" or "released" from the constraints of a traditional form."[9] The *Bacchae* stages the peril of trying to grapple with new ideas within old forms, yet tragedy itself as a genre is oddly situated within progress away from a poetic tradition. The audience needs the tragic spectacle to make sense of its intellectual reality, but that reality makes the tragic spectacle no longer possible.[10]

Regarding Pentheus's shocking dismemberment, Segal perceives the *Bacchae* to be grappling with irreconcilable principles, whether these are of god's nature, human gender, or the needs of the polis. Segal's study relies on a conceptualization of conflict in binary terms, much as the ancients seem to have done, but Victoria Wohl, for one, disputes the validity of the polarity itself. She points out that Dionysus's disruption in Thebes is not about the oedipal triangle of the family (and its larger mirror in terms of hierarchy in the state). Instead, identity bursts the integral boundaries of self through a process of "becoming-," an expression used by the psychoanalytic theorists Gilles Deleuze and Félix Guattari for the fertility of the unconscious that is not configured oedipally.[11] Thus Pentheus passes through stages of "becoming-other" with reference to gender, family, state, and self before ultimately "becoming-nothing" through *sparagmos*, a ritual honoring Dionysus that is ghastly perverted into his mother's shredding of his body.[12] If Wohl is correct, the *Bacchae* stages a version of unconscious anxiety that is utterly open and without polarities or any hierarchical structure to organize and in some sense alleviate it.

Dionysus is a crucial figure for this endless chasm of anxiety and as such gives us a new perspective on the romance of belonging. A god who is both the ultimate insider and the alien outsider, his abandonment and return signify how completely unbounded the possibilities might be in the romance of belonging. Structures usually stated as oppositions are exposed as illusory, strategic clichés to reassert boundaries.[13] In the *Ion*, Apollo and the other Olympians strain to shut down mortal anxiety about the hero's birth and abandonment in order to establish him as the token of Athenian destiny. In the *Bacchae*, however, the god himself is the abandoned child seeking reunion with his natal origins; instead of serving as the embodiment of imperial control, Dionysus marks the very lack of boundaries that seem to terrify the gods of the *Ion*. The romance of belonging, in short, need not be a study in how to make sure a master narrative of origins emerges from the unconscious; the very structures that should shut down the anxiety — the gods, in this case — announce that there is no final answer when it comes to identity. Such is the supple nature of this romance when it is dramatized as tragedy.

Freud designs "Moses and Monotheism" to deconstruct Jewish identity in the person of its greatest hero.[14] He states his intent at the outset: "To deprive a people of the man whom they take pride in as the greatest of their sons is not a thing to be gladly or carelessly undertaken, least of all by someone who is himself one of them. But we cannot allow any such reflection to induce us to put the truth aside in favour of what are supposed to be national interests" (*SE* 23: 7). Freud discovers in Moses' abandonment an effort to conceal the hero's true origins as an Egyptian. He argues for a kind of reverse family romance, by which the lowly Hebrew slaves are responsible for the abandonment, while the powerful and noble Egyptians give the nurture. The Jews are the neurotics who need to account for their association with such a strong and dynamic leader, an early and loyal adherent of the Pharaoh Akhenaton and his monotheism.

Freud does not explore the traumatic consequences of Moses' abandonment further than as a marker for a historical reality concealed within mythic tradition. His real interest is in the Jews themselves, those neurotics who eventually become the sternest adherents of true monotheism. Freud affiliates this monotheism with abstraction and symbol as the bases of thought.[15] The Jews' neurosis originates in their ancient repudiation and murder of Moses, the site of their guilt and longing, and abandonment is part of a system of signs and markers for this primal trauma. Freud argues further that this neurosis is the heart of the Jewish triumph: it takes tragic guilt to sharpen the longing to adhere or to belong (89–90).

Freud's deconstruction of Moses helps him to frame monotheism as man's liberation from "sensuality," that need to see and feel the evidence. This reliance on the sensual characterizes both the primitive human and the feminine.[16] Richard Armstrong has recently described the links between the intellectual progression involved, on the one hand, and the movement from "the mother to the father," in Freud's terms (*SE* 23: 113), on the other: "Freud's Moses furthers the rational trajectory of civilization in turn by insisting on a total prohibition against making images of God, thereby bringing it about that a 'sensory perception was given second place to what may be called an abstract idea — a triumph of intellectuality over sensuality or, more strictly speaking, an instinctual renunciation, with all its necessary psychological consequences.' "[17] In the intellectual polarity of the sensual and rational, one axis is occupied by the mother and the evidentiary. For the Jews, it yields to the sterner demands of the father and inferential logic on the other axis. For one last time in his life, Freud champions a hero whose career models psychoanalysis and its conquest over the neurotic longing to generate repetitions of past trauma. Abandonment, as finally staged by Freud theoretically, stands at the point where the image is obliterated.

Yet for all that Freud wishes to eliminate the sensual, he keeps recreating models for us to contemplate. When reading "Moses and Monotheism," one can't help wondering whether Freud honestly believed his romance of monotheism. It depends on such a topsy-turvy universe — Egyptian nobility co-opting a remnant nomadic tribe in the suburbs (18–19), and a convenient set of distant cousins worshipping Yahweh the volcano god in nearby Meribah-Kadesh, an oasis somewhere south of Palestine (33ff). Yet Freud has relied on his lifelong intellectual habits and done his scientific research, citing James Breasted and Eduard Meyer as well as Herodotus. Presumably he does accept these rationalized versions of Egyptian and Hebrew mythology.[18] Freud cannot get the fit right between "historical" structure and his theory of monotheism, but in the end it seems not to matter.[19] His passion is to define the Jews' unique status as the sternest adherents of monotheism. Theirs was a special alchemy of guilt and reliance on the intellectual abstract, such that they participate in a type of religious neurosis that draws its strength from "the return of the repressed" (78ff). In exposing the neurotic basis for Judaism, Freud offers them as a final, admirable image of the power of the unconscious.

Armstrong closes on the problematic nature of Freud's patent admiration for the Jews whose myth of the abandoned child he set about to deconstruct. He correctly reminds us that Freud's project in "Moses and Monotheism" is not to be read as a sort of "death-bed lapse into some suitably modified form of piety" (248). Rather, he sees Freud's deployment of Judaism as strategy for enriching psychoanalysis, such that we too understand "the narrative of psychoanalysis's development" better for having contemplated how Freud thought "his way out of Judaism" (248). I agree — for Freud, no spectacle of the neurotic recycling of repressed guilt is too sacred to be grist for the mill. Yet his continuing need for the neurotic spectacle is arresting. He swears that psychoanalysis, as the pinnacle of intellectuality, finally resolves and moves beyond the return of the repressed, but he cannot give up constructing models, even when he flees to Britain.

The longing to stop our quest for origins finally inheres in a strategy of abstraction but even that turns out to rely on seeing them. Typically, Euripides makes tragedy out of this spectacle and Freud argues for psychoanalysis. The consumption of the past by the present is terrifying to witness — it shatters all that comforts and structures. Or the process heals, because it imposes structures that allow the present to go forward into its own moment of choice and peril, when it chooses its future and is consumed by it. Either way, we always seem poised between the belonging that inheres in the image and that which accepts abstraction. Which of these is by analogy the embrace and which is abandonment? Euripides and Freud teach us that it scarcely matters, because in both choices there is violence and the recognition that we are where we belong.

Notes

Introduction

1. I use the term "primal scene" in Freud's original sense. For later, extended use of it, see Chapter 1 below.

2. See Armstrong (2005) and Winter (1999). "The intimacy of psychoanalysis and Greek tragedy almost goes without saying — whenever we think of Oedipus, we think of Freud," Winter writes (27), one of many such nods toward the obvious link. She goes on to question the self-evident nature of the link by pointing out that it "depends . . . upon the theoretical appropriation by psychoanalysis of a particular play," namely, Sophocles' *Oedipus Tyrannus* (28). Winter further discusses Freud's own sense of how tragedy's engagement of its audience models his aims for his readers. There are, of course, many psychoanalytic readings of *Oedipus Tyrannus*; see, e.g., Pucci (1992), Segal (1994), and Nussbaum (1994).

3. Winter (1999) 68.

4. Page duBois (1988) states Freud's links to antiquity as part of his "mythicizing" of the " 'metaphysical' opposition of the two sexes" (11); as a feminist, she challenges the intellectual hegemony created by those links.

5. Winter's (1999) emphasis on "parricide" and its continued tight focus on the oedipal moment is noteworthy; her express purpose, of course, is to study the Freudian construction ("institution") of knowledge, not to expand or correct it. She also argues for Freud's intent to establish psychoanalysis over against other emerging disciplinary studies of culture, such as anthropology and sociology. For other criticism by later psychoanalysts and by feminists of Freud's limits with respect to the oedipal, see Deleuze and Guattari (1977), Abraham and Torok (1986), and Sprengnether (1990).

6. Armstrong (2005), 253n5, defines "archive" as "the powers and principles that order [the physical archives of antiquity] into monuments, evidence, and information, or that deploy them to mediate historical consciousness"; he also quotes (9) Derrida's *Archive Fever* (1995), which uses the term "archontic principle."

7. Winter's (1999) discussion, 55–69, is crucial for the relationship between tragedy and psychoanalysis; she highlights tragedy's role of "modeling" the primal drama of parricide.

8. Freud, *SE* 4–5: 262.

9. Psychoanalysis also sets itself up as the new atheistic "tragic necessity"; see Winter (1999) 55. The issue of spectators' emotional engagement with the performance remains the subject of much study; see Konstan (2005) 13–26 and Bassi (2005) 251–270.

10. Spence (1994) 118, who studies the rhetorical strategy of the modern case history in 118–141.

11. Others have discussed the degree to which Freud understood this and structured

his case histories accordingly. In addition to Spence (1994), see also Armstrong (2005) 134ff, on the problematic of the case history as part of what psychoanalysis does to the relationship between past and present. See Johnson (2001) for a specific consideration of the Wolf Man's case history.

12. See Winter (1999) 27ff, for a theoretical discussion of this replacement.

13. The most comprehensive study of the typology is provided by Huys (1995), with further references. Euripides seems even to construct Ion as an anti-Oedipus on the basis of whom Athenians could think about their own destiny vis-à-vis their arch-rival Thebes. See esp. Segal (1999) 100–101, who notes, "The *Ion* reenvisages the action of the *Oedipus* through the eyes of Jocasta," and Zeitlin (1990), on the studied juxtaposition of Thebes's failed enterprise to Athens's glory, and (1996c), on the representation of Ion. Both children are cast out by their parents and end up as kings in their natal cities, but Ion is produced by an illicit and violent encounter with Apollo, while Oedipus is the product of legitimate but forbidden mating by king and queen. Oedipus is constructed as the consummate insider, and his childhood in the court of Corinth does not efface that fact; Ion must be redeemed and brought back into Athens's royal lineage, but through a kind of stealth that confirms his inherent outsider status. Each ends up with a family structure that symbolizes his civic role, Ion as the final founding father of Athens and Oedipus as the incestuous knot of Thebes's ruin. Oedipus is both fatherless and too closely affiliated with his mother and children; Ion gains two fathers, one public and acknowledged, one secret, and two roles for his mother, also one public, as threatening stepmother, and one secret, as his "real," natal mother.

14. On Oedipus as the hero of psychoanalysis, the man who solved the riddle of the unconscious by recognizing his foulest deeds (and our desires), and the role of the heroic in Freud's career generally, see Winter (1999) 30ff; Breger (2000) passim; and Armstrong (2005) 47–58. Recent studies of Freud's curriculum at his *Gymnasium* in Vienna suggest that he would never have read the *Ion* in Greek, as he did the *Oedipus Tyrannus*. See Johnson (2001) on the possible relationships among the real Pankejeff, Freud's "patient," and the Wolf Man.

15. On this matter, Kartiganer (1984), 12, already suggests an inherent conflict in Freud's relationship with the science of psychoanalysis: "From one perspective he [Freud] insists on the basically scientific nature of his work: he is in search of a causative moment in time, an event in the real world that can be discovered through a method of neutral, detached observation. Behind the uncanny arrangements of the self-deluding mind, which remembers and forgets in the same symptom, lies a concealed core of objectively recoverable evidence. But from another perspective Freud's quest seems not so much the scientist's search for facts as the romantic artist's determination to subvert any scene or structure that points too surely at bedrock and the end to all investigation." I investigate more thoroughly what we might understand about this "romantic" nature.

16. Armstrong (2005) 12–13. His first quotation uses Bourdieu's *Logic of Practice* (1990b) 55–57; his second uses Bourdieu's *In Other Words* (1990a) 63.

17. On the concept of "improvisation," see Armstrong (2005), 27–28 and 116–117, for the specific pattern of Heinrich Schliemann. Johnson (2001) uses the notion as the cornerstone of his argument on how Freud manipulated the patient known as the Wolf Man.

18. Armstrong (2005) 12; and although he uses a Freudian concept — of compulsion — he contextualizes it through Bourdieu: "Thus Freud's compulsive interest in antiquity is part of a complex social network that has a particular time and place, a network he both inhabits and creates through his social and scientific improvisations" (26).

19. As Winter (1999), 12, puts it, "Thus the dispositions of a given *habitus* provide for a fit between desires and socially available positions."

20. Winter (1999) 14.

21. Ibid. 12–14.

22. Breger (2000) 386.

23. Ibid. 2, 22ff.

24. Winter (1999) also acknowledges this practice of Freud's.

25. To use Winter's categories, instead of looking at the unconscious (or some other notion of our psyche), we study social processes that create our very sense of such a thing; we substitute the external for the internal. Winter (1999) 12–14.

26. Bourdieu, for instance, argues that even our sense that there might be a point of origin is constructed. As Winter summarizes Bourdieu's strictures on Freud's notion of unconscious: "To understand the unconscious as ultimate cause is explicitly to render internal what has already been incorporated through social processes" (Winter [1999] 13). See Bourdieu (1990b) 56 and (1977) 92–93.

27. Deleuze and Guattari (1977), 55–55, speak of the problem in terms of locating the point where psychoanalysis "started going bad." It is ever-receding, and they choose Freud's own moment, the "discovery of Oedipus."

28. See Armstrong (2005) 244, who notes Loraux (1995) 192, on the ancient awareness of origins. Freud constantly linked what he believed to be analogies in originary layers: primitives, infants, and neurotics all stand in the beginning of their own structures. Placing the ancient Greeks within this analogy was problematic, however; see Armstrong (2005) 48–52, and Winter (1999).

29. Griffith (2005) 98–110, esp. 108ff; his references are useful. He studies tragedy as an "oneiric realm," a phrase he borrows from Charles Segal, for exploring spectators' experience of the dramatic performance. For the "oneiric realm" as a site that approximates the work of dreaming for spectators, see Segal (1994) 88–89; see also Segal (1997).

30. Slater (1968) was an early sustained effort to understand Athenian society through the psychoanalytic dynamic; Alford (1992) 2–3, assesses Slater's success more favorably than that of Devereux (1976).

31. Alford (1992) 8–9.

32. DuBois (1988).

33. Wohl (2003) 19–29, for whom desire is "deeply ideological," but also a site where norms can be interrogated and challenged; on the unconscious and ideology, see esp. 26ff. See also Butler (1997). Wohl has done much to advance the enterprise of reading the ancient Athenians in psychoanalytic terms through varied approaches. In applying psychoanalytic principles to Athenian drama in *Intimate Commerce* (1998), she deliberately eschews Freudian categories as too constrained by Freud's nineteenth-century *habitus* (not her word), but nevertheless reads contests over women as sites of unconscious desire in men for status and control. Most recently (2005), Wohl has demonstrated how great the yield in provocative thought can be when later psychoanalytic theory, such as that of Deleuze and Guattari, is brought to bear on tragedy; see my Conclusion.

34. Armstrong (2005) 5; he also argues that Freud's psychoanalysis may well be "the return of repressed antiquity, distorted to be sure by modern desire, yet still bearing the telltale traces of the ancient archive."

35. See Armstrong (2005) 7, who articulates the issues with Freud particularly well. The question of Freud's relevance has been rehearsed yet again on the occasion of his 150th birthday in 2006. Other moments have arisen with the publication of further origi-

nal material of Freud's, such as Masson (1985), and, with particular relevance to the case of the Wolf Man, Obholzer (1982).

ONE: The Romance of Belonging

Epigraphs: Euripides, *Ion* 1291–1299, following ms order; Freud, "From the History of an Infantile Neurosis," *SE* 17: 9; the Wolf Man, quoted in Obholzer (1982) 32.

1. Dimock (1995) 54. This sense of something missed accelerated with the publication of the Wolf Man's various autobiographical works by Muriel Gardiner (1972) and then Karin Obholzer's account (1982) of her conversations with the elderly man. The work of Abraham and Torok (1986), for instance, springs from their assessment of the Wolf Man's accounts in Gardiner. For the impact of Obholzer's publication, see Lukacher (1986) 136ff.

2. See Katherina Zacharia's recent study of the *Ion* for a comprehensive survey of work on this tragedy through 2003.

3. See Johnson (2001) for a detailed study of the case history; Johnson's work has proved helpful, but his project relies, by design, on the work of Abraham and Torok (1986) and is consequently "strongly partisan."

4. In *SE* 17: 1–122; Freud had already published the dream of wolves in 1913, in "Fairy Tales in Dreams" (*SE* 12: 283–287), and discussed the case in 1914, in "On the History of Psycho-Analytic Movement" (*SE* 14: 54). He would continue to discuss it as late as 1937, in "Analysis Terminable and Interminable" (*SE* 23: 217ff).

5. See Gay (1998) 290.

6. See Armstrong (2005) 151ff, on the significance of Freud's fight with Jung for both the history and the myth of psychoanalysis; see also Lukacher (1986) 139ff, for the primal scene's importance in Freud's effort to retain control of the IPA. Johnson (2001), 2–3, disputes the accepted line on the significance of the political struggle in Freud's shaping of the case history.

7. Such as the age of the patient, the nature of the relationship of the sexual partners to each other and to the patient, and on whether the scene is to be understood literally or as a fantasy; see Norman (1998) 121.

8. Little (1993); see further in this chapter.

9. See esp. Lukacher (1986); in Chapter 2, I attempt to avoid this confusion in my discussion of the text's authoritative status by using the notion of a foundational narrative.

10. Obholzer (1982).

11. A dialogue most recently taken up by Johnson (2001) under the influence of Abraham and Torok (1976). See further in this chapter.

12. See Breger (2000) 121, on the brevity of Freud's early analyses; see also Gardiner (1972) 48–82, for the Wolf Man's own account of the years preceding his analysis; and Gay (1998) 285–84. In his fourth chapter, Lukacher (1986) studies the dialogue between doctor and patient.

13. Brunswick published her account of that re-analysis as "A Supplement to Freud's 'History of an Infantile Neurosis,'" *International Journal of Psycho-Analysis* 9 (1928); see Gardiner (1972) 263–307. Freud's only comment about the treatment in 1919–1920 was made in the final footnote added to "From the History of an Infantile Neurosis" in 1923 (121–22). After his analysis with Brunswick, Pankejeff's mental well-being was followed intermittently by the psychoanalytic community; see Gardner 311–366, for her encounters with him.

14. Periodically, Freud attempts a chronology, and at the end of the text, he gives a comprehensive summary; what is striking is the effort Freud must make repeatedly to clarify the complex sequence of what was going on in the Wolf Man's psyche; see 106ff and especially his closing note, added in 1923.

15. Not a belief, however, that Freud entirely accepted; the incident with Grusha, discussed in detail in Chapter 4, complicated matters in the analyst's opinion.

16. Freud in fact comments that the Wolf Man's response to his sister's suicide nearly forced him to concede Alfred Adler's claim that patients' neuroses developed from unresolved "will to power," or the "self-assertive instinct" (22–23).

17. Pankejeff never recalled the incident, although he claims that Freud promised him he would; Obholzer (1982) 36. See also the discussion of Lukacher (1986) 136–156.

18. There are a number of these additions throughout the case as well as a coda; Freud says that the case history was largely composed right after the analysis was completed, in 1914, but not published then because of the war. See Johnson (2001) 18–19, 29–30, who disputes this reasoning.

19. I quote the German from *GW* 12 (1986): 37.

20. See Armstrong (2005) 134–140, on Freud's use of the archaeological metaphor for a narrative of the past.

21. Blum (1980b) 368.

22. Norman (1998) 121.

23. Lukacher (1986), Johnson (2001), and Armstrong (2005) provide further discussions of studies raised here.

24. Brunswick's desire to affiliate her findings with Freud's have been seen in this title by others; see Lukacher (1986) 160–161.

25. See Esmen (1973), quoted in Blum (1980) 367; the possibility of the scene being either reality or fantasy seems to be part of this problem.

26. Johnson (2001), 7ff, reviews key developments.

27. Lacan (1977) 96–97; see also Lukacher (1986) 28ff.

28. Deleuze and Guattari (1977).

29. Kalinich (1991), 167, remarks in reference to the Wolf Man, "I can think of few fates worse than having one's life and psychology reviewed and re-interpreted by countless generations of psychoanalysts. To me, this is a vision of Hell that rivals both Dante and Steven Spielberg."

30. Abraham and Torok ([1976] 1986). For a consideration of their analysis see Mahony (1984); Johnson (2000), who develops the case further; and Lukacher (1986) 156–164.

31. Masson (1984). See also Kartiganer (1985) 27, who notes, "Now [Freud] is no longer the detached detective, methodically plugging symptoms and memories into a master plan, but a committed, desiring individual, caught up in a contemporary dispute within the psychoanalytic community and exercising a very personal and characteristic mode of behavior." Breger (2000), 273ff, assesses the difficulties of the primal scene from the perspective of modern work on memory and other factors as evidence that Freud's work as a therapist in this case is "static."

32. Johnson (2000) 18; see his account of the notion in Abraham and Torok, 15ff; he considers Freud's crypt to contain material concerning his infant brother's death. On Abraham and Torok, see also Lukacher (1986) 154ff.

33. Grene (1987), 7ff, calls the moment a "primal sin." The Lydian king Candaules forces his servant Gyges to witness his wife naked; she catches sight of Gyges watching her from behind the door and offers him a simple choice the next day: either he must die or he

must kill her husband and marry her. Gyges chooses the second option. Grene compares Herodotus's version of the story with Plato's in the *Republic* (359d). Devereux (1976), 299ff, also reads dreams in Euripidean tragedy as restagings of the primal scene.

34. Lukacher (1986) 35ff.

35. Little (1993) 306ff.

36. Little (1993) 305: "The 'primal scene of racism,' then, denotes the site (as well as the sight) where an audience at one and the same time reactively and proactively constructs the signification of race — in this instance, blackness. I am insisting on a noncausal relationship: an audience does not simply become reflexive *after* blackness is visualized. Response and creation are concurrent."

37. Sprengnether (1990); her discussion of the Wolf Man is on 72–74; the quotation is on 232. I discuss Sprengnether in greater detail below.

38. See duBois (1988) 8g, who draws on the work of Deleuze and Guattari in *Anti-Oedipus* (1977); see also Wohl (2005) 137–138, 145–146.

39. Johnson (2000) 11, who cites other critics in his second note.

40. That urgency, as we see in Chapters 2 and 3, can be written as a fight over authority or a matter of commerce. In either case, an aspect of belonging is spelled out. To belong is to submit to a structure, but who gets to write it? To belong is to agree to pay high and enduring costs. The urgency also, perversely, makes apparent the attractiveness of abandonment.

41. I do not mean to read Freud as a patient, however. If the Wolf Man's case history is like a romance in its need of analysis to make sense out of it, it is most definitely and consciously suffused by Freud's purposes and theoretical structures.

42. For Ion's parentage, see the Hesiodic *Catalogue of Women*, fr. 10a 20–23 (ed. Solmsen, Merkelbach, and West); see also West (1985) 57, 106–7. See also Parker (1986) 206–7, who summarizes what fifth-century Athenians probably knew about Ion; and Zacharia (2003) 48–55.

43. Euripides may actually create these origins for him; see Zacharia (2003) 48n1, and Parker (1986) 207n80, for the relevant materials and arguments.

44. The name in Greek is the present participle of the verb "to go"; see Lee (1997) at 661.

45. On the play's structure, see Solmsen (1934) and Wolff (1965) 172.

46. See the fourth chapter of Zacharia (2003), esp. 150–155, on the varying tones of comedy and tragedy within the single drama as a key Euripidean strategy for investigating the "dialogic vision of the truth," the subject of 176–182.

47. See Zacharia (2003) 183ff.

48. Earlier positions on either side of the question are succinctly summarized by Lloyd (1986) 33. See Neitzel (1988) 278–79, for a later attempt to justify Apollo's oracle. See also Yunis (1988) 122ff, for a reading of the relationship between Ion and Apollo as one of "reciprocal allegiance." For more recent attempts to read the play as an indictment of the god, however, see Hartigan (1991). See Saxenhouse (1986) 264, who reads Apollo's absence as symbolic of "what must be forgotten as cities and races are founded." For a discussion that centers on Apollo as if a character in the drama, see Sinos (1982); and see also Mastronarde (1975) 163 and n. 4, who discounts the utility of focusing on Apollo in interpreting the play. This focus is replicated in the recent comprehensive study by Zacharia (2003) 103–149; she devotes her entire third chapter to Apollo and reads the play "at least in part, as Euripides' meditation upon Apollo" (105). Zacharia also refers to the god's "absent presence" (104). Her study, however, incorporates other important perspectives, as indicated in notes below.

49. See esp. the second chapter of Zacharia (2003) 44–102, which thoroughly analyzes the play in these terms. See also Walsh (1978); Saxenhouse (1986); Loraux (1990); Ogden (1996) 170–172; and Zeitlin (1996c).

50. The *Ion* makes Erichthonios Kreousa's grandfather (267), but he is not in other tales about the founding of the city, which had a complicated and often contradictory set of stories about the lineage of its early kings. See Parker (1986) 187–214 for a reconstruction of the main lines; also Zacharia (2003) 60–65; and West (1985) 106–108, who calls Erechtheus, Kreousa's father, "the big spider at the heart of Attic myth."

51. Saxenhouse (1986), 259, 271, and passim, reads the study of autochthony as problematic. Loraux (1990) and Zeitlin (1996c) read it as a celebration of Athens's strength; both assume that the dominant culture watching the play—that of Athenian male citizens—would look for "drama . . . designed as an education for male citizens in the democratic city" (Zeitlin [1996d] 346). Hence the audience expected, beneath explorations of the travails of others, a confirmation of the ideologies that buttress this project. More specifically, Loraux (1990), 172ff, is interested in the representation of Kreousa as the site of a complex set of origins, both for Ion himself and for the city. Zeitlin concerns herself with the construction of social identities for Ion. See also Segal (1999). Zacharia (2003), 99–102, addresses the complexity in Euripides' creation of expectations that he then "is at pains to frustrate" (102); Euripides' project is "humanist" in its drive for honesty. See also Ebbott (2003) 80–81, on the play's ambiguity regarding the fertility of origins.

52. Thus Loraux (1990), 168, writes: "The sole subject of the play is Athens."

53. Rabinowitz (1993) 191. Other recent critics have not ignored Kreousa's suffering; see, e.g., Loraux (1990) 173, who locates "everything that is truly tragic" about the play in Kreousa's rape and suffering. Reading the *Ion* as a romantic comedy was popular among an older generation of critics, such as Conacher (1959, 1967) and, in a famously witty essay, Knox (1979). This perspective is considered again by Matthiessen (1990); see also, by implication although not explicitly, by Huys (1995); and Zacharia (2003).

54. Hoffer (1996) 316.

55. That is, Rabinowitz's feminist approach frankly aims at privileging Kreousa's pain as a woman and thus minimizing the pain inflicted upon Ion or upon the state; Hoffer's approach, by contrast, reads the damage done to the state.

56. As has been discussed recently by Segal (1999) 94ff. See also Ebbott (2003) and Ogden (1996) for two studies of illegitimacy in Greek culture that take account of the *Ion*.

57. The two references are vv 915 and 951.

58. On the multiple versions of Ion's abandonment and their disorienting effects, see Rabinowitz (1993) 203–204; but also Rosivach (1977) 289 and Loraux (1990) 175–177. Both Wolff (1965), 170–173, and Zeitlin (1996c), 293–300, remark on how the play simultaneously moves towards a symbolic reenactment of that act as Kreousa plots to kill Ion.

59. On the notion of the romance as a fantasy version of origins, see use of the term in Armstrong (2005) 24–25.

60. Lacan (1988), 6, 78–89, posits another "choice" that is traumatic, that of the child in its preference of erotic object, whether father or mother. The result is a "scar" over a loss or lack, that we can never be both the (physical) partner for both parents. See Wohl (2005) 138.

61. On the family as a "strategic" structure for studying the contours of a culture's community, see Slater (1968) x. See duBois (1988), however, on the possible tyranny of the family as a hegemonic structure in patriarchy; see also Deleuze and Guattari (1977).

62. In "Moses and Monotheism" (*SE* 23: 7–56), however, Freud deploys the myth of the abandoned hero to account for Moses' origins; see my Conclusion.

63. Human infants under foraging conditions must suckle almost constantly for sufficient hydration and nourishment, since their mothers produce a watery, low-fat milk, but newborns cannot cling to an adult's hair and have to be held constantly. Otherwise, they are at serious risk of predation. Kertzer (1993), 123, makes a similar point about the importance of suckling for babies abandoned more recently to "foundling homes" in Italy.

64. Hrdy (1999) 390.

65. As a whole, the tragedy could be seen as a precursor of Freud's family romance, for we have a child raised in mean circumstances, as a temple slave, who discovers that he has miraculous and noble origins. There are significant differences, particularly the absence of an idealization of Ion's natal parents from which his family romance devolves.

66. See Owen (1939) and Lee (1997), both at 1291.

67. And, to illustrate the nature of reciprocity in this romance, at one point Ion seems to answer, "And I nearly killed you"; but there are textual difficulties here. See Lee (1997) at 1499–50.

68. Or, as Page duBois (1988), 7, puts it: "Critics . . . must 'defamiliarize' the historical world for themselves and their readers." She is attempting to rethink categories of female representation outside of the binary opposition on which psychoanalytic theory depends.

69. Sprengnether (1999) 232.

70. With this insight, my own study goes in a direction rather different from Sprengnether, who wishes to articulate ways in which the mother is a subject or agent with respect to her child. She rejects the notion of preoedipal symbiosis as a fantasy of the child that eliminates the mother's autonomous experience of her body in conception and pregnancy. I agree with Sprengnether and in fact go further; see Chapter 4. Deleuze and Guattari (1977) 273–74, speculate about the same issue of responsibility and the predication of parents, and propose a cycle of sickness that begins with the father: "*Oedipus is first the idea of an adult paranoiac, before it is the childhood feeling of a neurotic.*" This structure that privileges the family is, however, what they challenge throughout their study as too linear and hierarchic.

71. See Wohl (2005) 140–143 on the hierarchical structure imposed by the oedipal as read in the *Bacchae*.

72. Even one of Freud's favorite epigram, "The child is the father of the man," which he borrowed from Wordsworth, privileges the child's experience at the expense of the adult's in a self-perpetuating cycle.

73. Huys (1995) 34, who has exhaustively studied the mythic type and its deployment in Euripides. I have benefited greatly from Huys's extraordinary assembling of comparative materials, although I disagree with his assessment of abandonment in the *Ion*.

74. Huys (1995) 38; the definition of exposure is that of Edmunds (1985) 28.

75. Fathers, such as Laius, or uncles, such as Pelias, are also possible; Huys (1995) passim, studies the motif in other cultures' myths as well.

76. I discuss the implications of defiance in this structure for both Euripides and Freud in greater detail in Chapter 3.

77. Studies of this literature are numerous; see Boheemen (1987) for an investigation particularly of the absent mother. Farah Mendlesohn and M. Katherine Grimes, both in Whited (2002), study the motif in children's literature with particular reference to the Harry Potter series; see further in this chapter.

78. Huys (1995), 34–38, suggests that this inevitable return to one's natal origins is not a requisite of the myth of the abandoned hero in other cultures.

79. Dever (1998) has taken up separation from the mother, but she does not speak of it in terms of abandonment: "Victorian novels almost invariably feature protagonists whose mothers are dead or lost. . . . The maternal ideal in fiction thus takes its shape and its power in the context of almost complete maternal absence, and I would argue, through the necessary vehicle of such a void" (xi). On 39–77, she discusses the relevance of the lost mother in the object-relations theories of Melanie Klein and D. W. Winnicott.

80. See Mendlesohn (2003) 161.

81. The point hardly needs illustrating, but we have seen how Freud develops the notion of the family romance around (the phantom of) abandonment, while Jung (1949) posits the Child as a major archetype driving development through separation and testing.

82. Bettleheim (1989) 66–69.

83. Unless the impulse is interpreted, as Bettelheim also does (145), as the child's anxiety about being left alone. See Huys (1995) 147–152, 246–258, on the matter of motivation in the ancient motif; he notes that the anguish of the maiden forced to expose her newborn out of shame or fear is rarely dramatized, the *Ion* being a significant exception, along with the fragmentary *Antiope* and *Melanippe Desmotis*.

84. The tendency to equate maturity with independence has been noted by feminists as an inherently male perspective on the matter. See, e.g., Foley (1994) with further references. Freud and later psychoanalysts, especially those of the object-relations school, studied the trauma of separation from the mother as a construction of normal childhood development; see Dever (1998) esp. 39–40.

85. Breger (2004), 14, quotes this passage from a late essay of Freud's, "Femininity," but argues that the vehemence of the language originates in Freud's own repressed sense of displacement from his mother's affection.

86. See esp. Jung (1949) on the Child.

87. In writing this, I am aware that my sense of the abandoned child's peril is predicated on a normative vision of a "proper" childhood. In calling attention to the norm as it exists in the "modern Western view," Catherine Panter-Brick defines it thus: "a child should a have a 'carefree, safe, secure and happy' existence (Somerville, 1982) and be raised by 'caring and responsible' adults." She rightly points out, however, that many alternatives to such a childhood exist throughout the world: this "discourse of childhood is quite clearly a construct, abstracted from the real-life circumstances of children. It is a model or ideal type which maps what is to be achieved and the paths to be followed" (Panter-Brick and Smith [2000] 4). It should be noted that her goal is to interrogate practical ways in which to allow real-life children to thrive regardless of culture (in whatever terms their culture defines thriving) — a goal I endorse in the real world. In my study, the normative defines both the proper childhood (with natal parents) and the life of the abandoned child (whose best option is with foster parents); I do not, however, perceive that norm to include the rosy categories of "carefree, safe, secure, and happy"; Panter-Brick may overstate her case here.

88. In this, Harry is much like Luke Skywalker, the young Jedi who fascinated an earlier generation. For Rowling, the scholarly discussions have begun but are somewhat premature given that the series is unfinished; see collections edited by Anatol (2003) and Whited (2002); for criticism with a colder eye, see Zipes (2001).

89. Marjorie Williams, "Babies in the Trash," *Washington Post*, February 4, 2000, A31;

Williams cites Hrdy (1999) as a radical new expression of what is *really* natural for mothers; see above in this chapter and further in Chapter 4.

90. There is evidence of a similar trend in northern Europe, where there is an increasing use of a "baby box," or "safe deposit box" at hospitals or social services offices. See "German Center Takes in Unwanted Babies," *Washington Post*, March 9, 2000, A2.

91. This trend toward decriminalizing abandonment challenges the modern context for examining the ancient Greek and Roman cultures' practice of not rearing all babies; see Oldenziel (1987), who surveys how varying sensibilities about the ancients in the twentieth century affected treatment of the subject of infant exposure.

92. One commonly cited statistic from the Department of Health and Human Services: in 1991, there were 65 "published reports of abandoned babies"; in 1998, there were 198.

93. The white couple, who abandoned their newborn in 1996, eventually received sentences of less than three years each through plea-bargains. In 2000, the Filipino couple were subject to prison terms of up to ten years until the judge demanded that prosecutors reconsider their charges in light of "other cases" in Delaware. See the opinion of Vivian Houghton at www.vivianhoughton.com/vivian/Articles/NJ_021020_Her_Words .htm (accessed October 7, 2006).

94. For the Illinois ad, see www.saveabandonedbabies.org (accessed May 27, 2005); it continues: "You can leave your unharmed baby, three days old or younger, at any hospital, emergency medical facility, staffed fire station, or police station in Illinois and walk away with no questions asked. The baby will be cared for and placed in a loving home for adoption. No attempt whatsoever will be made to contact you. No crime will have been committed. This is a truly safe process. This law was written to provide a safe alternative to abandonment for Illinois parents who feel they cannot cope with a newborn baby."

95. At www.crisispregnancy.com/birth-mother/legalized-abandonment-safe-haven-laws.html (accessed May 27, 2005, and June 6, 2006); at http://cfc.ky.gov (accessed June 6, 2006), the process is called "surrendering" a newborn.

96. It is clear, for instance, that Jodi Brooks made the difference in Mobile, Alabama, in November 1998, when she publicized the possibility that desperate mothers could leave unwanted children in area hospitals, although this was not then a legal act; see *Nursing Spectrum*, February 1, 2001, http://community.nursingspectrum.com/MagazineArticles/ article.cfm?AID=3186 (accessed May 27, 2005).

97. In August 2000, for instance, *Parents* magazine proclaimed Debi Faris "Parent of the Month." See her own website at www.gardenofangels.org/Home%20page.htm (accessed May 27, 2005); her comments are drawn from "Giving the Love They Lacked," *Parents*, August 2000, 16; see also *Washington Post*, February 17, 2002, F1. In addition to the accolades of *Parents*, the California Senate Republican Leader, Jim Brulte, got Faris named his district's "Woman of the Year" for being "instrumental" in the law's passage. She was also nominated for recognition as one of the "Ten Most Caring People of 2002," a nomination highlighted in "Matters of the Heart: The Caring Awards Honor Those Who Make Compassion Their Business," *Washington Post*, February 17, 2002, F1.

98. Williams (2000), 31, suggested that lawmakers might well reckon, "If we make it legal, every teenage mother will be abandoning her child." Lawmakers have overcome the widespread scruple she projects, but among the criticisms about the new spate of laws is precisely this, that indifferent parents will take advantage of them.

99. See, however, www.crisispregnancy.com/birth-mother/legalized-abandonment-safe-haven-laws.html (accessed May 27, 2005), for the states that do require basic family histories.

100. *Parents*, August 2000, 16; Faris is speaking about an incident in Indianapolis, in which a newborn froze to death in the parking lot of an emergency room: "If only his mother hadn't been afraid to go inside! That baby could have become someone else's blessing."

101. And the sense that the laws have been changed too quickly, without sufficient forethought for the adopted child's need to know about its birth circumstances or for the larger natal family's rights, is slowly emerging in web discussions; see, e.g., the *Christian Science Monitor* online opinion at www.csmonitor.com/2003/0404/01 1s010coop.html (accessed May 18, 2005). There are also the opinions of adopted children and men worried about their paternal rights; see http://home.socal.rr.com/huntingtonbeach/safeharbor .html (accessed May 18, 2005).

102. A further example of this tendency to redefine the identity of the abandoned child: when a woman went on trial for attempted first-degree murder because she put her child in a trash bag and dumped it in the garbage, the prosecution spelled out the revolting garbage with which the baby was placed in the bag, suggesting the dehumanizing of the baby by contact with it. More remarkably, both the defense and the prosecution tried to exploit the fact that the teenager named her infant Angel. The defense suggested that this naming indicated an intent to return and rescue the child, but the prosecution argued, "Isn't it a fact that you named your baby Angel because you planned for her to be dead?" *Washington Post*, August 1–4, 2000.

103. I am aware of no discussion by Freud of the real-life practice of abandonment, or of any study that raises the issue in relation to his intellectual and social acculturation, although the practice was certainly taking place in nineteenth-century Europe; see Kertzer (2000) for a description of the foundling's life based on Italian evidence, and Boswell (1986). Armstrong (2005), 103–109, 223–226, addresses the figure of Alexander the Great, however, as a model for Freud that incorporated the oedipal crisis.

104. Jung and Kerényi (1948) 121.

105. Ibid. 120; see also 113.

106. See Ebbott (2003) for a treatment of the motif in classical literature; see also Huys (1995) 377–394, for examples in other cultures of heroes who do not learn the identity of their natal parents, although even in these instances, the hero sometimes interacts with his natal family or destiny.

107. Yet the critical alternative, to deny that the real-life practice of abandonment had anything to do with spectators' experience of a play about abandonment, seems the choice of desperation. See Huys (1995) 15, who states: "Although we cannot exclude that certain details in Euripidean tragedy allude to contemporaneous practice, these statements are unverifiable, and do not contribute much to literary interpretation anyway." Huys does, however, summarize what is known about contemporary practices as he analyzes each component or motif in the "tale-pattern"; see 143, 199, and 239.

108. The literature on infant exposure in the ancient world is large and begins with Gustave Glotz's foundational article (1906). Ogden (1996) covers the matter in the larger legal and social context of illegitimacy. I found most useful the work of Patterson (1985) for her assessment of both the early evidence and earlier critical work, and Boswell (1988) for a larger framework. The evidence of the legality of the practice in Athens comes from Hermogenes 35 and Sextus Empiricus 36; it seems to be contradicted by another Solonic law prohibiting the sale of legitimate children; see, however, Patterson (1985) 104–5 and n. 6. The Athenian evidence is corroborated by the law code of Gortyn, which advises that a woman who was divorced while pregnant could expose her own child provided she first

offered it to the father. See also Harrison (1968) 70ff; Eyben (1980–81) 22 and n. 65; and MacDowell (1978) 91. Plutarch's *Life of Lycurgus* (30) describes the procedures by which Spartan elders decided, using physical criteria, whether newborns were to be reared or not. Aelian's notice that Thebes prohibited the exposure of infants, although not their sale, may also confirm the general acceptance of the practice in other cities (*Varia historia* 2.7). Scholarly efforts to recover a sense of the numbers by assessing their impact on the demographics of the Athenian population rely on varying assumptions and produce contradictory results; see Oldenziel (1987) 98–100 and Patterson (1985) 107–110 on the exchange among Engels (1980, 1984), Golden (1981), and Harris (1982), and the efficacy of statistical models for the effect of the practice on Athenian demographics. See also Boswell (1988) 133 on the fallacy of similar studies for the Roman period.

109. The early evidence consists exclusively of references in historical, philosophical, or dramatic texts. Using later sources as evidence about the likely shape of the practice of infant exposure in the fifth century must be done with caution, but since private or familial practices and rituals, particularly those involving women, are slow to change, historians currently working on fifth-century Athenian life have found the later evidence helpful; see esp. Patterson (1985) 104 and n. 3, and Golden (1990) 86–89. Oldenziel (1987) 88 describes how prejudices buttress scruples about using later evidence. She also criticizes the methodology found in the subject, particularly an overconfidence in a "scientific" method and the practice of "isolating a phenomenon in its smallest component," such as a specific time-frame or technical term (93). Blundell (1995), 12, argues for the slow nature of change throughout the broader topic of women's history.

110. See Patterson (1985) 108, who remarks on the "psychic cost" of infanticide, borrowing the phrase from Alvin Gouldner; see also Boswell (1986) 75ff and 134ff; and Golden (1990) 23 and 87–88. On the modern data, see Boswell (1988) 1 and n. 1, 7–12, and 20 and n. 42. See also Kertzer (1993) 10.

111. The ritual evidence is derived from inscriptional evidence; see Sokolowski (1969) 119 (*LSCG* 199), and Cameron (1932) 108. Menstruation and intercourse also incurred pollution; it is the relative length of the pollution surrounding the disposal of an infant that suggests the gravity of the act: the level of pollution is similar to that for abortion.

112. Plato *Theaetetus*, trans. Harold North Fowler; see also 157c–d and the *Republic* 5.460c (2.2), where his suggestion about "hiding the deformed child" away is more cryptic. Aristotle also recommends not rearing deformed children; see *Politics* 7.14.10, 1335b.19ff. Aristotle recommends in this same context that parents who simply do not want more children should prefer abortion before the fetus has "quickened" (*Politics* 7.6, 1335.19 and 25); see Germain (1969) 186. See also Boswell (1988) 40n96 on the arguments of Lacey (1968) 164 against the idea that deformed newborns might be killed.

113. Patterson (1985) 112; she makes the point about both Plato's metaphors and Aristophanes' jokes. See also Gardner (1989) 51.

114. Soranus *Gynecology* 2.10.5, trans. Owsei Temkin ([1956] 1991).

115. See Patterson (1985) 114, who also notes that it is difficult to imagine that a midwife or new parents would dispose of every baby who failed one or more of Soranus's criteria.

116. Soranus explains a barbaric custom of submersing a newborn in cold water to test its vitality (2.12 [81]); he considers this unnecessarily dangerous, but Aristotle thought subjecting children to cold when they are very young an "excellent" means of strengthening them (*Politics* 7.17, 1336a.12–18).

117. This ritual, which included a sacrifice, may have normally been on the fifth day. The *amphidromeia* and the *dekate*, a feast to which friends were invited on its tenth day, are discussed by Deubner (1952) and Golden (1986); their conclusions about the relationship of the two — that one was essentially private, the other public — are anticipated by Glotz (1906) 931. The significance of the ritual seems twofold, to accept the child as legitimate and to introduce it to the household's tutelary gods. In the *dekate*, the father named the child; the friends who attended could later be called on as witnesses to a man's citizenship; see below. As Mark Golden (1990), 23, puts it: "Being born, a biological event, was insufficient to make a child a member of an *oikos* or *oikia*, a household. Even those with two citizen parents had no automatic right of entry; they had to be accepted by the *kyrios* (the male head of household)." See also Harrison (1968) 70–71, 78–79.

118. See Golden (1990) 23, 86–87, and 95; also Patterson (1985) 115–121.

119. Patterson (1985), 119–121, does believe that more girls were exposed than boys. See also Golden (1981, 1990), who also believes that girls were more likely to be exposed, and Boswell (1988) 100ff, who notes that, while it is "plausible," there is little evidence to support the assumption. In favor of such a bias is evidence from the Hellenistic period, including the quip, "A son everyone raises, even if he happens to be poor, a daughter, however, even a rich man exposes" (*Hermaphroditus* of Poseidippos). See Boswell (1988) 102, who adds evidence from Lucian's *Dialogues of the Courtesans* (2.1), where a courtesan insists that she will not expose her newborn, "especially if it is a boy." See also a first-century b.c.e. letter from a mercenary to his wife that advises, "if by chance you give birth, rear it, if it is a son, but if it is a daughter, expose it." For this letter, see Eyben (1980–81) 16n43, citing similar evidence, mostly Roman; see also 26–27.

120. Huys (1995), 35, 62–63, notes that very little is known of the literary treatment of the myth of an exposed hero before Athenian drama. In Herodotus as well, exposed infants are male; Huys, 88, calls this pattern "in sharp contrast with historical reality."

121. Boswell (1988), 6–12, discusses the problematic nature of either position; see also Murray (1943) 46–54 for a brief survey of abandonments in tragedy and later comedy; Huys (1995), passim, is much more comprehensive. Earlier treatments of abandonment assumed that comedy provided a reliable picture of the real-life practice; see Glotz (1906) for how detailed a discussion can be made based on such assumptions. But see also Golden (1990) xvi, 179, who assumes that the frequency of the motif in New Comedy is not an indication of its practice in real life: "it is precisely such out-of-the-ordinary occurrences which spice up the stage"; and Fantham (1975) 44–46, who draws a similar inference. In arguing for preferential exposure of girls, Golden (1990) 94–95, points to the greater frequency of archaic and classical Athenian funerary monuments in honor of sons, but this statistic is pertinent for suggesting a prejudice in favor of sons whom parents chose to rear; see Golden's own caution at 86–87. See also Ridgway (1987) 405–406; memorials to girls, however, show the same overall fine quality as those to boys, and there are also monuments of families with multiple children, including multiple girls. A similar problem occurs with fourth-century oratory. Private civil cases mention many more male children than female, suggesting that selective exposure skewed the normal demographic balance, but Isager (1981–1982), 88–89, argues that this skewing is illusory, because the Greek practice seems to have been to mention daughters primarily when they are relevant to the facts of the case. Ogden (1996), 64–65, concludes that girls were preferentially exposed based on "[w]hat we know of relative exposure rates," but I am not sure what he considers this knowledge to be.

122. Patterson (1985) 116–119; Boswell (1988), 104–106, detects a similar paradox in

the Roman evidence, that the poor seemed more likely to take up and rear exposed children as their own. On the rich abandoning their children, the third-century historian Polybius accuses wealthy Greeks of "pretentiousness, avarice, and indolence" because they either do not marry or raise only one or two children in order to "leave these in affluence"; *Hist* 36.17.5–10. At 10, Polybius even recommends a law "making it compulsory to rear children." See the even more categorical indictment of Musonius Rufus (fr. 15); and Eyben (1980–81) 24, 41. See, however, the quotation from Poseidippus above; this witticism, if taken at face value, suggests what we might expect; see Patterson (1985) 120n50.

123. Plutarch *De amore prolis* 497e. This comment must remind us of the premise of Toni Morrison's *Beloved*, in which slavery is such a "disease."

124. See Ogden (1996) 106–110.

125. See Isaios 3.30, as well Demosthenes 39, 40. See also n. 117 above and Patterson (1985) 115. The Demonsthenic "Against Neaira" (59) is our most elaborate evidence for the scenario of a man up to no good trying to enroll a child in his phratry.

126. See Golden (1986) 252–256; he interprets the gesture at 253n25; see also Patterson (1985) 105.

127. As with the metaphor of philosophy, the comic jokes must also draw upon common assumptions, prior knowledge, and attitudes to succeed; see Gardner (1989) 51ff, on using comic evidence to detect underlying male anxieties; she discusses the jokes from the *Thesmophoriazusae* in terms similar to those I employ.

128. Aristophanes *Thesmophoriazusae*, trans. Sommerstein (1994). The First Woman pronounces a curse upon anyone who informs on a woman trying such a substitution (339–340); she later complains about the interference of an overly zealous husband in the procedure (407–409). At vv 564, the Kinsman specifies that one's own female slaves may be a source for such substituted babies. These jokes imply the availability of newborns for the substitution, leading to modern speculation about a kind of underground market in unwanted babies among women, both freeborn and slave. See Patterson (1985) 116; see also Sommerstein at 503: "The baby . . . would be some slave-woman's child whom her owner had no wish to rear."

129. Gardner (1989) 52–54, who also detects another anxiety associated with a wife's infidelity, namely, that she might give her lover the opportunity to steal from her husband's *oikia;* her evidence is drawn from Lysias 1.33; see also Sommerstein (1994) at 564–565.

130. This comic fantasy represents an inversion of Hippolytus in Euripides' play, who wishes that men could do without sex and buy their children from temples, pledging gold, silver, or bronze depending on how valuable a child they wanted (*Hippolytus* 616ff); see Rabinowitz (1992) 157–158. This more familiar fantasy of reproduction — that of the male who can get his heirs without sex — can also be seen Hesiod's *Theogony*, 886–900. The fantasy as such has been discussed by many; see Zeitlin (1996b) 78–86.

131. Gardner (1989), 56–57, argues that a woman would substitute babies as a means of safeguarding their "material security" (or so the male anxiety would have it), because without producing an heir, she might be divorced and sent back to her father's *oikos* with the stigma of barrenness to block any other marriage.

132. The First Woman's mock prayer against any man who informs on an attempt at substitution, preceded by real treacheries against the state, plays into this tension between (a woman's) private aims and the state's need for legitimate citizens; see Sommerstein, ad loc. for the mixture of the comic with "real" portions of the prayer, especially curses upon

anyone who plots against the *demos* (335), negotiates with the Persians (337), or attempts a dictatorship (338–339).

133. Apollodorus's peroration in "Against Neaera" is an instructive reminder of how a skillful speaker can use the single event as a powerful example of harm to the state; see Demosthenes 59.111–117.

134. Patterson's remarks (1985), 103n1, are a good example of the process; although she understands that there is a difference of purpose between infanticide and infant exposure, she decides that "given that 'exposure' does seem to have been the prevailing way of disposing of unwanted infants and to have been viewed as an act of violence against the newborn comparable to the abortion of the fetus . . . I think it is fair to continue the practice of referring to the issue as one of infanticide."

135. See Boswell (1988) 111–131, who infers this from epigraphic and historical evidence as well as literary texts; see esp. 123–124. Concerning the legal evidence, Boswell comments: "it is probably not unreasonable to conclude that recovery occurred often enough to attract considerable attention from legists, and therefore to constitute a not unrealistic hope on the part of parents (and a not extravagant plot device on the part of writers)" (124). He concludes: "The overwhelming belief in the ancient world was that abandoned children were picked up and reared by someone else" (131). See, however, Hrdy (1999) 297–299, who faults Boswell for discounting the difficulty of keeping newborns alive without an available nurse; see also Kertzer (1993) 123. But the point is not so much the numbers themselves, which Boswell acknowledges might well be low, as the *expectation* that a child might survive. The need to find a nurse is dealt with in the mythic and historical tales about heroes abandoned at birth often enough to indicate that the ancients were well aware of its significance. See Huys (1995) 299–306.

136. For instance, to thank his audience for its support for an earlier comedy, Aristophanes likens himself to a young woman forced to abandon a child: his play, like the child, was rescued and raised by the spectators themselves. The cliché may engage the spectators' impression (or hope) that babies abandoned in public view, where rescue might occur, were indeed saved. See Huys (1995) 239, who assumes that "logically . . . unmarried girls . . . secretly nursed the hope of rescue. The most frequently attested places of abandonment—streets, squares and temples—strongly suggest the expectation that a passer-by would take up the child." See Huys (1995) 2.2.3, for a detailed discussion of all the dramatic evidence for the presence or absence of tokens; he notes that tokens can also be read as grave gifts, or as bribes to anyone who finds the child, again suggesting that parents not only expected that a child might survive but also wanted to promote that survival. See also Boswell (1988) 125–124 and Fantham (1975) 56–63 for differing opinions about the reliability of New Comedy for gauging historical practice. Finally, there is the tragic rhetoric against weak-willed parents in the face of an omen or prophecy that a child to be born is dangerous. Such parents are excoriated for their reliance on the chance of abandonment, as Helen taunts Hecuba: "And the next person responsible for destroying both Troy and me was that old man who didn't kill Alexander as an infant—that bitter copy of a firebrand" (*Troiades* 920–922; see also *Andromache* 293–300).

137. Although Oldenziel (1987), passim, uses it. Boswell (1988), 133, argues strongly on the need to distinguish infanticide from abandonment; he discusses the differences in effect both in terms of impact on individual families and on the demographics. Patterson (1985), passim, however, uses them synonymously and explains why in her first note (103).

138. Boswell (1988), 125, notes that during the Roman empire, most families did not move far from their origins, and "many parents may have known the foster parents of abandoned children . . . as epigraphy and legal materials suggest." Bearak (2002), 208–209, provides a modern parallel in a story for the *New York Times* on parents selling their children in Afghanistan and then visiting them in the homes of their new owners.

139. See Huys (1995) 244, e.g., and 267–270. Huys's evidence documents many stories, both from the Greeks and other Mediterranean cultures, in which a desperate mother's motive was to *save* the life of her child from an angry grandfather or ruler. Huys argues that her gesture places the child in sufficient peril that the intent to kill is the same — as is the ambiguity; see 240ff, esp. 242: "The objective purpose of the [exposure] thus cannot coincide with one of these subjective intentions but somehow includes both. Objectively speaking, indeed, it always aims in a sense at the child's death, even if a mother abandoning her child eagerly hopes for its rescue, for the danger must be menacing enough to give the opportunity to demonstrate the child's miraculous election."

140. Huys (1995), 34–35, denies that this is an intrinsic part of the exposure tale.

141. See Zacharia (2004) for a recent analysis of repetition in the *Ion;* see Lukacher (1986) and Johnson (2001) on Freud's case history.

142. Wohl (2002) 19–29. See also Butler (1997).

143. Brooks (1987), 13–14, opens his essay by remarking that traditional psychoanalytic criticism tends to be "embarrassing," because it subjects the wrong object to "analysis."

144. Brooks (1987), 13, does speak of the text and reader as switching roles between analyst and analysand, and recognizes that the analyst will participate in his own "delusional system." See also Kartiganer (1985).

145. Brooks (1987) 16.

146. See Little (1993). In addition to whatever shared or collective antecedent experiences of the audience may be implicated in its perception of the text, readers who opt out of the dominant structure bring their own unruly agenda.

147. States (1985) 25.

148. Freud makes this argument in "On a History of the Psychoanalytic Movement" (*SE* 14); I return to it in Chapter 2. Freud did not, of course, refrain from such analysis himself.

T W O : Competing Accounts

Epigraphs: Freud, "From the History of an Infantile Neurosis," *SE* 17: 50; Euripides, *Ion* 542–544; the Wolf Man, quoted in Obholzer (1983) 31.

1. See Zacharia (2003) 66–70 on the repetitions and the differences among them. The amount of stichomythia in the play is very high, the two longest extant examples being 264–368 and 934–1028. See also Lee (1997) 186.

2. Johnson (2001), 43ff, provides a provocative account of the case history as psychoanalysis's challenge to biography, a genre of which Freud was notoriously skeptical; see also Armstrong (2005) 134ff and Breger (2000) 1–2. Johnson himself reads the case history as Freud's and the Wolf Man's "life-writings" (51ff), and sees in this process Freud's construction of the Wolf Man as a necessary adversary. Lukacher's study (1986) of the primal scene was particularly influential on the readings in this chapter.

3. Noting how easily most patients are able to adopt "an attitude of uncritical self-observation," Freud comments, "I myself can do so very completely, by the help of writing down my ideas as they occur to me" (*SE* 4–5: 103).

4. Freud also stresses in "From the History of an Infantile Neurosis" (*SE* 17: 52) that the task of construction is not the patient's — that is, that of the eyewitness, traumatized by his primal scene — but the analyst's, who can realize the significance of each detail from the fantastic language of the analytic dialogue.

5. Freud added the quotation from Schiller, which he received from Otto Rank, to his 1909 edition of *The Interpretation of Dreams*.

6. See Breger (2000) 184.

7. See also Kartiganer (1985) 14–17, on Freud's discovery of the value of this profusion as he developed his notion of psychoanalysis.

8. Lacan (1978) 41; see also the remark of Sheridan, his translator, on the nature of the "real" for the phrase "residue of all articulation" (280).

9. See also Gay (1998) 264.

10. See Lukacher (1986) 141ff. Kartiganer (1985), esp. 32–35, discusses Freud's insistence "on maintaining [the primal scene's] literalness — even as he marches out all the arguments against it," as an answer against the deconstructionists who would claim the primal scene as pure "Undecidability" (33–34).

11. See Johnson (2001), however, who reads the case history very differently and discusses Freud's staging of the Wolf Man as his chief enemy.

12. Whatever immediate dissent or contradiction the Wolf Man voices is absorbed by the conventions of psychoanalysis themselves. As Werbert (1998), 223, remarks: "Neither a *yes* or a *no* on the part of the analysand can help us to decide the correctness of the construction: a *no* can be an expression of resistance, a *yes* of a hypocritically agreeable attitude. The only confirmation we can expect is that at best the analysand responds with new material that is in accord with the construction or can contribute to the gap being filled in more completely." After the fact, Werbert points out, the psychoanalytic literature can fall back on the claim that what is said in analysis is a unique congruence of two persons and a moment, and thus beyond challenge (187). This in itself is troubling, however, in light of Freud's desire to treat his analyses, particularly that of the Wolf Man, as an "empirical test" of his basic psychoanalytic theory (226). See also Winter (1999) 138–140.

13. Adler was one of the original members of the "Wednesday Psychoanalytic Society"; see Gay (1998) 174 and esp. 216–23; also Breger (2000) 173ff. Armstrong (2005) discusses how Freud in his appropriation of ancient figures, especially Empedocles, "dodges any question of indebtedness to his followers Adler or Stekel" (93). For Adler's names for his version of psychoanalysis and Freud's distress, see "On a History of the Psycho-Analytic Movement," *SE* 14: 51–52.

14. The Wolf Man's history is particularly crucial in Freud's attack on Adler, because he seeks to refute his colleague's notion of the "masculine protest"; the primal scene is mentioned to support the notion of the infant's early experience of desire (*SE* 14: 54). On the struggles with these two pupils, see Breger (2000) 194–207, 217–232.

15. See "On the History of the Psycho-Analytic Movement," *SE* 14, 60, where Freud accuses Jung of producing not "fresh observations" but "fresh interpretations."

16. I discuss examples of these incorporated voices later. See Lukacher (1986) 138ff; critics have claimed similar tensions in Freud's analysis of Dora, for instance; see Szecsödy (1998) 58.

17. Transference plainly did its work: the Wolf Man saw the analysis rather differently from Freud's theoretical construction of him. As far as he could judge, Freud took him seriously as an intellectual and treated him, in his own words, as the "younger comrade of

an experienced explorer setting out to study a new, recently discovered land." The Wolf Man credits Freud's "outstanding personality" for the ease and strength of the transference, as well as the fact that he himself had just lost his father when he began his analysis. See Gardiner (1972), esp. 88–89 and her note to "The Memoirs of the Wolf Man," on Freud's personality and the death of his father. The Wolf Man's comments in this context, which were written in 1970, seem aimed at diminishing Freud's success. On Freud's admiration for the Wolf Man's intellectual depth, however, see "My Recollections of Sigmund Freud," written in 1952 (Gardiner, 140).

18. See Breger (2000) 185.

19. See "Analysis Terminable and Interminable" (*SE* 23: 217–218), where Freud applies this bold metaphor: "The saying that a lion only springs once must apply here." On this gesture, see also Lacan (1977) 96–97; Lukacher (1986) 28ff. Breger (2000), 347ff, faults Freud severely for threatening patients.

20. Freud characterizes the material's effect by saying it enabled the Wolf Man "clear up his inhibitions and remove his symptoms" (*SE* 17: 11). His language in discussing these two ploys suggests — but no more — that the sequence in which these two strategies were deployed was first the promise and then the threat.

21. Gardiner (1972) 304; see also Lacan (1977) 96–97; Lukacher (1986) 28–29; and Gay (1998) 291–292. On the Wolf Man's psychosis, see Blum (1980a).

22. See Johnson (2001) 16 on the Wolf Man's use of gifts.

23. Critics have been quick to point out the "blackmail" nature of Freud's interactions at this point; see Breger (2000) 274.

24. It is also a detail that others believe accounts for the infant's sense of trauma as well as the primal scene; see Breger (2000) 274. Later, when the Wolf Man was troubled by his failure to recall the primal scene, he also dwelt on the fact that he *could* remember the illness's symptoms.

25. See Johnson (2001) 16.

26. For instance, an important memory from this period, in which a nursery-maid knelt before him, provided crucial confirmation, as constructed by Freud, that the Wolf Man 's oedipal longing had once been masculine and hence "normal," but, as we shall see in Chapter 4, that event could not serve as the site of trauma itself. See Gay (1998) 288. Again, much later, the Wolf Man preferred to think of his seduction by his sister when he was two and a half as this originary trauma and hence, his "primal scene." On the doubts of more modern psychoanalysts, see Blum (1980a) 35–36; see also Lukacher (1986) 137; Gay (1998) 288–289.

27. See Werbert (1998) 233–237; on the absence of the Wolf Man's mother from the case history, see Sprengnether (1990) 72–74.

28. The Wolf Man (Sergei Pankejeff), "My Recollections of Sigmund Freud," in Gardiner (1978) 136–137.

29. According to Freud, the Wolf Man long associated his mother's gastrointestinal complaints and vaginal bleeding with her experiences in the primal scene, and near the end of his analysis with Freud, he revisited the primal scene with compassion for his father, seeing the latter's castration in it (88).

30. See *SE* 17: 12: "I requested the patient to make the strictest criticism of his recollections, but he found nothing improbable in his statements and adhered closely to them."

31. On Freud's use of analogy, particularly from antiquity, see Armstrong (2005).

32. Freud recasts the primal scene to represent different aspects of these symptoms,

and the tensile strength of the true account shows in its seemingly endless adaptability: its pathogenic effect on the patient (43ff); its status as a site of anxiety (46); or the affect of its participants (45n).

33. Lukacher (1986); see also now Johnson (2001).

34. I draw Jung's remarks from Gay (1998) 752, who reports them in his bibliographical notes; he draws them from an interview Jung gave to "his friend John M. Billinsky," which took place in 1957, published in *Andover Newton Quarterly* 10 (1969) 39–43; the quotation is from p. 42.

35. Freud, "On the History of the Psycho-Analytic Movement," *SE* 14: 58; he also quotes Adler (51), "I may even speak publicly of the personal motive for his work, since he himself announced it in the presence of a small circle of members of the Vienna group: — 'Do you think it gives me such great pleasure to stand in your shadow my whole life long?'"

36. On the strategy of this "personal dimension," see Armstrong (2005) 37, where he defines the issue, and passim.

37. The primal scene of their voyage is not Jung's only effort to get a picture of Freud's sex life; Jung also writes to Freud, commenting on the third edition of *The Interpretation of Dreams*, that he and his students "badly missed" the "(personal) essential meaning," the "libidinal dynamics" of such dreams as the Irma dream, and "the personal-painful in your own dreams." See Gay (1998) 124–125.

38. See Armstrong (2005) 239–44 for a discussion of Freud's attempt to deal with the concept of matriarchy as an origin when constructing his own primal narrative for human culture; on Freud's use of antiquity as an "analogy" in his psychoanalytic argument, see 38–42 and passim.

39. See also Caldwell (1989) 129ff for a symbolic interpretation of Chaos that seeks to read Hesiod's *Theogony* in Freudian terms.

40. On the succession myth as a struggle over reproduction, see Zeitlin (1996b) 78–79; and Katz (1982). That women control a man's knowledge about his breeding is a bitterness already to be found in the *Odyssey*; see Zeitlin (1996a) 24–27, 35–40, 43–48, for its implications in Homer; and (1996b) 62–72, for Hesiod. The struggle finally ends with Zeus's development of an immortality in which he, as the father, can have all the sex he wants and engender children but never be supplanted by them. Sex is decoupled from its biological consequences, because the father does not breed his successor. Zeus can thus simultaneously embody both of his chief epithets, Father of Gods and Men, and Ageless — never yielding to those who come after. Such are the consequences of Zeus outfoxing his first consort, Metis, to prevent her giving birth to one greater than himself, and then exercising the self-restraint not to make Thetis his consort, so that her male offspring, destined to supplant its father, is not his own. See Zeitlin (1996b) 79–80.

41. Gay (1998), 752, outlines the contradictions in Jung's story that cast doubt upon portions of it, although he cites other evidence that Freud did indeed refuse to "help interpret one of his own dreams aboard ship" (Jung to Freud, December 12, 1912, Freud and Jung [1974] 583–84, 584n). Whether Freud had an affair with Minna Bernays is less relevant here than Jung's narrative of his confrontation with Freud, but see Gay's note (1998) 753, about the lack of primary sources (the letters between Freud and Bernays); and Armstrong (2005) 37.

42. On Gay's implication in Freud's official mythology of psychoanalysis, see Breger (2000) 381–383.

43. Gay (1998) 202; see also Breger (2000) 225; and Brooks (1990) 138–141, 160–163, who discusses Freud's Jewish identity with reference to his jokes and parodies the notion of psychoanalysis as the "Jewish science."

44. Thus Xouthos rescued Athens at its time of military need and won the city as his kingdom; Oedipus saved Thebes from the Sphinx and gained its rule and its queen. On the process dramatized as a therapy for Athens, see Zacharia (2003) 101–102. The *Ion* presents two different plots for introducing Ion as an heir. First, Xouthos intends to pass off this boy as his legitimate heir to the Athenian kingship; see Zeitlin (1996c) 288–289, who comments on the gender inversions in this plot. Then Kreousa and Ion must deceive Xouthos about his "parentage" of the youth (a divinely sanctioned and perpetually successful deceit), but Apollo makes this version of Ion's paternity into adoption (ibid. 334–335).

45. Gay (1998), 202 and 234, tracks the deterioration: Jung writes, "let me enjoy your friendship not as that of equals but as that of father and son. Such a distance appears to me appropriate and natural." Later, however, he writes: "I would like to call your attention to the fact that your technique of treating your pupils like your patients is a *blunder*. In that way you produce slavish sons or impudent rascals . . . I am objective enough to see through your trick. . . . Meanwhile you are sitting pretty on top, as father" (quoted by Gay, 238).

46. Breger (2000) and Gay (1998) offer their own competing accounts of the rupture, with Gay slanting it toward Freud's needs and Breger emphasizing Jung's.

47. In his version, however, Euripides makes Xouthos exclusively the outsider with military experience. In the *Athenian Constitution*, attributed to Aristotle, Ion's foreign origins are twice asserted (41.2 and in the *Epitome* of Heraclides). This text claims that Ion was selected by the first Athenian kings because of their weakness in military matters; 3.2. See Thucydides 1.3.2, who describes how descendents of Hellene ingratiated themselves into Greek cities as military allies, although he does not name Ion.

48. Foley (2001), 5–6, remarks on this process, which she firmly outlines for each of her discussions of women's tragic acts.

49. Zacharia (2003) 99–102; the quotation is found on 102. See also Ebbott (2003) 80–81, who assesses the tension in terms of the respective fertility of abandonment and autochthony.

50. See Zeitlin (1996) 289.

51. The term "humanist" is Zacharia's (2003) 101.

52. Mastronarde (1975) 165: "The monologue of Hermes . . . contains the precise narrative and genealogical detail which may be expected in Euripides." See also Hartigan (1991) 70. Thus the importance of the early link created between Ion's destiny and that of Erichthonios, an autochthonous king. One of Athens's most ancient and cherished myths about itself, that its people are so indigenous that the royal line sprang from the earth itself, is insinuated here into a more obscure myth about a later ruler, Ion, because Euripides wants to explore the meaning of that autochthonous myth in light of human suffering. Eventually, the Athenian audience is treated to the spectacle of its early ancestors finding that they "may have it all ways," as Zeitlin (1996c), 337, puts it. See also Zacharia (2003) 62–65. Ion becomes a king who is both divinely engendered and a legitimate citizen, autochthonous, at least symbolically, yet possessed of a human mother and himself fruitful — not always a sure thing for autochthons. See Peradotto (1977) 92–95; and Ebbott (2003) 77ff on Ion as a strategy to restore fertility to Athens's royal line.

53. As others point out, Hermes is symbolically the appropriate figure to open the play, since he was present at Ion's first rebirth, to rescue him from the cave where he was

left to die; now he appears to preside over a second rebirth that is also a resurrection to full royal status in Athens. See Loraux (1990) 170, 178; also Zeitlin (1996c) 331n127; and Rabinowitz (1993) 216, who stresses Hermes' role in matters of "exchange." Huys (1995), 147ff, also discusses Hermes' role as Apollo's servant, which parallels that of the servant who often assists in exposing infants.

54. For Hermes' speech in full, see Erbse (1984) 73–76. For contrast, in the prologue to *Hippolytus*, Aphrodite announces that she set up Phaedra's passion. See also the *Alcestis*, in which Apollo predicts, after meeting Death, that he will salvage things.

55. Hermes' exit line, announcing his plan to hide in nearby bushes to see what happens, marks the parallel between himself and the audience; see Rabinowitz (1993) 216. Huys (1995), 147–148, observes that Hermes' watch here parallels other mythic and legendary tales in which the servant charged with the exposure watches, or is ordered to watch, to witness the fate of the child; Huys sees "a direct connection between Hermes' act of exposure and Ion's appearance . . . as if time had stood still ever since, the audience will now witness together with the spying god what will become of this abandoned child." He makes a similarly good point about a displaced motif in connection with Kreousa's conversation with the pedagogue; this represents the "typical" conversation *before* exposure between maiden and trusted servant (149).

56. Erbse (1984), 78, notes that as soon as Kreousa enters and a rapport between queen and youth develops so rapidly that their recognition as mother and son seems inevitable, the spectator is on notice.

57. See Lee (1997) for Hermes' language; other versions of the abandonment dwell in greater detail on the rape itself, especially Kreousa's monody. See Loraux (1990) 196–199 on the symbolic significance of space on and beneath the Acropolis.

58. See Wolff (1986) 33–34, who particularly stresses the importance of Apollo's plans, "because Apollo is often accused during the play of having failed to look after his son." Mastronarde (1975), 164–165, discusses the images of orderliness in Hermes' prologue as a prelude to the disorder that human emotion is going to introduce. Segal (1999), 72, calls the prologue "distanced, antiseptic."

59. See Lee (1997) at 20–5 and 26, the tokens as the first evidence of the important theme of autochthony; see also Loraux (1990) 196–199 on the ambiguity between life and death in the play's use of these symbols.

60. The queen is later precise and detailed about what she put in the basket (1417–1436).

61. Athena as deus ex machina confirms this rosy view of abandonment's essential healthiness when she adds the detail that Kreousa gave birth "without illness" by Apollo's design (ἄνοσον; 1596).

62. See Huys (1995) 162ff, who discusses how this choice for an infant's abandonment typically signals intent about the child's survival.

63. Hermes' aside confirms that the god did intervene in the former way by helping the Pythia overcome her revulsion (47–48). Note that Owens (1939) at 47 suggests that this aside may not be Hermes' but the Pythia's, to account for her change of heart.

64. When the priestess later gives them to Ion, they still mean nothing to her: the basket is a colorless container (ἄγγος) to her (1337), and she urges him to begin the search for his mother at Delphi, where she still believes him to have been abandoned (1365–1366).

65. As indeed Delphi was in historic times a repository for cities' and individuals'

wealth. The Athenians themselves, among others, maintained a treasury there. The significance of Delphi as a place of safety is noted, although put differently, by Zeitlin (1996c) 295–296 and by Segal (1999) 74–77. See now Zacharia (2003), chap. 1, which deals with the representation of Delphi in contrast to Athens. Loraux (1990), 177–178, minimizes the significance of the specific identities inhering in site of Delphi.

66. Compare Xouthos's words to Ion (530) and Athena's confirmation of Apollo's claim (1560); and see Golden (1990) 23, on the *amphidromeia.*

67. The verb is in part an expression of outrage arising from the Pythia's revulsion at the pollution of Apollo's sanctuary; it also signals the maiden's intent concerning her newborn child. Kreousa's first words about her ancient travail echo the nuances of suffering and outrage: ὦ τλήμονες γυναῖκες ὦ τολμήματα / θεῶν. ("O, suffering women, O, outrages of / the gods! 252–253). Her intent emerges more gradually. See 958, 960, and 1497. Her unwillingness to open her eyes or to be frank certainly are poignant signs of her own entrapment in the past. As Hoffer (1996), 303, puts it, "A repressed mind is the psychological cost of social oppression"; see his further discussion at 304–306.

68. See Pucci (1992) 90–104 on the mother as the figure of chance in Oedipus's tale.

69. On the direct challenge to Hermes' account posed by Kreousa's entrance, see Erbse (1984) 78. On Kreousa's "riddling" manner, see Hoffer (1996) 304–306.

70. See Hoffer (1996) 305.

71. For the role of Ion's monody in establishing his opening characterization, see Mastronarde (1975) 166; Hartigan (1991) 70–71; and Segal (1999) 69, 75–76. See also Hoffer (1996) 295–299, who argues that Ion's purity is linked intrinsically with violence in his monody.

72. See Lee (1997) at 139–40; Ion uses the phrase "true father" to express what he thinks is a relationship constructed purely out of benefaction.

73. As such, this construction of self is to be distinguished from the process usually noted about Ion, that his identity is constructed in the course of the play.

74. See also Hoffer (1996) 304–309 for a detailed discussion of this scene.

75. Hoffer (1996), 310, speaks of Xouthos's intrusion on "the tentative intimacy of Ion and Creusa, based on a shared experience of oppression and a shared feeling of repression and yearning." See also Erbse (1984) 78: "Mutter und Sohn kommen einander so nahe, daß die Anagnorisis unmittelbar bevorzustehen scheint." In fact, in a dramaturgical tour de force, this sympathy expresses itself throughout the scene in a kind of surface irony, so piquant to the audience, in the comments between unrecognized mother and son ("How I bless the woman who bore you!" "That experience [of your friend] is in exact harmony with my own!"). See 308 and 359 and cf. 330 and 354.

76. Ion eagerly questions this queen about her family's autochthonous history until his reference to Athens's long cliffs provokes a cry of pain (258–284). An outpouring of experience from Kreousa seems imminent, a recollection of abandonment from the lips of an eyewitness. Instead, their conversation veers from ancient pain to the current circumstance that brings the queen to Delphi, her childlessness. It is in this context of childlessness that an abandonment finally appears, but it is the foundling's tale, not the queen's. Only after Ion and Kreousa have constructed his abandonment does she finally indulge in her recollection of the past. Yet she offers a story that is a fiction deliberately designed to conceal memory. This complicated layering of Kreousa's memories and fictions under and over Ion's construction expresses the surface "truth" about the identity of these two, felt once again as delicious irony by spectators. It is also is a dramaturgical instantiation of an

underlying psychic turbulence that is compressed and, at least initially, motionless because of the compression — a perfect expression of Kreousa's prevailing mechanism for handling her suffering as a memory.

77. Her verb — ὤλβισα — is important in the context of economic calculation concerning foundlings, a subject of Chapter 3; as Hoffer (1996), 307, notes, Ion also employs economic metaphor in their conversation to encourage Kreousa to be more forthcoming in her revelations about herself.

78. See Lee's remark (1997) at 322–327: "Kr.'s attention to the concrete detail of Ion's upbringing, food and clothing is expressive of a woman obsessed with her failure to provide for [her] own child." See also Segal (1999) 82–83, who speaks of Kreousa' "initiating" Ion into the world of "adult sexual relationships."

79. Ion's lack of a nurse does not trouble him now; later he dwells on this loss (1372).

80. Lee (1997) at 325 notes that the Greek is "perhaps intentionally ambiguous"; the language allows us to understand that Ion could be saying either that he is the product of a wrong done *by* a woman, or *to* her. Lee continues, "If Kr. is responding to this line in 330, it is interesting that she assumes the latter."

81. See Segal (1999) 77, who remarks on how Kreousa "intertwines her own life story . . . with his."

82. Kreousa's verb in 328 — literally, to rush or dart toward something — and Ion's reason for never making a search collectively express a powerful desire. And it is precisely the interaction between her discourse and his that expresses the desire: while the verb is hers, the emotion is his. See, however, Lee (1997) at 328: "Kr. projects her eagerness to find her son onto Ion."

83. The effect here is partly due to the surface irony pervading this scene, whereby neither character is as fully aware of the import of his or her claims and concerns vis-à-vis the other as is the audience, but the transformation in Ion's curiosity about his real parents and his newfound zeal for the hunt must also strike spectators. Pucci (1992), 80n1, has a fine description of this play in "tragic irony."

84. Ion's language marks the activation: although in his monody he reveled in his toils, he now feels a burden he would love to share with a mother. The repetition of πόνος as an expression of his work for Apollo seems key; see 102, 128, 131, and 134 in his monody, but πόνος as burden or suffering appears at 331. Earlier, he consistently values such efforts as well, calling them "pious" (εὐφάμους) at 134 and, at 128 and 131, in reference to his entire service (πόνον), "fair" (καλόν), and "glorious" (κλεινός). See Hoffer (1996) 299.

85. See Hoffer (1996) 308, who attributes her use of the fiction more specifically to "shame."

86. Huys (1995), 110, notes that in Euripides' fragmentary *Melanippē Sophē*, the heroine also apparently uses a fictional maiden as a screen for her own history when arguing against her father's inclination to burn her (unidentified) babies. On the use of "maiden" or even "virgin" to refer to seduced or raped girls, see Sissa (1990) 73–123.

87. On the monody and its role in changing Kreousa's intent, particularly on the role of "opening up" locked boxes, see Gibert (1995) 164–189 and Rabinowitz (1993) 194–195. On the larger theme of maidens and vessels, see Ebbott (2003) 13–22, who addresses the *Ion* on 19–20.

88. When Kreousa "finally" speaks openly of her own suffering, she offers two versions of the rape and abandonment, one lyric, one dialogic, which are not quite identical, calling into question which is the more correct. Plus, the queen is beginning to operate, by

that time, under the influence of provocation that motivates her to act like a conventional murderous stepmother (see further below in this chapter). Also see Zacharia (2003) 66–70 on the function of these repetitions.

89. I print Diggle's text here, but note that Lee (1997) at 355 retains νιν as a reference to the abandoned child, "even with Diggle's order of verses." I prefer the MS order, as does Murray, since in keeping with my line of argument, Ion's swerve back to abandonment following the reference to childlessness is a nice bit of pointed irony. Precisely this action of Apollo's has kept Kreousa from being childless.

90. Lee (1997) at 353 points to these illogicalities, but to make a different point: "Here . . . Euripides stresses the fallibility of human reason . . . Kr. exposed the child, assuming it would die (18), but hoping at the same time that Apollo might save it (965). When she returned to the cave, presumably seeking confirmation of its fate, she found exactly the signs suggesting that Apollo had acted as she wished — the baby gone and no sign of bloodshed. But her fear led her to conclude that the baby had been killed." Lee relies, however, on a conflation of three different constructions of the abandonment, Hermes', Kreousa's here, and a later one of hers.

91. Ion's "rationalizing" explanations are seen as a feature of his youthful, naïve character, but he can entertain the incredible as well. See Walsh (1978) 301–302; Lloyd (1986) 39. For instance, he shows eager curiosity about Athens's autochthonous beginnings and Kreousa's own miraculous childhood (265–282), and his initial incredulity here does not prevent him from participating fully in Kreousa's emphasis on Apollo's role, even to the point of assessing neatly the entire story in terms that, while ostensibly his, sound exactly like hers: "The god wrongs him; and the mother herself is wretched" (ἀδικεῖ νιν ὁ θεός· ἡ τεκοῦσα δ' ἀθλία; 355, reading νιν instead of Diggle's νυν).

92. Hoffer (1996), 309, calls the entire encounter a "tender non-conversation." Lee (1997) at 357–358 comments, "Ion's suggestion that the child might be alive provokes an outburst [by Kreousa] against Apollo. Recognition is now prevented by her bitterness against the god: if the child is dead, it is his fault; if it is alive and cared for by him, he is selfish, even though she later says that this is precisely what she wanted (965). [Kreousa] continues to be blinded by her tears (cf. 241f.), unable to see the truth because she is consumed by misplaced grief and bitterness." Lee notes, at 350–3, 353, 354, how the characters' individual preoccupations foreclose recognition.

93. See Lee (1997) at 359: "while 356 establishes the similarity of the 'friend's' fate to Kreousa's, it is scarcely congruent with Ion's. He must be talking vaguely of the general situation."

94. Huys (1995), 94, remarks: "it is of immense importance that Kreousa's rape and exposure go undetected and she lives on without loss of honour." See also Ebbott (2003).

95. See Little (1993) for this interaction between audience and text with reference to Shakespeare.

96. The audience's role here is crucial. It is unlikely that anyone in it was ever abandoned, but highly likely that many were parents who had made the decision at the heart of the romance, one way or the other. That is why Kreousa's fate is so disturbing.

97. Although not all of this speech may be original; see Kovacs (1979) 116–123 for cuts. For a survey of the issues of Athenian legitimacy and citizenship, see Foley (2001) 73ff.

98. See Foley (2001) 85; Ogden (1996) 188–199.

99. See, e.g., Owen (1937) passim, who even notes places where he supposes the

Chorus should have protested at the Old Man's dishonesty but does not. The Old Man's construction has been called a "paranoid fantasy," consistent with a servant's loyalty to his family's fortune; see Walsh (1978) 303–305; Zeitlin (1996c) 320–321; Segal (1999) 77.

100. See Lee (1997) at 1537.

101. There is, of course, loss, especially of loved ones, an event whose traumatic effect on the unconscious Freud addresses in "The Ego and the Id" (1923), *SE* 19: 1–59; see Butler (1990) 57ff.

102. And it has been studied as such by others; for the primal scene, see Lukacher (1986); on abandonment, see Zacharia (2003).

103. See Sprengnether (1990). Abraham and Torok (1986) reconstruct the primal scene on the Wolf Man's sister. See Breger (2000), who infers that Freud's longing for and anger toward his mother had a greater influence on his theory than Freud was willing to recognize.

THREE: Profit and Loss in Belonging

Epigraphs: Euripides, *Ion* 523; the Wolf Man quoted in Gardiner (1972) 149; Ruth Mack Brunswick, ibid. 294–295.

1. A point that Freud stresses (*SE* 17: 72ff).

2. See Bowdler (1996) 419ff; and esp. now Armstrong (2005) for the importance of Freud's archaeological collection as a reflection of his understanding of psychoanalysis. See Gay (1998) 170–173, for Freud's use of the Latin phrase in a 1896 lecture on hysteria (172).

3. MacGillivray (2000) 102; see also 115 for Evan's attitude toward antiquities. See Bowdler (1996) 420 and Armstrong (2005) 194–195.

4. Armstrong (2005) 194–195; at 14–15, he suggests that more may be going on with ownership of the object than intellectual pleasure; he unpacks the erotics behind possessing the ancient artifact as Freud himself handled the issue in his analysis of a fictional archaeologist in Wilhelm Jensen's *Gravida:* "Given the historical tenor of Christian sexual mores and the Jewish abhorrence of idolatry, the traces of alternative sexualities that persist in the ancient archive create a situation whereby the study of ancient culture brings on a veritable 'return of the repressed.' The repressed which returns is not just a matter of sexual interests and indulgences, but also the compulsive fascination with the sensuous image itself and the insistent immediacy of its hedonic properties."

5. See Poovey (1998) 27, who studies the beginnings of the process, in the eighteenth century, of weakening the biblical narrative through "nontheological discourse." Winter (1999) situates Freud's construction of psychoanalysis within the competition for supremacy among other disciplines. See Armstrong (2005) 139 on how the "archaeological model enabled" the drive of psychoanalysis to narrate.

6. On Freud's budgeting for the purchase of antiquities, see Gay (1998) 170–172; see also MacGillivray (2000) 71ff, 82, and 166–166, for Evans's varying efforts at money-raising. Armstrong (2005) at 121 and 220, discusses Evans in terms of personal finance as a contrasting figure to Freud.

7. Poovey (1998) 30.

8. Ibid. 43, quoting John Mellis's *A Briefe Instruction and Maner How to Keepe Bookes of Acompts after the Order of Debitor and Creditor* (1588). Here the "superfluous" is the criterion for eliminating individual details from transactions as they are rerecorded from the

"Memorial," a detailed and chronologically maintained daybook of transactions, to the "Journal," a periodic summary with an index and a standardized currency, to the "Ledger," where the double-entry bookkeeping actually took place.

9. Winter (1999), 269, quotes Freud from "Instincts and Their Vicissitudes" on the acquisition of "phenomena" and their classification and interpretation on the basis of "abstract ideas," which become increasingly "precise" as more material is observed. The key matter seems to be getting enough material.

10. The Wolf Man's own experience is worth noting: he was his father's co-heir with his mother, who was also made the executor of the estate, to the Wolf Man's fury, but apparently out of concern for his disability.

11. For a recent discussion of Freud's theory of the family romance and its adaptation for classical texts, see Davis (1993) 11–12.

12. There is a mythic pedigree for this structure, to be found, e.g., in Aeschylus's *Agamemnon*, which condemns the house of Atreus for its squandering of wealth generally and that of its children in particular. See Jones (1988) 8–14, but also Taplin (1977) 311ff, esp. 313–314; and Goldhill (1992) 27–32, who speaks about the family's murder of its children within the context of recompense.

13. "Thus in these phantasies the over-valuation that characterizes a child's earliest years comes into its own again," Freud writes ("Family Romances," *SE* 9: 241).

14. The development of modern economics and the story of its replacement of ancient, divinely sanctioned structures with "reason-of-state arguments" begins well before the late nineteenth century, of course; for the phrase, see Poovey (1998) 27, who traces its development in the seventeenth and eighteenth centuries, especially among English and Scottish thinkers.

15. See Chapter 2 above; this preoccupation also reminds us of the nineteenth -century struggle about the structures of the mind, especially about the relationship of free will and whatever force lay behind such phenomena as dreaming; see Locke (2001) 23–28. On Freud's particular efforts to articulate the relationship, see also Lukacher (1986) 24–28, 136–141.

16. It is this possibility of comparison among fostering and natal parents, as well as this denouement, that makes the structure of the family romance such a supple interpretive tool for examining nineteenth-century fiction; see Boheemen (1987) and Dever (1998).

17. Freud further insists that such a "present" *always* interrupts the primal scene of lovemaking (82).

18. The Wolf Man's earliest memories betray his original male orientation, but his sister's molestation converts him to a passive role for receiving libidinal pleasure. I study these memories in Chapter 4.

19. Breger (2000), 165–166, for instance, comments, "the conflict of this stage ['anality'] are not so much the pleasures and frustrations of an 'erotogenic zone' as they are battles that pit the young child's emerging autonomy against adult authority."

20. Freud quoted in Gay (1998) 287; the letter to Sandor Ferenczi is dated February 13, 1910 (Gay, 689). Ruth Mack Brunswick comments that the Wolf Man commenced his analysis with her by a bout of diarrhea, which she interpreted as signifying the importance once again of the economic and, more specifically, as a kind of debt repayment; see Gardiner (1972) 282. The Wolf Man much later denied ever making these comments; see Obholzer (1982) 169.

21. Johnson (2001) also studies the importance of gift-giving in the case, although to a different end than the one pursued here.

22. See also Brunswick's remarks, Gardiner (1972) 303.

23. At *SE* 17: 23, 73, 83. Abraham and Torok (1986) assess the significance of this erotic site differently, as a version of the primal scene in which the Wolf Man witnessed his father's seduction of his sister; see esp. 36–40; and Johnson (2001) 12ff. See also Lukacher (1986) 156–159.

24. Gardiner (1972), 167, remarks in a note to Freud's case history that the German here — *dienende Personen* — "would include Therese, a nurse in a sanatorium," who became the Wolf Man's wife.

25. Gardiner (1972) 149–150. See also Armstrong (2005) 139–140, on this gift as part of the Wolf Man's "narrative web."

26. In discussing the reactions of H.D. to Freud's collection of antiquities, Armstrong (2005), 195ff, notes the problem of "*artifactual economy*" surrounding their presence in Freud's office.

27. Winter (1999) 140; her subsequent discussion (141ff) of Freud's wish to analyze the middle and upper classes instead of the poor is richly provocative regarding how class explicitly influenced his development of theory.

28. Armstrong (2005), 194–196, discusses similar efforts by H.D. to acquire a particularly apt artifact.

29. Armstrong (2005) 197; he adds, "The Wolf Man was, after all, obedient enough later to produce paintings of his wolf dream that corresponded better to Freud's interpretation than his original drawing." See also Johnson (2001) 137–140, who stresses the importance of this picture as another gift-giving gesture in his interpretation of the relationship between Freud and the Wolf Man. See also below on Abraham and Torok's assessment of this "gift."

30. The literature on this subject is enormous; see Mauss (1967). For its application to tragedy, see Wohl (1998).

31. Brunswick's analysis, in Gardiner (1972), focuses to an extraordinary degree precisely on this matter of entitlement and financial recompense, such that she comments frequently on the Wolf Man's attitudes to Freud and his responsibilities, past, present, and future. On the Wolf Man's sense of entitlement to the free analysis provided by Freud in 1919–1920, see 294. On the loss of his fortune and Freud's supposed responsibility for this, see 282. On the Wolf Man's place in psychoanalysis, the words are Brunswick's own assessment of Freud's motives; see 266.

32. Gardiner (1972) 282.

33. Gardiner (1972) 303; Brunswick has this to say on Freud's contributions: "The craving for presents from the father was the prime expression of the son's passivity. . . . Had the patient been as cured of his feminine attitude to the father as he seemed to be, those contributions [from Freud] would have been devoid of emotional significance" (ibid.).

34. See "Analysis Terminable and Interminable," *SE* 23: 217–219. Other psychoanalysts have been more dubious; see Lacan (1977) 96–97, who warns against the lure of impatience in analysis, and urges "time for understanding" be given to the patient. See also Lukacher (1986) 28–30.

35. Gardiner (1972) 140; see Armstrong (2005) 138–140, who discusses how Freud used antiquity's artifacts to promulgate this sense in his patients.

36. See Gardiner's note to the Wolf Man's autobiography (1972) 88n3; also Lukacher (1986) 144.

37. Freud admits that, absent the final emphasis he and the Wolf Man were able to give to the primal scene, he would have had to accede to Adler's views concerning power and

"object-choice" (22). Lukacher (1986), 162, comments on the Wolf Man's lack of awareness of the "debt" Freud owed him "for his theory."

38. On that key detail being the fact that he *witnessed* something, see Chapter 2 above and Abraham and Torok (1986); Johnson (2001), 16, calls the detail "something hidden, something left to analyze."

39. We know enough about the Wolf Man's early history to sense that Freud's threatened abandonment replicated his parents' neglect and disregard of him. Even his father's pronounced preference for his sister, whether that took the form of incest or not, enacted that kind of abandonment within the family that is being relegated to a humiliating role. See Johnson (2001) 124ff, who lists the discrepancies in characterization and detail between Freud's account of the Wolf Man and his own, as these are collated by Esterson (1993). Johnson recognizes that neither man gave the fully factual account.

40. Lukacher (1986), 158, provides a crucial discussion of the mutual entanglement.

41. On her technique and what may have lain under it, see Lukacher (1986) 160–161.

42. Brunswick notes: "He talked at great length about the marvels of analysis as a science, the accuracy of my technique, which he professed to be able to judge at once, his feeling of safety at being in my hands, my kindness in treating him without payment, and other kindred topics" (Gardiner [1972], 279–280).

43. Ibid. 284.

44. Ibid. 294–295.

45. Johnson (2001) 164–167, discusses Freud's handing of his patient over to Brunswick as a great if cryptic "gift."

46. Gardiner (1972) 279–280; see also 266–267, esp.: "He took his wife's advice [that he conceal the recovery of the jewels] because, as he admitted, it coincided with some inner feeling of his own. And from this time on his greed for money from Freud increased: he was always wondering how large the next present would be."

47. See Johnson (2001) and Kalinich (1991). Abraham and Torok (1986), 14–15 and 65ff, suggest that the Wolf Man was being "paid for his silence," first, by his family, in the matter of his father's rape of his sister; Freud's gifts seem to continue that payoff. By their reckoning, Brunswick's great success was in enabling him to see, not that he witnessed the rape, which lies permanently concealed, but that Freud as the father was at least not also the seducer. Lukacher (1986), 156ff, has an excellent review of Abraham and Torok's argument (as well as those of others who believe that Freud missed the correct content of the primal scene). The Wolf Man himself came to believe the scene was his own molestation by his sister.

48. Gardiner (1972) 300–301.

49. The new version of the primal scene also replaces, however, a scene of the toddler eavesdropping on a rival sister being paid by the father for her services; see Abraham and Torok (1986). Brunswick accepts the patient's need for a female analyst because, "It was indeed safer now for him to be analysed by a woman, because he hereby avoided the homosexual transference which at this point was evidently so strong that it would have become a danger to the cure, rather than an instrument of it" (Gardiner [1972] 280). See Abraham and Torok (1986) 10.

50. Abraham and Torok (1986) 52–53.

51. Lacan (1977), 96–97, makes the connection as well as, and although he does not elaborate his point in this context, he does connect the payments with the "initiative of Freud's" — i.e., the setting of an end to the analysis. See Lukacher (1986) 29.

52. Gardiner (1972) 267.

53. In reference to Freud's very gesture of threatening to terminate analysis, Bruns-wick postulates that the Wolf Man produced the necessary material, but also "that an inaccessibility which necessitates a time limit will most often use this limit for its own ends. . . . This [the ending of the analysis] resulted in the patient's bringing sufficient material to produce a cure, but it also enabled him to keep just that nucleus which later resulted in his psychosis" (ibid. 304). The truth of her remarks about Freud's attitude toward the Wolf Man is not in question (although it might be), nor the therapeutic value of forcing the Wolf Man to relax his attachment to his former analyst.

54. In "Analysis Terminable and Interminable" (*SE* 23: 219).

55. See Johnson (2000) 2.

56. Masson (1984), for one, infers that Freud overlooked evidence that would support a seduction theory. More recently Dimock (1995), 59, has argued a similar point. As we shall see in Chapter 4, Freud had to minimize the significance of another early memory, but, I suggest, for different reasons.

57. See also Lukacher (1986) 138–140, who explains that Freud could not admit that "with the notion of the primal scene he had formally and finally moved beyond recollec-tion. . . . Freud was constrained from making such an admission for fear of losing control over the International Psychoanalytic Association. When he writes that 'many people will think that this single admission decides the whole dispute,' he is thinking of the analysts sympathetic to Jung or Adler who would eagerly exploit such a break from recollection, seeing it as confirmation of Freud's failure as an analyst" (139). Lukacher also remarks in detail on Freud's stress upon the exact equivalency of the primal scene to recollection, although to make a different point about Freud's interest in hermeneutic authority.

58. Poovey (1998), 61–63, writes about the power of abstraction as a key to the success of double-entry bookkeeping in the development of the modern fact through its capacity to substitute for details and render them "superfluous."

59. See Lukacher (1986) 136ff.

60. In his autobiography, the Wolf Man notes, "'My' Egyptian immediately struck my eye, the figure which for me symbolized my analysis with Freud, who himself called me 'a piece of psychoanalysis'" (Gardiner [1972] 150). See Armstrong (2005) 197, on Freud's obsession with artifacts as tokens of psychoanalytic destiny.

61. I would disagree with Johnson (2001) 16 when he argues that the Wolf Man gave Freud "something hidden, something left to analyze" (all the while keeping concealed with the "crypt" what could not be revealed; the crypt as part of the defense of "incorpora-tion," is a notion that Johnson borrows from Abraham and Torok; see his n. 4).

62. See Winter (1999), whose second chapter discusses this relationship in these terms.

63. Millett (1991), 79–80, remarks on how limited Athenians' "movable property" actually seems to have been. The object has recently been the subject of inquiry as a form of conspicuous wealth within the ideology of reciprocity that marked high-status Athen-ians. See esp. Ober (1989) 226–230, who, speaking of the practice of the *litourgia*, notes, "the rich man's ability and willingness to contribute to the state, and the sense of gratitude the recipients [the *demos*] felt toward the donor, were primary sources of the positive impressions which interacted with the negative impression of wealth to produce a constant tension within the ideology of wealth." The study's beginning was marked by Morris (1986); see esp. 8ff. See also Reden (1995) 79–80, 83ff; Mitchell (1995) 3–21; Wohl (1998)

59–82; and Millett (1998) 243ff, esp. 246–245, on the display of "choregic tripods" set up to celebrate victories in tragic competitions.

64. In the ancient Greek economy, in other words, there was not as yet an established standard medium, such as coined money, for evaluating all other possessions. Greek coinage existed well before the late fifth century, but our modern understanding of its symbolic value is greatly disputed. See Reden (1995) 171–175, for an articulation of the important difference between coin and money in the ancient world, and a detailed discussion of the issues and response by Kurke (1999) 6–22. See also Macve (1994) 58–59 for discussion by a historian of accounting.

65. A good example is found in Sophocles' *Philoctetes:* Heracles' bow, which he gave to Philoktetes after he agreed to ignite the pyre that would release the great hero from his suffering, established an immutable link between them, implicating the younger hero in Troy's destined fall as well as marking his role in it; see 1422ff, where Herakles as the deus ex machina spells out these links.

66. Ameinokles' windfall was cups of gold and silver (χρύσεα ποτήρια . . . πολλὰ δὲ ἀργύρεα), as well as other untold weath (ἄλλα τε ἄφατα χρήματα) (7.190), but Herodotus goes on to contrast his new exceptional prosperity (μέγα πλούσιος ἐγένετο) with his lack of good fortune (τἆλλα οὐκ εὐτυχέων) owing to the slaying of his child (apparently by himself, although Herotodus does not make this detail clear).

67. See Millett (1991) 31–32.

68. The verb also means to steal; see Owen (1939) ad loc.; and Lee (1997) *ad loc.* for the joke. In the *Iliad*, Nestor uses ῥύσι' ἐλαυνόμενος (11.674) to describe a retaliatory cattle raid.

69. For a good discussion of the problems this body of forensic evidence presents for the social historian, since, while it is a treasure trove of information about life in Athens, it rarely presents the whole of the picture, see Millett (1991) 2–3, 19ff.

70. Cohen (1992), 3–8, summarizes the transformation between the fourth and fifth centuries.

71. Our evidence about the Athenian economy before the fourth century comes from evidence drawn from literature and art, and it is slanted to reflect the mores and tastes of citizens of high status. Recent studies argue that the literature of the fifth century in particular privileges those forms of wealth based on land ownership and its husbandry; see Xenophon *Oeconomicus* 7.20–22. Critics vary as to the degree to which this aristocratic ideology was competing with other forms of prosperity and commerce for control of what it meant to be the best sort of citizen; see the somewhat opposing surveys of the topic by Reden (1995) 1–9 and Kurke (1999) 18–23; also Mitchell (1997) 3–21 and esp. Millett, whose work on credit clarified my own understanding of the distinctions to be made. Morris (1999), xiii–xix, has a concise but useful discussion of the notion of "status," as opposed to class. On craftsmen and shopkeepers as citizens of low status, see Pomeroy (1999) 241. For the notion of the citizen whose self-interest outweighs that of the polis, see Wohl (1998) 152ff on competing ideologies of ownership in the *Alcestis*. While the case is strong for such an ideology, different texts exploit the elite imagination of the good citizen and his wealth to rather different ends, and a complete view of Athens's economy in the fifth century is obscured by the perspective of the evidence we must use to construct it. Many citizens were craftsmen or in trade, and Athenians engaged in overseas trade from early on. These citizens' view of wealth is harder to recover in available literature, but such men were in Euripides' audience too. See Millett (1991) 39, where he distinguishes the "theory" of lending from the reality; and Pomeroy et al. (1999) 241.

72. See Millett (1991) passim, who uses the common term, "an embedded money economy," for his picture of Athens. See also Macve (1994) 58–59 on such an economy in which money itself had not yet been conceptualized as a "common measurement unit," such that abstract notions of overall profitability or the relative profitability of any single transaction could be measured once assets and commodities, or capital and income, were converted into this unit. See also Reden (1995) 171ff.

73. See Millett (1991) 36ff, who cites Aristophanes *Ecclesiazusae* 446ff and evidence as early as Hesiod's *Works and Days* for the informal practice of loaning equipment and thereby creating obligations (which could be discharged by similar loans in return). See also Sommerstein at 446–9, for further references. In this culture, certain groups of citizens are seen to participate in exchanges with the intent of securing "social union" rather than "financial profit"; see Wohl (1998) xxvii.

74. Millett (1991) 3; he remarks on 40: "As relationships became increasingly tenuous, a position would eventually be reached at which the 'personal knowledge' [of lender and borrower that serves as security for the loan] ceased to exist. Beyond that point it became legitimate for the lender to require some formal sanction to guarantee repayment." The fourth-century case "Against Timotheus" recorded in [Demosthenes] 49 provides examples of lending property and transactions without witnesses; see Millett (1991) 213–215 and Cohen (1992) passim.

75. [Dem.] 49.5, trans. A. T. Murray, Loeb Classical Library (Cambridge, Mass.: Harvard University Press, 1939).

76. Millett (1991) 96. The issue of whether ancient men could predict net profitability is vexed; for opposing arguments, see Finley (1999) 115–118 and Macve (1994) 58.

77. Macve (1994) 70–75; see also 62, 84.

78. Poovey (1998), 29–91, studies the invention of double-entry bookkeeping as the beginning of the modern "fact," with its reliance on the numerical and abstract for verity. She distinguishes between ancient and modern facts by assuming that ancient ones "referred to metaphysical essences, [while] modern facts are assumed to reflect things that actually exist," a distinction she bases on Aristotle (29, 336n4); she discusses the phenomena of the abstraction and the arbitrary on 57ff. See also Macve (1994) 57.

79. But, as Macve (1994), 70–75, notes, double-entry bookkeeping is a convenience, not a necessity for recognizing such things as profitability, which he argues ancient businessmen certainly understood.

80. See Poovey (1998) 62ff, who discusses how the numerical is deployed to guarantee veracity. See also Baekker (1992).

81. Macve (1994) 58–59. Such a record could prevent external fraud — attempts by creditors and debtors to cheat bankers — because it provided a narrative of each transaction and its later corresponding transaction, whether in repayment or credit. It might also help a banker against the charge of internal fraud, such as a denial of repayment; see Millett (1991) 96, who surmises that "embezzlement" was the main crime against which such records were kept.

82. See particularly the discussions of the distinction in Gabrielson (1986) 99–114; Cohen (1992) 8 and 191–194; also Kurke (1991) 225–239, who stresses the use of the distinction in underpinning the ideological concerns of the aristocrats; see also below in this chapter.

83. Eventually, Athenians came to want or need records that tracked wealth rendered invisible through deposit, loan, or investment. Such narratives of financial transactions may have been useful for many different reasons, including overseas investments and

concealing one's true wealth. This latter concern is already evident in the fifth century due to the radical democracy's use of the *litourgia* (a service or assessment for public expense) to supplement public funds by requiring men with wealth to finance portions of public service with their personal own resources. See Cohen (1992) 196ff, who sees concealment from a possible *litourgia* as a principal motive (or from an *antidosis*, a civil suit by which one citizen could force another to exchange property with him in order to prove that the other man was better equipped for an expensive liturgy); see Lysias 3 and 20.23. Millett (1991) 64–67, however, reminds us that Athenians actually went into debt in order to perform these liturgies, because, especially for those with political ambition, the faithful or even extravagant performance of one was a shrewd use of visible wealth. The sale of property was considered fraudulent in the context of an *antidosis;* see Isaeus 6.3, 7.71, and 11.48; Dem. 5.8; Aeschin. 1.101; and Millett (1991) 79.

84. See Cohen (1992) passim, but esp. 23n99; see also Millett (1991) 209.

85. Apollodorus states that his father did not press for repayment because he knew that Timotheus did not have the cash; see 23–24, 27. Somewhat disingenuously, Apollodorus also says that the loan to Timotheus was due to inadvertency on the part of a slave.

86. Cohen (1992) 23.

87. Apollodorus's account also underscores the fact that formal business — even investments — could be conducted with an eye to the intangible yield of social and political goodwill.

88. Aristotle explains this association with a metaphor: as children are to their parents, so yield (*tokos*) grows from the invested principal; *Politics* 1.1258b5. See also Cohen (1992) 45.

89. The male child inherited, of course, but girls, after the rituals initiating them into the family, could not be alienated either, except for lost virginity. The ancient Athenian lawgiver Solon forbade their sale into slavery. The girl could also be crucial as an *epikleros* in preserving her father's name and property intact. See Demand (1979) 3, 13; Pomeroy (1997) 36–39; and Cox (1998) 91–99.

90. Others, however, could have been adduced, such as Aeschylus's *Agamemnon;* see Wohl (1998) on the intersection of commerce and psyche there.

91. Lateiner (1989), 142–142, comments on Herodotus's deployment of children in the context of "extirpation of the house" as "*tisis*" for the "seven violators of supra-national *nomoi.*" Flory (1987) 23–48, focuses rather upon the historian's use of women.

92. By Herodotus's own reckoning; he begins with a survey of yet more ancient, mythic examples of rape and counter-rape. See Flory (1987) 24–29, for the juxtaposition.

93. The legend of Cyrus's birth, taken in isolation, conforms closely to Huys's reading of the mythic meaning (1995) 38ff. See also Burkert (1979) 6–7.

94. See Lateiner (1989) 142, on Herodotus's moral judgment expressed through the "extirpation of the house of the aggrandizing wrongdoer; from Book I he cites Astyages' lack of a male heir as well as Solon's famous citation of Tellus as the happiest of mortals, "in part because he had sons and grandsons (1.30.4)."

95. Gera (1997), 187–204, has a good summary and interpretation of Herodotus's account, as well as references to the most important recent discussions; see also Blok (2002) 236ff on Herodotus's use of women in his ethnographies. Munson (2001), 11, situates Cyrus's death at the Araxes river within the theme of rivers in his life.

96. Gera (1997), 195, calls Tomyris's challenge here a mark of her "self-assurance and strength. On the Araxes as both a symbolic and geographic limit of empire, see Flory (1987) 94; Lateiner (1989) 129–132; Gould (1989) 102ff; and Gera (1997) 189–190.

97. Tomyris's self-confidence is revealed in the detail of a three-days' journey from the river. She will give up the strategic value that natural barrier gives her if her enemy is willing to do the same. Flory (1987), 90, discusses the propensity for stupidity of more civilized aggressors, which manifests itself in part in their inability to recognize other forms of motivation than their own.

98. Flory (1987), 13–14, 57–58, and 95–96, discusses the preoccupation of modern scholars with the value of Croesus's advice extensively and argues for its essential soundness. Gera (1997), 193, believes that Croesus's advice is seriously flawed and argues that Tomyris herself is "the only wise figure in this story" (193).

99. In particular, σπεύδων becomes ἄπληστε αἵματος (206 and 212). Evans (1991), 54–56, notes the arch of Cyrus's life as beginning and ending in blood.

100. Flory (1987), 97ff and 100ff, discusses the typology of the "prosperous aggressor" unable to comprehend what a "noble savage" is really saying. Flory's reliance on various tropes — such that he attempts to read figures like Tomyris as versions of the ignored wise advisor, the witty and vengeful queen, and the naïve but noble savage — leads eventually to confusion. I prefer rather to read Tomyris's "advice" to Cyrus as a military challenge, whose import he and his courtiers fail to comprehend.

101. Just as Tomyris's actions close book 1, Candaules's wife opens its historical beginning in a similar style. Flory (1987) 36, 42; see also Lateiner (1989) 138ff. See, however, Gera (1997) 197, who suggests that Herodotus actually depicts Tomyris as the "more masculine" of the two rulers in her refusal to use deceit.

102. For many critics, this trick, with its use of wine to beguile savages accustomed only to milk, is the heart of the episode; see esp. Hartog (1989) 167, and Romm (1998) 107–108. See also Munson (2001) 101–103, on Herodotus's relativistic treatment of the Massagetae's customs.

103. Croesus's assumption that the Massagetae will succumb to wine's intoxicating novelty is confirmed both by their actions and by Tomyris's inability to find the right words for the drink. Hartog (1988) 162–170; the quotation is to be found on 167. See also Romm (1998) 107–108.

104. At one level, there seems to be a continuation of the dichotomy between the cultured, which has refined its weaponry from human blood to wine, and the primitive, which still thinks in terms of blood sacrifice; see Hartog (1988).

105. Herodotus explicitly marks Cyrus's delusion about his dream (210). I thank Temple Wright for his illumination of this provocative scene.

106. Croesus does arrange a marriage for his son, we are told, but as a means to distract the youth with pleasures.

107. See Lateiner (1989) 142–143, on the theme of childlessness in conjunction with the "aggrandizing wrongdoer."

108. In reference to the larger theme, see the apt term "oikocide" used by Lateiner (1989) 143.

109. Benardete (1999), 144, calls attention to the role of children in rise and fall of the Pisistratids and links it with the character of a tyranny, which must rely on its personal resources or on foreign ones.

110. See Lateiner (1989) 143, who argues that the "dreadful" incident "justifies" Harpages' treason.

111. See Gibert (1995) 173–189, for an excellent discussion of the deployment of imagery of storing up and opening in the play; see too Ebbott (2003) 13ff on the use of

"vault" as a metaphor for the maiden as treasure and for her enclosure in other classical literature. On the significance of Ion's tent, see Goff (1988) and Zeitlin (1996c) 324–331.

112. Golden (1990) 93 and n. 63.

113. Diggle (1994) 114. See, however, Lee (1997) at 476, who defends the manuscript's καρποτρόφοι because it continues the "commercial metaphor of the preceding verse."

114. On the use of wealth so invested, see Cohen (1992) 116.

115. Cohen (1993) 111ff; see also 52–60 for the distinction; he also argues, however, 140–143, that the risk should not be overstated, given the return of "20–30 percent (plus repayment of the principal)" that we find stipulated in terms for maritime loans, a gross profit that had to cover many expenses.

116. The phrase διαδέκτορα πλοῦτον (478) balances and glosses ὑπερβαλλούσας . . . εὐδαιμονίας (472–473): as invisible property, children make an excellent investment.

117. "Risk-free venture" sounds more ominous in the Greek, in which both words evoke motion, but the noun insists on it (*aphorman*, a starting-off or a setting-out) while the adjective cancels it out (*akinēton*, unmoved or unmovable). See Lee (1997) ad loc.: "a commercial metaphor referring to capital which keeps producing and so need never be disturbed . . . i. e. reduced." On the noun, see the scholiast on *Medea* 342; Cohen (1993) 184; and Millett (1983) 46. On *akinēton*, see Lee ad loc.

118. In this play, the oxymoron is naïve: Ion illustrates how movable children are if their parents discard them in abandonment. Raising a child is not always a sure thing, the parents may decide. Or, more bluntly, raising *this* child is not a safe bet.

119. On the ideology, see Kurke (1991) esp. 228ff. Lee (1997), at 490, puts it well: "They are unsentimental about the benefits of children: they are desirable because they bring considerable advantages, forming a link in the chain of inheritance ... and defending their country."

120. See Kurke (1991) 229, who also discusses this passage in terms of visible and invisible wealth.

121. See Lee (1997) at 485–487, who calls attention to *Hercules* 643–645 and Bond's comments at 642–643 and 645.

122. Note then that children are not "top-rank" possessions, that is, possessions that cannot be traded for or evaluated in terms of goods of lesser rank. For the concept, see, e.g., Kurke (1991) 94–95 and Morris (1986).

123. Simoeisios's inability to repay his parents for his upbringing when Aias kills him is only the first such reckoning in the *Iliad* (4.478).

124. Huys (1995), 172, discusses the weird juxtaposition of an "idyllic tableau" of dancing maidens with "the contrasting horror of a mother abandoning there her baby" as evidence of the emotional turmoil felt by the mother.

125. Kreousa's choice, as an unwed maiden, is particularly "natural," and the Chorus seems to prefer legitimate children in 487 (but the text is troubled), so that even in this context, Kreousa's choice is not as skewed as her father's. See Ebbott (2003) 19–20.

126. As discussed in Chapter 1, the ambiguity in the child's fate is the feature that seems to have both haunted and comforted parents. The possibility that the child survived to someone else's benefit screened parents from worse fates; the possibility that it might actually return to resume its inalienable place in their own *oikos* disturbed their dreams and myths.

127. On the practical element in the play, see Segal (1999) 99–100.

128. Cf. 562, where Xouthos proclaims that this day has made him at least "pros-

perous" (μακάριόν γ'); see also Lee (1997) ad loc. for a treatment of the word as "blissful." Both meanings, of course, are possible. See Saxonhouse (1986) 268–272 on Xouthos's complete lack of interest in Ion's mother as an appropriation of procreation by the male — hence, cultural — over the female — hence, biologic and natural; see also the comments of Zeitlin (1996c) 336.

129. For the questions that assimilate chance and mother, see vv 539 and 540, also 669. Pucci (1992), 90ff, who discusses the mother as the figure of *tukhē* or randomness (chance) in psychoanalytic terms, points to Oedipus's claim that he is the child of *Tukhē* (*OT* 1080–83), and recognizes that the mother's "generosity" is both natural, in terms of nurture, and promiscuous.

130. οὐ πέδον τίκτει τέκνα "the ground does not bear children" (542). This line is a sign of Xouthos's utterly alien status in Athens, for in this city, the ground has given birth repeatedly, and to the royal line, no less. Among the many scholars who note this point, see esp. Loraux (1990) 185; Saxonhouse (1986) 270; and Zeitlin (1996c) 325, who focuses on Ion's "affinity" with autochthony. The line also characterizes the king succinctly. He is willing to believe the oracle without pressing its logic, but utterly without faith in the larger mythology of either Delphi or his adopted state, Athens; see Lee (1997) at 542. Notice that Ion's premise contains a sort of abandonment: the earth bore him and then left him there to be found by someone kind enough to bring him to Delphi.

131. A variation of this scenario, here a means to account for unexpected offspring, later becomes in the hands of the Old Man a site of malicious calculation; see below in this chapter.

132. This scenario is used by later comedy; see Loraux (1990) 169, who cites the *Epitrepontes* of Menander as a parallel for the whole of the *Ion*, and Fantham (1975) 58, who adduces parallels from Plautus.

133. At least with women; their experience with other men and boys is another issue beyond this topic, but recall that Xouthos's approach to Ion has the appearance of a lover coming on to a potential beloved — see Chapter 4 and Knox (1979).

134. On the legal necessity of wedded sexual intercourse, see Demand (1994) 13 and duBois (1988) 65ff, esp. 79–80 on the *Ion*.

135. See Ebbott (2003) 19–20.

136. See Zeitlin (1996c) 334–337, on the language of adoption here and later (1532–1543, 1560–1562).

137. See Zacharia (2003) 137, who notes the similarities as well. Another sign of Ion's naïveté here is that autochthony creates possibilities regarding Ion's first question that he is unaware of or ignores: crops and children are two valuable commodities about which the king and queen of a city might be concerned; in Athens, however, children might *be* the crop itself, a point discussed especially by Loraux (1990) 191.

138. See Ebbott (2003) 17–21, on concealment as the means to restore a maiden's virginal state. Kreousa misses the further irony that that same mechanism might mean that she is not childless after all.

139. On the ideology of this gesture, see Kurke (1999) 93: "In contrast to commodity exchange, gift exchange depends on a personalized relationship between transaction partners which endures over time."

140. On Kreousa's ritual enclosure of Ion, much has been written; see, e.g., Loraux (1990) 75–76, 195–205; also Zeitlin (1996c) 294–297; and Gibert (1995) 185–189, who discusses the "cradle" as part of Euripides' representation of Kreousa's change of mind.

141. The nominative can hardly be construed with Apollo, although Owen (1939), ad loc., takes it as an apostrophe; the adjective in its normal meaning of "uneducated, ignorant," and hence "brutish," suits him in this bitter context. To have it modify the infant requires a forced sense of "without a trace," "unconscious of its woes," or "unknown"; see Owen (1939) and Lee (1997) ad loc. Diggle (1981) obelizes the word.

142. οἴμοι, μέγας θησαυρὸς ὡς ἀνοίγνυται / κακῶν (Oh, what a great treasure box of evils is opening!). See esp. Gibert (1995) 173ff.

143. Kreousa and her retainer equate the death of the child with consumption by wild animals and a childhood among the dead; all become equivalents as failures by the god to help. Kreousa's language suggests that Apollo should have picked up his child and acknowledged it as his — made him a part of his *oikos* in something like an *amphidromeia*. In keeping with the irony of the play, however, Apollo has matched and completed Kreousa's gestures through his agent Hermes: she sealed the *antipex* — Hermes opens it; she left it in one sanctuary (Pan's) — Hermes removes it to Apollo's; she threatened the god with the child's mutilation and death — he answered with a silence that eliminates her recouping anything from the gesture, since she is the one tormented by the child's supposed suffering.

144. Xouthos imagines recouping Ion as an ornament and credit to his house, because his own wealth and status allow for a freeborn son to accrue as profit, not blight (576–581); see Loraux (1990) 185. But Kreousa does not enjoy this luxury. Her justification to Ion, once they are reunited, about Apollo's evasive prophecy to Xouthos explains it well: a child born in dubious circumstances needs a rich, well-placed father (1540–1545).

145. Kreousa's father sacrificed her sisters for his victory against Eumolpos, but Poseidon then killed him; Kreousa and Ion rehearse these events in brief at 277–282.

146. At 523 and 1406–1407, where Ion uses the verb as an accusation against the woman he still does not know is his mother.

147. Lee (1997), at 523, notes Xouthos's tactlessness in the first context, given Ion's servile status; see also at 1406.

148. See Boswell (1988) 61ff, on Roman laws requiring that natal parents, if they wished to reclaim a child, repay foster parents for the costs they had incurred in raising it.

149. Ion's abandonment leaves nothing to chance in this construction, which calls Xouthos's arrangements "having engaged with a guest-friend" (ἐξενωμένον; 820). This is another more nefarious mystification of Ion's identity, no more an abandonment than Apollo's arrangements, as described by Hermes, and no more anonymous than Kreousa's ritualized exposure.

150. On Apollo's perspective, see Zacharia (2003) 128ff, who outlines the god's "dual aspect" toward Kreousa and Ion, whom he treats with "violence" or "care," and concludes that we are not to privilege one view of the god's behavior over the other. See also Segal (1999) 94–98.

151. Compare 1540–1544 (Kreousa's) with 1560–1562 (Athena's).

152. Athena's observation that Apollo chose not to appear himself to explain, "lest blame for earlier events come into the open" (1558), is a tantalizing ambiguity whose meaning has long been disputed; see Lee (1997) ad loc.; and Zacharia (2003), chap. 3.

153. Ion's superfluity of parents is much discussed. Zeitlin (1996c) has one of the best recent discussion on the intricacies of parentage in the drama; see also Ebbott (2003) and Zacharia (2003).

154. He is unmoved by denials of calculation or claims of *philia* (friendship), and he refuses initially to be embraced by either, a strong visual signal that he cannot be possessed

simply by claims. *Philia* also reverberates economically, as a relationship of belonging. The term that would de-commercialize reunion with Ion in fact reinforces that aspect of it.

155. See 137; 183; 319–321; 1324; Ion even acknowledges his debt to inanimate buildings (109–110). This calculation seems to be the analogue to the Chorus's assessment of children's worth as visible property.

156. ὡς γὰρ ἀμήαηωρ ἀπάτωρ τε γεγὼς; used of an orphan, an evocative, if an unusually strong, phrase.

157. Ion's monody establishes his characteristics of youth, naïveté, and utter devotion to the god whose shrine he tends. According to Burnett (1971) 104, his song has a timeless, "enchanted world" quality to it that is in sharp contrast both to Hermes' tale and to what is about to happen to him. See Gibert (1995) 189–201 for an excellent discussion of arguments for and against the education of Ion as a kind of stripping away of his naïve faith in the essential wholesomeness of his world in Delphi.

158. Others have noted how this structure is weirdly skewed in reference to the normal Athenian's sense of identity. For the dependence of a child's future rights as a citizen on his father's status, see Foley (2002) 73ff.

159. The Old Man's account of Ion in Xouthos's plot makes him the worst thing of all, a motherless no-account as the usurper of her royal line (836–838). Loraux's essay (1990) perhaps best emphasizes Kreousa's paramount role as mother in determining Ion's Athenian identity, despite the fact that, as all ancient spectators would have known and felt, it took *both* parents to establish citizenship, and the father's role was paramount.

160. See Kovacs (1979) 116ff for significant deletions.

161. See Lee (1997) ad loc. for other tragic instances of this platitude, but given the play's emphasis on calculating profit and loss, it is strange: how can great things be an equal blessing to small things? It is not a matter of attitude, as the Chorus prays for at 490–491, because Ion includes that in his calculation.

162. The extra, mortal father is needed for the child to be well-born (or legitimate; εὐγενῆ; 1540ff); and he is a sign of Apollo's good intentions 1540; This reasoning is exactly that claimed by Athena for Apollo; it is also exactly the inverse of Ion's when calculating the cost of not having a known mother.

163. Zeitlin (1996c), 287–293, offers the best account of this playfulness.

164. Ion finally accepts this account: "This is a worthy possession I'm getting" (ἄξιον τὸ κτῆμά μοι; 1618). On whether these are his words, which the MSS deny, see Lee (1997) ad loc., who, like Diggle (1981) and Owen (1939), accepts Hermann's attribution.

165. The gesture parallels adoption, as Zeitlin (1996c), 335, discusses, and Apollo's kindly gesture balances the Old Man's account, which posited Xouthos's ill intent (808ff).

166. The power of choice may be the point of the false oracle, which is a symbol for Ion's constructed, unnatural identity, at least as far as the gods are concerned: how silly of Xouthos to ask whether he can have a son — the first person he meets can be his son; he has only to embrace someone to make him his.

167. In the *Theaetetus* 160e; see Chapter 1 above.

168. And for us now to speak of infantile development in language that makes separation the equivalent of abandonment is to domesticate the latter and to privilege the child's progress as a screen over the adult's hidden trauma; see Chapter 1 above.

169. See esp. Hoffer (1996).

170. Again, see Armstrong's discussion (2005) of ancient culture as such a source for Freud.

F O U R : Recognition

Epigraphs: Lacan (1978) 59; Euripides, *Ion* 1292–1293.

1. Freud calls this figure a *Kindermädchen* (*GW* 12: 124); she is distinct from the Wolf Man's *Kinderfrau*, his "Nanya," who played such a large role in introducing him to religion (*SE* 17: 61–62) and the English governess (*Gouvernante*) who was remembered with fear and loathing and was dismissed from her duties when the Wolf Man was still a toddler (see *GW* 12: 37–38, 123–124). I retain "nursery-maid" from the translation in the Standard Edition, because our "babysitter" seems too casual to designate her formal and permanent relationship in the Wolf Man's household.

2. That fire is physically present is suggested by 1258; see Owen (1939) ad loc., who notes that πυρά here is a synonym for "altar," and so it is, but not a coincidental one. Hoffer (1996), 300–301, also remarks on the parallelism of fire in the eyes of the two contestants.

3. Since urination is the child's understanding of ejaculation; see Freud, "Civilization and Its Discontents," *SE* 21: 90n1.

4. Jean Laplanche calls fire "the paradigmatic figure for the perception of the traumatic event." See Lukacher (1986) 129–130, who cites Laplanche (1980–81) 3: 194–196. Lukacher also corrects Felman (1980) 148, who remarks that fire *"eliminates the center"* (her emphasis) by noting that, on the contrary, fire marks the presence of the something that fuels it; it never leaves simply "emptiness and loss." See further below in this chapter.

5. Such as a mother's love for her son being the "most perfect, easily the most ambivalence-free of all human relationships"; see Gay (1998) 505ff. On the problem, see Sprengnether (1990) and Armstrong (2005), esp. 69ff, for Freud's treatment of the mythic structures of the mother. Breger's biography (2000) passim, makes a thoroughgoing case for Freud's inability to deal with his own early trauma with his mother as the great absence in psychoanalysis.

6. In her study of the absent mother in nineteenth-century novels, Dever (1998), 45, concludes: "the embodied mother is completely irrelevant within the psychoanalytic *Bildungsroman*, while the metaphor of maternal benevolence, constructed through and as her willful passivity, is essential"; see 40–51. On Freud's sentimentality regarding the mother, see Gay (1998) 505ff. Breger (2000) studies Freud's replacement of his true feelings about his mother with his theory as a systematic, lifelong therapeutic strategy.

7. The phrase is the title of Sprengnether's chap. 3 (1990, 39–85); she discusses the case of the Wolf Man on 72–74. She also concludes, in reference to the patient whom Freud calls Dora, that "his own narrative displays the symptoms he attributes to the hysteric" (40).

8. See Sprengnether (1990) 230–232.

9. Ibid.; the second part of Sprengnether's book (179–221) studies object-relations, Lacan, and Luce Ingaray in particular. Not all psychoanalytic theorists, however, fall prey to this structure. For two examples, see Deleuze and Guattari (1977), who directly challenge the oedipal triangle's hegemony, and Butler (1990) who discusses how psychoanalysis participates in the hegemony of heterosexual structures in defining identity.

10. Dever (1998) 51; at 39–77, she provides a good summary of Freud's own thinking about the loss of the mother and the contrasting positions of Melanie Klein and D. W. Winnicott.

11. Object-relations theorists differ about the nature of the crisis. Melanie Klein erot-

icized the moment as an anticipation of "the dramas that constitute the later, Oedipal-genital phase" (Dever, 52). The mother and her breast take the place of the father and the phallus as central figures in the development of the child's consciousness. The need to outgrow the breast and nursing is perceived as more natural and thus beneficial than the castration anxiety defined by Freud. D. W. Winnicott was more concerned with the "absolute dependency" of the child on the mother, which renders the mother exceptionally and dangerously powerful as long as she is an attachment; see Winnicott (1986) 124–125; see also Dever (1998) 53ff.

12. Winnicott in fact, through his notion of the "good enough mother," invites the mother's active participation in her own effacement in her child's separation from her; see Dever (1998) 65ff.

13. See Sprengnether (1990) 233ff, who relies on the theory of Julia Kristeva in formulating her ideas.

14. Hrdy (1999) 125–129; although newborns possess vestiges of an instinct to cling "for dear life," the human species lost the body hair to which most infant primates cling as insurance against their mother's careless or sudden movement, so that human babies must be constantly held as well as suckled. See also Kertzer (1993) 123. As for the "allomother," Hrdy (1999) considers the dynamics of this option in her chap. 6. Even today, when human babies are unlikely to be eaten by carnivores, they are difficult to keep alive if they cannot be nursed, absent such modern technologies as the rubber nipple and infant formula, as well as the availability of clean drinking water; see Hrdy (1999) 298–304. As for ancient so-called "feeding bottles," these are unlikely to have been effective; see Demand (1994) 7–8 and n. 28, where she observes that these may well have been lamps rather than bottles.

15. Hrdy (1999), 390, argues that humans sacrificed newborn capacity for autonomous survival in favor of brain size. She spells out the strategies: "By crying out, signaling, clasping tight, and in emotional terms, by caring desperately, baby primates do whatever it takes to feel secure" (96). And the infant's anxiety at separation at the physical level may instead be a manifestation of fear that its mother's attention and life-saving care may be wandering.

16. Such an image of mother and child also differs from the typology at the heart of object-relations, with its preoccupation with the child's movement from its primal sense of symbiosis with the mother to separation. See Stern (2000) 42ff, who notes, however, that the object-relations theorists, particularly Klein, do posit the subjectivity of the newborn.

17. Stern (1998) 17–18; see also his assessment in Stern (2000) 54–61.

18. Such was the fate of all such threats by women in the Wolf Man's early life, according to Freud. His mother and his Nanya both threatened castration to ward him off masturbation.

19. In both cases, the memory screened by later anxiety is recognized as important well before the scenes themselves can be recovered.

20. In 1918, Freud added another comment on the power of the Grusha scene to confirm the reality of his construction of the primal scene.

21. On Armstrong's discussion on the primacy of "intellectuality" (2005), which is fundamentally of the father, over the "sensuality" of the mother, and thus the primacy of theory over evidence, see the Conclusion.

22. As is plain in Freud's efforts to distinguish his reliance on the phylogenetic from Jung's; see *SE* 17: 97. Freud's rhetoric here concerning the ubiquity of the primal scene is misleading. He wrote these remarks, as an addition to the original text of the case history,

in 1918, when he was finally able to publish it after World War I. It is possible that in the intervening four years, he had heard more patients speak about primal scenes, but the claim of parallels raises suspicion, especially given that this case was to introduce the world to the notion. See Lukacher (1986) 140, for Freud's tendency to substitute "theoretical hope" for clinical evidence.

23. As Freud systematically transfers all such threats in "From the History of an Infantile Neurosis"; see 86.

24. Gay (1998), 505, also reminds us of how little we know about the Wolf Man's early history with his natal mother. In his later career, she was an object of intense rivalry for his father's money, but after the Russian revolution, she lived with the Wolf Man and his wife Therese until her death in the 1950s.

25. It is also tempting to hear in these two characterizations the two outcomes of the romance of belonging — the tease suggesting a bond, the scold suggesting anger and separation.

26. Note discussions of his identification with the suffering of Christ, esp. 64–67; and the confusion suffered over the German word for wasp (94, quoted above).

27. Armed with the Wolf Man's own later recollections, psychoanalysts have nonetheless embarked on just such a hunt, a process that accelerated after the Austrian journalist Karin Obholzer (1982) interviewed the Wolf Man extensively just before his death. Many have concluded that Freud did not hear "the cries of the Wolf-Man" correctly, but the results of these various reanalyses of the Wolf Man are so disparate that none is finally compelling. *Cries of the Wolf Man* is the title of Mahony (1984). See also Kanzer (1980), Masson (1984), and Kartiganer (1985). For the reassessment of the Wolf Man's primal scene by the psychoanalytic community itself, see Blum (1980a). See the more recent Johnson (2001), who begins from the work of Abraham and Torok (1976). Yet each is put forward with "delusional certainty," as Lila Kalinach (1991), 186, calls these futile quests in her critique of the process. See also Lukacher (1986). The delusion lies in the lure of the narrative, both Freud's and the Wolf Man's, but Freud's restaging has been too effective and thorough.

28. In "Totem and Taboo" (*SE* 13: 1–161), Freud theorizes extreme physical violence as a crucial element in identity and enshrines murder as the primal event in human culture, but the murder lies between a father and his sons, who both long for and fear the act of violence.

29. The primal scene itself is a cardinal instance of this process, in which Freud admits that he had to discard some details that were not confirmed by the Wolf Man's response to the scene constructed out of them; see *SE* 17: 62n1, 89, 95.

30. Lacan (1978) 70, with the apt phrase, "the solicitation of the gaze." In this discussion, the paradox that fascinated Lacan himself is that the patient has only words to effect spectacle.

31. Freud, "Civilization and Its Discontents," *SE* 21: 90n1. Thus to the connection between fire and urination had to be added ambition: political power begins in a control over the body and its impulses. This scenario allows Freud to account for the persistent association of women with hearths in Western cultural myths: they were put in charge of the communal or family fire precisely because their anatomy did not allow them to extinguish it on a whim or in a "homosexual competition." Freud develops the conjecture further in "The Acquisition and Control of Fire" (*SE* 22: 187–193), in which he interprets the Promethean myth of fire to account for the libidinal meaning of early man's relation to

fire. His association of urination and ambition appears as early as "The Interpretation of Dreams": see *SE* 4: 218 and 5: 469; in the latter passage, he links his own dreaming about urination with Gulliver's extinguishing of a fire for the Lilliputians. See also "Character and Anal Erotism," *SE* 9: 175.

32. See n. 4 above. The connections between flames and trauma that later psychoanalysts have articulated more explicitly seem already inherent in Freud's formulation as well, if elusive.

33. By the "psychology of dreams," Freud addresses the role of well-known psychological phenomena, such as condensation and regression, as they occur in dreaming, as well the requirements that a dream be "sensory images" and "though not invariably . . . that the structure of the dream shall have a rational and intelligible exterior" (533).

34. It recurs most recently in Mark Buchan's engaging discussion of the deaths of Odysseus's enemies in the *Odyssey* (2005) 171; Buchan relies on Slavoj Žižek's analysis of the dream in *Enjoy Your Symptoms! Jacques Lacan in Hollywood and Out* (1992).

35. The dream thus functions as a drama fulfilling wishes, in this case, Freud's wish to illustrate the psyche of dreams.

36. For Lacan, the dream better illustrates the principle that it keeps the person asleep and thus forestalls its own end.

37. Thus Lacan understands the term as an extension of his definition of its root, *tuché* (1978) 69–70. While he notes the more normal translation of this noun, "chance" or "misfortune," Lacan derives his sense from the verbal root of the word, τυγχάνω, which he takes to mean "to encounter" or "to meet."

38. In Lacan's theory, there is an equivalence between the origin and an encounter of the "real," and the play of flames upon their fuel suggests the "real," which is the beginning of symbols but lies beyond our grasp. To avoid confusion, I have consistently used Freudian terms and omitted this concept of the real, but Alan Sheridan, Lacan's translator, clarifies (Lacan [1978], 280): "[the real] stands for what is neither symbolic nor imaginary, and remains foreclosed from the analytic experience." Hence, "the real" is used "to describe that which is lacking in the symbolic order, the ineliminable residue of all articulation, the foreclosed element, which may be approached, but never grasped." Lacan himself was troubled by a haste in psychoanalysis to apply labels; he considers the effort to pinpoint the "actuality of the situation" as an aid in the "demystification of that artifact of treatment known as the transference" (69) to be of little value. "The real has to be sought beyond the dream — in what the dream has enveloped, hidden from us, behind the lack of representation of which there is only one representative. This is the real that governs our activities more than any other, and it is psychoanalysis that designates it for us." (60) Such is the paradox of his chosen field: the real is unrecoverable, but psychoanalysis must still diagnosis it.

39. Freud acknowledges that in 1919 they discovered a fragment that required further work; for subsequent analysis by Brunswick, see Chapter 3 above.

40. On Freud's habits of mind at the center of the development of psychoanalysis, see the studies of Winters (1999), Johnson (2001), and Armstrong (2005).

41. Lacan, who avoided "the potential dangers of narrative case histories," could play with the notion of the perpetually unrecoverable and fault Freud for his sense of timing and authoritarian ways, but the founder of psychoanalysis had no such luxury. See Lukacher (1986) 28–31, who contrasts Freud and Lacan in greater detail.

42. We never find out whether the mother-figure and child were about to embrace or

reject one another, but we don't need to because Freud ingenuously implicates the encounter in the primal scene of the father's embrace. As for the fire burning at the site, although it seems a provocative symbol of a longing to see something before it becomes a reproach, Freud deems it to signify merely the presence of a stereotype.

43. From this violation flow others, particularly the Chorus's decision to disobey a direct injunction to conceal Xouthos's good news from Kreousa. This convention itself solves problems arising from another convention that requires the dramatic chorus to remain on stage throughout the action. Zeitlin (1996), 315, suggests that these two violated conventions are deliberately set up against one another: Apollo's, that is, requires (and is requited by) the Chorus's. In fact, the entire structure of the play suggests a putting to right of the god's initial bad dramatic taste: the "false" recognition, between Ion and Xouthos, leads to the Chorus enflaming Kreousa with the news; the intrigue of the murder plot then comes *before* the "true" recognition — again, uniquely in extant tragedy.

44. See Zeitlin (1996c). Loraux (1990) structures her discussion of identity's construction in the play around Kreousa's status as an *epikleros*, that is, a daughter attached to her father's estate because of the absence of a male heir. Zacharia (2003) studies the contributions of all Ion's parents, natal, foster, and fraudulent, and surveys previous work as well.

45. Segal (1999) 93.

46. Ogden (1996) studies the legal status of the bastard in Athenian society; Ebbott (2003) studies deployment of the figure in literature. Fourth-century court cases indicate, of course, that a man's legitimate status could also be challenged by political enemies later in his life. Slater (1968) studies the dynamic between mother and son in his early years.

47. Murnaghan (1992) 249.

48. See Alexiou (1974), Holtz-Warhaft (1992), and Derderian (2001). That there is anything inherent or natural about the link is called into question by Stears (1998) 113ff.

49. Murnaghan (1992) 245–246, on Demophoön's fate in the "Homeric Hymn to Demeter"; and 246–249, on Meleager's. See also Foley (1994) and Clay (1989).

50. On the cliché, see Zeitlin (2005). Her gesture also reverses the father's ritual embrace attending the introduction of a child into a household in the *amphidromeia*, and in expressing her longing for a witness, Kreousa may also evoke a ritual intended to preserve the sanctity of the *oikos:* her refusal to embrace her newborn was necessary for a larger good. Finally, we should recall that Meleager's mother, Althea, has an instant in which to do one of two things: snatch a burning log from her hearth or simply watch it burn; see Murnaghan (1992) 247ff.

51. Recognition is not the normal climax in a play about an abandoned child who is reunited with his natal family. In the more familiar structure, the reunion of child and parent precedes their plotting to punish or overthrow a (now) common enemy as the play's climax. Sophocles' *Oedipus Tyrannus* is one notable exception to this pattern, since this royal child's apprehension of the truth about his identity is the play's climax. Instead of reunion, mother and son must dissolve their awful bonds, and Oedipus, having long since killed his father, the man who ordered his exposure, has no enemy but himself. But the *Ion* calls a greater attention to its exceptional structure by including within its own action an attempt at murder before the reunion in the absence of true recognition. See Gibert (1995) 92 on the skill with which the *Ion* postpones the "release" of Kreousa from her "doomed attempt to remain silent." See also Huys (1995) 37, 47–48, and 335–343 on the more expected structure of recognition preceding the plotting.

52. But it is a detail he shares with the other Athenian autochthon used in the play as symbol of Athens's foundation, Erichthonios, who was born from the earth as a baby — an unusual beginning for autochthons — and immediately stashed in his box.

53. See Hrdy (1999) 298, who criticizes Boswell for neglecting this aspect of the foundling's peril when optimistically assuming the prospects of its survival. Of course, the verb τρέφειν need not only indicate strictly "nurturing," but a more general "rearing"; see Huys (1995) 271, who suggests that it can simply signify "rescuing." I prefer the stricter meaning because of the verb's proximity to "breast." One can apply various sorts of logic to eliminate the paradoxical quality of Ion's remark: that infants do not "*know*" that they're breast-feeding; or, that Euripides is merely applying a dramatic economy here — the Pythia provided for a wet-nurse, of course, but the detail would be irrelevant and intrusive — and so on. The importance of nursing can be seen in other mythic tales about infant gods and mortals abandoned at birth, in which the question of who nursed the newborn is rarely neglected. Some wet-nurse or kindly animal is nearly always provided for in the story. No account explains who immediately nursed Oedipus, but his eventual placement in the royal household of Corinth was perhaps sufficient explanation for an ancient listener. The infant Zeus is nurtured by bees and a she-goat in his Cretan cave; Iamos is also given honey, although by serpents (Pind. *O.* 6.44–46); Cyrus is given to a shepherd whose wife has just lost her newborn (Hdt. 1.122, who rejects the "folktale" that Cyrus was nursed by a dog); Pelias is suckled by a mare (schol. A *Il.* 10.334); Paris, by a she-bear or perhaps, based on the fragments of Sophocles' *Alexandros*, a human wet-nurse (see Huys, 1995, 278); Telephos was nursed by a doe (Soph. *Aleadai*, fr. 89). I draw these references from Huys (1995) chap. 2.1, 270ff, whose focus in surveying the evidence of wild animals is, however, from the perspective of the child's miraculous survival. His comments on the *Ion* in this regard are suggestive, for this play places heavy emphasis upon the ravaging of wild animals, in contrast to their miraculous care for helpless newborns in other myths (cf. 279ff). Since this care usually takes the form of nursing, it may be that the *Ion* is deliberately negating a possibility for Ion's care that would have been familiar to the audience. See also Pomeroy (1997) 121 and 185n92, who comments on the ancient evidence both for attempts at baby bottles (in clay) and for wet-nurses. See also Segal (1999) 95–96 on nursing and issues of "male" versus "female parenthood" in the play.

54. This is as close as he comes to criticizing Kreousa. The distinction between nursing and embracing is clear in Kreousa's lament; just before these lines, she states that she did wrap Ion up in swaddling (1489–1490).

55. On the displacement of Kreousa's body as a site for Ion's natal identity, see Rabinowitz (1993) 194–195.

56. Mutilation by wild beasts is a formulaic fate for the fallen in epic and therefore may haunt the spectators' imaginations, but this haunting is perhaps made more disturbing because they also abandoned newborns.

57. On the interplay of the embrace and the enclosure, see esp. Zeitlin (1996c) 294ff, 300–307, on the theme of Ion as a second Erichthonios, born again from his entombment in the cave; and Gibert (1995) 185ff. See Price (1978) 59–60, for representations of Athena with Erichthonius; see also 2–9, where she notes that Earth herself was also *kourotrophos*. This magisterial approach to the problem of the foundling's identity — converting it into a symbolic object that satisfies the needs of the community — is oddly present within one very fruitful approach to understanding the *Ion* in the past fifteen years, one that studies how the play itself performs a similar conversion on Ion into a sacred relic of Athens's

glorious ancestry. While critics such as Loraux (1990) or Zeitlin (1996c) cogently argue that the dramatization of Ion's miraculous reunion with his natal mother and his entry into the city of Athens celebrates all that it means to be Athenian, with all the most important and venerable symbols of that city and its special relationship to its guardian gods insinuated into the complicated constructions of Ion's familial and political identity, this process of conversion is one that we as readers and critics are heavily implicated in. Although we don't think we need a foundling whose identity evokes desperate women and unwanted children, we would like to know more about the strange, distant culture of fifth-century Athens. And thus we build in Ion the identities useful to this project, relying on evidence in the play that others — gods and mortals — have converted the abandoned child into symbols before us.

58. Cf. 1324–1325 for her participation in this reciprocity. Lee (1997), at 319–330, sees in Ion's statement a distinction made between a *real* mother's care and that of a foster mother: "the point of this statement is to put limits on the maternal role of the Priestess; though she treated Ion like a mother (321), she was unable to nurture him as his own mother could have." But Ion's words state what he understands more flatly than an opposition between the missing mother, who refused to nurse him, and the Pythia, who couldn't but somehow raised him and who therefore counts as his mother to him. Still, the Pythia believes she enjoys a privileged position from which to counsel him. When she enters, she presumes that her superior relationship gives her a right to order the youth to search for his natal mother, as a gesture that will turn him from his new savagery and make him "pure" (καθαρός; 1333). The Pythia's power is more limited than she knows, however. The operation she recommends will not turn Ion away from this stereotypical stepmother; instead, embracing the *antipex* will lead to the more intimate and humane embrace of mother and son. See Watson (1995) 35–37, who reviews the opinions of scholars troubled by Kreousa's abrupt reversion to type.

59. Here the sense of space and gestures is very strong, and the comic possibility of stage business has long been recognized; it is perhaps most engagingly stated by Knox (1979) 260–263.

60. Knox (1979), 260, notes that Xouthos's approach to Ion could be mistaken for a lover's come-on, an effect, he correctly argues, that would have been much more strongly felt by the fifth-century audience, steeped as it would have been in ways and means of homoerotic courtship. Ion's gesture overtly stands as midpoint in tone between his scouring the temple precinct of the birds who might befoul it and his baleful threat to seize Kreousa and hurl her from Parnassus's heights (158ff; 1266ff); see Lee (1997) ad loc., who calls Ion's threat here "light-hearted," in contrast with his later threat to Kreousa.

61. Knox (1979), 260, first stressed the point that the spectators would see an attempt at erotic assault in Xouthos's excited gestures and language; it has been taken up by others — see Hoffer (1996) 298.

62. What may startle us later is to learn that the delusion is to be permanent and enshrined in Athens's official history of its origins.

63. At 151 b–c, he suggests that new mothers feel this most of all.

64. So-called by Owen (1939) ad loc., who sees the same effect in 1293. Lee (1997), ad loc. cites as parallel Kreousa's command at 1404; references to *Euripides'* Andromache 258, 260, where the threats come from Hermione, seem less apt, since she will be the agent of the burning.

65. Although the audience does learn of his future from Athena, it is a future shrouded by deceit.

66. See esp. Zacharia (2003) 31–39, who draws on earlier studies; see also Mastronarde (1975) 169; Goff (1988) 42–54; Loraux (1990) 175–176; Alford (1992) 46; Zeitlin (1996c) 319–320.

67. The poison hangs alongside a potent universal healing potion; the meaning of this imagery has been much studied. See Burnett (1971) 115–116; Mastronarde (1975) 168; Loraux (1990) 200–201.

68. This sense of morality is false, however; see Hoffer (1996) 299–303.

69. The vessel is a symbol of Ion, safely embraced in her arms, just as Kreousa was saved in the embrace of her mother; see Lee (1997) at 1337. On the Pythia as a kind of deus ex machina, see Lee (1997) 298, who cites Schmid-Stählin (3.554); see also Halleran (1985) 36–37. Kreousa's revelation of the *antipex* also inverts the image of its counterpart in the play, the tent. At the level of dramatic structure, the balance between these two contestants is necessary to generate a dramatic impasse that can only be resolved by the miraculous intervention of the god's human agent, the Pythia, with her tokens from the past. Ion is as frustrated and helpless in the face of Kreousa's defiance as he is determined, after her revelations, to confront Apollo about who his father is (cf. 1312–1319 and 1546–1548).

70. The Chorus's language suggests this with the metonymy of "torch" (πυρᾶς) for altar (1258). See also Hoffer (1996) 300–301, who suggests that we are meant to imagine Ion with the same "hereditary glare."

71. The audience heard the whole tale from Kreousa when she planned the murder (989–998). This highly eccentric version of the Gorgon's story may well have been invented by Euripides precisely for this moment, since each detail of the story is too thematically significant to be coincidental. See Segal (1999) 80–81, Mastronarde (1975) 168, and Lee (1997) at 991. The heirloom situates the destiny of Athens's royal household on and in the person of its sole survivor — a female who could normally not inherit such a role with all its trappings. Nevertheless, she must be the mortal vessel through which the ancient line of autochthonous beings passes into a reality of Athens's early kings, and in token of that, murder and healing inhere in her person. The ways in which the drama loads meaning onto the person of Kreousa have been much discussed; see esp. the studies of Walsh (1978) and Loraux (1990).

72. For other discussions of thematic significance of this imagery, see Zeitlin (1996c) and Loraux (1990).

73. See States (1985) 54–58, in relation to Shakespeare's art, on the way in which dramatic language "creates a verbal world that bathes what we see before us in its quality" (57).

74. See Zeitlin (1996) 314ff.

75. See Lee (1997) at 1404–1405.

Conclusion

Epigraph: Keva Rosenfeld, "Cleaning out the House," *Day to Day*, National Public Radio, August 18, 2005, www.npr.org/templates/story/story.php?storyId=4805166 (accessed October 14, 2006).

1. I claim this while keeping in mind here the warning of Panter-Brick (2000) on the dangers of assuming a normative family structure. Her warning only reinforces my sense of the universal I am positing: whatever structure of familial belonging a culture offers, every single child in it or of it was chosen for keeping or not.

2. It is no wonder then that we prefer to see the romance from the perspective of the

child, the miraculous survivor. Psychoanalysis comforts its adherents with the fiction that its goal is the heal the suffering of the child, caught between its fantasies and its parents. Myth comes up with the comforting fictions of its own that the gods deploy the fatal child as sign that their awareness of destiny allows them to control it.

3. See Breger (2000) 358–362, who notes that despite his gesture, which Freud refused, Jung's collaboration with the Nazis in other respects makes this "not his finest hour" (359).

4. See Gay (1998) 632–651.

5. See the largely fictitious lives by Satyrus (*Life of Eur.* fr. 39) and Philodemus (*de vitiis*, col. 13). It should be noted that Euripides' final, victorious set of plays included the extant *Iphigenia at Aulis* and the lost *Alcmaeon in Corinth*. Segal (1997), 212–213, does not speculate why Euripides might have left but does detect a change in the man's thinking about civic "leadership."

6. An Oedipus or a Paris may be an ominous sign of the gods' displeasure or of destiny's inevitability, but can a god signify his own irresistible godhead?

7. The work on the play is enormous. See Segal (1997) for earlier studies, and Wohl (2005).

8. Segal (1997) 246. And if the mythic terms of abandonment hold true, then Euripides depends on a conceptualization of his exposure as the desperate measure by the genre itself to stave off the demise, but this is not to suggest that Dionysus is the champion of prose (or that Segal suggests anything like that!). The very return of the child to his natal origin disrupts regardless of intent.

9. Segal (1997) 272ff.

10. If Euripides stages tradition's death for his spectators, he is notorious for having killed off the genre of tragedy itself. The Athenians themselves knew this even before they saw the *Bacchae*: that tragedy was gone with the death of the man who had made it impossible for tradition to be staged any longer. Aristophanes' *Frogs* in 405 fantasizes about the possibility of bringing him and his well-written poetry back from the dead (but ends up choosing Aeschylus instead because the kind of men he offers to save the city from its self-destructive war are not the clever, modern sort offered by Euripides). But if Euripides is responsible for the death of tragedy, by exploding the terms that structured the first manifestation of this genre, the *Bacchae* seems to contradict this notion, because it is, at first glance, starkly traditional: an offended god exacts horrific punishment to the ruin of characters and the edification of the audience. Yet despite its traditional form the play explodes categories of symbols and boundaries that earlier tragedies rely on. Or is the deconstruction in the person of the god? Rather than a return to traditional values, as some early critics read the play (a late conversion from all that fresh mountain air), is this play the tragedian's subtlest and deadliest subversion of Athens's official religious codes? See most recently Segal (1997).

11. Acknowledging that the oedipal triangulation is a hegemony blocking awareness of the "polymorphously perverse human desire," Wohl charts the *Bacchae*'s exuberance of an imagined or created otherness that challenges the very possibility of (Greek) structures and polarities to contain the "Real of sexual difference" (151). Such an application of psychoanalysis defies the very notion of what Freud was about, because it frees itself from structure itself.

12. Wohl (2005).

13. To take an obvious example, one cliché asserts that the god's ritual celebrates

Athenian greatness as a polis when it resides in its heart but dissolves the cultural strictures on sexuality and citizenry when it retreats to the mountainside. The *Bacchae*, however, confounds this structure by sending the citizen women into madness outside the city and bringing an alien chorus of Maenads into the city to speak—apparently—of the moderation (or *sophrosyne*) in Dionysiac worship. See Segal (1997) 78–124.

14. Freud had been working on "Moses and Monotheism" since 1934 and had published the first two sections. It was the last and longest section, two versions of reflections on the origin of monotheism, that he found he could finish once in London with the expectation of actually publishing it.

15. Freud also shows signs of distrust and disdain for the structures of abandonment, perhaps because these had been most thoroughly studied from a psychoanalytic point of view by Otto Rank ([1909] 2004), whom Freud cites but despised.

16. On Freud's relationship to Judaism and especially on his appropriation of Moses, chap. 11 of Armstrong's discussion (2005) is crucial; I am in debt to his discussion of the Freudian Moses' role in "the triumph of intellectuality" (244ff).

17. Armstrong (2005), 245, continues: "It seems clear that matriarchy is implicated in sensuality from a remark he makes on the next page concerning the historical passage to patriarchy. 'But this turning from the mother to the father points in addition to a victory of intellectuality over sensuality—that is, an advance in civilization, since maternity is proved by the evidence of the senses while paternity is a hypothesis, based on an inference and a premise. . . .' (SE 23:114)."

18. The references are to James Breasted, *History of Egypt* (1906), and Eduard Meyer, *Die Entstehung des Judentums* (1906). Freud also makes use of Breasted's *The Dawn of Conscience* (1934).

19. The crucial third part of "Moses and Monotheism" shows signs of the struggle. It was repeatedly revised, he tells us, and added to; in fact, it consists of two sections, which repeat each other's arguments. Freud could not bring himself to publish it either; he says he delayed for fear of offending the Catholic Church in Austria, which was protecting him. See the editor's remarks, *SE* 234–235.

Works Cited

Abraham, Nicolas, and Maria Torok. 1986. *The Wolf Man's Magic Word. A Cryptonymy.* Translated by Nicholas Rand. Minneapolis. Originally published as *Le Verbier de l'Homme aux loups. Cryptonymie* (Paris, 1976).

Alford, C. Fred. 1992. *The Psychoanalytic Theory of Greek Tragedy.* New Haven, Conn.

Alexiou, Margaret. 1974. *The Ritual Lament in Greek Tradition.* Cambridge, England.

Anatol, Giselle, ed. 2003. *Reading Harry Potter. Critical Essays.* Westport, Conn.

Andreades, A. [1933] 1979. *A History of Greek Public Finance.* Vol. 1. Translated by Carroll N. Brown. New York.

Armstrong, Richard. 2005. *A Compulsion for Antiquity. Freud and the Ancient World.* Ithaca, N.Y.

Arnott, W. Geoffrey. 1996. "Realism in the *Ion:* Response to Lee." In Silk (1996) 110–118.

Austin, M. M., and P. Vidal-Naquet. 1977. *Economic and Social History of Ancient Greece.* London.

Baecker, Dirk. 1992. "The Writing of Accounting." *Stanford Literary Review* 9: 157–178.

Bakker, Egbert, Irene de Jong, and Hans van Wees, eds. 2002. *Brill's Companion to Herodotus.* Leiden.

Bassi, Karen. 2005. "Visuality and Temporality: Reading the Tragic Script." In Pedrick and Oberhelman (2005) 251–270. Chicago.

Bearak, Barry. 2002. "Children as Barter." In *The New York Times: A Nation Challenged. A Visual History of 9/11 and Its Aftermath*, ed. Mitchel Levitas, 208–209. New York.

Benardete, Seth. [1969] 1999. *Herodotean Inquiries.* South Bend, Ind.

Bettelheim, Bruno. 1989. *The Uses of Enchantment: The Meaning and Importance of Fairy Tales.* New York.

Biehl, W. 1992. "Textprobleme in Euripides' *Ion.*" *Philologus* 136: 14–30.

Blake, Andrew. 2002. *The Irresistible Rise of Harry Potter.* London.

Blok, Josine. 2002. "Women in Herodotus' *Histories.*" In Bakker et al. (2002) 225–242. Leiden

Blum, Harold P., M.D. 1980a. "The Borderline Childhood of the Wolf Man." In Kanzer and Glenn (1980) 341–352. New York.

———. 1980b. "The Pathogenic Influence of the Primal Scene: A Reevaluation." In Kanzer and Glenn (1980) 367–372. New York.

Blundell, Sue. 1995. *Women in Ancient Greece.* Cambridge, Mass..

Boheemen, Christine van. 1987. *The Novel as Family Romance. Language, Gender, and Authority from Fielding to Joyce.* Ithaca, N.Y.

Bolkestein, Hendrik. 1922. "The Exposure of Children at Athens and the ἐγχυτρίστριαι." *Classical Philology* 17: 222–239.

——. 1958. *Economic Life in Greece's Golden Age.* 2nd ed. Leiden.

Bond, Godfrey, ed. 1981. *Euripides Heracles, with Introduction and Commentary.* Oxford.

Boswell, John. 1988. *The Kindness of Strangers. The Abandonment of Children in Western Europe from Late Antiquity to the Renaissance.* New York.

Bourdieu, Pierre. 1977. *Outline of a Theory of Practice.* Translated by Richard Nice. New York.

——. [1987] 1990a. *In Other Words. Essays Towards a Reflexive Sociology.* Translated by Matthew Adamson. Stanford.

——. [1980] 1990b. *The Logic of Practice.* Translated by R. Nice. Stanford.

Bowdler, Sandra. 1996. "Freud and Archaeology." *Anthropological Forum* 7: 419–438.

Breger, Louis. 2000. *Freud. Darkness in the Midst of Vision.* New York.

Bremmer, Jan-Martin. 1983. "Scapegoat Rituals in Ancient Greece." *Harvard Studies in Classical Philology* 87: 299–320.

——, ed. 1986a. *Interpretations of Greek Mythology.* Totowa, N.J.

——. 1986b. "Oedipus and the Greek Oedipus Complex." In Bremmer (1986a) 41–59.

Brooks, Peter. 1984. "Fictions of the Wolf Man: Freud and Narrative Understanding." In *Reading for the Plot. Design and Invention in Narrative,* 264–285. New York.

——. 1987. "The Idea of a Psychoanalytic Literary Criticism." In *Discourse in Psychoanalysis and Literature,* edited by Shlomith Rimmon-Kenan, 1–18. London.

——. 1990. *Reading Freud.* New Haven, Conn.

——. 1994. *Psychoanalysis and Storytelling.* Oxford.

Brunswick, Ruth Mack. [1928] 1972. "A Supplement to Freud's 'History of an Infantile Neurosis.'" In Gardiner (1972) 263–307. London.

Buchan, Mark. 2004. *The Limits of Heroism. Homer and the Ethics of Reading.* Ann Arbor, Mich.

Burnett, Anne. 1971. *Catastrophe Survived. Euripides' Plays of Mixed Reversal.* Oxford.

Butler, Judith. 1990. *Gender Trouble. Feminism and the Subversion of Identity.* New York.

——. 1997. *The Psychic Life of Power. Theories in Subjection.* Stanford.

Calame, Claude. 2003. *Myth and History in Ancient Greece. The Symbolic Creation of a Colony.* Translated by Daniel Berman. Princeton, N.J.

Calhoun, G. M. [1926] 1968. *The Business Life of Ancient Greece.* New York.

——. 1930. "Risk in Sea Loans in Ancient Athens." *Journal of Economics and Business History* 2: 561–584.

Caldwell, Richard. 1989. *The Origin of the Gods. A Psychoanalytic Study of Greek Theogonic Myth.* New York.

Cameron, A. 1932. "The Exposure of Children and Greek Ethics." *Classical Review* 46: 105–114.

Casson, L. 1984. *Ancient Trade and Society.* Detroit.

Castledon, Rodney. 1990. *The Knossos Labyrinth: A New View of the "Palace of Minos" at Knossos.* London.

Cavaignac, E. 1951. *L'Économie grecque.* Paris.

Christ, M. R. 1990. "Liturgical Avoidance and *Antidosis* in Classical Athens." *Transactions of the American Philological Association* 120: 147–169.

Clay, Jenny Strauss. 1989. The *Politics of Olympus: Form and Meaning in the Major Homeric Hymns.* Princeton, N.J.

Coen, Stanley J. 1994. *Between Author and Reader. A Psychoanalytic Approach to Writing and Reading.* New York.

Cohen, Edward E. 1992. *Athenian Economy and Society. A Banking Perspective.* Princeton, N.J.

Conacher, D. J. 1959. "The Paradox of Euripides' *Ion.*" *Transactions of the American Philological Association* 90: 20–39.

———. 1967. *Euripidean Drama. Myth, Theme, and Structure.* Toronto.

Cox, Cheryl Anne. 1998. *Household Interests: Property, Marriage Strategies, and Family Dynamics in Ancient Athens.* Princeton, N.J.

Damour, Lisa. 2003. "Harry Potter and the Magical Looking Glass: Reading the Secret Life of the Preadolescent." In Anatol (2003) 15–24. Westport, Conn.

Davies, J. K. 1981. *Wealth and the Power of Wealth in Classical Athens.* Salem, N.H.

Davis, Robert Con. 1993. *The Paternal Romance. Reading God-the-Father in Early Western Culture.* Urbana, Ill.

Deleuze, Gilles, and Félix Guattari. 1977. *Anti-Oedipus. Capitalism and Schizophrenia.* Translated by Robert Hurley, Mark Seem, and Helen R. Lane. New York. Originally published as *L'Anti-Oedipe* (Paris, 1972).

Demand, Nancy. 1994. *Birth, Death, and Motherhood in Classical Greece.* Baltimore.

Derderian, Katharine. 2001. *Leaving Words to Remember: Greek Mourning and the Advent of Literacy.* Leiden.

Derrida, Jacques. 1995. *Archive Fever. A Freudian Impression.* Translated by Eric Prenowitz. Chicago.

Deubner, Ludwig. 1952. "Die Gebräuche der Griechen nach der Geburt." *Rheinisches Museum* 95: 374–377.

Dever, Carolyn. 1998. *Death and the Mother from Dickens to Freud. Victorian Fiction and the Anxiety of Origins.* Cambridge, England.

Devereux, George. 1976. *Dreams in Greek Tragedy. An Ethno-Psycho-Analytical Study.* Berkeley.

Diggle, James, ed. 1981. *Euripidis Fabulae.* Vols. 1–3. Oxford.

———. 1994. *Euripidea. Collected Essays.* Oxford.

Dimock, George. 1995. "Anna and the Wolf Man: Rewriting Freud's Case History." *Representations* 50: 53–75.

DuBois, Page. 1988. *Sowing the Body. Psychoanalysis and Ancient Representations of Women.* Chicago.

Ebbott, Mary. 2003. *Imagining Illegitimacy in Classical Greek Literature.* Lanham, Md.

Edmunds L. 1985. *Oedipus. The Ancient Legend and Its Later Analogues.* Baltimore.

Engels, Donald. 1980. "The Problem of Female Infanticide in the Greco-Roman World." *Classical Philology* 75: 112–120.

———. 1984. "The Use of Historical Demography in Ancient History." *Classical Quarterly* 34: 386–393.

Erbse, Hartmut. 1984. *Studien zum Prolog der euripideischen Tragödie.* Berlin.

Esterson, Allan. 1993. *Seductive Mirage. An Exploration of the Work of Sigmund Freud.* Chicago.

Eyben, Emiel. 1980–81. "Family Planning in Graeco-Roman Antiquity." *Ancient Society* 11–12: 1–82.

Evans, J. A. S. 1991. *Herodotus, Explorer of the Past.* Princeton, N.J.

Fantham, Elaine. 1975. "Sex, Status, and Survival in Hellenistic Athens: A Study of Women in New Comedy." *Phoenix* 29: 44–74.

Faraone, Christopher. 1992. *Talismans and Trojan Horses. Guardian Statues in Ancient Greek Myth and Ritual.* New York.

Felman, Shoshana. 1980. "Turning the Screw of Interpretation." In *Literature and Psycho-analysis. The Question of Reading: Otherwise*, 94–207. Baltimore.

Fine, J. V. A. 1951. *Horoi. Studies in Mortgage, Real Security, and Land Tenure in Ancient Athens. Hesperia*, supp. 9.

Finley, Moses I. [1951] 1985. *Studies in Land and Credit in Ancient Athens.* With a new introduction by P. Millet. New Brunswick, N.J.

———. [1973] 1999. *The Ancient Economy.* Updated edition with foreword by Ian Morris. Berkeley.

Flory, Stewart. 1987. *The Archaic Smile of Herodotus.* Detroit.

Foley, Helene. 1994. *The Homeric Hymn to Demeter. Translation, Commentary, and Interpretive Essays.* Princeton, N.J.

———. 2001. *Female Acts in Greek Tragedy.* Princeton, N.J.

Forehand, Walter E. 1979. "Truth and Reality in Euripides' *Ion*." *Ramus* 8: 174–187.

Fowler, Harold North, trans. [1921] 1987. *Plato. Theaetetus and Sophist.* Cambridge, Mass.

French, A. 1991. "Economic Conditions in Fourth-Century Athens." *Greece & Rome*, 2nd ser., 38: 24–40.

Freud, Sigmund. 1900. "The Interpretation of Dreams." In *The Standard Edition of the Complete Psychological Works of Sigmund Freud* (elsewhere cited as *SE*), translated and edited by James Strachey et al., vols. 4 and 5. London.

———. 1908. "Character and Anal Erotism." *SE* 9: 169–175.

———. 1909. "Family Romances." *SE* 9: 236–241.

———. 1913. "Fairy Tales in Dreams." *SE* 12: 281–287

———. 1913. "Totem and Taboo." *SE* 13: 1–161.

———. 1914. "On the History of the Psycho-Analytic Movement." *SE* 14: 7–66.

———. 1918. "From the History of an Infantile Neurosis." *SE* 17: 7–122.

———. 1918. "The 'Uncanny.'" *SE* 17: 218–256

———. 1923. "The Ego and the Id." *SE* 19: 1–59.

———. 1930 (1929). "Civilization and Its Discontents." *SE* 21: 64–145.

———. 1932. "The Acquisition and Control of Fire." *SE* 22: 187–193.

———. 1937a. "Analysis Terminable and Interminable." *SE* 23: 211–253.

———. 1937b. "Constructions in Analysis." *SE* 23: 257–269.

———. 1939. "Moses and Monotheism." *SE* 23: 7–56.

———. [1940] 1986[6]. "Aus der Geschichte einer infantilen Neurose." In *Gesammelte Werke* (cited as *GW*), 12: 27–157. [London] Frankfurt.

———. [1941] 1993[7]. "Der Familienroman der Neurotiker." In *Gesammelte Werke* (cited as *GW*), 7: 225–231. [London] Frankfurt.

Freud, Sigmund, and C. G. Jung. 1974. *The Freud/Jung Letters: The Correspondence Between Sigmund Freud and C. G. Jung.* Edited by William McGuire. Translated by Ralph Manheim and R. F. C. Hull. Originally published as *Briefwechsel [von] Sigmund Freud [und] C. G. Jung*, ed. William McGuire and Wolfgang Sauerländer (Frankfurt am Main, 1974).

Furley, William. 1999–2000. "Hymns in Euripidean Tragedy." *Illinois Classical Studies* 24–25: 183–197.

Gabrielson, V. 1986. "Φανερά and Ἀφανὴς Οὐσία in Classical Athens." *Classica et Mediaevalia* 37: 99–114.

Gardiner, Muriel, ed. 1972. *The Wolf Man and Freud.* London.

Gardner, Jane F. 1989. "Aristophanes and Male Anxiety—The Defence of the *Oikos*." *Greece and Rome* 36: 51–62.

Gay, Peter. [1988] 1998. *Freud: A Life for Our Time.* New York.

Gellie, George. 1984. "Apollo in the *Ion.*" *Ramus* 93–101.

Gera, Deborah. 1997. *Warrior Women. The Anonymous "Tractatus de Mulieribus."* Leiden.

Germain, Louis. 1969. "Aspects du droit d'exposition en Grèce." *Revue historique de droit français et étranger* 47: 177–197.

———. 1980. "L'Exposition des enfants nouveau-nés dans la Grèce ancienne. Aspects sociologiques." In *L'Enfant au Moyen âge. Littérature et civilisation,* 211–246. Aix-en-Provence.

Gernet, Louis. 1981. " 'Value' in Greek Myth." In *Myth, Religion and Society.* Translated by R. L. Gordon. Cambridge.

Gibert, John. 1995. *Change of Mind in Greek Tragedy.* Göttingen.

Glen, Jules. 1980. "Concepts and Styles in Freud's Case Histories." In Kanzer and Glenn (1980) 5–13. New York.

Glotz, Gustave. 1906. "L'Exposition des enfants." In id., *Études sociales et juridiques sur l'antiquité grecque,* 187–228. Paris.

Goff, Barbara. 1988. "Euripides' *Ion* 1132–65: The Tent." *Proceedings of the Cambridge Philological Society* 34: 42–54.

Golden, Mark. 1981. "Demography and the Exposure of Girls at Athens." *Phoenix* 35: 316–331.

———. 1986. "Names and Naming at Athens: Three Studies." *Echos du monde classique* 30: 245–269.

———. 1990. *Children and Childhood in Classical Athens.* Baltimore.

Goldhill, Simon. 1992. *Aeschylus. The Oresteia.* Cambridge, England.

———. 1996. "East Coast Oedipus: Suspicious Readings." *Arion* 4.2: 155–171.

Goldsmith, R. W. 1987. *Premodern Financial Systems: A Historical Comparative Study.* Cambridge, England.

Gomme, A. W. 1933. *The Population of Athens in the Fifth and Fourth Centuries B.C.* Oxford.

Gould, John. 1989. *Herodotus.* London.

Grene, David, trans. 1987. *The History of Herodotus.* Chicago.

Griffith, Mark. 2005. "The Subject of Desire in Sophocles' *Antigone.*" In Pedrick and Oberhelman (2005) 91–135. Chicago.

Gupta, Suman. 2003. *Re-Reading Harry Potter.* New York.

Halleran, Michael. 1985. *Stagecraft in Euripides.* Totowa, N.J.

Hanson, J. O. de Graft. 1975. "Euripides' *Ion:* Tragic Awakening and Disillusionment." *Museum Africum* 4: 27–42.

Harris, William. 1982. "The Theoretical Possibility of Extensive Infanticide in the Greco-Roman World." *Classical Quarterly* 32: 114–116.

———. 1988. "When Is a Sale Not a Sale? The Riddle of Athenian Terminology for Real Security Revisited." *Classical Quarterly* 39: 39–43.

Harrison, A. R. W. 1968. *The Law of Athens,* vol. 1: *The Family and Property.* London.

Hartigan, Karelisa V. 1991. *Ambiguity and Self-Deception. The Apollo and Artemis Plays of Euripides.* Frankfurt am Main.

Hartog, François. 1988. *The Mirror of Herodotus. The Representation of the Other in the Writing of History.* Translated by Janet Lloyd. Berkeley.

Hoffer, Stanley E. 1996. "Violence, Culture, and the Workings of Ideology in Euripides' *Ion.*" *Classical Antiquity* 15: 289–318.

Holtz-Warhaft, Gail. 1992. *Dangerous Voices: Women's Laments and Greek Literature.* London.

Horwitz, Sylvia L. 1981. *The Find of a Lifetime. Sir Arthur Evans and the Discovery of Knossos.* New York.

Hrdy, Sarah Blaffer. 1999. *Mother Nature. A History of Mothers, Infants, and Natural Selection.* New York.

Hude, Charles. 1926³. *Herodoti Historiae*, Vols. 1 and 2. Oxford.

Huys, Marc. 1995. *The Tale of the Hero Who was Exposed at Birth in Euripidean Tragedy. A Study of Motifs.* Symbolae Facultatis Litterarum Lovaniensis 20. Louvain, Belgium.

Isager, Signe, 1981–1982. "The Marriage Pattern in Classical Athens. Men and Women in Isaios." *Classica et Mediaevalia* 30: 81–96.

Jens, W., ed. 1971. *Die Bauformen des griechischen Tragödie.*

Johnson, Lawrence. 2001. *The Wolf Man's Burden.* Ithaca, N.Y.

Jones, Ernest. 1953–1957. *The Life and Work of Sigmund Freud.* 3 vols. New York.

Jones, John. [1962] 1988. "The House of Atreus." In *Aeschylus' "The Oresteia,"* edited by Harold Bloom, 5–29. New Haven, Conn.

Jung, C. G., and C. Kérenyi. 1949. *Essays on a Science of Mythology. The Myth of the Divine Child and the Mysteries of Eleusis.* Translated by R. F. C. Hull. New York.

Just, Roger. 1989. *Women in Athenian Law and Life.* New York.

Kalinich, Lila. 1991. "Where Is Thy Sting? Some Reflections on the Wolf-Man." In *Lacan and the Subject of Language*, edited by Ellie Ragland-Sullivan and Mark Bracher, 167–187. New York.

Kanzer, Mark. 1980. "Further Comments on the Wolf Man: The Search for a Primal Scene." In Kanzer and Glenn (1980) 359–366. New York.

Kanzer, Mark, and Jules Glenn, eds. 1980. *Freud and His Patients.* New York.

Kartiganer, Donald M. 1985. "Freud's Reading Process: The Divided Protagonist Narrative and the Case of the Wolf-Man." In *The Psychoanalytic Study of Literature*, edited by Joseph Reppen and Maurice Charney, 3–36. Hillsdale, N.J.

[Katz], Marilyn Arthur. 1982. "Cultural Strategies in Hesiod's *Theogony:* Law, Family, Society." *Arethusa* 15: 63–82.

Kertzer, David. 1993. *Sacrificed for Honor. Italian Infant Abandonment and the Politics of Reproductive Control.* Boston.

———. 2000. "The Lives of Foundlings in Nineteenth-century Italy." In Panter-Brick and Smith (2000) 41–56. Cambridge, England.

Keuls, Eva. 1985. *The Reign of the Phallus: Sexual Politics in Ancient Athens.* New York.

Knox, Bernard. 1979. "Euripidean Comedy." In *Words and Action. Essays on the Ancient Theater*, 250–274. Baltimore.

Konstan, David. 2005. "Aristotle on the Tragic Emotions." In Pedrick and Oberhelman (2005) 13–25. Chicago.

Kovacs, David. 1979. "Four Passages from Euripides' *Ion.*" *Transactions of the American Philological Association* 107: 111–124.

Künstler, Rolf. 1998. "Horror at Pleasure of His Own of Which He Himself Is Not Aware: The Case of the Rat Man." In Matthis and Szecsödy (1998) 127–162. Northvale, N.J.

Kurke, Leslie. 1991. *The Traffic in Praise. Pindar and the Poetics of Social Economy.* Ithaca, N.Y.

———. 1999. *Coins, Bodies, Games, and Gold. The Politics of Meaning in Archaic Greece.* Princeton, N.J.

Lacan, Jacques. 1977. *Écrits. A Selection.* Translated by Alan Sheridan. New York.

———. 1978. *The Four Fundamental Concepts of Psycho-analysis.* Translated by Alan Sheridan. New York.

———. 1988. *Encore: The Seminar of Jacques Lacan XX.* Edited by J.-A. Miller. Translated by B. Fink. New York.

Lacey, W. K. 1968. *The Family in Classical Greece.* Ithaca, N.Y.

Langs, Robert J. 1980. "The Misalliance Dimension on the Case of the Wolf Man." In Kanzer and Glenn (1980) 373–385. New York.

Lapatin, Kenneth. 2002. *Mysteries of the Snake Goddess. Art, Desire, and the Forging of History.* Boston.

Laplanche, Jean. 1980–81. *Problématiques.* 4 vols. Paris.

LaRue, Jene. 1963. "Creusa's Monody: *Ion* 859–922." *Transactions of the American Philological Association* 94: 126–136.

Lateiner, Donald. 1989. *The Historical Method of Herodotus.* Toronto.

Lee, Kevin H. 1996. "Shifts of Mood and Concepts of Time in Euripides' *Ion.*" In Silk (1996) 85–109.

———, ed. 1997. *Euripides' Ion, with Introduction, Translation, and Commentary.* Warminster, England.

Levin, A. J. 1948. "The Oedipus Myth in History and Psychiatry: A New Interpretation." *Psychiatry* 11: 283–299.

Lewis, N. 1960. "*Leitourgia* and Related Terms." *Greek, Roman, and Byzantine Studies* 3: 175–184.

Little, Arthur L., Jr. 1993. " 'An essence that's not seen': The Primal Scene of Racism in *Othello.*" *Shakespeare Quarterly* 44: 304–324.

Lloyd, M. 1986. "Divine and Human Action in Euripides' *Ion.*" *Antike und Abendland* 32: 33–45.

Locke, Nancy. 2001. *Manet and the Family Romance.* Princeton, N.J.

Loraux, Nicole. 1990. "Creousa the Autochthon: A Study of Euripides' *Ion.*" In Winkler and Zeitlin (1990) 168–206. Princeton, N.J.

———. 1995. *The Experiences of Tiresias. The Feminine and the Greek Man.* Translated by Paula Wissing. Princeton, N.J.

Lowry, Eddie. 1988. "Euripides' *Ion* and Rank's Hero Myth." *Classical Bulletin* 64: 15–20.

Lukacher, Ned. 1986. *Primal Scenes. Literature, Philosophy, Psychoanalysis.* Ithaca, N.Y.

MacDowell, Douglas M. 1978. *The Law in Classical Athens.* London.

MacGillivray, Joseph A. 2000. *Minotaur. Sir Arthur Evans and the Archaeology of the Minoan Myth.* New York.

Macve, R. H. [1985] 1994. "Some Glosses on 'Greek and Roman Accounting.' " In *Accounting History. Some British Contributions,* edited by R. H. Parker and B. S. Yamey, 57–87. Oxford.

Mahony, Patrick J. 1984. *Cries of the Wolf Man.* New York.

Manlove, Colin. 2003. *From Alice to Harry Potter. Children's Fantasy in England.* Christchurch, New Zealand.

Masson, Jeffrey Moussaieff. 1984. *The Assault on Truth: Freud's Suppression of Seduction Theory.* New York.

———, trans. and ed. 1985. *The Complete Letters of Sigmund Freud to Wilhelm Fliess, 1877–1904.* Cambridge, Mass.

Mastronarde, D. 1975. "Iconography and Imagery in Euripides' *Ion.*" *Classical Studies* 8: 163–176.

Matthiessen, Kjeld. 1990. "Der *Ion* — eine Komödie des Euripides?" In *Opes Atticae. Miscellanea philologica et historica Raymondo Bogaert et Hermanno Van Looy oblata,* edited by M. Geerard, 271–291. Steenbrugge, Holland.

Matthis, Iréne, and Imre Szecsödy, eds. 1998. *On Freud's Couch. Seven New Interpretations of Freud's Case Histories.* Translated by Sheila Smith. Northvale, N.J.

Mauss, Marcel. 1967. *The Gift. Forms and Functions of Exchange in Archaic Societies.* Translated by Ian Cunnison. New York.

Mendlesohn, Farah. 2002. "Crowning the King. Harry Potter and the Construction of Authority." In Whited (2002) 159–181. Columbia, Mo.

Millett, Paul. 1991. *Lending and Borrowing in Ancient Athens.* Cambridge, England.

———. 1998. "The Rhetoric of Reciprocity in Classical Athens." *Reciprocity in Ancient Greece,* ed. Christopher Gill, Norman Postlethwaite, and Richard Seaford, 227–253. Oxford.

Mills, Alice. 2003. "Archetypes and the Unconscious in *Harry Potter* and Diana Wynne Jones's *Fire and Hemlock* and *Dogsbody.*" In Anatol (2003) 3–13. Westport, Conn.

Mitchell, Lynette G. 1995. *Greeks Bearing Gifts. The Public Use of Private Relationships in the Greek World, 435–323 BC.* Cambridge, England.

Morris, Ian. 1986. "Gift and Commodity in Archaic Greece." *Man* 21: 1–17.

———. 1999. "Foreword." Finley (1999) *ix–xxxvi.* Berkeley.

Mueller, Gerhard. 1983. "Bemerkungen zum 'Ion' des Euripides." *Würzburger Jahrbucher* 9: 33–48.

Munson, Rosaria. 2001. *Telling Wonders. Ethnographic and Political Discourse in the Work of Herodotus.* Ann Arbor, Mich.

Murnaghan, Sheila. 1992. "Maternity and Mortality in Homeric Poetry." *Classical Antiquity* 11: 242–264.

Murray, Gilbert. 1943. "Ritual Elements in the New Comedy." *Classical Quarterly* 37: 46–54.

Neitzel, Heinz. 1988. "Apollons Orakelspruch im 'Ion' des Euripides." *Hermes* 116: 272–279.

Norman, Johan. 1998. "Little Hans: The Dramaturgy of Phobia." In Matthis and Szecsödy (1998) 93–126. Northvale, N.J.

Nussbaum, Martha. 1994. "The *Oedipus Rex* and the Ancient Unconscious." In Rudnytsky and Spitz (1994) 42–71. New York.

Ober, Josiah. 1989. *Mass and Elite in Democratic Athens. Rhetoric, Ideology, and the Power of the People.* Princeton, N.J.

Obholzer, Karin. 1982. *The Wolf-Man. Conversations with Freud's Patient — Sixty Years Later.* Translated by Michael Shaw. New York.

Ogden, Daniel. 1996. *Greek Bastardy in the Classical and Hellenistic Periods.* Oxford.

Oldenziel, Ruth. 1987. "The Historiography of Infanticide in Antiquity. A Literature Stillborn." In *Sexual Asymmetry: Studies in Ancient Society,* 87–107. Amsterdam.

Owen, A. S., ed. 1939. *Euripides' "Ion."* Oxford.

Panter-Brick, Catherine, and Malcolm T. Smith, eds. 2000. *Abandoned Children.* Cambridge, England.

Parker, Robert. 1986. "Myths of Early Athens." In *Interpretations of Greek Mythology,* edited by Jan Bremmer, 187–214. Totowa, N.J.

Patterson, Cynthia. 1985. " 'Not Worth the Rearing': The Causes of Infant Exposure in Ancient Greece." *Transactions of the American Philological Association* 115: 103–123.

Pedrick, Victoria, and Steven Oberhelman, eds. 2005. *The Soul of Tragedy. Essays on Athenian Drama.* Chicago.

Peradotto, John. 1977. "Oedipus and Erichthonius: Some Observations on Paradignmatic and Syntagmatic Order." *Arethusa* 10: 85–101.

Polanyi, K. 1968. *Primitive, Archaic, and Modern Economies. Essays of Karl Polanyi.* Edited by G. Dalton. Garden City, N.Y.

Pomeroy, Sarah B. 1983. "Infanticide in Hellenistic Greece." In *Images of Women in Antiquity,* edited by Averil Cameron and A. Kuhrt, 207–22. London.

———. 1986. "Copronyms and the Exposure of Infants in Egypt." In *Studies in Honor of A. Arthur Schiller,* edited by Roger Bagnall and W. Harris, 147–162. Leiden.

———. 1997. *Families in Classical and Hellenistic Greece. Representations and Realities.* Oxford.

Pomeroy, Sarah B., Stanley M. Burstein, Walter Donlan, and Jennifer Tolbert Roberts. 1999. *Ancient Greece. A Political, Social, and Cultural History.* New York.

Poovey, Mary. 1998. *A History of the Modern Fact: Problems of Knowledge in the Sciences of Wealth and Society.* Chicago.

Price, Theodora Hadzisteliou. 1978. *Kourotrophos: Cults and Representations of the Greek Nursing Deities.* Leiden.

Pucci, Pietro. 1992. *Oedipus and the Fabrication of the Father.* Baltimore.

———. [1987] 1995. *Odysseus Polutropos: Intertextual Readings in the Odyssey and the Iliad.* Ithaca, N.Y.

Rabinowitz, Nancy Sorkin. 1993. *Anxiety Veiled. Euripides and the Traffic in Women.* Ithaca, N.Y.

Rank, Otto. [1909] 2004. *The Myth of the Birth of the Hero. A Psychoanalytic Exploration of Myth.* Translated by Gregory C. Richter and E. James Lieberman. Baltimore.

Reden, Sitta von. 1995. *Exchange in Ancient Greece.* London.

Reppen, Joseph, and Maurice Charney, eds. 1984. *The Psychoanalytic Study of Literature.* Hillsdale, N.J.

Revermann, Martin. 1999–2000. "Euripides, Tragedy and Macedon: Some Conditions of Reception." *Illinois Classical Studies* 24–25: 451–467.

Ridgway, B. S. 1987. "Ancient Greek Women and Art: The Material Evidence." *American Journal Archaeology* 91: 399–409.

Rihll, R. E. 2001. "Making Money in Classical Athens." In *Economies Beyond Agriculture in the Classical World,* edited by David J. Mattingly and John Salmon, 115–142. New York.

Rimmon-Kenan, Shlomith, ed. 1987. *Discourse in Psychoanalysis and Literature.* New York.

Romm, James. 1998. *Herodotus.* New Haven, Conn.

Rosenmeyer, Thomas G. 1963. *The Masks of Tragedy. Essays on Six Greek Dramas.* Austin.

Rosivach, V. 1977. "Earthborns and Olympians: The Parodos of the *Ion.*" *Classical Quarterly* 27: 284–294.

Rowling, J. K. 1997. *Harry Potter and the Sorcerer's Stone.* New York.

———. 1998. *Harry Potter and the Chamber of Secrets.* New York

———. 1999. *Harry Potter and the Prisoner of Azkaban.* New York.

———. 2000. *Harry Potter and the Goblet of Fire.* New York.

———. 2003. *Harry Potter and the Order of the Phoenix.* New York.

———. 2005. *Harry Potter and the Half-Blood Prince.* New York.

Rudnytsky, Peter L., and Ellen Handler Spitz, eds. 1994. *Freud and Forbidden Knowledge.* New York.

Saxonhouse, Arlene. 1986. "Myths and the Origins of Cities: Reflections on the Autochthony Theme in Euripides' *Ion.*" In *Greek Tragedy and Political Theory,* edited by J. Peter Euben, 252–273. Berkeley.

Segal, Charles. 1994. "Sophocles' *Oedipus Tyrannus:* Freud, Language, and the Unconscious." In Rudnytsky and Spitz (1994) 72–95. New York.

———. [1982] 1997. *Dionysiac Poetics and Euripides' Bacchae.* Expanded ed. Princeton, N.J.

————. 1999. "Euripides' *Ion*: Generational Passage and Civic Myth." In *Rites of Passage in Ancient Greece: Literature, Religion, Society*, edited by Mark Padilla, 67–108. *Bucknell Review 43, no. 1*. Lewisburg, Pa.

Shipton, K. M. W. 1997. "The Private Banks in Fourth-Century B. C. Athens: A Reappraisal." *Classical Quarterly* 47: 396–422.

Silk, M. S., ed. 1996. *Tragedy and the Tragic: Greek Theatre and Beyond*. Oxford.

Sinos, Dale S. 1982. "Characterization in the *Ion*: Apollo and the Dynamism of the Plot." *Eranos* 80: 129–134.

Sissa, Giulia. 1990. *Greek Virginity*. Translated by Arthur Goldhammer. Cambridge, Mass.

Slater, Philip. 1968. *The Glory of Hera. Greek Mythology and the Greek Family*. Boston.

Sokolowski, Francisek. 1969. *Lois sacrées des cités grecques*. Paris.

Solmsen, Friedrich. 1934. "Euripides' Ion im Vergleich mit anderen Tragödien." *Hermes* 69: 390–419.

Sommerstein, Alan, ed. and trans. 1994. *Thesmophoriazusae*. Vol. 8 of *The Comedies of Aristophanes*. Warminster, England.

————, ed. 1998. *Ecclesiazusae*. Vol. 10 of *The Comedies of Aristophanes*. Warminster, England.

Spence, Donald. 1994. *The Rhetorical Voice of Psychoanalysis: Displacement of Evidence by Theory*. Cambridge, Mass.

Sprengnether, Madelon. 1990. *The Spectral Mother: Freud, Feminism, and Psychoanalysis*. Ithaca, N.Y.

Stears, Karen. 1998. "Death Becomes Her: Gender and Athenian Death Ritual." *The Sacred and the Feminine in Ancient Greece*, edited by Sue Blundell and Margaret Williamson, 113–127. London.

Stahl, Hans-Peter. 1975. "Learning Through Suffering? Croesus' Conversations in the History of Herodotus." *Yale Classical Studies* 24: 1–36.

States, Bert. 1985. *Great Reckonings in Little Rooms. On the Phenomenology of Theater*. Berkeley.

Stern, Daniel N. 1998. *Diary of a Baby*. New York.

————. 2000. *The Interpersonal World of the Infant. A View from Psychoanalysis and Developmental Psychology*. New York.

Strohm, Hans. 1976. "Epikritisches zur Erklärung von Euripides' 'Ion.'" *Wiener Studien* 10: 68–79.

Szecsödy, Imre. 1998. "Dora: Freud's Pygmalion or the Unrecovered Patient of a Famous Analyst?" In Matthis and Szecsödy (1998) 57–92. Northvale, N.J.

Taplin, Oliver, 1978. *Greek Tragedy in Action*. Berkeley.

————. 1977. *The Stagecraft of Aeschylus. The Dramatic Use of Exits and Entrances in Greek Tragedy*. Oxford.

Temkin, Owsei, trans. [1956] 1991. *Soranus' Gynecology*. Baltimore.

Thornburn, John E. 2001 "Apollo's Comedy and the Ending of Euripides' *Ion*." *Acta Classica* 44: 221–236.

Todorov, Tzvetan. 1973. *The Fantastic. A Structural Approach to a Literary Genre*. Translated by Richard Howard. Ithaca, N.Y.

Toohey, Peter. 2004. *Melancholy, Love, and Time. Boundaries of the Self in Ancient Literature*. Ann Arbor, Mich.

Troiano, E. 1985. "The *Ion*: The Relationship of Character and Genre." *Classical Bulletin* 61: 45–52.

Van Hook, La Rue. 1920. "The Exposure of Infants at Athens." *Transactions of the American Philological Association* 41: 36–44.

Vernant, J.-P. 1976. "Remarks on Class Struggle in Ancient Greece." *Critique of Anthropology* 7: 67–81.

———. 1982. "From Oedipus to Periander: Lameness, Tyranny, Incest in Legend and History." *Arethusa* 15: 19–38.

Viljoen, G. van N. 1959. "Plato and Aristotle on the Exposure of Infants at Athens." *Acta Classica* 2: 58–69.

Walsh, G. B. 1978. "The Rhetoric of Birthright and Race in Euripides' *Ion.*" *Hermes* 106: 301–315.

Watson, Patricia. 1995. *Ancient Stepmothers. Myth, Misogyny and Reality.* Leiden.

Werbert, Andrzej. 1998. "Where the Horsetails Grow as High as Palms: The Case of the Wolf Man." In Matthis and Szecsödy (1998) 185–246. Northvale, N.J.

Whited, Lana A., ed. 2002. *The Ivory Tower and Harry Potter: Perspectives on a Literary Phenomenon.* Columbia, Mo.

Whitehead, D. 1983. "Competitive Outlay and Community Profit: Φιλοτιμία in Democratic Athens." *Classica et Mediaevalia* 32: 55–74.

Winkler, John, and Froma Zeitlin, eds. 1990. *Nothing to Do with Dionysus? Athenian Drama in Its Social Context.* Princeton, N.J.

Winter, Sarah. 1999. *Freud and the Institution of Psychoanalytic Knowledge.* Stanford.

Wohl, Victoria. 1998. *Intimate Commerce. Exchange, Gender, and Subjectivity in Greek Tragedy.* Austin.

———. 2002. *Love Among the Ruins. The Erotics of Democracy in Classical Athens.* Princeton, N.J.

———. 2005. "Beyond Sexual Difference: Becoming-Woman in Euripides' *Bacchae.*" In Pedrick and Oberhelman (2005). 137–154. Chicago.

Wolff, Christian. 1965. "The Design and the Myth in Euripides' *Ion.*" *Harvard Studies in Classical Philology* 69: 169–194.

Young, Rodney S. 1941. "ANTIΠHX: A Note on the *Ion* of Euripides." *Hesperia* 10: 138–142.

Yunis, Harvey. 1988. *A New Creed: Fundamental Religious Beliefs in the Athenian Polis and Euripidean Drama.* Göttingen.

Zacharia, Katerina. 1995. "The Marriage of Tragedy and Comedy in Euripides' *Ion.*" In *Laughter Down the Centuries,* edited by Siegfried Jäkel and Asko Timonen, 45–62. Turku, Finland.

———. 2003. *Converging Truths. Euripides' "Ion" and the Athenian Quest for Self-Definition.* (*Mnemosyne Supplementum* 242). Leiden.

Zeitlin, Froma. 1990. "Thebes: Theater of Self and Society in Athenian Drama." In Winkler and Zeitlin (1990) 130–167. Princeton, N.J.

———. 1996a. "Figuring Fidelity in Homer's *Odyssey.*" In id., *Playing the Other. Gender and Society in Classical Greek Literature,* 19–52. Chicago.

———. 1996b. "Signifying Difference: The Case of Hesiod's Pandora." In id., *Playing the Other. Gender and Society in Classical Greek Literature,* 53–86. Chicago.

———. 1996c. "Mysteries of Identity and Designs of the Self in Euripides' *Ion.*" In id., *Playing the Other. Gender and Society in Classical Greek Literature,* 285–338. Chicago.

———. 1996d. "Playing the Other: Theater, Theatricality, and the Feminine in Greek Drama." *Playing the Other. Gender and Society in Classical Greek Literature,* 341–374. Chicago.

Zipes, Jack. 2001. *Sticks and Stones. The Troublesome Success of Children's Literature from Slovenly Peter to Harry Potter.* New York.

Index

From a History of an Infantile Neurosis is abbreviated HIN within index entries.

Nanya (*Kinderfrau*) 18; nursery maid (*Kindermädchen*), 19, 155, 160; real-life finances of, 113; sister, 16–17, 197nn16, 19; and Ruth Mack Brunswick, 115–20; as valuable object, 112. See also *From a History of an Infantile Neurosis*

Xouthos: accounting maneuvers, 146; and choosing his son, 149–50, 226n166,

228n144; construction of public account for Ion, 98–99; delusion of, 177; embrace of Ion, 176, 236n60; practical mind of, 141; as treacherous schemer, 100; use of technical language, 145. *See also* father; infant abandonment

Zacharia, K., 80–81
Zeitlin, 171, 183